THE BAVLI'S UNIQUE VOICE

SOUTH FLORIDA STUDIES IN THE HISTORY OF JUDAISM

Edited by
Jacob Neusner
William Scott Green, James Strange
Darrell J. Fasching, Sara Mandell

Number 71
THE BAVLI'S UNIQUE VOICE
A Systematic Comparison of the Talmud of Babylonia
and the Talmud of the Land of Israel
Volume One

by
Jacob Neusner

THE BAVLI'S UNIQUE VOICE

A Systematic Comparison
of the Talmud of Babylonia
and the Talmud of the Land of Israel

Volume One

Bavli and Yerushalmi Qiddushin
Chapter One
Compared and Contrasted

by

Jacob Neusner

Scholars Press
Atlanta, Georgia

THE BAVLI'S UNIQUE VOICE
A Systematic Comparison of the Talmud of Babylonia and the Talmud of the Land of Israel
Volume One

Publication of this book was made possible by a grant from the Tisch Family Foundation, New York City. The University of South Florida acknowledges with thanks this important support for its scholarly projects.

Library of Congress Cataloging in Publication Data
Neusner, Jacob, 1932-
   The Bavli's unique voice: a systematic comparison of the Talmud of Babylonia and the Talmud of the land of Israel/ by Jacob Neusner.
         p. cm. — (South Florida studies in the history of Judaism; no. 71-72)
   Includes index.
   Contents: v. 1. Bavli and Yerushalmi Qiddushin chapter one compared and contrasted — v. 2. Yerushalmi's, Bavli's, and other canonical documents' treatment of the program of Mishnah tractate Sukkah chapters one, two, and four compared and contrasted: a reprise and revision of The Bavli and its sources.
   ISBN 1-55540-834-6 (v. 1). — ISBN 1-55540-835-4 (v. 2)
   1. Talmud—Comparative studies. 2. Talmud Yerushalmi—Comparative studies.   I. Title.   II. Series: South Florida studies in the history of Judaism; 71-72.
BM501.N45   1993
296.1'2506—dc20   93-20017
                                                                     CIP

Printed in the United States of America
on acid-free paper

Table of Contents

Preface

Beginning here I undertake a seven-volume analysis of the intellectual relationship between the second of the two Talmuds and the first. What I want to know is whether the framers of the Talmud of Babylonia have found in the work of their predecessors guidance on how to read the Mishnah and on what questions to raise in response to that reading. At stake in the answer to that question is whether the second of the two Talmuds stands on its own or carries forward a received tradition of Mishnah exegesis handed on by the first of the two. And the upshot will be to determine whether the Bavli makes a statement in behalf of its authorship in particular or stands within a tradition – hermeneutical, but also theological – that speaks for an indeterminate time and circumstance, but not the occasion and situation of the framers of the Bavli in particular. There is no point in reading the Bavli in its distinctive context if it forms a link in a chain of tradition; but if the Bavli takes a stand of its own, then the setting in which its writers take their stand and make their statement proves consequential. So while most of this monograph addresses small matters, the issue is a formidable one, and the outcome governs the next important step in the inquiry into the formation of Judaism, in its historical and theological context, to which I have devoted my life.

The upshot, then, is that the Bavli forms a singular, cogent, systematic, systemic statement: it speaks for itself, for its authorship, for all those who, over a long period of time, wrote up materials used in it, and its message is contained in the ways in which the received materials were turned from inert to active components in that systemic statement. Let me place this work into its context, since that simple sentence completes the inquiry begun in *The Bavli's One Voice: Types and Forms of Analytical Discourse and Their Fixed Order of Appearance* (Atlanta, 1991: Scholars Press for South Florida Studies in the History of Judaism).

Here I further conclude the entire monographic experiment in the description of the Bavli contained in the following ad hoc works: probes of sample data on problems characteristic of the documents overall:

The Talmud of the Land of Israel. A Preliminary Translation and Explanation (Chicago: University of Chicago Press: 1983. XXXV). *Introduction. Taxonomy.*

Canon and Connection: Intertextuality in Judaism (Lanham, 1986: University Press of America. Studies in Judaism Series).

The Bavli and Its Sources: The Question of Tradition in the Case of Tractate Sukkah (Atlanta, 1987: Scholars Press for Brown Judaic Studies).

Making the Classics in Judaism: The Three Stages of Literary Formation (Atlanta, 1990: Scholars Press for Brown Judaic Studies).

The Yerushalmi. The Talmud of the Land of Israel. An Introduction (Northvale, 1992: Jason Aronson, Inc.).

The Tosefta. An Introduction (Atlanta, 1992: Scholars Press for South Florida Studies in the History of Judaism).

The Bavli. The Talmud of Babylonia. An Introduction (Atlanta, 1992: Scholars Press for South Florida Studies in the History of Judaism).

The Canonical History of Ideas. The Place of the So-called Tannaite Midrashim: Mekhilta Attributed to R. Ishmael, Sifra, Sifré to Numbers, and Sifré to Deuteronomy (Atlanta, 1990: Scholars Press for South Florida Studies in the History of Judaism).

The Talmud: Close Encounters (Minneapolis, 1991: Fortress Press).

Tradition as Selectivity: Scripture, Mishnah, Tosefta, and Midrash in the Talmud of Babylonia. The Case of Tractate Arakhin (Atlanta, 1990: Scholars Press for South Florida Studies in the History of Judaism).

Language as Taxonomy. The Rules for Using Hebrew and Aramaic in the Babylonian Talmud (Atlanta, 1990: Scholars Press for South Florida Studies in the History of Judaism).

The Bavli That Might Have Been: The Tosefta's Theory of Mishnah Commentary Compared with that of the Babylonian Talmud (Atlanta,

1990: Scholars Press for South Florida Studies in the History of Judaism).

The Rules of Composition of the Talmud of Babylonia. The Cogency of the Bavli's Composite (Atlanta, 1991: Scholars Press for South Florida Studies in the History of Judaism).

The Bavli's One Voice: Types and Forms of Analytical Discourse and their Fixed Order of Appearance (Atlanta, 1991: Scholars Press for South Florida Studies in the History of Judaism).

The Bavli's One Statement. The Metapropositional Program of Babylonian Talmud Tractate Zebahim Chapters One and Five (Atlanta, 1991: Scholars Press for South Florida Studies in the History of Judaism).

How the Bavli Shaped Rabbinic Discourse (Atlanta, 1991: Scholars Press for South Florida Studies in the History of Judaism).

The Bavli's Massive Miscellanies. The Problem of Agglutinative Discourse in the Talmud of Babylonia (Atlanta, 1992: Scholars Press for South Florida Studies in the History of Judaism).

Sources and Traditions. Types of Composition in the Talmud of Babylonia (Atlanta, 1992: Scholars Press for South Florida Studies in the History of Judaism).

The Law Behind the Laws. The Bavli's Essential Discourse (Atlanta, 1992: Scholars Press for South Florida Studies in the History of Judaism).

The Bavli's Primary Discourse. Mishnah Commentary, Its Rhetorical Paradigms and Their Theological Implications in the Talmud of Babylonia Tractate Moed Qatan (Atlanta, 1992: Scholars Press for South Florida Studies in the History of Judaism).

The Discourse of the Bavli: Language, Literature, and Symbolism. Five Recent Findings (Atlanta, 1991: Scholars Press for South Florida Studies in the History of Judaism).

How to Study the Bavli: The Languages, Literatures, and Lessons of the Talmud of Babylonia (Atlanta, 1992: Scholars Press for South Florida Studies in the History of Judaism).

The Bavli's Intellectual Character. The Generative Problematic in Bavli Baba Qamma Chapter One and Bavli Shabbat Chapter One (Atlanta, 1992: Scholars Press for South Florida Studies in the History of Judaism).

Decoding the Talmud's Exegetical Program: From Detail to Principle in the Bavli's Quest for Generalization. Tractate Shabbat (Atlanta, 1992: Scholars Press for South Florida Studies in the History of Judaism).

The Principal Parts of the Bavli's Discourse: A Final Taxonomy. Mishnah Commentary, Sources, Traditions, and Agglutinative Miscellanies (Atlanta, 1992: Scholars Press for South Florida Studies in the History of Judaism).

The Torah in the Talmud. A Taxonomy of the Uses of Scripture in the Talmuds. Tractate Qiddushin in the Talmud of Babylonia and the Talmud of the Land of Israel. I. Bavli Qiddushin Chapter One (Atlanta, 1992: Scholars Press for South Florida Studies in the History of Judaism).

The Torah in the Talmud. A Taxonomy of the Uses of Scripture in the Talmuds. Tractate Qiddushin in the Talmud of Babylonia and the Talmud of the Land of Israel. II. Yerushalmi Qiddushin Chapter One. And a Comparison of the Uses of Scripture by the Two Talmuds (Atlanta, 1992: Scholars Press for South Florida Studies in the History of Judaism).

With the completion of this seven-volume monograph, I shall regard as having been settled and closed the question of the Bavli's relationship to the Yerushalmi. For the results are clear even with the completion of Parts One and Two, which are published simultaneously. These results should be set forth briefly.

The Bavli stands entirely on its own, pursuing its own program, through its own modes of thought and inquiry; it speaks of the same Mishnah and draws upon the same Scripture; it may use episodic sayings or even stories and other brief compositions that make their way into the other Talmud. But the Bavli does with these things whatever it wishes, and knowing a saying in the Yerushalmi, or a problem investigated by the Yerushalmi, or a proposition espoused by the Yerushalmi, in no way permits us to predict the morphology and structure of the Bavli's writing that makes use of ths same saying, investigates the same problem, or argues in behalf of or against the same proposition. The Bavli does not stand in a relationship of dependence to the Yerushalmi.

The evidence that I have accumulated here and in the other parts of this monograph leaves no reasonable doubt on that score; every time we compare the Bavli's compositions or composites to the Yerushalmi's counterparts (joined as they are at a common Mishnah pericope or at a common verse of Scripture, for example, prooftext for a shared proposition), we find in common only the common Mishnah pericope or prooftext or (less frequently) ad hoc saying. The Bavli therefore is not a traditional document, taking up its position at the end of a long chain of formulation and transmission, glossing what it has received, shaped by the dictates of an earlier age.

The differences between the two Talmuds are so ubiquitous, stunning, and profound, that one may well wonder, at the end, why they should be compared at all. The Bavli may be compared with the Yerushalmi because it looks like the Yerushalmi, forming a commentary to the same Mishnah, drawing upon the same Written Torah (Scripture, "Old Testament"), appealing at points to the same circulating sayings. But the Bavli does with its inheritance, shared with the Yerushalmi, precisely what its authors, framers, and authorships wish to do, rarely if ever taking up and revising a received composition, never, so far as I can see, borrowing a received composite. In its proportions, in its intellectual morphology (a term explained in due course), in its structure, program, points of stress and emphasis, the Bavli makes its own statement, in its own language, using its own forms, for its own purposes. And that statement is independent of the Yerushalmi's statement, forms, and (so far as the framers of the Yerushalmi's compositions and composites may be said to have done their work purposefully), intellectual purpose.

With this work of literary analysis and description complete, I open the way to a large-scale account of the systemic statement of the Bavli. The Bavli certainly is one of the most successful writings in the history of religions. It took over an entire antecedent canon and restated it, setting forth as an orderly, proportioned, coherent system what had earlier circulated as bits and pieces of a religious worldview. Out of religion, the Bavli's framers produced theology.

And evidence of their success is stunning. From the Bavli forward, not only did everybody refer back to the Bavli as the starting point. More astonishing still, no one produced documents like the documents that had been written before the Bavli and taken over by the Bavli – taken over, or merely supplanted. That is to say, there was never another Mishnah, or Tosefta, or Talmud; there would be commentaries to these closed and finished writings, but no one produced another Talmud after this one. And, more to the point, there also would never be Midrash compilations like the Midrash compilations superseded by the Bavli: no more Sifras or Leviticus Rabbahs or Genesis Rabbahs or Song of Songs Rabbahs, that would argue through exegetical form a single sustained proposition. The Midrash compilations that would follow would constitute collections and arrangements of this and that, this authority's collection ("Yalqut") and that authority's scrapbook. But there would never be another Midrash compilation like Sifra, to take one example, or like Ruth Rabbah or Lamentations Rabbah – commentaries in form, propositional exercises in intent and outcome – to take another. The writing of Judaism would proceed along other lines, different lines. The Bavli marked the end of one kind of writing, the beginning of other kinds of writing: the definitive conclusion of a vast canonical process. And, as we shall see in this account, the Bavli's framers found a unique voice for themselves, one that would serve to deliver a message that was both unique but also authoritative: a consensus formed, induced, demonstrated, challenged and defended, never stipulated but always shown to cohere and proved consistent, orderly, compelling, ineluctable in all details, a single, unitary, systematic, systemic statement – one imposed, insisted upon: theology.

I plan to approach the problem by an account of what I conceive to be the context: the problem solved by the framers of the Bavli, defined in the setting of the problem solved by their Zoroastrian counterparts at roughly the same epoch, that is, the final phases of what we now define as late antiquity: the systematization and the writing down of the great tradition. So from this monograph, I turn not into the Bavli but away from it and outward toward its historical context, defined – so it seems to me – by what was happening in Iran, inclusive of Babylonia, in the same age: what the Zoroastrian were sages doing at the moment of turning, in the hour of nascent Islam. But that work, now germinating, will come in due course, in the right setting, and for the right purpose. Of only one thing am I now certain: no progress can be made in the description of the Bavli, to which I have devoted some thirty monographs, not to mention my entire life, without a sustained and systematic comparison to cognate writings: writings that do the same thing, solve the same problem.

The next phase in the description of the Bavli requires comparison with documents that are not like it (in the way that the Yerushalmi is like it), but that – so it seems to me – also propose to solve the same problem of an ancient, continuous culture. The planned projects addressing synchronic issues are three:

The Bavli and the Denkart. A Comparison of the Systemic Statements of Judaism and Zoroastrianism.

From Old Order to New: Judaism, Zoroastrianism, Islam at the End of Antiquity.

All of this is aimed at the project of placing the Bavli into its own diachronic context and forming of the document a well-analyzed component in the formative history of Judaism: the climax and conclusion of the formation of the Judaism that would emerge from antiquity to dominate for all time to come, down to our own day. It is the description of the Talmud's statement, its "Judaism," its system, a description that is not mere paraphrase but true characterization, in the model of *The Transformation of Judaism. From Philosophy to Religion* (Champaign, 1992: University of Illinois Press):

The Definition of Judaism. From the Yerushalmi's Religion to the Bavli's Theology. The Autonomous Discourse of the Bavli and its Associated Midrash Compilations. The Traits and Program of the Normative, Dual Torah in Conclusion.

While I did not undertake this work in order to discover a theological truth, let alone demonstrate a theological proposition, I should be remiss if I did not state what I conceive to be one striking normative result of this descriptive inquiry. The implicit theological result is obvious: any notion that "Judaism," that is, the Torah, governs all places from one place is contradicted by the sages of the Bavli, who did not even concede that the Mishnah, a document of the Land of Israel, would be read in Babylonia in the way in which it was read in the Land of Israel. The Torah was everywhere one and the same. But to the sages of the Bavli that fact never meant that it would be read only in one place for all places. And since what the Bavli's framers rejected was the reading of the Mishnah in the Land of Israel, their clear intent was to declare their independence of intellect from even the Holy Land's sages, the autocephalous character of their right to judgment. True, when the Messiah would come, Torah once more would go forth from Zion and God's word from Jerusalem. But that would be because God would give the Torah – God, not sages.

And, in the interim, in their Talmud, the sages of Babylonia through power of intellect established for their region's community not mere equality but priority over the Land of Israel. And their success was complete. Babylonia's Talmud, not that of the Land of Israel – held sway and governs today, even in the Land of Israel. So what mattered then was force of intellect and above all else, the ineluctable hegemony of criticism. And – though people over there today substitute pride of place for wit and intellect – that is true today, too. Applied reason and practical logic, defining the morphology of mind of the Bavli and marking that document's incomparable superiority over the other Talmud, settled the question – because they persuaded people about what was, and is, true and compelling.

The Bavli won out because it is a more profound and more compelling writing, owing to the power of its sustained and unforgiving critical reasoning, and the Yerushalmi lost out even though it came from the Holy Land. So in matters of wit and intellect, mind matters, circumstance doesn't.

It remains to express my continuing thanks to the University of South Florida for providing ideal conditions in which to pursue my research, and to my colleagues in the Department of Religious Studies and in other departments for their ongoing friendship and stimulating conversation. They show me the true meaning of the word collegiality: honesty, generosity, sincerity. In the long, prior chapter in my career, now closed, I never knew such people of character and conscience.

JACOB NEUSNER
Distinguished Research Professor of Religious Studies
UNIVERSITY OF SOUTH FLORIDA
Tampa, FL 33620-5550 USA

July 28, 1992
My sixtieth birthday

Introduction

In this seven-volume monograph I prove that the second of the two Talmuds stands completely independent of the first. The Bavli's statement is its own; its voice, in context, is unique. We know that fact because when we compare the two Talmuds, we find that they are entirely unlike one another. They intersect at some verses of Scripture – but then not always for the same purpose; at many paragraphs of the Mishnah – but without a shared result far more often than with; and at episodic sentences of eminent authorities or stories or brief compositions, but then what is shared is mostly inert and rarely permits us to predict what both Talmuds will do with the same item. The Bavli does not build upon the Yerushalmi, refer to it, comment upon it, take issue with it, invoke its name or its ideas, find guidance in its intellectual program or compliment, by imitation, its modes of thought, reasoning, inquiry, and criticism. Similar in its form – a commentary to the Mishnah – the Bavli is unique in everything that counts. So the Talmuds differ because they're different.

But in that case, on what basis is comparison legitimate to begin with? That question stands at the head of any account of results such as these: How justify the comparison if in the end there proves to be little or nothing to compare? For before any labor of differentiation comes the answer to the simple question: How are the two Talmuds alike? Legitimating comparison takes priority over establishing contrast. And, as a matter of fact, if we had to describe either of the two Talmuds, our inductive procedure would be the same, so in what follows, by "the Talmud" I mean either one or the other.

The Talmuds look alike, so can be compared. But they are not alike, so they should be contrasted. For both documents fall under the following analytical considerations. They are alike, but in their canonical context, different from all other documents: a genus made up of two species. Among Mishnah centered writings – the Tosefta, Sifra, the two Sifrés, the Bavli and the Yerushalmi – only the two Talmuds conduct

1

sustained analytical inquiries over a broad range of problems. The Tosefta is not an analytical document; we have to supply the missing analytical program (as the authors of the two Talmuds, but particularly the Bavli, themselves discovered early on). Sifra and the two Sifrés treat the Mishnah in only a single aspect,[1] while the two Talmuds cover that aspect generously, along with a far more elaborate program. So the two Talmuds are unique in context. And they are unique in a second, somewhat more subtle way: both are made up mainly, though not exclusively, of writing we may call "talmud" or "a talmud," which is a moving ("dialectical") argument, from point to point, in which all possibilities are systematically taken up and examined. What is Talmudic about the two Talmuds is that mode of thought, which is a critical, systematic application of applied reason and practical logic, moving from a point starting with a proposition and (ordinarily) ending with a firm and articulated conclusion.

So let us speak of the Talmud as a genus, describing both species at one and the same time. In that way I prepare the way for the differentiation between the species of the genus Talmud, to which this seven-volume monograph is devoted.

The first point is the simplest but the most fundamental, since among all the canonical writings of Judaism, only the Talmud exhibits this trait: the systematic, formal, persistent mode of establishing order and structure: commentary to words and phrases of the (prior) Mishnah, always differentiated in the expected, intratextual manner of the rabbinic writers in general, for whom the conception of intertextuality is alien and repulsive (because arrogant). Looking at the Talmud whole, we notice two totally distinct sorts of materials: statements of law, then discussions of and excursus on those statements. We bring no substantial presuppositions to the text, if we declare these two sorts of materials to be, respectively, primary and constitutive, secondary and derivative. Calling the former the declaration of laws, the Mishnah passage, and the latter the exegesis of these laws, the Talmud proper, imposes no a priori judgment formed independently of the literary evidence in hand. We might as well call the two "the code" and "the commentary." The result would be no different.

In fact, as we see everywhere, the Talmud (once again: both Talmuds) is made up of two elements, each with its own literary traits

---

[1]This is spelled out in *Uniting the Dual Torah: Sifra and the Problem of the Mishnah* (Cambridge and New York, 1989: Cambridge University Press). Where the Mishnah intrudes in the two Sifrés, it is in this same regard; otherwise the Mishnah passage in the two compilations is cited for purposes of mere illustration.

and program of discussion. Since the Mishnah passage at the head of each set of Talmudic units of discourse defines the limits and determines the theme and, generally, the problematic of the whole, our attention is drawn to the traits of the Mishnah passages as a group. Here, of course, a certain measure of descriptive work has been done. But even if we for the first time saw these types of pericopes of the Mishnah (embedded as they are in the Talmud and separated from one another), we should discern that they adhere to a separate and quite distinctive set of literary and conceptual canons from what follows and surrounds them. Hence at the outset, with no appreciable attention to anything beyond the text, we should distinguish two "layers" of the Talmud and recognize that one "layer" is formed in one way, the other in another way. (I use "layer" for convenience only; it is not an apt metaphor.)

As I just said, if then we were to join together all the Mishnah pericopes, we should notice that they are stylistically and formally coherent and also different from everything else in the compilation before us. And, in point of fact, both Talmuds are like one another and different from every other document of the Judaism of the Dual Torah that reached closure in ancient times, down to the seventh century. Accordingly, for stylistic reasons alone we are on firm ground in designating the "layer" before us as the base point for all further inquiry. For the Mishnah "layer" has been shown to be uniform, while the Talmud "layer" is not demonstrably so. Hence, itself undifferentiated, the former the Mishnah "layer"provides the point of differentiation. The latter, the Talmud "layer," presents the diverse materials subject to differentiation.

To describe either Talmud we have to begin with its relationship to the Mishnah, which is the Talmuds' own starting point. While the Mishnah admits to no antecedents and neither alludes to nor cites anything prior to its own materials, a passage of the Talmud is often incomprehensible without knowledge of the passage of the Mishnah around which the Talmud's discourse centers. Yet in describing and defining the Talmud, we should grossly err if we were to say it is only, or mainly, a step-by-step commentary on the Mishnah, defined solely by the Mishnah's interests. We may not even say though it is a step closer to the truth that the Talmud is a commentary on or secondary development of, the Mishnah and important passages of the Tosefta. Units of discourse which serve these sorts of materials stand side by side with many which in an immediate sense do not. Accordingly, while a description of the Talmud requires attention to the interplay between the Talmud and the Mishnah and Tosefta, the diverse relationships between the Talmud and one or the other of those two documents constitute only one point of description and differentiation. For the Talmud is in full command of its own program of thought and inquiry. Its framers, responsible for the units of discourse, chose what in the Mishnah will be analyzed and what ignored. True, there could be no Talmud without the Mishnah and Tosefta. But knowing only those two works, we could never have predicted in a systematic way the character of the Talmud's discourse at any point.

To develop a taxonomy of the units of discourse contained within either of the two Talmuds we begin by describing gross redactional traits. These are visible to the naked eye. The question then is simple: What kinds of units of discourse does the document exhibit and how are they arranged? The answer to this question should yield a first glimpse of the redactional program of the ultimate framers of the Talmud. Once we differentiate by type among the materials in the hands of the arrangers of the whole, we also may observe what principles, if any, guide their work of arrangement.

What was the exegetical repertoire of the two Talmuds? The Talmud – that is, both Talmuds – invariably does to the Mishnah one of these four things:

1. Text criticism
2. Exegesis of the meaning of the Mishnah, including glosses and amplifications
3. Addition of scriptural prooftexts of the Mishnah's central propositions
4. Harmonization of one Mishnah passage with another such passage or with a statement of Tosefta.

The first two of these four procedures remain wholly within the narrow frame of the Mishnah passage subject to discussion. The second pair take an essentially independent stance vis-à-vis the Mishnah pericope at hand. Speaking of both Talmuds whole and complete, I state very simply that we do not find a single usable category in which the Talmud treats the Mishnah as a whole, either viewing it as a complete document, or taking up entire tractates or at least entire chapters. The Mishnah is read by the Talmud as a composite of discrete and essentially autonomous rules, a set of atoms, not an integrated molecule, so to speak. In so doing, the most striking formal traits of the Mishnah are obliterated. More important, the Mishnah as a whole and complete statement of a viewpoint no longer exists. Its propositions are reduced to details. Then, on occasion, the details may be restated in generalizations encompassing a wide variety of other details across the gaps between one tractate and another. This immensely creative and imaginative approach to the Mishnah vastly expands the range of discourse. But, as I said, the first, and deepest, consequence is to deny to the Mishnah both its own mode of speech and its distinctive and coherent message.

Both Talmuds' framers dealt with Mishnah tractates of their own choice, and neither provides a Talmud to the entirety of the Mishnah. What the Mishnah provided, therefore, was not received in a spirit of humble acceptance. Important choices were made about what to treat, hence what to ignore. The exegetical mode of reception did not have to obscure the main lines of the Mishnah's system. But it surely did so. The discrete reading of sentences, or, at most, paragraphs, denying all context, avoiding all larger generalizations except for those transcending the specific lines of tractates, this approach need not have involved the utter reversal of the paramount and definitive elements of the Mishnah's whole and integrated worldview (its "Judaism"). But doing these things did facilitate the revision of the whole into a quite different pattern. To use a different metaphor, they shifted the orbit of the Mishnah from one path to another.

The Talmud provides some indication of effort at establishing the correct text of various passages of the Mishnah. This nearly always is in the context of deciding the law. It is not a random search for a "perfect" text. It rather represents a deliberate and principled inquiry into the law as revealed by the phrasing of a passage. That is why, in the bulk of these passages, the legal consequences of one reading as opposed to another are carefully articulated, sometimes even tied to a range of other points subject to dispute.

The Mishnah, as is well known, rarely finds it necessary to cite a scriptural prooftext for its propositions. Just as the Mishnah ignores the scriptural ways of stating propositions in general, and laws in particular, favoring instead its own highly distinctive and disciplined syntax and morphology and word choices, so the Mishnah rephrases whatever it borrows from Scripture into its own terms. It rarely invokes in behalf of its own ideas the authority of Scripture. That occurs more commonly in discussions of theological than narrowly legal matters. The Talmud of our probe, by contrast, finds it appropriate whenever possible to cite scriptural prooftexts for the propositions of the Mishnah. The best we can say is that the Talmud's approach to a given passage of the Mishnah, two out of three times, is to provide some sort of gloss or exegesis, and one out of three times a prooftext as well. The provision of exegetical remarks is hardly surprising. Given the traits of the Mishnah, we must find remarkable the interest in adding what the framers of the Mishnah, for their part, found unnecessary.

For the Mishnah is hardly an independent code, totally autonomous of Scripture. On the contrary, viewed one by one, the tractates of the Mishnah exhibit diverse relationships to the facts presented in Scripture. While the various tractates of the Mishnah relate in different ways to Scripture, the view of the framers of the Talmud on the same matter is not differentiated. So far as they are concerned, prooftexts for Mishnaic rules are required. These will be supplied in substantial numbers. And that is the main point. The Mishnah now is systematically represented as not standing free and separate from Scripture, but dependent upon it. The authority of the Mishnah's laws then is reinforced. But the autonomy of the Mishnah as a whole is severely compromised. And that is the main point. Just as the Mishnah is represented in the Talmud as a set of rules, rather than as a philosophical essay, so it is presented, rule by rule, as a secondary and derivative development of Scripture.

So the undifferentiated effort to associate diverse Mishnah laws with Scripture is to be viewed together with the systematic breakup of the Mishnah into its diverse laws. The two quite separate activities produce a single effect. That is, they permit the Talmud to represent the state of affairs pretty much as the framers of the Talmud wish to do. Everything is continuous: Scripture, Mishnah, Talmud itself. Then all things, as now shaped by the rabbis of the Talmud, have the standing of Scripture and represent the authority of Moses (now called "our rabbi"). Accordingly, once the Mishnah enters either of the two Talmuds it nowhere emerges intact. It is wholly preserved, but in bits and pieces, shaped and twisted in whatever ways the Talmud wishes. The sages of the Mishnah read the Scripture as closely and as honestly as can be imagined. To be sure, that is not to claim their results always, or even often, coincide with the original intent of the diverse writers and framers of the scriptural law codes. It is only to allege that the trait of mind of the Mishnaic exegetes of Scripture was no different from our own: to do their best, in an honest and forthright way, to say what the passage meant, and therefore must continue to mean.

First, when does the Talmud speak for itself, not for the Mishnah? Second, what sorts of units of discourse contain such passages of "Talmudic" in the two Talmuds?

1. Theoretical Questions of Law Not Associated with a Particular Passage of the Mishnah.

There is some tendency to move beyond the legal boundaries set by the Mishnah's rules themselves. More general inquiries are taken up. These of course remain within the framework of the topic of one tractate or another, although there are some larger modes of thought characteristic of more than a single tractate. To explain what I mean, I point to the mode of thought in which the scriptural basis of the law of the Mishnah will be investigated, without regard to a given tractate. Along these same lines, I may point to a general inquiry into the count under which one may be liable for a given act, comments on the law governing teaching and judging cases, and the like. But these items tend not to leave the Mishnah far behind.

2. Exegesis of Scripture Separate from the Mishnah.

It is under this rubric that we find the most important instances in which the Talmud presents materials essentially independent of the Mishnah. The repertoire produced by our probe is substantial and striking. While, as I said, many items on the foregoing list may be linked to a theme of the Mishnah, if not to a specific rule, virtually all of the items on this list stand totally separate from the Mishnah. They pursue problems or themes through what is said about a biblical figure, expressing ideas and values simply unknown to the Mishnah. Moreover, as we shall see in due course, most of what is said in response to verses of Scripture reveals right on the surface fundamental values of what we may call, for convenience's sake, Rabbinic Judaism.

3. Historical Statements.

The Talmud contains a fair number of statements that something happened, or narratives about how something happened. While many of these are replete with biblical quotations, in general they do not provide exegesis of Scripture, which serves merely as illustration or reference point.

4. Stories about, and Rules for, Sages and Disciples, Separate from Discussion of a Passage of the Mishnah.

The Mishnah contains a tiny number of tales about rabbis. These serve principally as precedents for, or illustrations of, rules. The Talmud by contrast contains a sizable number of stories about sages and their relationships to other people. Like the items in the second and third lists, these, too, may be adduced as evidence of the values of the people who stand behind the Talmud, the things they thought important. These tales rarely serve to illustrate a rule or concept of the Mishnah. The main, though not the only, characteristic theme is the power of the rabbi, the honor due to the rabbi, and the tension between the rabbi and others, whether the patriarch, on the one side, the heretic on the second, or the gentile on the third. When the Talmud presents us with ideas or expressions of a world related to, but fundamentally separate from, that of the Mishnah, that is, when the Talmud wishes to say something other than what the Mishnah says and means, it will take up one of two modes of discourse. Either we find exegesis of biblical passages, with the value system of the rabbis read into the scriptural tales; or we are told stories about holy men and paradigmatic events, once again through tales told in such a way that a didactic and paranaetic purpose is served.

If, therefore, we want to point to what is Talmudic in either of the two Talmuds it is the exegesis of Scripture, on the one side, and the narration of historical or biographical tales about holy men, on the other. Since much of the biblical exegesis turns upon holy men of biblical times, we may say that the Talmud speaks for itself alone, as distinct from addressing the problems of the Mishnah, when it tells about holy men now and then. But what is genuinely new in the Talmud, in comparison and contrast to the Mishnah, is the inclusion of extensive discourse on the meaning imputed to Scripture. Our Talmuds therefore stand essentially secondary to two prior documents: Mishnah, on the one side, and Scripture, on the other. Mishnah is read in the Talmud pretty much within the framework of meaning established by the Mishnah itself. Scripture is read as an account of a world remarkably like that of the rabbis of the Talmud. When the rabbis speak for themselves, as distinct from the Mishnah, it is through exegesis of Scripture. (But any other mode of reading Scripture, to them, would have been unthinkable. They took for granted that they and Scripture's heroes and sages lived in a single timeless plane.)

It follows that the Talmuds are a composite of three kinds of materials: exegeses of the Mishnah, exegeses of Scripture, and accounts of the men who provide both. Perhaps one might wish to see the Talmud as a reworking of its two antecedent documents: the Mishnah, lacking much reference to Scripture, and the Scripture itself. The Talmud brings the two together into a synthesis of its own making, both in reading Scripture into Mishnah, and in reading Scripture alongside of, and separate from, Mishnah. Further, since, as we know, the next major phase, beyond the Talmud, in the formation of the literature of Judaism, will be the making of compilations of scriptural exegeses (midrash collections), we may say that the Talmud forms the bridge from the formation of the Mishnah to the making of the earliest midrash collections. Focused upon the Mishnah, it opens the way to the creation of compilations of midrash passages. But the question of how to define and describe the Talmud's own system remains to be answered.

First, when we seek to define and describe what is both Mishnaic and Talmudic in either of the two Talmuds we cannot turn chiefly to the substance of the document, the points at which the Talmud as we know it shares or does not share themes and conceptions found also in the Mishnah.

Second, it does not suffice to allege, as I did above, that what is distinctively Mishnaic is identified in the discussion of the simple meaning of a Mishnah rule or an analysis of the interplay of two or more rules of the Mishnah.

Third, when we catalogue issues essentially independent of the Mishnah, the result is a glimpse at a world definitive not of the Talmud as such but rather of the *context* of the Talmud as we know it. That is to say, lacking systematic tractates, chapters, or even an abundance of units of discourse, on the distinctively rabbinic themes and exercises, we cannot describe out of the resources of the Talmud itself a system we may call Talmudic, in contradistinction to the system we properly call Mishnaic. The materials are not sufficient. They are not represented as structurally definitive. They are episodic and hardly articulated.

Fourth and most decisive, what is Talmudic in our Talmuds must be located, then defined and described, at that very point at which the distinctively Talmudic is itself Mishnaic. If, as we now know, the bulk of the Talmud's materials focuses upon the Mishnah, it must follow that the system everywhere expressed within the Talmud *also* will be revealed when the Talmud addresses the Mishnah. Specifically we must once more seek to taxonomize and then catalogue those passages in which the Talmud's framers carry out that exercise that is paramount and predominant, defining the character of approximately 90 percent of the whole of the document: Mishnah exegesis. What we want now to know is how to describe the worldview of the framers of the document when at issue is the exegesis of the Mishnah.

To phrase the questions from the top to the bottom: What do rabbis in particular do when they read the Mishnah? What are their modes of thought, their characteristic ways of analysis? Finally, what do we learn about their worldview from the ways in which they receive and interpret the worldview they have inherited in the Mishnah? These are the very questions, we now realize, that the Talmud answers. So when we wish to describe the Talmud's system as a whole, we must answer them. It goes without saying that in differentiating the two documents, we shall also raise the same question: How is the treatment of the Mishnah in the later Talmud different from that in the earlier one (if it is)? Having come this far, let me now state the upshot of the initial inquiry, Chapter One of this book: if we want to know how the later Talmud differs from the earlier one, it will be in the way in which the two Talmuds treat the Mishnah (and by analogy any other document or proposition), there and there alone. But that statement will make sense only when we have considered both Talmuds' reading of M. Qiddushin 1:1.

The Talmudic exegetes of the Mishnah brought to the document no distinctive program of their own. At least, I perceive no hidden agenda. To state matters negatively, the exegetes did not know in advance of their approach to a law of the Mishnah facts about the passage not contained (even implicitly) within the boundaries of the language of the Mishnah passage itself (except only for facts contained within other units of the same document). Rejecting propositions that were essentially a priori, they proposed to explain and expand precisely the wording and the conceptions supplied by the document under study. I cannot point to a single instance in which the Talmudic exegetes appear to twist and turn the language and message of a passage, attempting to make the words mean something other than what they appear to say anyhow. Whether the exegetical results remain close to the wording of a passage of the Mishnah, or whether they leap beyond the bounds of the passage, the upshot is the same. There is no exegetical program revealed in the Talmud's reading of the Mishnah other than that defined, to begin with, by the language and conceptions of one Mishnah passage or another.

That simple fact calls into question whether we may ever define what is Talmudic about the Talmuds. That is hardly an operative category. For, at the end, the whole, seen whole, appears to be nothing more than a secondary development of the Mishnah. To be sure, the Talmud contains a merely episodic and negligible corpus of distinctively rabbinic, hence Talmudic, tales about rabbis and references to verses of Scripture read as rabbis read them. But that paltry and occasional set of "tacked-on" units of discourse merely underlines the main and definitive trait of the whole. The Talmud overall slavishly adheres to the program, canons of thought, and (so far as we may judge) "values" of the Mishnah itself. So that on the face of it appears to be the whole story: the Mishnah speaks about life, and the Talmud speaks about the Mishnah.

If there is nothing *in particular* that is Talmudic, there is much *in general* that is Talmudic. Distinguishing the Mishnaic from the Talmudic components of the Talmuds shows us that the Talmudic sages' reading of the Mishnah, their hermeneutic, takes shape within the wording and contents of the Mishnah. For these set forth the problems to be solved and furthermore guided the exegete to solutions of them. But the entire approach of the Talmud to the Mishnah is itself profoundly Talmudic, and this in several fundamental respects.

First, the Mishnah was set forth by Rabbi whole and complete, a profoundly unified, harmonious document. The Talmud insists upon obliterating the marks of coherence. It treats in bits and pieces what was originally meant to speak whole. That simple fact constitutes what is original, stunningly new and, by definition, Talmudic.

Second, the Mishnah, also by definition, delivered its message in the way chosen by Rabbi. That is to say, by producing the document as he did, Rabbi left no space for the very enterprises of episodic exegesis undertaken so brilliantly by his immediate continuators and heirs.

True, a rather limited process of explanation and gloss of words and phrases, accompanied by a systematic inquiry into the wording of one passage or another, got underway, probably at the very moment, and within the very process, of the Mishnah's closure. But insofar as the larger messages and meanings of the document are conveyed in the ways Rabbi chose through formalization of language, through contrasts, through successive instances of the same normally unspecified, general proposition, for example, the need for exegesis was surely not generated by Rabbi's own program for the Mishnah. Quite to the contrary, Rabbi chose for his Mishnah a mode of expression and defined for the document a large-scale structure and organization, which, by definition, were meant to stand firm and autonomous. Rabbi's Mishnah speaks clearly and for itself.

For the Mishnah did not merely come to closure. At that moment it also formed a closed system, that is, a whole, complete statement. It does not require facts outside of its language and formulation, so makes no provision for commentary and amplification of brief allusions, as the Talmud's style assuredly does. The Mishnah refers to nothing beyond itself. It promises no information other than what is provided within its limits. It raises no questions for ongoing discussion beyond its decisive, final, descriptive statements of enduring realities and fixed relationships. The Talmud's single, decisive, irrevocable judgment is precisely opposite. The Talmud's first initiative is to reopen the Mishnah's closed system, almost at the moment of its completion and perfection. That at the foundations is what is Talmudic about the Talmuds: their daring assertion that the concluded and completed demanded clarification and continuation. Once that assertion was made to stick, nothing else mattered very much.

What was to be clarified was obvious. What was to be continued must go forward along an essentially straight line from the starting point. No matter. The message was clear not solely in the character of the whole, still less in its contents, its assertions about the meaning of the Mishnah's laws. At every point, from the simplest gloss to the most far-ranging speculative inquiry, the message was the same. It was conveyed (we have learned to perceive) in the very medium of the Talmud: a new language, focused upon a new grid of discourse. The language was what it was: anything but patterned and thus anything but Mishnaic, even when (viewed redactionally) in Tosefta.

The grid of discourse lay across, rather than within, the inner boundaries of the Mishnah itself, a profound and fundamental revolution in thought, as I have already stressed. Accordingly, the Talmud's distinctive traits, separate from those defined by the Mishnah for the age beyond the Mishnah's closure, lie not in the depths of what was said, but on the very surface, in the very literary formulation of the Talmud itself. Yet the judgment of the Talmud upon the Mishnah, that is, what is Talmudic in the Talmud, is not fully described when we have seen what lies scattered on the surface. When we return to the taxa just now found exhaustive, we discover a program of criticism of the Mishnah framed by independent and original minds. Let us bypass the obvious points of independent judgment, the matter of insistence that the very word choices of the Mishnah require clarification, therefore prove faulty. The meanings and amplification of phrases represent the judgment that Rabbi's formulation, while stimulating and provocative, left much to be desired. These indications of independence of judgment among people disposed not merely to memorize but to improve upon the text provided by Rabbi hardly represent judgments of substance.

Rather, let us turn to the two most striking lists: first, the provision of scriptural prooftexts for the propositions of various passages of the Mishnah, a matter that has captured our attention many times; second, the rewriting, in the Mishnah's own idiom, if not in its redactional and disciplinary patterns, of much of the law, through the supplementary materials we call Tosefta, a matter treated here in only a preliminary way. As to the former, of course, the message is clear. The propositions of the Mishnah cannot stand by themselves but must be located within the larger realm of scriptural authority. If Rabbi presented his Mishnah without prooftexts in the belief that such texts were either self-evident or unnecessary, his continuators and successors rejected his judgment on both counts. So far as the Mishnah was supposed to stand as a law code independent of the revelation of Torah to Moses at Mount Sinai, it was received by people to whom such a supposition was incredible. So far as Rabbi took for granted the scriptural facticity of the facts of his law code, that was regarded as insufficient.

What was implicit (if it was implicit) had to be made explicit. As to the latter, the Tosefta's numerous passages, serving as an exegetical complement to the Mishnah's corresponding passages, phrased in the way in which the Mishnah's sentences are written (as distinct from the utterly different way in which the Talmud's sentences are framed), show equivalent independence of mind. They indicate that, where sages of the time of the Talmuds took up Mishnaic passages, they were not at all limited to the work of gloss and secondary expansion. They recognized and exercised a quite remarkable freedom of initiative. In the Tosefta they undertook to restate in their own words, but imitating the Mishnah's style, the propositions of the Mishnah passage at hand. That is, they both cite what the Mishnah had said and also continue, in imitation of the Mishnah's language, the discourse of the Mishnah passage itself.

These Toseftan complements to the Mishnah are Talmudic, just as much as the rhetorically unrelated passages listed in the other catalogues, in two senses. First, they come to expression in the period after the Mishnah had reached closure, as is clear from the fact that the exact language of the Mishnah is cited prior to the labor of extension, expansion and revision. So they are the work of the Talmud's age and authority. Second, they self-evidently derive from precisely the same authorities responsible for the formation of the Talmud as a whole. That is the fact, by definition. Accordingly, both the insistence upon adducing prooftexts for passages Rabbi judged not to need, and the persistent revision and expansion of the Mishnah, even in clumsy imitation of the Mishnah's syntax, rhetoric, and word choices, tell us once more that simple truth we saw at the outset. The Talmud is distinctively Talmudic precisely when the Mishnah itself defines the Talmud's labor, dictates its ideas, displays its rhetoric, determines its results. The very shift in usable language, from "the Mishnah" (as a whole) to "the Mishnah passage" or "the Mishnaic law at hand" indicates the true state of affairs. On the surface, in all manner of details, the two Talmuds are little more than secondary and derivative documents, explaining the Mishnah itself in trivial ways, or expanding it in a casuistic and logic-chopping manner. But viewing that same surface from a different, more distant perspective and angle, we see things quite differently. In detail the Talmud changed nothing. Overall, the Talmud left nothing the same.

So, as I said at the outset, in the Talmud we find little to deem Talmudic in particular. But there is much that is Talmudic in general. The particular bits and pieces are Mishnaic. But the Talmud leaves nothing of the Mishnah whole and intact. Its work upon the whole presents an essentially new construction. Through the Mishnah, Rabbi contributed to the Talmud most of the bricks, but little of the mortar, and none of the joists and beams. The design of the whole bore no relationship to Rabbi's plan for the Mishnah. The sages of the Talmud did the rest. They alone imagined, then built, the building. They are the architects, theirs is the vision. The building is a monument to the authority of the sage above all.

I have left for last the single fact, spread over the whole, superficial beyond all others, thus indicative of the Talmudic sages' freedom of imagination: the exercise of free choice even among the Mishnah's tractates awaiting exegesis. We do not know why some tractates were chosen for Talmudic expansion and others left fallow. We may speculate that the omission of all reference to the entire division of Holy Things, on the everyday conduct of the Temple, and to most of the division of Purities, on the sources of uncleanness, objects subject to uncleanness, and modes of removing contamination, constitutes a radical revision of the law of Judaism. What for Rabbi was well over 40 percent of the whole story in volume, forming two of his six divisions in structure, for the Talmud's designers (I assume early as much as late), was of no importance.

Both Talmuds address Appointed Times, Women, and Damages, the second, third, and fourth divisions of the Mishnah. That is then where the comparisons and contrasts have to take place. Interest in the division of Appointed Times involved extensive discussion of the conduct of the cult on extraordinary days. Perhaps at issue here was not what had to be omitted (the cult on appointed times) but what people wanted to discuss, the home and village on those same holy occasions. So the former came in the wake of the latter. Inclusion of the divisions of Women, on the family and the transfer of women from father to husband and back, and Damages, on civil law and institutions, is not hard to explain. The sages fully expected to govern the life of Israel, the Jewish people, in its material and concrete aspects. These divisions, as well as some of the tractates of the division on Appointed Times, demanded and received attention. Ample treatment of the laws in the first division, governing the priests' rations and other sacred segments of the agricultural produce of the Holy Land, is to be expected among authorities living not only in, but also off, the Holy Land.

Accordingly, when we describe the selection of divisions, at the very same moment we interpret the principle of selection: relevance to the setting of the nation of Israel in its Land. Here, too, as before, the details of how the Mishnah is received are only moderately interesting. But the central fact is stunning: whole divisions were dropped. There is evidently nothing in the particularity of the details to be regarded as definitive of the mind and imagination of the group behind our Talmud. But the Talmud as a whole tells us what we wish to know. Having labored in the underbrush of a document in form and substance totally subservient to its own principal focus, the Mishnah itself, we reach this simple conclusion. In accepting authority, in centering discourse upon the ideas of other men, in patiently listing even the names behind authoritative laws from olden times to their own day, the sages and framers of the Talmud accomplished exactly the opposite of what they apparently wished to do.

The two Talmuds form a single genus because they both made a commentary. But they both obliterated the text. So theirs is a different kind of commentary from, for example, the genius Rashi's, whose commentary always highlights the wholeness and integrity of the text on which he comments. They loyally explained the Mishnah. But they turned the Mishnah into something else than what it had been. They patiently hammered out chains of tradition, binding themselves to the authority of the remote and holy past. But it was, in the end, a tradition of their own design and choosing. That is, it was not tradition but a new creation. And so this Talmud of ours, so loyal and subservient to the Mishnah of Rabbi, turns out to be less a reworking of received materials than a work of remarkably independent judgment. The Talmuds speak humbly and subserviently about received truth, always in the name only of Moses and of sages of times past. But in the end it is truth not discovered and demonstrated, but determined and invented and declared.

Since the Talmuds carry forward and depend upon the Mishnah, to describe the Talmuds we have to begin with its relationship to the Mishnah, which is the Talmuds' own starting point. While the Mishnah admits to no antecedents and neither alludes to nor cites anything prior to its own materials, a passage of the Talmud is often incomprehensible without knowledge of the passage of the Mishnah around which the Talmud's discourse centers. Yet in describing and defining the Talmud, we should grossly err if we were to say it is only, or mainly, a step-by-step commentary on the Mishnah, defined solely by the Mishnah's interests. We may not even say though it is a step closer to the truth that the Talmud before us is a commentary on or secondary development of, the Mishnah and important passages of the Tosefta. Units of discourse which serve these sorts of materials stand side by side with many which in an immediate sense do not. Accordingly, while a description of the Talmud requires attention to the interplay between the Talmud and the Mishnah and Tosefta, the diverse relationships between the Talmud and one or the other of those two documents constitute only one point of description and differentiation. For the Talmud is in full command of its own program of thought and inquiry. Its framers, responsible for the units of discourse, chose what in the Mishnah will be analyzed and what ignored. True, there could be no Talmud without the Mishnah and Tosefta. But knowing only those two works, we could never have predicted in a systematic way the character of the Talmud's discourse at any point.

The Mishnah nonetheless permits us at the outset to gain perspective on the character of Talmuds. For the Mishnah does exhibit a remarkable unity of literary and redactional traits. By that standard our Talmud presents none. Accordingly, while whatever materials reached the framers of the Mishnah ca. 175-200 were revised by them in line with a single and simple literary and redactional program, the same is not the case for the Talmuds. Whatever the stages of redaction of the document as a whole, let alone of its components, we may say with certainty that the people ultimately responsible for the document as we have it did not do to the materials in their hands what the framers of the Mishnah did to theirs. The ultimate redactors did not participate in the work of formulation. Units of discourse framed in some prior setting have been preserved as is (though we do not know to what extent as to detail). They were drawn together whole and complete with other such essentially fixed and final units of discourse.

The redactional program of the men responsible for laying out the materials of Talmuds may now be described in simple terms. Most important, there was such a program and it is essentially the same in both writings. There is nothing random. That is clear because, within the differentiation of units of discourse I have defined, diverse types of units of discourse are not mixed together promiscuously. There is a pronounced tendency in both Talmuds to move from close reading of the Mishnah and then Tosefta to more general inquiry into the principles of a Mishnah passage and their interplay with those of some other, superficially unrelated passage, and, finally, to more general reflections on law not self-evidently related to the Mishnah passage at hand or to anthologies intersecting only at a general topic. Now while that program may appear self-evident and logical, we must not assume there were no choices in how to lay things out.

The program I have described exhibits sufficient variation to rule out the possibility that our Talmud's way is the better way of doing things. The redactors knew precisely how they wished to lay out the materials that they drew together into the Talmud. Accordingly, the work of redaction was active and followed a program. If therefore we now take as fact that the Talmud before us is the result of a generation, or several generations, of redaction, it is because we see the evidence of active participation in the formation of the document: a plan, a program. The contrary possibility, that this is just how things happened to come to hand, seems unlikely, given the disproportionate replication of a single logical, self-evident pattern. The second question flows from the first. If the redactors participated in the organization of units of discourse, did they also place their mark upon the formulation of those same units of discourse?

The Talmuds are phrased so differently that a comparison of the syntax of the Mishnah with that of the Talmud is incongruous. Unlike the Mishnah, the Talmud reveals no effort to systematize sayings in larger constructions, to impose a pattern upon all individual sayings. If the Mishnah is framed to facilitate memorization, then we must say that the Talmud's materials are not framed with mnemonics in mind. If the Mishnah focuses upon subsurface relationships in syntax, the Talmud in the main looks like notes of a discussion. These notes may serve to recreate the larger patterns of argument and reasoning, a summary of what was thought and perhaps also said. The Talmud preserves and expresses concrete ideas, reducing them to brief but usually accessible and obvious statements. The Mishnah speaks of concrete things in order to hint at abstract relationships, which rarely are brought to the surface and fully exposed.

The Mishnah hides. The Talmud spells out. The Mishnah hints. The Talmud repeats, *ad nauseam*. The Mishnah is subtle, the Talmud obvious; the one restrained and tentative, the other aimed at full and exhaustive expression of what is already clear. The sages of the Mishnah rarely represent themselves as deciding cases. Only on unusual occasions do they declare the decided law, at best reticently spelling out what underlies their positions. The rabbis of the Talmud harp on who holds which opinion and how a case is actually decided, presenting a rich corpus of precedents. They seek to make explicit what is implicit in the law. The Mishnah is immaterial and spiritual, the Talmud earthy and social. The Mishnah deals in the gossamer threads of philosophical principle, the Talmud in the coarse rope that binds this one and that one into a social construction.

The comparison and contrast of the Mishnah to the Talmud presents us with a set of opposites, captured in the simple contrast that has emerged at one point after another, between exemplifying a pattern as against providing a precedent, speculating on the implications of principles as against deciding the law and declaring whose opinion counts. My interpretation of the matter beyond the evidence is this: the Mishnah speaks of stasis and eternity to whom it may concern. The Talmuds address Israel in the here and now of ever-changing times, the gross matter of disorder and history. Clearly, the central traits of the Mishnah, revealed in the document at its time of closure in ca. A.D. 200, were revised and transformed into those definitive of the Talmud at its time of closure in ca. A.D. 400 for the earlier Talmud, 600 for the later. So much for how the Talmuds are alike: in every possible way. How are they different? The burden of this seven-volume monograph is, they scarcely intersect. In common is form, different is substance, beginning, middle, and end. So, as I say, the Talmuds differ because they're different.

The way forward lies in a rereading of a complete, large chapter of a major tractate, for which purpose I begin with Bavli and Yerushalmi to Mishnah-tractate Qiddushin Chapter One. The Bavli for that tractate, more than forty folios, is equivalent to all but the largest tractates of the

Bavli. The Yerushalmi's counterpart is of respectable dimensions, certainly not so perfunctory as the Yerushalmi's treatment of the Babas. We take special interest in the description of types of Mishnah commentary (and willy-nilly, other compositions and composites as well). This will take a variety of directions. First, given a common Mishnah pericope, do we find the two Talmuds asking the same question or different questions? If the same question, do they then go about their work in the same way or in different ways? If in different ways, what do we learn in the difference, specifically about the second of the two Talmuds? If they ask different questions, then what interests characterize the one but not the other? Does the second of the two Talmuds acknowledge a program received from the first, or do its framers address the Mishnah without the mediation of a prior authorship and its program?

These then form two distinct paths of inquiry, the one into the types of compositions and composites, a question of form-analysis writ large, the other into the specific intellectual programs characteristic of each document. The second of the two inquiries is the more difficult to define at the outset, but its outlines will rapidly take shape. In the opening analysis, we read each of the Talmuds in succession, and I take the time to spell out what I see and why. The results are given for the reading of M. 1:1. In the later ones, I approach matters in a succinct way, utilizing signals and comparison tables, rather than fully spelling out what is before us. I also undertake ad hoc comparisons of points at which the two Talmuds refer to the same verse of Scripture, make the same point, or respond to the same problem, and show that, so far as I can see, at none of these points of concrete intersection does the Bavli borrow anything from the Yerushalmi. By that point, anyone with the patience to work through the evidence as I represent it will know precisely what I see and why it bears the meaning that I impute to it.

1

Mishnah-Tractate Qiddushin 1:1 in the Yerushalmi and the Bavli

Our initial probe carries us to a long and important Talmud passage, and that justifies our treating the first step as a test of a familiar procedure. It is my way to analyze the formal patterns of documents, and I have shown in a variety of works that the organizing and large-scale forms of one compilation differ markedly and purposefully from those of another.[1] Any work of comparison should therefore begin with the governing formal program of each of the Talmuds. So at the end of the presentation of the texts, I compare the formal preferences of the two Talmuds. A second, equally familiar procedure of mine is to translate the particular into the general, and here, again, I generalize on the intellectual programs of the two Talmuds and then compare the generalizations. These procedures will tell us whether we take the correct approach in our attempt to differentiate one Talmud from the other.

1:1

A. A woman is acquired [as a wife] in three ways, and acquires [freedom for] herself [to be a free agent] in two ways.

B. She is acquired through money, a writ, or sexual intercourse.

---

[1]The work of comparative form-analysis is in these works: *The Integrity of Leviticus Rabbah. The Problem of the Autonomy of a Rabbinic Document* (Chico, 1985: Scholars Press for Brown Judaic Studies); *Comparative Midrash: The Plan and Program of Genesis Rabbah and Leviticus Rabbah* (Atlanta, 1986: Scholars Press for Brown Judaic Studies); *From Tradition to Imitation. The Plan and Program of Pesiqta deRab Kahana and Pesiqta Rabbati* (Atlanta, 1987: Scholars Press for Brown Judaic Studies). [With a fresh translation of Pesiqta Rabbati *Pisqaot* 1-5, 15.]; *Canon and Connection: Intertextuality in Judaism* (Lanham, 1986: University Press of America. Studies in Judaism Series); and *Midrash as Literature: The Primacy of Documentary Discourse* (Lanham, 1987: University Press of America Studies in Judaism series).

C.   Through money:
D.   The House of Shammai say, "For a denar or what is worth a denar."
E.   And the House of Hillel say, "For a perutah or what is worth a perutah."
F.   And how much is a perutah?
G.   One eighth of an Italian issar.
H.   And she acquires herself through a writ of divorce or through the husband's death.
I.   The deceased childless brother's widow is acquired through an act of sexual relations.
J.   And acquires [freedom for] herself through a rite of removing the shoe or through the levir's death.

I. The Talmud of the Land of Israel to M. Qiddushin 1:1

[I.A]   The meaning of the language of the Mishnah [at M. 1:1B] is [that a woman is acquired] either through money, or through a writ, or through sexual intercourse, [but all three are not required for such a transaction].

[B]   And so, too, did R. Hiyya teach, "It is not the end of the matter that all three are involved, but even through any one of them [the transaction is carried out]."

[C]   Through money: How do we know [that time on the basis of Scripture]?

[D]   "If any man takes a wife" (Deut. 22:13) tells us that a woman is acquired through money.

[E]   Through sexual relations: How do we know [that item on the basis of Scripture]?

[F]   "And goes in to her [having sexual relations with her]" (Deut. 22:13) tells us that a woman is acquired through sexual relations.

[G]   I should then have reached the conclusion that the transaction is effected both through this means and through that [together].

[H]   How do I know that money effects acquisition without sexual relations, or that sexual relations effect acquisition without money?

[I]   R. Abbahu in the name of R. Yohanan: "It is written, 'If a man is found lying with a woman who has had sexual relations with her husband' (Deut. 22:22).

[J]   "Now take note: Even if the man has acquired her only through sexual relations, the Torah has decreed that he who has sexual relations thereafter is [guilty of having sexual relations with a married woman and is subject to the death penalty through] strangling."

[K]   [No, J's reading will not suffice. For] it is not the end of the matter that [the sexual relations take place] in the normal manner. But even [if the husband had sexual relations] not in the normal manner, [the woman is deemed fully wed to him].

[L]   [The following statement will indicate that the cited verse serves the purpose of proving that sexual relations not in the normal manner have the same effect. Consequently, the proof for H remains to be adduced.] R. Abbahu in the name of R. Yohanan: "The verse is required to indicate that sexual relations not in the normal manner [effect acquisition of the woman]. If you maintain [to the contrary] that the verse refers to a relationship effected through sexual relations in the normal manner, why should Scripture refer to a woman 'who has had sexual relations with her husband'? Even someone else [than the husband] may [through an act of normal sexual relations] render her 'a woman who has had sexual relations.'"

[M] As what we have learned there:

[N] If two men had sexual relations with a betrothed girl in succession, the first is liable to be put to death by stoning, and the second by strangling [M. San. 7:9]. "[The latter has had sexual relations with a nonvirgin who has the legal status of one 'who has had sexual relations with her husband,' although it is not her husband. See M. San. 11:1.]"

[O] Thus we have learned that sexual relations without payment of a money fee [effect acquisition of the woman].

[P] Payment of money without sexual relations, whence?

[Q] "And if he does not do these three things for her, she shall go out for nothing, without payment of money" (Ex. 21:11). "If he takes another wife to himself..." (Ex. 21:10).

[R] Just as the woman [slave girl] mentioned first involves a money payment, so the woman [wife] mentioned second involves a money payment. [That is, in context the acquisition is through payment of money.]

[S] "[When a man takes a wife and marries her, if then she finds no favor in his eyes because he has found some indecency in her,] and he writes her a bill of divorce and puts it in her hand and sends her out of his house, and if she goes and becomes another man's wife..." (Deut. 24:1, 2).

[T] The "becoming" [another man's wife] is so joined to the sending forth. Just as the sending forth is through a writ, so the "becoming" [another man's wife] is through a writ.

[II.A] [Having proved the rules through scriptural exegesis, we now turn to the experiment of proving the same rules through logical argument.] Said R. Abin, "And Hezekiah taught: 'When a man takes a wife' (Deut. 24:1) tells us that a woman is acquired through a money payment.

[B] "Now, it is a matter of logical argument, if a Hebrew slave girl. who is not acquired through sexual relations, is acquired through a money payment [Ex. 21:7: 'When a man sells his daughter'], this one, who may be acquired through sexual relations, is it not reasonable to suppose that she should be acquired through a money payment?

[C] "The childless brother-in-law's widow will prove [to the contrary], for she indeed is acquired through an act of sexual relations, but she is not acquired through a money payment.

[D] "This one, too, should cause no surprise, that even though she is acquired through sexual relations, [on the analogy with the childless sister-in-law] she still is not acquired through a money payment.

[E] "Accordingly, Scripture is required to state, 'When a man takes a wife' – indicating that she is acquired through a money payment.

[F] "'And has sexual relations with her' – indicating that she is acquired through an act of sexual relations.

[G] "Now is it not logical to argue as follows: If the childless widow, who is not acquired through a money payment, is acquired through an act of sexual relations, this one, who is acquired through a money payment, is it not logical that she should also be acquired through an act of sexual relations?

[H] "The Hebrew slave girl proves to the contrary. For she is acquired through a money payment and is not acquired through an act of sexual relations.

[I] "This one, too, should cause no surprise, for even though she is acquired through a money payment, she is not to be acquired through an act of sexual relations.

[J] "Accordingly, Scripture is required to state, 'When a man takes a wife' – indicating that she is acquired through a money payment.

[K] "'And has sexual relations with her' – indicating that she is acquired through an act of sexual relations.

[L] "As to a writ: Now if a payment of money, which does not have the power to free the woman from her husband, has the power to bring her under the domain of her husband, a writ, which does have the power to take her out of his domain – is it not logical that it should also have the power to bring her into his domain?

[M] "No, if you have stated that rule in regard to a money payment, which has the power to remove what has been sanctified from consecrated status through redemption [substitution], will you say the same of a writ, which does not have the power to redeem what has been consecrated and so remove it from its consecrated status?

[N] "The argument a fortiori has been shattered, and, accordingly, you must return to Scripture.

[O] "So it was necessary for Scripture to state: 'When a man takes a wife and marries her, if then she finds no favor in his eyes because he has found some indecency in her, and he writes her a bill of divorce and puts it in her hand and sends her out of his house, and she departs out of his house, and if she goes and becomes another man's wife...' (Deut. 24:1, 2).

[P] "The 'becoming' [another man's wife] thus is joined to the sending forth. Just as the sending forth is through a writ, so the becoming another man's wife is through a writ."

[III.A] Said R. Yudan, "It is possible to construct an argument a fortiori that a free woman may be acquired through an act of usucaption [in this context: Through performing an act of service that a wife is expected to perform for the husband].

[B] "[The argument rests upon the mode of acquisition of a Canaanite slave girl, which is through usucaption.] Now if, in the case of a Canaanite slave girl, who is not acquired through sexual relations, the girl is acquired through usucaption, this one, who is acquired through an act of sexual relations – is it not logical that she should be acquired through usucaption?

[C]   "Accordingly, Scripture is required to state, 'When a man takes a wife and has sexual relations with her' (Deut. 24:1), meaning, it is through sexual relations that this one is acquired, and she is not acquired through usucaption.

[D]   "[Similarly] we may construct an argument a fortiori in the case of a Canaanite slave girl that she should be acquired through an act of sexual relations.

[E]   "Now it is a matter of logic. If a free woman, who is not acquired through usucaption, is acquired through an act of sexual relations, this one, who is acquired through usucaption, is it not logical that she should be acquired through an act of sexual relations?

[F]   "Accordingly, Scripture is required to state, 'As for your male and female slaves whom you may have, you may buy male and female slaves from the nations that are round about you.... You may bequeath them to your sons after you, to inherit as a possession forever' (Lev. 25:46).

[G]   "It is through usucaption that a Canaanite slave girl is acquired, and she is not acquired through an act of sexual relations."

[IV.A] Lo, we have now proved that a woman is acquired as a wife in three ways...through money, writ, or sexual intercourse [see M. 1:1B].

[B]   Up to now we have dealt with Israelites. [What is the law as to] gentiles?

[C]   R. Abbahu in the name of R. Eleazar: "It is written 'Behold, you are a dead man, because of the woman whom you have taken; for she has had sexual relations with her husband' (Gen. 20:3).

[D]   "For those who are acquired through sexual relations, they are liable [for having sexual relations with a married woman], but they are not liable [for having sexual relations with] those who are [merely] betrothed."

[E]   The following statement of R. Eleazar [H-L] implies that that rule applies only when in the act of sexual relations the man has had the intention of effecting acquisition of the woman, while the following statement of Samuel [F-G] implies that that rule applies even when the man did not have the intention of effecting acquisition of the woman.

[F]   For R. Jonah said in the name of Samuel, "If a whore is standing at the window, and two men had sexual relations with her, the first is not put to death, while the second is put to death on account of the first [who through the act of sexual relations has acquired the woman as his wife, even though he did not intend to do so]."

[G]   Now did the former party actually intend through his act of sexual relations to acquire the whore as his wife? [Obviously not!]

[H]   "No man of you shall approach any one near of kin to him to uncover a nakedness" (Lev. 18:6).

[I]   Why does Scripture say, "No man ['man,' appearing twice in the verse]?"

[J]   It is to place under the jurisdiction of the laws of the nations gentiles who have had sexual relations with the connections prohibited to gentiles, and to place under the jurisdiction of the laws of Israel [58c] gentiles who have had sexual relations with the connections prohibited to Israelites.

[K]   Said R. Eleazar, "Among all of them, you have only a betrothed Israelite woman [for whom a gentile is liable].

[L]   "[That is to say,] if a gentile had sexual relations with an Israelite woman who is betrothed, he is liable. If he had sexual relations with a gentile woman who was betrothed, he is exempt."

[M]   Now if he had sexual relations with a betrothed Israelite woman, on what count is he liable? Is it under their laws or under the laws of Israel?

[N]   If you say that they are tried under Israelite law, then they must be subject to the testimony of two witnesses, to the judgment of twenty-three judges, to appropriate admonition, and, if guilty, to execution through stoning.

[O]   If you say that they are tried under gentile law, then they must be subject to the testimony of only one witness, to the judgment of only one judge, to no admonition, and, if guilty, to execution through decapitation by a sword.

[P]   R. Judah bar Pazzi adds, "[They are put to death] through strangulation, by reason of that very verse [cited at Q]."

[Q]   "What is the scriptural basis for this position? 'Whoever sheds the blood of man, by man his blood shall be shed' (Gen. 9:6) – [and this is through strangulation]."

[R]   [As to further differences, along the lines of N-O,] if you say that they are tried under Israelite law, then if he converted, he remains liable.

[S]   If you say that they are tried under gentile law, then if he converted he becomes exempt.

[T]   For R. Haninah said, "If a Noahide cursed [God] and converted he is exempt, because his status under the law has changed."

[U]   R. Eleazar in the name of R. Haninah said, "How do we know that Noahides are subject to admonition to avoid prohibited connections as are Israelites?

[V]   "'Therefore...a man cleaves to his wife' (Gen. 2:24) – and not to his fellow's wife.

[W]   "'Therefore...a man cleaves to his wife' – and not to a male, or to a beast."

[X]   R. Samuel, R. Abbahu, R. Eleazar in the name of R. Haninah: "A Noahide who had sexual relations with his wife not in the usual way is put to death.

[Y]   "What is the scriptural basis for that view? 'Therefore...a man cleaves to his wife and they become one flesh' (Gen. 2:24) –

[Z]   "It is to be at the place at which the two of them become one."

[AA]   R. Yosé raised the question, "Sexual contact with a male – what is the law?

[BB]   "Sexual contact with a beast – what is the law?

[CC]   "Now all prohibited sexual relations were derived from the prohibition of having sexual relations with a menstruating woman. That covering a male or a beast likewise derives from the same analogy."

[DD]   Now up to now we have raised the question concerning Israelites. What is the law regarding gentiles?

[EE] Said R. Mana, "Is it not from [the exegesis of the verse,] 'And he will cleave to his wife' – and not to the wife of his fellow? [That is, 'cleaving'] in any manner [is forbidden]."

[FF] Similarly, [there is also a prohibition of any sexual contact] with a male or an animal.

[V.A] Lo, we have learned that gentiles are not subject to the laws of consecrating a woman as betrothed [through money, IV.A-D]. What about their being subject to the laws of divorce?

[B] R. Judah b. Pazzi and R. Hanin in the name of R. Huna the Great of Sepphoris: "Either they are not subject to the law of divorce at all, or [unlike Israelite practice] each issues a writ of divorce to the other."

[C] R. Yohanan of Sepphoris. R. Aha, R. Hinena in the name of R. Samuel bar Nahman: "'For I hate divorce, says the Lord, the God of Israel' (Mal. 2:16).

[D] "Among Israelites I have framed the law of divorce, and I have not given the law of divorce to the nations of the world."

[E] R. Hananiah in the name of R. Pinhas: "The entire pericope makes use of the language 'the Lord of Hosts,' while here it uses the language 'the God of Israel.'

[F] "This is to teach you that the Holy One, blessed be He, has designated the use of his name in regard to divorces only with respect to Israelites alone."

[G] A statement of R. Hiyya the Elder implies that [in his view] gentiles are not subject to the law of divorce.

[H] Rather: For R. Hiyya taught, "A gentile... who divorced her, and the both of them [the first husband and the woman] converted to Judaism, I do not invoke the rule, 'Then her former husband, who sent her away, may not take her again [to be his wife]' (Deut. 24:4). [The rule is not applied because she is not regarded as having been divorced by him to begin with, when they both were gentiles]."

[I] And so, too, it has been taught: A case came before Rabbi, and he declared it valid for [the husband to remarry her].

[VI.A] With a writ: That is to say, with a writ that is not worth a perutah.

[B] But as to a writ that is worth a perutah, it is tantamount to money.

[C] This is in line with what R. Hiyya taught:

[D] **By a writ [– how so?]**

[E] **One must say that it is a writ worth a perutah.**

[F] **But is a woman consecrated with anything worth a perutah? Rather, even if one wrote it on a shard or on wastepaper [both of which have a value less than a perutah], and he gave it to her,**

[G] **lo, this one is consecrated [T. Qid. 1:2].**

[H] If he wrote [a writ of divorce] on something from which one may not derive benefit at all, [what is the law]?

[I] Is one deemed divorced or not?

[J] R. Eliezer said, "She is not divorced."

[K] [Now as to the use of such a thing for a writ of betrothal,] said R. Zeira, "Rabbis were at variance on this issue.

[L] "The one who said 'She is not betrothed with such a thing' maintains that she also may not be divorced with such a thing.

[M] "And the one who said 'She may be betrothed' also maintains that she may be divorced therewith."

[N]   Colleagues say [that such an analogy is null, for you cannot compare the law governing betrothal with the law governing divorce, and so they rule] to the strict side.

[O]   R. Yosé raised the question, "What is the meaning of 'ruling to the strict side'?

[P]   "[Shall we say that] she will not be betrothed [by such a writ] but she may be divorced by such a writ, and that is the meaning of 'rule to the strict side'?

[Q]   "Or do we maintain that she is not divorced [by such a writ] but she may be betrothed [by it], and that is 'ruling to the strict side'?" [This is not worked out.]

[R]   What is the law in the present matter [of betrothals]?

[S]   The rabbis of Caesarea in the name of R. Jacob bar Aha [maintain that there really is no dispute at all:] "The one who said that she may be divorced is of the opinion that it is permitted to betroth with a document written on material from which the scribes prohibited benefit.

[T]   "The one who said that she may not be divorced is of the opinion that it is prohibited to betroth with a document written on material from which the Torah prohibited benefit, but the scribes permitted such betrothal."

[U]   If you say so, does this statement not stand at variance with what Rab has said?

[V]   For Rab said, "In the view of R. Meir, 'He who effects a betrothal by handing over leaven [worth a perutah] from the sixth hour and onward [on the fourteenth of Nisan when, in point of fact, Israelites no longer may derive benefit from leaven, but this by ruling of scribes, not by the Torah's law] has done nothing whatever.'" [Now if the prohibition is merely on the basis of scribes' ruling, then the betrothal should be valid.]

[W]   There [in the case of handing over leaven] it is with the object itself that the man effects betrothal. Now leaven from the sixth hour and onward is worthless, [and that is why the betrothal is null].

[X]   But here it is with the conditions stated in the writ that the man has effected the betrothal.

[Y]   If that is the case, then even if it is with something from which benefit is prohibited by the Torah, [why] should the woman [not] be betrothed?

[Z]   What difference is there between such a thing and a writ that is not worth a perutah?

[AA] There [in the case of a writ composed on something that may not be utilized at all] the material is not suitable for completing the value of the perutah, [for it is totally worthless,]

[BB] while here [in the case of something not worth a perutah but with some slight value] the material is suitable for completing the value of the perutah. [It is offensive to give a woman something with no worth whatever, and on that account the materials forbidden for Israelite use or enjoyment may not be used at all.]

[VII.A] There we have learned: **An oath imposed by judges is imposed if the claim is at least for two pieces of silver, and the concession on** the part of the defendant is that he owes at least a perutah's worth [M. Shebu. 6:1A].

[B]   As to the claim:

[C]   The House of Shammai say. '[Money means] a maah."

[D]   And the House of Hillel say, "Two maahs."

[E]   The opinions assigned to the House of Shammai are at variance with one another.

[F]   For there [at M. Qid. 1:1] the House of Shammai maintain that "money" means a denar, and here they say it means a maah.

[G]   The opinions assigned to the House of Hillel are at variance, for there [at M. Qid. 1:1] they say "money" means a perutah, and here they say that it means two maahs.

[H]   R. Jacob bar Aha in the name of R. Haninah: "The House of Shammai derive [their position] from the rule governing the selling of a Hebrew slave girl. Just as the operative price at the original sale of such a girl is a denar, so betrothal affecting her is for a denar.

[I]   "The House of Hillel derive their position from the law governing the payoff [in redeeming such a girl]. Just as the operative price at the payoff [in redeeming] her is a perutah, so betrothal affecting her is for a perutah."

[J]   What is the scriptural basis for the position of the House of Shammai?

[K]   It is said, "[And if he does not do these three things for her,] she shall go out for nothing, without payment of money" (Ex. 21:11).

[L]   Now do we not know that it is without payment of money? Why then should Scripture state, "Without payment of money"?

[M]   It is on the basis of this that we learn that she is sold for a sum of money greater than the minimum sum understood by the word "money." And how much is that? It is a denar.

[N]   Or perhaps "money" refers to a perutah, and "more than a minimum sum of money" would then mean two perutahs?

[O]   The smallest value of a minted coin is a maah.

[P]   In that case, let it be a maah?

[Q]   R. Bun in the name of R. Judah bar Pazzi: 'The reason is that if she wishes to work off what she owes, she deducts [from the debt] at the rate of a maah a year and goes free."

[R]   And let her deduct at the rate of a perutah.

[S]   Said R. Bun, "Take note. If she wanted to deduct what is owing on her debt at the beginning of the sixth [and final] year of service, then the sum owing at the beginning of her calculation would be a perutah, and the sum owing at the end of that same process of deducting from the debt will be a perutah. [That anomaly must be avoided.]

[T]   "Rather at the beginning of the last year, her debt will be a maah, and at the end she will deduct a perutah."

[U]   What is the basis for the position of the House of Hillel?

[V]   On the basis of the fact that at the end of the process of deduction from the original debt, a perutah remains, you know that the sum required for betrothing her also is a perutah.

[W]   If at the end [of the process of working off the debt over a six year period], there remains only what is worth a perutah, is it possible to suppose that she does not deduct that amount and go forth free? [Obviously not.]

[X]   Accordingly, just as the sum owing at the end of the six-year period of deduction is a perutah, so the sum required for betrothing her is a perutah.

[Y]   The opinions imputed to the House of Hillel are at variance.

[Z]   It is written, "If a man delivers to his neighbor money or goods to keep [and it is stolen out of the man's house...if the thief is not found the owner of the house shall approach the judges to show whether he has put his hand to his neighbor's goods]" (Ex. 22:7-8).

[AA] Now if [the language, money or goods] is used to indicate that a court need not trouble with a claim of less than a perutah in value, it already is stated, "and thereby become guilty" (Lev. 6:7) – excluding what is worth less than a perutah.

[BB] Accordingly, why does Scripture specify "money"?

[CC] On the basis of that statement we derive the fact that at issue is more than a minimum sum of money. And how much is more than a minimum sum of money? It is two maahs.

[DD] Or perhaps a minimum sum of money is a perutah, and more than a minimum sum of money would be two perutahs?

[EE] The smallest minted coin is a maah.

[FF] So let it be a maah.

[GG] "Or goods" [stated in the plural] means two. So in the case of "money" it must be two [coins].

[HH] How do the House of Shammai interpret the passage, "or goods"?

[II]   It is in line with the following, as it has been taught: R. Nathan says, "'Or goods' seems to encompass under the law even clay pots."

[JJ]   Samuel said, "If one has laid claim for two needles, and the bailee confesses that he received one of them, he is liable for an oath."

[KK] Said R. Hinena, "And that ruling applies if the two were worth two perutahs, so that the claim should be for at least a perutah, and the concession should cover an object worth at least a perutah."

[LL] And this accords with the position of the House of Shammai, who do not derive the rule governing "money" from that governing "goods."

[MM] But in accord with the view of the House of Hillel, who do derive the rule governing "money" [58d] from that governing "goods," just as "goods" must be two, so "money" must be two.

[NN] Along these same lines, just as "money" refers to two maahs, so "goods" refers to what is worth two maahs.

[VIII.A] **Even though the House of Shammai and the House of Hillel disputed concerning the co-wives, concerning sisters, concerning the married woman, concerning a superannuated writ of divorce, concerning the one who betroths a woman with something of the value of a perutah, and concerning the one who divorces his wife and spends a night with her in an inn,**

[B]   **the House of Shammai did not refrain from taking wives among the women of the House of Hillel, and the House of Hillel from the House of Shammai [M. Yeb. 1:41].**

[C]   **But they behaved toward one another truthfully, and there was peace between them,**

[D] Since it is said, "They loved truth and peace" (Zech. 8:19) [T. Yeb. 1:10].

[E] There is the matter of the genealogically illegitimate status of children between them, and yet you say this? [Incredible!]

[F] What would be a practical case?

[G] If a girl was betrothed to the first man with what is worth a perutah, and to the second with what is worth a denar, in the opinion of the House of Shammai, she is betrothed to the second man, and any offspring she has by the first are deemed illegitimate.

[H] In the opinion of the House of Hillel, she is betrothed to the first man, and any offspring she has by the second are deemed illegitimate.

[I] R. Jacob bar Aha in the name of R. Yohanan: "The House of Shammai concede to the House of Hillel as to the stringent side of things."

[J] On the strength of that concurrence, the House of Shammai may marry women from the House of Hillel, for [the latter] concede [the position of the former].

[K] But the House of Hillel should not marry women from the House of Shammai, for [the latter indeed still] do not concede [their position].

[L] R. Yohanan in the name of R. Yannai: "Both these and these behaved in accord with the law. [That is why they could intermarry.]"

[M] If they behaved in accord with the law, then note the following:

[N] [Said R. Judah b. Betera, "There is the following precedent: A trough of Jehu was in Jerusalem, and it was perforated with a hole as large as the spout of a water skin. And everything that required preparation in conditions of cleanness in Jerusalem was prepared depending upon it for immersion.] And the House of Shammai sent and broke it down. For the House of Shammai say, 'Until the greater part of the object is broken down, it still is regarded as a utensil' [M. Miq. 4:5P-S]."

[O] [The story, cited to indicate that the House of Hillel did not indeed adopt the stringent position of the House of Shammai in the conduct of the law, does not prove its point. For] R. Yosé b. R. Bun said, "Before the case came to the House of Hillel, the House of Shammai [had reason to] object [to the condition of the trough]. Once the case came to the House of Hillel, the House of Shammai had no [further reason to] object. [That is, once the matter was brought to the attention of the house that took the less stringent position, it changed its ways.]"

[P] Said R. Abba Meri, "And that is right. What do we learn? That they declared unclean all the clean things prepared relying on the purification power of the trough in the past. But not from this time onward [that is, once the case came to the House of Hillel]."

[Q] R. Yosé b. R. Bun said, "Rab and Samuel differed. One of them said, 'These and those conducted themselves in accord with the law,' and the other one said, 'These conducted themselves in accord with their view of the law, and those conducted themselves in accord with their view of the law.'"

[R] [As to this latter view,] there is the matter of the genealogically illegitimate status of children between them, and yet you say this [that they both intermarried and also followed diverse views of the law]? [Incredible!]

[S] The Omnipresent watched out for them, and a practical case [involving illegitimacy] never actually took place.

[T] It has been taught: [**Under all circumstances the law is in accord with the House of Hillel.**]

[U] **To be sure, he who wants to impose a stricter rule on himself, to follow the law in accord with the opinion of the House of Shammai and in accord with the House of Hillel – concerning such a one, Scripture says, 'The fool walks in darkness' (Qoh. 2:14).**

[V] **He who holds by the lenient rulings of the House of Shammai and the lenient rulings of the House of Hillel is out-and-out evil.**

[W] **But if it is to be in accord with the teachings of the House of Shammai, then let it be in accord with both their lenient rulings and their strict rulings.**

[X] **And if it is to be in accord with the teachings of the House of Hillel, then let it be in accord with both their lenient rulings and their strict rulings [T. Suk. 2:3K-O].**

[Y] What you have stated [about following the opinions of both houses one way or the other] applies before the echo went forth [and declared the law to accord with the House of Hillel].

[Z] Once the echo had gone forth [saying,] "In all circumstances the law accords with the position of the House of Hillel, and whoever violates the position of the House of Hillel is liable to the death penalty," [that statement no longer applied].

[AA] It was taught: The echo went forth and declared, "These and those are both the words of God. But the law still accords with the position of the House of Hillel."

[BB] Where did the echo go forth?

[CC] R. Bibi in the name of R. Yohanan: "In Yavneh did the echo go forth."

[IX.A] **And how much is a perutah? One-eighth of an Italian issar [M. 1:1F-G].**

[B] It is taught [**A perutah of which they have spoken is one out of eight perutahs to an issar**];

[C] an issar is one twenty-fourth of a denar [T. B.B. 5:11].

[D] A silver denar is one twenty-fourth of a gold denar.

[E] R. Hiyya taught [in the Tosefta's version,] "**A sela is four denars.**

[F] "**Six silver maahs are a denar.**

[G] "**A silver maah is two pondions.**

[H] "**A pondion is two issars.**

[I] "**An issar is two mismasin.**

[J] "**A mismas is two quntronin.**

[K] "**A quntron is two perutahs.**"

[L] Said R. Zeira, "In the days of R. Simai and our rabbis, they declared that the perutah was one out of twenty-four to a maah."

[M] **Rabban Simeon b. Gamaliel says, "The perutah of which they have spoken is one of six perutahs to the issar.**

[N] "There are three hadrasin to a maah,

[O] "two hannassin to a hadras,

[P] "two shemanin to a hannas,

[Q] "two perutahs to a shemen" [T. B.B. 5:1].

[R] So it comes out that there are one out of twenty-four to a maah.

[S] R. Haninah and R. Mana: R. Haninah says, "As to copper perutahs, they stand at their assigned value [without rising or falling, contrary to the views given just now that Simai and our rabbis added to their value]. But silver [issars] may decrease or increase in value."

[T] R. Mana says, "[Issars made out of] silver stand in their assigned value. [Perutahs made out of] copper may increase or decrease in value."

[U] In the view of R. Haninah, in all circumstances six women may be betrothed with a single issar [since it is worth six perutahs at all times].

[V] In the opinion of R. Mana, sometimes it will be six, sometimes eight.

[W] Hilpai said, "Set me down at the shore of the river; if I cannot demonstrate that whatever is said in the Mishnah of R. Hiyya [the Tosefta] may in fact be derived from our Mishnah, then throw me into the river."

[X] They said to him, "And lo, R. Hiyya taught, 'A sela is four denars.'"

[Y] He said to them, "So, too, have we learned: How much may a sela be defective and still not fall under the rule of fraud? R. Meir says, "Four issars at an issar to a denar [M. B.M. 4:5A-B]. [That is one twenty-fourth of a sela, for a denar is six maahs, and a maah is four issars, so it is one twenty-fourth. Four denars make up a sela.]"

[Z] They said to him, "And has not R. Hiyya taught: 'Six maahs are a denar'?"

[AA] He said to them, "So we learn in our Mishnah: **Over reaching is an overcharge of four pieces of silver out of twenty-four pieces of silver to the sela, one sixth of the purchase price [M. B.M. 4:3A-B].** [So a denar is six maahs.]"

[BB] They said to him, "And has not R. Hiyya taught: 'Two pondions make up a maah'?"

[CC] He said to them, "**So we learn in our Mishnah: If one sanctified a field two or three years before the Jubilee, he gives a sela and a pondion for each year [M. Ar. 7:11].** [There are forty-eight pondions to a sela, twenty-four maahs to a sela, so two pondions to a maah.]"

[DD] They said to him, "And has not R. Hiyya taught: 'Two issars make up a pondion'?"

[EE] He said to them, 'So we learn in our Mishnah: **He who sets aside an issar [in the status of second tithe and takes it to Jerusalem] and ate [as second-tithe produce purchased] against half of its value, and then went to another area [in Jerusalem], and lo, [an issar] is worth a pondion. [That is, twice its previous value, so that the money remaining is worth a full issar of produce he eats against its value as second-tithe produce worth another issar [M. M.S. 4:6A-C].]** [So an issar is worth two pondions.]"

[FF] They said to him. "And has not R. Hiyya taught: 'Two mismasin are an issar; two quntronim are a mismas; two perutahs are a quntron'?"

[GG] He said to them, "So we learn in our Mishnah: **And how much is a perutah? One-eighth of an Italian issar [M. Qid. 1:1F-G]."**

[X.A] **And she acquires herself through a writ of divorce [M. 1:1H].**

[B] This is in line with what is written, "And he writes her a bill of divorce" (Deut. 24:2).

[C] **Or through the death of the husband [M. 1:1H].**

[D] This is in line with what is written, "Or if the latter husband dies, who took her to be his wife" (Deut. 24:3).

[E] That proves that the death of the second husband [frees her to remarry]. How do we know that the death of the first husband does so as well [in context]?

[F] Now if in the case of the second husband, whose [death] does not constitute an ample release [of the woman, since she still may not remarry the original husband, who had divorced her], you say that death permits [her to remarry] the first husband, who has the power to release her more fully – is it not a matter of logic that his death should also permit her to remarry?

[G] Said R. Huna, "Scripture itself has said that the death of the husband permits the wife to remarry,

[H] "For it is written, 'If brothers dwell together, and one of them dies and has no son, the wife of the dead shall not be married outside the family to a stranger.' (Deut. 25:5). Lo, if he does have a son, his death frees [the wife to marry anyone she wants].

[I] Said R. Yosé b. R. Bun, "If you say that death does not permit the wife to remarry, then how shall we declare that a widow is prohibited [only] to a high priest, or a divorcée or a woman who has undergone the rite of removing the shoe [Deut. 25:1ff.] to an ordinary priest? [For lo, the widow would be prohibited from marrying anyone, not merely a high priest, as Scripture specifies.]"

[J] [Objecting to this argument regarding the widow and the high priest,] said R. Yohanan bar Mareh, "Interpret [the rule of the widow's not marrying the high priest] to apply [solely] to the case of a deceased childless brother's widow. [That is, such a childless widow may not marry her brother-in-law when he is high priest. She is permitted to the other levirate brothers and prohibited to all others. Accordingly, the attempted proof need not stand.]"

[XI.A] [With regard to M. 1:1, **The deceased childless brother's widow is acquired through an act of sexual relations,** we turn to the exegesis of Deut. 25:5: "Her husband's brother shall go in to her, and take her as his wife, and perform the duty of a husband's brother to her."] "Her husband's brother shall go in to her" – this is the act of sexual relations.

[B] "And he shall take her as his wife – this refers to the act of bespeaking [that is, he says to her, 'Behold you are sanctified to me.']" [For the levirate marriage, bespeaking is the equivalent to an act of betrothal in an ordinary marriage.]

[C] May one say that, just as the act of sexual relations completes the transaction of acquiring her as a wife, so the act of bespeaking [by itself] also will accomplish the thing [so that the levir inherits his brother's property]?

[D] Scripture states, "[take her as his wife] and perform the duty of a husband's brother to her" [meaning, even after he has taken her as his wife through betrothal, he remains in the status of the husband's brother and must have sexual relations and does not accomplish the marriage merely by an act of betrothal].

[E] The entire passage, therefore, indicates that, as to the levir, the act of sexual relations completes acquisition of the widow as his wife, and mere bespeaking does not complete the acquisition of the woman as his wife.

[F] If so, what value is there in the act of bespeaking at all?

[G] It serves to betroth her, as against the claim of the other brothers.

[H] R. Simeon says, "Bespeaking either fully effects acquisition or does not." [Thus the foregoing position is rejected.]

[I] What is the scriptural basis for R. Simeon's position?

[J] "Her husband's brother shall go in to her" – this refers to an act of sexual relations.

[K] "And take her as a wife" – this refers to an act of bespeaking.

[L] [So the two are comparable, with the result that] just as an act of sexual relations effects complete possession of her as his wife, so does the act of bespeaking completely effect her acquisition as his wife.

[M] Or "her husband's brother shall go in to her" and lo, "he takes her as a wife," with the result that the act of bespeaking has no standing in her regard at all.

[N] R. Eleazar b. Arakh said, "The act of bespeaking effects a complete acquisition in the case of the childless brother's widow."

[O] What is the scriptural basis for R. Eleazar b. Arakh's position?

[P] "And take her as his wife" – lo, it is tantamount to the act of betrothing a woman.

[Q] Just as in the case of betrothing a woman, one effects total possession, so in the case of a deceased childless brother's widow, also the act of bespeaking [which is the parallel, as explained above] effects total possession.

[R] **What is "bespeaking"?**

[S] **If the brother says, "Lo, you are sanctified to me by money," or "by something worth money" [T. Yeb. 2:1].**

[XII.A] [M.1:1J: **The deceased childless brother's widow acquires freedom for herself through a rite of removing the shoe** omits reference to the act of a co-wife. Yet if the co-wife goes through the rite, the other co-wives are exempt. Accordingly,] R. Isaac asked, "And why do we not say that that is the case, whether it is the act of removing the shoe done by herself or by her co-wife?"

[B] He reverted and said, "We learn, 'through a rite of removing the shoe,' and not 'through her rite of removing the shoe.' So here the meaning is that it is sufficient whether it is her rite of removing the shoe or whether it is the rite performed by her co-wife."

[C] And lo, we have learned, The deceased childless brother's widow is acquired through an act of sexual relations [M. 1:2].

[D] Now do you have the possibility of ruling that that is the case whether it is an act of sexual relations with her or an act of sexual relations with her co-wife? [Obviously not!]

[E] The Mishnah pericope speaks [only] of the case where there is only one surviving childless widow.

[F] "Why did [R. Isaac] ask about a case of two surviving childless widows [when our Mishnah deals with only one]?"

[XIII.A] R. Samuel bar R. Isaac asked, "As to a betrothed slave girl ['If a man lies carnally with a woman who is a slave, betrothed to another man and not yet ransomed or given her freedom, an inquiry shall be held [an inquiry is also understood to mean that a flogging takes place]. They shall not be put to death, because she was not free; but he shall bring a guilt-offering for himself to the Lord' (Lev. 19:20-21)], by what means does she acquire full ownership of herself, to be exempt from a flogging, and her lover from a guilt-offering?"

[B] It is self-evident that she does not go forth by means of a writ of divorce.

[C] For R. Hiyya in the name of R. Yohanan said, "He who is half-slave and half-free – if he betrothed a woman, they do not scruple as to his act of betrothal, and, along these same lines, if he divorced a woman, they do not scruple as to his act of divorce. [Accordingly, an act of divorce is meaningless in this case.]"

[D] It is self-evident that she goes forth when her husband dies.

[E] This is in line with what R. Yosé said in the name of R. Yohanan, "Aqilas the proselyte translated before R. Aqiba, 'And she is a slave, betrothed to another man' as 'laid by a man' [hence the act of sexual relations has made the owner into her husband, and therefore when he dies she no longer is subject to flogging and the like]."

[F] This is in line with what you say, "And the woman took and spread a covering over the well's mouth and scattered grain" (2 Sam. 17:19).

[G] [Along these same lines] said R. Hiyya in the name of R. Yohanan, "So, too, did R. Eleazar b. R. Simeon explain the matter before sages: 'And she is a slave, betrothed to another man' as 'laid by a man.'

[H] "This is in line with what you say, '[Crush a fool in a mortar with a pestle] along with crushed grain.'"

[I] What is the law as to her acquiring ownership of herself at the death of her master or at the completion of the six years?

[J] What is the force of this question?

[K] Is it in accord with the view of R. Aqiba? [Surely not.]

[L] For R. Aqiba said, "Scripture speaks of a case in which she is half-slave and half-free, betrothed to a free boy. [In such a case what bearing does the death of the master have upon her status?]"

[M] But in the view of R. Ishmael, it is a serious question.

[N] For R. Ishmael said, "Scripture speaks of a Canaanite slave girl married to a Hebrew slave."

[O] The issue then is whether the marriage has standing under the law of the Torah.

[P] "If his master gives him a wife" (Ex. 21:4) [indicates that the marriage most certainly does have standing under the law of the Torah].

[Q] No, the question remains pressing: What is the law as to her acquiring full ownership of herself when her master dies or the six years are fulfilled, in accord with the view of him who said that a Hebrew slave does not serve the heir [of his original master]?

Unit I takes up the exegetical basis for the Mishnah's law, and, as we have noted, unit II, continuous with the foregoing, asks whether logic alone might have provided the foundation for the same facts. The consistent result is negative. Unit III takes up a further possibility of a mode of acquisition outside of the ones listed in the Mishnah and proves through Scripture that that mode is not valid. Unit IV then turns to the status of gentiles, asking (in the main) whether they are subject to the same rules. As to betrothing a woman, they are not. Unit V introduces the issue whether gentiles are subject to the rules of divorce. Unit VI distinguishes a writ from something worth a perutah, since the monetary requirement is such that the former may well be worth a perutah. The argument unfolds in terms of something totally without value; its logical potentialities are fully realized. Unit VII takes up M. 1:1C-D and accounts for the positions of the houses, at the same time comparing what they say here with a relevant position at M. Shebu. 6:1. The main point is that the minimum sum at issue in a case in which the judges impose an oath, so far as the two Houses are concerned, is different from the minimum sum to serve as betrothal money. Unit VIII amplifies unit VII. Unit IX proceeds to M. 1:1F-G. Its purpose is to introduce the Tosefta's materials and then to show that the Mishnah and Tosefta accord on the details of coinage. I present the Tosefta's version of the matter of what is assigned to Hiyya. Unit X proceeds to M. 1:1H, supplying its scriptural base. Units XI and XII take up the concluding materials of the Mishnah. Only unit XIII moves entirely beyond the limits of the Mishnah's language and problems. So what we have is a sustained analysis of the Mishnah and a rich anthology of relevant materials.

II. The Talmud of Babylonia to M. Qiddushin 1:1

I.1   A.   **A woman is acquired [as a wife]:**

B.   *What differentiates the present passage, in which case the Tannaite formula commences,* **A woman is acquired [as a wife]**, *from the passage to come, in which case the Tannaite formula uses the language,* **A man effects betrothal [lit.: consecrates] on his own or through his agent** [M. 2:1A]? [Why not say, a woman is betrothed, rather than, is acquired?]

C.   *Since the Tannaite framer of the Mishnah passage planned to introduce the matter of acquiring through money [he used language appropriate to a monetary transaction]. For how do we know that a monetary token serves* to effect betrothal? The fact derives from the verbal analogy established by the use of the word "purchase" [or take] with reference to the field of Ephron. Here we have, "if any man take a wife" (Deut. 22:13), and there, "I will give you money for the field, take it from me" (Gen. 23:13). [Freedman: Just as 'take' in the latter verse refers to money, so in the former too, the wife is taken, betrothed, by money.] *And "taking" is referred to as acquisition, in line with the verse, "The field that Abraham acquired" (Gen. 49:30). Or, also, "Men shall acquire fields for money" (Jer. 32:44). Therefore the framer of the Mishnah passage has used the word choice: A* **woman is acquired [as a wife].**

D. *Well, then, why not use the same word choice in that other passage [at M. 2:1A], namely,* A man acquires...?

E. *To begin with the Tannaite framer of the whole makes uses of the language of the Torah, and then, the language of rabbis.*

F. *And what is the meaning of the rabbinical word choice?*

G. *Through the act of betrothal the husband forbids the woman to everyone else in the world as that which has been consecrated is forbidden to everyone else in the world [but the Temple].*

H. *And why not use the Tannaite formulation here,* a man acquires [just as M. 2:1 uses the language, a man acquires]?

I. *The reason is that the framer of the passage planned at the end to present as the Tannaite formulation the rule,* **And she acquires herself through a writ of divorce and through the husband's death.** *Now this refers to her, so the Tannaite framer likewise refers in the opening clause to her.*

J. *Well, then, why not commence,* a man acquires and also transfers ownership [of the woman to herself]?

K. *The reason is that there also is the matter of the death of the husband, which restores the woman's title to herself, and that is not a transfer of title that the husband carries out! That is a transfer of title that is carried out by Heaven.*

L. *And if you prefer, I shall say, had the Tannaite framer used the language,* [the man] acquires, *I might have supposed that that is even against the woman's will. In using the Tannaite formulation,* **A woman is acquired,** *he has implied, that is only with her knowledge and consent, but otherwise, not.*

I.2 A. *And how come the Tannaite framer of the passage uses the feminine form of the word three, rather than the masculine form?*

B. *The reason is that he will use the word way, which is feminine too, in the following verse of Scripture:* "And you shall show them the way wherein they must walk" (Ex. 18:20).

C. *Well, what about that which is taught on Tannaite authority, where the word three is used in the masculine form:* **In seven ways do they examine the Zab before he is confirmed as to flux [M. Zab. 2:2A]?** *Why not use the feminine form?*

D. *The reason is that he proposes to speak of way, which appears in the masculine form in the following verse:* "They shall come out against you in one way and flee before you in seven ways" (Deut. 28:27).

E. *Well, then, the two verses prove contradictory, and the Mishnah passages are likewise contradictory!*

F.   *The two verses are not contradictory. Where we find the feminine form, the reference point is the Torah, which is feminine in the verse, "The torah of the Lord is perfect, restoring the soul" (Ps. 19:8), and hence the feminine form is employed. There, the reference is to war-making, which men, not women, do, so the masculine form is used. The Mishnah passages are not contradictory: Since the reference here is to a woman, the word is given the feminine form; the reference in the intersecting passage is to a man, for a man is examined, but a woman isn't; a woman contracts that form of uncleanness even though there is no external cause [so no examination is necessary]. Hence the masculine form is used.*

I.3   A.   *Well, then, the Tannaite formulation uses three? It is because the word "ways" is to be used in the feminine? Then let the Tannaite formulation make reference to "things," which is a masculine noun, and use the masculine form of the word for three?*

     B.   *The reason is that the framer of the passage wanted to formulate the Tannaite rule with reference to sexual relations, and sexual relations is called "way," in the verse, "And the way of a man with a maid...such is the way of an adulterous woman" (Prov. 30:19-20).*

I.4   A.   *So there is no problems with respect to betrothal through sexual relations. What is to be said about betrothal through a monetary token or a document of betrothal?*

     B.   *They are formulated as they are in conjunction with the formulation on sexual relations.*

     C.   *And will two items be so formulated because of one?*

     D.   *These, too, are preliminaries to the sex act.*

     E.   *And if you like, I shall say, who is the authority behind the unattributed passage? It is R. Simeon, as has been taught on Tannaite authority:*

     F.   R. Simeon says, "How come the Torah has said, 'If a man take a wife' (Deut. 22:13), and not, 'when a woman is taken by a man'? It is because it is the way of a man to go looking for a woman, but it is not the way of a woman to go looking for a man. The matter may be compared to the case of someone who has lost something: Who looks for whom? The owner of the lost object looks for what he has lost."

     G.   *Well, then, we have learned in the Mishnah:* **In seven ways do they examine the Zab before he is confirmed as to flux [M. Zab. 2:2A].** *Why not use the language,* things *there?*

     H.   *In using the language they do there, we are informed that it is the way of gluttony to cause a flux, and it is the way of drunkenness to cause a flux.*

     I.   *But lo, we have learned in the Mishnah:* **A citron [tree] is like a tree in three ways, and like a vegetable in one way [M. Bik. 2:6A].** *Why not use the language,* things, *there?*

     J.   *It is because he wants to go onward,* **and like a vegetable in one way.**

     K.   *Big deal – so use the language,* things, *there too!*

     L.   **[3A]** *There we are informed that it is the way of a citron to be like that of vegetables. Specifically, just as it is the way of vegetables to grow through any sort of water [even artificial irrigation, which cannot be done for wheat and vines], and when it is picked it is to be tithed, so it is the way of the citron to grow through any sort of water [even artificial irrigation, which cannot be done for wheat and vines], and when it is picked it is to be tithed.*

M.   *And lo, as we have learned in the Mishnah [using the word way rather than thing or aspect]:* **A koy [a beast that falls into the taxon of a wild beast and also into that of a domesticated beast] – there are ways in which it is like a wild animal, and there are ways in which it is like a domesticated animal; and there are ways in which it is like [both] a domesticated animal and a wild animal; and there are ways in which it is like neither a domesticated animal nor a wild animal [M. Bik. 2:8].** *Why not use the word "thing" here, too? And furthermore we have learned in the Mishnah [using the word way rather than thing or aspect]:* **This is one of the ways in which writs of divorce for women... [M. Git. 1:4C].** *Why not use the word "thing" here, too? Rather, in any passage in which there is a point of differentiation, the word* ways *is used as the Tannaite formulation, and in any passage in which there is no point of differentiation, the word* things *is used. The formulation of the Mishnah, closely examined, sustained that view:* **R. Eliezer says, "It is like a tree in every thing" [M. Bik. 2:6E].**

I.5   A.   *What exclusionary purpose – three, no more – is served by specifying the number at the opening clause and at the consequent one?*

      B.   *The exclusionary purpose of specifying the number at the opening clause serves to eliminate as a means of betrothal the marriage canopy [and its rite of consummating the marriage] itself.*

      C.   *Well, then, from the perspective of* R. Huna, who has said, "The marriage canopy effects acquisition of title to the woman, on the strength of an argument a fortiori," *what is eliminated by the specification of the number of modes of betrothal?*

      D.   *It serves to exclude the possibility of barter [trading the betrothal of a woman in exchange for an object]. It might have entered your mind to say, since we have derived the use of the word "take" from the use of the word "take" in connection with the field of Ephron, just as the title of a field may be acquired through barter, so title to a woman may be acquired through barter. Thus we are informed that that is not the case.*

      E.   *Yeah, so maybe it is the case?*

      F.   *There is the possibility of an act of barter of something worth less than a penny, but through something worth less than a penny [3B] a woman cannot be acquired.*

I.6   A.   *The exclusionary purpose of specifying the number at the concluding clause serves to eliminate the rite of removing the shoe. For it might have entered your mind to suppose that the possibility of the rite of removing the shoe should derive by an argument a fortiori from the case of the levirate wife. If a levirate wife, who is not freed by a divorce, is freed by the rite of removing the shoe, than this one [the levirate wife] who is freed by divorce surely should be freed by a rite of removing the shoe. Thus we are informed that that is not the case.*

      B.   *Yeah, so maybe it is the case?*

      C.   Scripture is explicit: "Then he shall write her a writ of divorce" (Deut. 24:1) – through a writ he divorces her, but he doesn't divorce her in any other way.

II.1 A.   **She is acquired through money:**

      B.   *What is the scriptural source of this rule?*

C. And furthermore, we have learned in the Mishnah: **The father retains control of his daughter [younger than twelve and a half] as to effecting any of the tokens of betrothal: money, document, or sexual intercourse [M. Ket. 4:4A]** – *How on the basis of Scripture do we know that fact?*

D. Said R. Judah said Rab, "Said Scripture, 'Then shall she [the Hebrew slave girl] go out for nothing, without money' (Ex. 21:11). No money is paid to this master, but money is paid to another master, and who would that be? It is the father."

E. *But might one say that it goes to her?*

F. *But how can you suppose so? Since the father has the power to contract her betrothal, as it is written,* "I gave my daughter to this man" (Deut. 22:16), *can she collect the money? [Obviously she cannot, so the father gets the money.]*

G. *But maybe that is the case only for a minor, who has no domain ["hand," with which to effect acquisition], but in the case of a girl, who has a domain for the stated purpose, she may contract the betrothal and also get the money paid for the betrothal?*

H. Said Scripture, "Being in her youth, in her father's house" (Num. 30:17) – every advantage accruing to her in her youth belongs to her father.

I. *Then what about what* R. Huna said Rab said, "How on the basis of Scripture do we know that the proceeds of a daughter's labor go to the father? 'And if a man sell his daughter to be a maidservant' (Ex. 21:7) – just as the proceeds of the labor of a maidservant go to the master, so the proceeds of the labor of a daughter go to the father"? *What need to I have for such a proof, when the same proposition may be deduced from the phrase,* "Being in her youth, in her father's house" (Num. 30:17)?

J. *Rather, that verse refers to releasing her vows [and not to the matter at hand, as the context at Num. 30:17 makes clear].*

K. *And, furthermore, should you say, so let us derive the rule covering money from the rule covering other propositions, in fact, we do not ever derive the rule covering money from the rule covering other propositions!*

L. *And, furthermore, should you propose, so let us derive the rule governing the disposition of monetary payments from the rule governing fines, it is the simple fact that the rule governing monetary payments is not to be derived from the rule governing the disposition of fines.*

M. *Then here is the reason that compensation for humiliation and damages is assigned to the father:* [Add: *If he wanted, he could hand her over [for marriage] to an ugly man or to a man afflicted with boils].* [Since he himself could subject her to indignity and benefit from it, he gets the compensation from someone who does that to her (Slotki).]

N. *Rather, it is more reasonable that, when the All-Merciful excluded another "exodus" [from the household],* [4A] *it was meant to be like the original.* [Slotki: As in the original, it is the master, not the slave girl, who would have received the money for her redemption, but a specific texts states to the contrary, so in the implication it must be the father, corresponding to the master, who gets the money when she leaves his control at betrothal.]

O.   *Yes, but the one "exodus" is not really comparable to the other. For in the case of the master, the slave girl entirely exits from his control, while in the exodus from the domain of the father, the exit to the bridal canopy has not yet been completed.*

P.   *Nonetheless, so far as it concerns his power to remit her vows, she does entirely exit his domain, for we have learned in the Mishnah:* **A betrothed girl – her father and her husband annul her vows [M. Ned. 10:1A-B].**

II.2   A.   *But does the verse, "She shall go out for nothing" serve the present purpose? Surely it is required in line with that which is taught on Tannaite authority, as follows:*

B.   "And she shall go out for nothing" – this refers to the days of her puberty; "without money" refers to the days of just prior to puberty. [Freedman: Thus the verse merely teaches that something else, not money, frees her, but implies no other conclusion.]

C.   *Said Rabina, "If so, Scripture ought to have said, 'no money.' Why formulate matters as 'without money'? It is to indicate, 'No money is paid to this master, but money is paid to another master, and who would that be? It is the father.'"*

D.   *And on what basis do we perform such an exegesis? It is as has been taught on Tannaite authority:*

E.   "And have no children" (Lev. 22:13) – I know only that that pertains to her own child, what about her grandchild? Scripture says, "And have no child," meaning, any child whatsoever.

F.   So far I know that that is the case only of a valid offspring, what about an invalid one?

G.   Scripture says, "And have no child," meaning, "hold an inquiry concerning her."

H.   *But lo, that clause has yielded the deduction concerning the grandchild!*

I.   *In point of fact it is not necessary to present a verse of Scripture to prove that grandchildren are in the status of children. Where a verse of Scripture is required is to deal with invalid offspring.*

J.   *And how does the Tannaite authority himself know that such an exegesis is undertaken?*

K.   *Say:* It is written, "Balaam refuses" and "my husband's brother refuses" (Num. 22:14, Deut. 25:7). In these instances, the words are written without the Y that they could have had. *Now hear in the verses treated above, the Y is used, which proves that the Y, which is dispensable, is included for exegetical purposes.*

II.3   A.   *And it was necessary to provide a verse of Scripture to indicate that the minor daughter's token of betrothal is assigned to her father, and it also was necessary to find a verse of Scripture to indicate that her wages are assigned to her father. For if the All-Merciful had made reference to the assignment of the token of betrothal to her father, I might have supposed that that was because she has not labored for that item, but as to her wages, for which she has labored, I might have said that they are assigned to her. And if we had been informed of the matter of her wages, in which matter, after all, she is provided for by him, [I might have supposed that since he supports her, she gets her wages], but as to the matter of tokens of betrothal given to her from a third party, I might have supposed that these go to her. So both proofs were required.*

II.4 A. *Reverting to the body of the foregoing:* "And she shall go out for nothing" – this refers to the days of her puberty; "without money" refers to the prepubescent time [days just prior to puberty].

B. *But why should the All-Merciful simply make reference to the prepubescent time [days just prior to puberty], and it would not have been necessary to make reference to the time of her puberty?*

C. Said Rabbah, "The one comes along to impart meaning to the other. *It may be comparable to the case of the words, a sojourner or a hired servant [Lev. 22:10: Toshab, sakir,] as has been taught on Tannaite authority:*

D. "'One word refers to a Hebrew slave acquired permanently, the other to one purchased for six years [at Lev. 22:10: "A slave purchased in perpetuity belonging to a priest or a slave purchased for six years shall not eat of the Holy Thing"]. If Scripture had referred to the former and not the latter, I would reason, if a slave acquired permanently may not eat Holy Things, how much more so is one acquired only for six years forbidden to do so! And if that were so, I would say, the former word refers to a slave purchased for a limited period, but one acquired in perpetuity may eat. So the word that refers to the slave purchased for a period of six years comes along and illuminates the meaning of the word for the one purchased in perpetuity, by contrast to the one purchased for a period of six years – and neither one may eat.'"

E. *Said to him Abbayye, "But are the cases truly parallel? In that case, they are two distinct classes of persons, so that, even if Scripture had made explicit reference to a sojourner whose ear had been pierced's not eating, and then made explicit reference to the other, then the hired hand might have been derived by an argument a fortiori. Such matters Scripture does take the trouble to spell out. But here, by contrast, the maidservant is one and the same person. Once she has left the prepubescent period, what business does she have to do with him when she becomes pubescent?"*

F. *Rather, said Abbayye, "It was necessary to make this point only to deal with the case of a woman who exhibits no signs of puberty even after she has reached the age of twenty years. It might have entered your mind to suppose that when she reaches pubescence, she goes free, but not merely by reaching her majority. So we are informed to the contrary."*

G. *Objected Mar bar R. Ashi to this proposition:* "But is this not attainable through an argument a fortiori? If the appearance of puberty signs, which do not remove the girl from the domain of the father, do remove the girl from the domain of the master, reaching maturity, which does remove her from the domain of the father, surely should remove her from the domain of the master!"

H. *Rather, said Mar bar R. Ashi, "The proof is required only to deal with the matter of the sale of a barren woman* [Freedman: a minor who shows symptoms of constitutional barrenness]. *It might have entered your mind to suppose that with one who will later on produce puberty signs, the sale is valid, but with one who won't, the sale is null.* [4B] *So we are informed by the verse, 'and she shall go out for nothing' that that is not the case."*

I. *But to Mar bar R. Ashi, who has said, "But is this not attainable through an argument a fortiori?," haven't we established the fact that*

*something that can be proved through an argument a fortiori Scripture
will nonetheless trouble to make explicit?*

J.   *Well, that's true enough where there is no other possible reply, but if there
     is, we give that possible reply* [making the verse pertain to some other
     matter than the one under discussion (Freedman)].

II.5   A.   *[That she is acquired through money] is derived by the following Tannaite
            authority on a different basis, as has been taught on Tannaite authority:*

       B.   "When a man takes a wife and has sexual relations with her, then
            it shall be, if she find no favor in his eyes, because he has found
            some unseemly thing in her" (Deut. 24:1) – the sense of "take"
            refers only to acquisition through a payment of money, in line
            with the verse, "I will give the money for the field; take it from
            me" (Gen. 23:13).

       C.   But cannot the same be proven by an argument a fortiori: If a
            Hebrew slave girl, who cannot be acquired by an act of sexual
            relations, can be acquired by money, a wife, who may be acquired
            in marriage by an act of sexual relations, surely can be acquired
            by money!

       D.   A levirate wife proves the contrary, since she may be acquired by
            sexual relations but not by a money payment.

       E.   But what distinguishes the levirate wife is that she cannot be
            acquired by a deed, and can you say the same of an ordinary wife,
            who can be acquired by a deed? So it is necessary for Scripture to
            teach, "When a man takes a wife and has sexual relations with
            her, then it shall be, if she find no favor in his eyes, because he
            has found some unseemly thing in her" (Deut. 24:1) – the sense of
            "take" refers only to acquisition through a payment of money, in
            line with the verse, "I will give the money for the field take it
            from me" (Gen. 23:13) [Sifré Deut. CCLXVIII:1.1].

       F.   *But what need to I have for a verse of Scripture, since it has been
            yielded by the argument a fortiori [the case of the levirate wife having been
            refuted]?*

       G.   *Said R. Ashi, "It is because one may raise the following disqualifying
            argument to begin with: Whence have you derived proof for the matter?
            From the case of the Hebrew slave girl?* But what distinguishes the
            Hebrew slave girl is that she goes out from bondage with a money
            payment. Will you say the same in this case, in which she does not
            go forth through a money payment? So it is necessary for Scripture
            to teach, 'When a man takes a wife and has sexual relations with
            her, then it shall be, if she find no favor in his eyes, because he has
            found some unseemly thing in her' (Deut. 24:1) – the sense of 'take'
            refers only to acquisition through a payment of money, in line with
            the verse, 'I will give the money for the field take it from me' (Gen.
            23:13)."

       H.   *And it was necessary for Scripture to deal with the case,* "and she shall
            go out for nothing" *and also* "when a man takes." *For had Scripture
            made reference to* "when a man takes," *I might have thought, the token
            of betrothal that the husband gives to her is her own; therefore Scripture
            states,* "and she shall go out for nothing." *And if Scripture had said
            only,* "and she shall go out for nothing," *I might have supposed, if the
            wife gives him the money and betroths him, it is a valid act of betrothal.*

Therefore Scripture stated, "when a man takes," but not, "when a woman takes."

II.6   A.   "...And possesses her [has sexual relations with her]":

B.   This teaches that a woman is acquired through an act of sexual relations.

C.   One might have reasoned as follows:

D.   If a deceased childless brother's widow, who may not be acquired through a money payment, may be acquired through an act of sexual relations, a woman, who may be acquired through a money payment, logically should be available for acquisition through an act of sexual relations.

E.   But a Hebrew slave girl will prove the contrary, for she may be acquired through a money payment, but she is not acquired through an act of sexual relations. [On that account, you should not find it surprising for an ordinary woman, who, even though she may be acquired through a money payment, may not be acquired through an act of sexual relations] [Sifré Deut. CCLXVIII:1.2].

F.   What characterizes the Hebrew slave girl is that she is not acquired for a wife. But will you say the same in this case, in which the woman is acquired for a wife?

G.   So Scripture states, "...And possesses her [has sexual relations with her]?"

H.   But then why do I need a verse of Scripture [in light of F]? *Lo, the matter has been proven without it!*

I.   *Said R. Ashi, "Because there is the possibility of stating that at the foundations of the logical argument there is a flaw, namely, from whence do you derive the case? From the deceased childless brother's widow. But what characterizes the levirate widow is that she is already subject to a relationship to the levir, but can you say the same in this instance, where the woman hardly is subject to any relationship whatever to this unrelated man? So it is necessary to state: '...And possesses her [has sexual relations with her]' – This teaches that a woman is acquired through an act of sexual relations."*

III.1   A.   [5A] And how on the basis of Scripture do we know that a woman may be acquired by a deed?

B.   It is a matter of logic.

C.   If a payment of money, which does not serve to remove a woman from a man's domain [as does a writ of divorce], lo, it has the power of effecting acquisition,

D.   a deed [namely, a writ of marriage or a marriage contract], which does [in the form of a writ of divorce] have the power to remove a woman from the domain of a man, surely should have the power of effecting acquisition.

E.   No, if you have made that statement concerning the payment of money, which does have the power of effecting acquisition of things that have been designated as Holy and of produce in the status of second tithe [there being an exchange of money for such objects, by which the objects become secular and the money becomes consecrated], will you make the same statement concerning a writ, which does not have the power of effecting acquisitions of Holy Things and produce in the status of second tithe, for it is written, "And if he who sanctifies the field will in any manner redeem it, then he shall add the fifth part of the money of your estimation, and it shall be assigned to him" (Lev. 27:19)?

F. Scripture says, "And he writes her a bill of divorcement, hands it to her, and sends her away from his house; she leaves his household and becomes the wife of another man."

G. Her relationship to the latter is comparable to her leaving the former. Just as her leaving the former is effected through a writ, so her becoming wife to the latter may be effected through a writ [Sifré Deut. 268:1.3].

H. *Well, why not draw the comparison in the opposite direction, namely,* the going forth from the marriage to the establishment of the marriage: Just as the establishment of the marriage is through money, so the going forth from the marriage is through money?

I. Said Abbayye, "People will say, money brings the woman into the marriage and money takes her out of it? Then will the defense attorney turn into the prosecutor?"

J. *If we accept that argument, then the deed of betrothal likewise will be subject to the saying, a writ removes her from the marriage, and a writ brings her into it? So will the prosecutor turn into the defense attorney?*

K. *Yes, but the substance of this document is distinct from the substance of that document.*

L. *Yeah, well, then, the purpose of this money payment is different from the purpose of that money payment!*

M. *Nonetheless, all coins have the same mint mark! [So who knows the difference? But the documents contain different wordings.]*

III.2   A. Raba said, "Said Scripture, 'And he shall write for her' (Deut. 24:1) – through what is in writing a woman is divorced, and she is not divorced through a money payment."

B. *Why not say:* Through writing a woman is divorced, but she is not betrothed through what is in writing?

C. Lo, it is written, "And when she goes forth, then she may marry" so comparing divorce to marriage.

D. Why choose that reading rather than the contrary one [excluding money for divorce and but accept a deed for marriage? why not reverse it?]

E. *It stands to reason that when we deal with divorce, we exclude a conceivable means for effecting divorce; when dealing with divorce should we exclude what is a means of effecting a betrothal?*

F. *Now how, for his part, does R. Yosé the Galilean attain that same principle, [since he interprets the language of the verse at hand for another purpose], how does he know that a woman is not divorced through a money payment?*

G. *He derives that lesson from the language,* "a writ of divorce," *meaning,* "A writ is what cuts the relationship, and no other consideration cuts the relationship."

H. *And rabbis – how do they deal with the language,* "a writ of divorce"?

I. *That formulation is required to indicate that the relationship is broken off through something that effectively severs the tie between him and her. For it has been taught on Tannaite authority:* [If the husband said], "Lo, here is your writ of divorce, on the condition that you not drink wine, that you not go to your father's house for ever," this is not an act of totally severing the relationship. [If he said,] "... for thirty days...," lo, this is an act of severing the relationship. [The husband cannot impose a permanent condition, for if he could do so, then the relationship will not have been completely and finally severed.]

J. And R. Yosé?

K. *He derives the same lesson from the use of the language, "total cutting off" as against merely "cutting off."*

L. And rabbis?

M. *The rabbis do not derive any lesson from the variation in the language at hand.*

III.3 A. *While it is not possible to derive the rule governing one mode of acquisition from another [the various arguments having failed], maybe it's possible to infer one from two others [so that if we can show that it is possible to effect acquisition through two modes that work elsewhere and also that work in respect to a betrothal, then a third, that works elsewhere, can work in this case too]?*

B. *Which two?*

C. *Perhaps the All-Merciful should not make reference in Scripture to a deed, and that might be derived from the other two modes of acquisition [sexual relations, money payment]? But then one might argue that what characterizes these other two modes of acquisition is that a good deal of benefit derives from them, which is not the case for a mere piece of paper.*

D. *Then perhaps Scripture should not make written reference to the mode of sexual relations, and that might be derived from the other two? But then one might argue that what is characteristic of the other two is that they serve to effect acquisition in a wide variety of matters, while that is not so in the instance of sexual relations!*

E. *Then let Scripture not make reference to the matter of money, and let that derive from the other two? But what characterizes the other two is that they take effect even contrary to the woman's will, which is not the case of money [she must be willing to accept it]. And should you say that money, too, may take effect willy-nilly in the case of a Hebrew slave girl, nonetheless, in the matter of effecting a marriage, we find no such instance.*

III.4 A. Said R. Huna, "The marriage canopy effects acquisition of title to the woman, on the strength of an argument a fortiori: If a money payment, which on its own does not confer the right to eat priestly rations, effects transfer of title to the husband over the woman, the marriage canopy, which does confer the right to eat priestly rations, surely should effect the transfer of title."

B. But doesn't acquisition through a money payment confer the right to eat priestly rations? And hasn't Ulla said, "By the law of the Torah, a girl of Israelite caste who was betrothed to a priest is permitted to eat priestly rations: 'But if a priest buy any soul, the purchase of his money...' (Lev. 22:11) – *and this one also falls into the class of* 'purchased of his money.' And what is the reason that they have said that she may not eat priestly rations? Lest a cup of wine in the status of priestly rations be mixed for her in her father's house and she share it with her brother or sister [who are not in the priestly caste]"?

C.   *Then raise the following question:* What characterizes a money payment is that it does not effect the completion of the acquisition of the wife but nonetheless effects transfer of title, [5B] the marriage canopy, which does effect the completion of the acquisition of the wife, surely should effect transfer of title and hence betrothal!

D.   The particular trait of a money payment is that with it things that have been consecrated and second tithe may be redeemed.

E.   But sexual relations proves to the contrary [having no bearing on that matter].

F.   The distinguishing trait of sexual relations is that that is a means for acquiring a levirate widow as a wife.

G.   A money payment, inoperative there, proves the disqualifying exception.

H.   So we find ourselves going around in circles. The distinctive trait that pertains to the one is not the same as the distinctive trait that applies to the other, and the generative quality of the other is not the same as the generative quality of the one. But then, the generative trait that pertains to them all is that they effect transfer of title in general and they also effect transfer of title here. So I shall introduce the matter of the marriage canopy, which effects transfer of title in general and should also effect transfer of title here.

I.   But the generative quality that is characteristic of the set is that they produce a considerable benefit.

J.   A writ, a mere piece of paper, proves the disqualifying exception.

K.   The distinctive quality of the deed is that it can remove an Israelite woman from a marriage.

L.   A money payment and sexual relations provide the disqualifying exceptions.

M.   So we find ourselves going around in circles. The distinctive trait that pertains to the one is not the same as the distinctive trait that applies to the other, and the generative quality of the other is not the same as the generative quality of the one. But then, the generative trait that pertains to them all is that they effect transfer of title in general and they also effect transfer of title here. So I shall introduce the matter of the marriage canopy, which effects transfer of title in general and should also effect transfer of title here.

N.   But the generative quality that is characteristic of the set is that they serve under compulsion.

O.   And R. Huna?

P.   *In any event, we don't find any aspect of compulsion when it comes to the money payment.*

III.5   A.   [As to R. Huna's statement,] said Rabbah, "There are two refutations of what he has said: First, *we learn in the Mishnah the language,* **three,** *not four; and furthermore, isn't it the simple fact that the marriage canopy completes the relationship only in consequence of an act of betrothal? But can the marriage canopy complete the relationship not in the aftermath of an act of betrothal, so that we may deduce that, when it is* not in consequence of an act of betrothal, there is the same result as the marriage canopy following such an act?"

B. Said Abbayye, "As to what you have said, namely, first, we learn in the Mishnah the language, three, not four, the Tannaite authority makes explicit reference only to what is explicitly stated in Scripture, but not what is not explicitly stated [and we have shown that the media of money and deed derive from exegesis, if not from an explicit statement of Scripture, but the validity of the marriage canopy is only derived by an argument a fortiori]. And as to your statement, isn't it the simple fact that the marriage canopy completes the relationship only in consequence of an act of betrothal? as a matter of fact, that is R. Huna's argument: If a money payment, which does not complete the relationship after a prior payment of a money payment, the marriage canopy, which does complete the relationship after a money payment, surely should effect transfer of title just as well!"

III.6 A. Our rabbis have taught on Tannaite authority:

B. With money, how so?

C. If he gave her money or what is worth money and said to her, "Lo, you are consecrated to me," "Lo, you are betrothed to me," "Lo, you are for me as a wife," Lo, this one is consecrated. But if she gave it to him and said to him, "Lo, I am consecrated to you," "Lo, I am betrothed to you," "Lo, I am yours as a wife," she is not consecrated [T. Qid. 1:1B-D].

III.7 A. Objected R. Pappa, "So is the operative consideration only that he gave the money and he made the statement? Then if he gave the money and she made the statement, she is not betrothed? Then note what follows: But if she gave it to him and said to him, "Lo, I am consecrated to you," "Lo, I am betrothed to you," "Lo, I am yours as a wife," she is not consecrated! So the operative consideration is that she gave the money and she made the statement. Lo, if he gave the money and she made the statement, there would be a valid betrothal!"

B. The opening clause describes precisely the details of the transaction, and the concluding one states them in more general terms.

C. Yeah, well, then, can you make a statement in the second clause that contradicts the implications of the first!? But this is the sense of the statements before us: If he gave the money and he made the statement, it is obvious that the betrothal is valid. If he gave the token and she made the statement, it is treated as a case in which she gave the money and made the statement, and there is no valid betrothal.

D. And if you wish, I shall say, if he gave the money and he made the statement, she is betrothed. If she gave the token and she made the statement, she is not betrothed. If he gave the token and she made the statement, it is a matter of doubt, and, on the authority of rabbis, we take account of the possibility of a valid transaction.

III.8 A. Said Samuel, "In the matter of a betrothal, if he gave her money or what is worth money and said to her, 'Lo, you are sanctified,' 'Lo you are betrothed,' 'Lo, you are a wife to me,' Lo, this woman is consecrated. 'Lo, I am your man,' 'Lo, I am your husband,' 'Lo, I am your betrothed,' there is no basis for taking account of the possibility that a betrothal has taken place. And so as to a writ of divorce: If he gave her the document and said to her, 'Lo, you are sent forth,' 'Lo, you are divorced, 'Lo, you are permitted to any man,' Lo, this woman is divorced. 'I am not your man,' 'I am not your husband,' 'I am not your betrothed,' there is no basis for taking account of the possibility that a divorce has taken place."

B. *Said R. Pappa to Abbayye, "Does this bear the implication that Samuel takes the view,* 'Inexplicit abbreviations [such as the language that is used and then spelled out, for example, "I am forbidden by a vow from you" *means, "I am not going to speak to you."* "I am separated from you by a vow" *means, "I am not going to do any business with you"*; "I am removed from you" *means, "I am not going to stand within four cubits of you"*] are null [and take effect only if they are made explicit]'? *And have we not learned in the Mishnah:* **He who says, "I will be [such]" – lo, this one is a Nazir [M. Naz. 1:1B]?** *And in reflecting on it, we stated: 'But maybe the sense of,* **I will be [such]**, *is I will fast?' And said Samuel,* 'But that rule that the Mishnah states pertains to a case in which a Nazirite was walking by at just that moment.' *So the operative consideration is that* a Nazirite was walking by at just that moment. Lo, if that were not the case, it would not be the rule! [So Samuel maintains that inexplicit abbreviations are valid only if made explicit.]"

C. *Here with what case do we deal? It is a case in which he said, "...to me."*

D. *If so, what's the point [that we didn't already know]?*

E. *That [6A] is his position with respect to the latter formulations. Here it is written,* "when any man takes a woman" (Deut. 24:5), *not that he takes himself as a husband; and there* "and when he sends her away" *and not when he sends himself away.*

III.9 A. *Our rabbis have taught on Tannaite authority:*

B. "Lo, you are my wife," "Lo, you are my betrothed," "Lo, you are acquired by me," she is consecrated.

C. "Lo, you are mine," "Lo, you are in my domain," "Lo, you are subject to me," she is betrothed.

III.10 A. *So why not form them all into a single Tannaite statement?*

B. *The Tannaite had heard them in groups of three and that is how he memorized them.*

III.11 A. *The question was raised:* "If he used the language, 'Singled out for me,' '...designated for me,' '...my helpmate,' 'you are suitable for me, ' 'you are gathered in to me,' 'you are my rib,' 'you are closed in to me,' 'you are my replacement, ' 'you are seized to me,' 'you are taken by me,' [what is the consequence]?"

B. *In any event you can solve one of these problems on the basis of that which has been taught on Tannaite authority:* If he said, "You are taken by me," she is betrothed, in line with the language, "when a man takes a wife."

III.12 A. *The question was raised,* "If he said, 'You are my [betrothed] bondmaid,' what is the law?"

B. *Come and take note of what has been taught on Tannaite authority:*

C. If he said, "You are my [betrothed] bondmaid," she is consecrated, for in Judea a betrothed woman is called a betrothed bondmaid.

D. *So is Judah the majority of the world at large?*

E. *This is the sense of the statement:* If he said, "You are my [betrothed] bondmaid," she is consecrated, for it is said, "that a betrothed bondman belonging to a man" (Lev. 19:20). Moreover, in Judea a betrothed woman is called a betrothed bondmaid.

F. *So do I need to know a custom in Judea in order to sustain what Scripture says?*

G. *This is the sense of the statement:* If in the territory of Judea he said, "You are my [betrothed] bondmaid," she is consecrated, for it is said, "that a betrothed bondman belonging to a man" (Lev. 19:20), for in Judea a betrothed woman is called a betrothed bondmaid.

III.13 A. *With what situation do we deal [in the interpretation of the language just now cited as effective]? Should I say that it is a situation in which* he is not talking with her about business having to do with her writ of divorce or her betrothal? *Then how in the world should she know what he is talking about with her?! But rather, it is a case in which* he is talking with her about business having to do with her writ of divorce or her betrothal. *Then, even if he said nothing at all, but merely gave her money, she is still betrothed, for we have learned in the Mishnah:* [If] he was speaking to his wife about matters relevant to her divorce contract or her bride price and did not make it explicit – R. Yosé says, "It is sufficient for him [simply to give her the contract or bride price without a declaration." R. Judah says, "He must make it explicit" [M. M.S. 4:7]. And said R. Huna said Samuel, "The decided law accords with R. Yosé."

B. *Say:* In point of fact, *it is a case in which* he is talking with her about business having to do with her writ of divorce or her betrothal. *If he had given her money and then shut up, that would indeed be the rule [she would be divorced or betrothed], but here with what situation do we deal? It is one in which he gave her the item and stated to her the language that has just now been set forth, and this is what is at issue here: When he used this language, was it for purposes of betrothal? Or was it for purposes of work? And that question stands over.*

III.14 A. *Reverting to the body of the foregoing:*

B. [If] he was speaking to his wife about matters relevant to her divorce contract or her bride price and did not make it explicit –

C. R. Yosé says, "It is sufficient for him [simply to give her the contract or bride price without a declaration]."

D. R. Judah says, "He must make it explicit" [M. M.S. 4:7].

E. Said R. Judah said Samuel, "And that is the case in which they were engaged in discussing that very same matter."

F. And so said R. Eleazar said R. Oshayya, "And that is the case in which they were engaged in discussing that very same matter."

G. *There is a Tannaite dispute on the same matter:*

H. Rabbi says, "And that is the case in which they were engaged in discussing that very same matter."

I. R. Eleazar b. R. Judah says, "Even though they were not engaged in discussing that very same matter" [cf. T. Qid. 2:8]].

III.15 A. *Well, if they were not engaged in discussing that very same matter, then how in the world should she know what he is talking about with her?*

B. Said Abbayye, "It is a case in which they moved from one topic to another in the same context."

III.16 A. Said R. Huna said Samuel, "The decided law accords with R. Yosé."

B. *Said R. Yemar to R. Ashi, "But what about what R. Judah said Samuel said, 'Whoever is not expert in the character of writs of divorce and betrothals should not get involved in dealing with them' – is that the case even if he has heard nothing of this ruling of R. Huna in Samuel's name?"*

C. He said to him, Yes indeed."

III.17 A. And so as to a writ of divorce: If he gave her the document and said to her, "Lo, you are sent forth," "Lo, you are divorced," "Lo, you are permitted to any man," lo, this woman is divorced.

B. *It is obvious that if he gave her her writ of divorce and said to his wife, "Lo, you are a free woman," [6B] he has not said anything effective. If he said to his female slave, "Lo, you are permitted to any man," he has not said anything effective. If he said to his wife, "Lo, you are your own property," what is the law? Do we say that he made that statement with respect to work? Or perhaps, he meant it to cover the entirety of the relationship?*

C. *Said Rabina to R. Ashi, "Come and take note of what we have learned in the Mishnah:* **The text of the writ of divorce [is as follows]: "Lo, you are permitted to any man." R. Judah says, "[In Aramaic]: Let this be from me your writ of divorce, letter of dismissal, and deed of liberation, that you may marry anyone you want." The text of a writ of emancipation [is as follows]: "Lo, you are free, lo, you are your own [possession]"** [cf. Deut. 21:14] [M. Git. 9:3]. *Now if, in the case of a Canaanite slave, whose body belongs to the master, when the master says to him,* lo, you are your own [possession], *he makes that statement covering the entirety of the relationship, when he makes such a statement to his wife, whose person he does not acquire as his possession, all the more so should it yield the same meaning!"*

III.18 A. Said Rabina to R. Ashi, "If he said to his slave, 'I have no business in you,' *what is the upshot? Do we say that the sense is,* I have no business in you in any way whatsoever? *Or perhaps he made that statement with respect to work?"*

B. *Said R. Nahman to R. Ashi, and other say, R. Hanin of Khuzistan to R. Ashi, come and take note:* **He who sells his slave to gentiles – the slave has come forth to freedom, but he requires a writ of emancipation from his first master. Said Rabban Simeon b. Gamaliel, 'Under what circumstances? If he did not write out a deed of sale for him, but if he wrote out a deed of sale for him, this constitutes his act of emancipation'** [T. A.Z. 3:16A-C]."

C. *What is a deed of sale?*

D. *Said R. Sheshet, "He wrote for him the following language: 'When you escape from him, I have no claim on you.'"*

III.19 A. Said Abbayye, "If someone effects a betrothal with a loan, the woman is not betrothed. If it is with the benefit of a debt, she is betrothed, but this is not to be done, because it constitutes usury accomplished through subterfuge."

B. *What is the definition of the benefit of a debt? Should I say that he treated the interest as a loan, saying "I am lending you four zuz for five"? But that is actual usury. And it in fact a debt.*

C. *The rule pertains to a case in which he gave her extra time to pay the debt.*

III.20 A.   Said Raba, "If someone said, 'Take this maneh on the stipulation that you return it to me,' in regard to a purchase, he does not acquire title [for example, real estate would not be acquired if the money has to be returned]; in the case of a woman, she is not betrothed; in the case of redeeming the firstborn, the firstborn is not redeemed; in the case of priestly rations, he has carried out the duty of handing it over, but it is not permitted to do it that way, since it appears to be the case of a priest who assists in the threshing floor [in order to get the priestly rations, and that is not permitted because of the indignity]."

     B.   *What is Raba's operative theory? If he maintains that* a gift that is made on the stipulation that it will be returned is classified as a gift, *then even the others, too, should be valid; and if he maintains that it is not a valid gift, then even in the case of priestly rations, it should not be valid. Not only so, lo, Raba is the one who* said, "A gift that is given on the stipulation that it is returned is classified as a gift," for said Raba, "'Here is this citron [as a gift to you] on condition that you return it to me' – if one has taken it and carried out his obligation and returned it to the other, he has carried out his obligation, but if he did not return it, he did not carry out his obligation." [So a conditional gift is entirely valid.]

     C.   *Rather, said R. Ashi, "In all cases the gift that rests on a stipulation is valid, except the case of a woman, because* a woman is not acquired through barter."

     D.   *Said R. Huna Mar b. R. Nehemiah to R. Ashi, "This is what we say in Raba's name, precisely as you have said it."*

III.21 A.   Said Raba, "If a woman said, 'Give a maneh to Mr. So-and-so [7A] and I shall be betrothed to you,' she is betrothed under the law of surety, *namely: Even though a surety does not derive benefit from the loan, he obligates himself to repay it; so this woman too, though she derives no benefit from the money, still obligates and cedes herself as betrothed.*

     B.   "If someone said, 'Here is a maneh, and be betrothed to Mr. So-and-so' – she is betrothed under the law governing a Canaanite slave, *namely: In the case of a Canaanite slave, even though he himself loses nothing when someone else gives his master money to free him, nonetheless acquires ownership to himself, so even though this man personally loses nothing, he acquires the woman.*

     C.   "If a woman said, 'Give a maneh to Mr. So-and-so, and I shall be betrothed to him,' she is betrothed on the basis of the law governing both classes of transactions; *as to a pledge, even though he personally derives no benefit, he obligates himself, and this woman, too, though she gains nothing cedes herself. Should you object, how are the cases parallel? In the case of a pledge he who acquires title loses money [paying off the debtor], but this man is acquiring the woman at no cost to himself – then the Canaanite slave proves the contrary, since he loses nothing but gains his freedom. And if you object, how are the cases parallel? In that case he who gives title acquires the money given for the slave, but here, does the woman cede herself and acquire nothing? Then the surety proves it, though he personally gets nothing, he still obligates himself."*

III.22   A.   *Raba raised this question:* "'Here is a maneh and I'll become betrothed to you' [Freedman: and the man accepted it saying, 'Be betrothed to me with it'], [what is the law?]"

         B.   Said Mar Zutra in the name of R. Pappa, "She is betrothed."

         C.   *Said R. Ashi to Mar Zutra, "If so, you have a case in which property* that is secured [real estate] is acquired along with property that is not secured [movables], *while in the Mishnah we have learned the opposite, namely:* **Property for which there is no security is acquired along with property for which there is security through money, writ, and usucaption. And property for which there is no security imposes the need for an oath on property for which there is security [M. 1:5C-D]."** [Freedman: A creditor could collect his debt out of the debtor's real estate, even if sold after the debt was contracted, but not out of movables, if sold; hence the former is termed property that ranks as security, the latter, not. Human beings are on a par with the former, and Ashi assumes that the woman is acquired in conjunction with the maneh.]

         D.   *He said to him, "Do you suppose that she said to him, '...along with...'? Here we deal with a person of high standing. In exchange for the pleasure that she derives from his accepting a gift from her, she has determined to give him title over her person."*

         E.   *So, too, it has been stated in the name of Raba: The rule is the same in monetary matters.* [Freedman: If A says to B, "Give money to C, in return for which my field is sold to you," the sale is valid, by the law of surety.]

         F.   *And it was necessary for the rule to be stated in both instances. For if we had been informed of the rule only in connection with betrothals, that might have been thought that it is because the woman accepts the most meagre compensation, in line with what R. Simeon b. Laqish said, for said R. Simeon b. Laqish, "Better to live together than to live a widow," but as to a monetary transaction, I might have said that that is not the case. And if it had been only with respect to a monetary transaction that we had been informed of the law, that might have been because it is possible to remit a debt if one chooses, but that would not be the case with regard to a betrothal [in which instance a woman must receive a token of betrothal]. So it was necessary for the rule to be stated in both instances.*

III.23   A.   Said Raba, "If a man said, 'Be betrothed to half of me,' she is betrothed, 'half of you be betrothed to me,' she is not betrothed."

         B.   *Objected Abbayye to Raba, "What's the difference between the language, 'Be betrothed to half of me,' and the language, 'half of you be betrothed to me,' so that in the latter case she is not betrothed? Is it because Scripture has said, 'when a man take a wife' (Deut. 24:1) but not half a wife? Then Scripture also says, 'a man,' but not half a man!"*

         C.   *He said to him, "How are the cases parallel! In that case a woman cannot be assigned to two men, but can't a man be assigned to two or more women? So this is what he meant to say to her: 'If I want to marry another woman, I'll do just that.'"*

         D.   *Said Mar Zutra b. R. Mari to Rabina, "Why not consider that the betrothal spreads through the whole of the woman? Has it not been taught on Tannaite authority: 'If one says, "The foot of this animal shall be a* burnt-offering," the whole becomes a burnt-offering'? *And even in the opinion of him who says that* the whole of the beast is not then classified as a burnt-offering, that is the case in which one has sanctified a part of the beast on which life does not depend, but he who sanctifies a part of the beast on which life depends – the whole of it is indeed a burnt-offering!"

E. *But are the cases comparable? In that case, we deal with a mere beast. But in this case, we have a third party opinion in play [so the woman would have to concur that the betrothal spread through the whole of her]. The matter is comparable only to the case of which R. Yohanan spoke, namely,* "In the case of a beast that belongs to two partners, if one of them consecrated his own half, and then he went and bought the half belonging to the other party and consecrated that part, it is indeed deemed consecrated, but it is not offered up. Still, it has the power to effect an act of substitution [with a secular beast with which it is exchanged], and the beast that is exchanged for it is in the same status. *Three rules are to be derived from this ruling.* One may deduce, [7B] first of all, that a beast that is consecrated can be removed forever from sacred use [and even though later on they became fit to be offered, they cannot be offered, since they have prior been suspended from use on the altar for some reason]. And one may deduce, second, that if to begin with [at the point of its consecration] an animal is removed from sacred use, then the suspension remains valid forever. And you may deduce, third, that the consecration of animals that have been dedicated as to their value can be removed."

III.24 A. *Raba raised the question,* "If one said, 'Half of you is betrothed with half of this penny, and half of you is betrothed with the other half,' what is the law? *Once he said to her, 'a half penny,' he has divided the money [and there is no valid betrothal], or maybe what he was doing was just counting out the matter [betrothing her for the penny, half for half]? If, then, you should maintain that he was just counting the matter out, what if he said, 'half of you for a penny, and half of you for a penny,' what is the law? Since he has said, 'for a penny,' and 'for a penny,' he has divided his statement [and it is null], or maybe, if the procedure was on a single day, what he was doing was counting out the matter? And if you say that, if it was on the same day, he was counting out the matter, then what if he said, 'Half of you for a penny today, and the other half* of you for a penny tomorrow'? *Since he said, 'tomorrow,' he has divided it up and the transaction is null, or perhaps this is what he meant: The betrothal starts right away but won't be finished until tomorrow? And if he said, 'both halves of you for a penny,' here he certainly has made the entire proposition all together, or maybe a woman can't be betrothed by halves?"*

B. *The questions stand.*

III.25 A. *Raba raised the question,* "What if a man said, 'Your two daughters are betrothed to my two sons for a penny'? *Do we invoke as the operative criterion the one who gives and the one who receives, so there is a valid monetary transaction [one person gives and one person receives the penny], there is no transaction under that sum? Or perhaps we invoke the criterion of the one who betroths and the one who is betrothed, so there is no monetary transaction here?"*

B.   *The question stands.*

III.26 A.   *R. Pappa raised the question,* "What if a man said, 'Your daughter and your cow are mine for a penny'? *Do we interpret the language to mean, 'Your daughter for a half-penny and your cow for a half-penny," or perhaps 'your daughter for a penny,' and ownership of title to your cow by the act of drawing it?"*

B.   *The question stands.*

III.27 A.   *R. Ashi raised the question,* "What if a man said, 'Your daughter and your real estate are mine for a penny'? *Do we interpret the language to mean, 'Your daughter for a half-penny and your property for a half-penny," or perhaps 'Your daughter for a penny, and ownership of title to your property through usucaption'?"*

B.   *The question stands.*

III.28 A.   *There was a man who betrothed a woman with a token of silk. Said Rabbah, "It is not necessary to perform an act of Valuation in advance [to inform the woman of its value]."*

B.   *R. Joseph said, "It is necessary to perform an act of Valuation in advance [to inform the woman of its value]."*

C.   If he said to her, "Be betrothed for what is worth any piddling sum," all parties concur that it is not necessary to make an up-front Valuation of the silk. If he said to her, "For fifty zuz," and this silk is not worth that much, then it isn't worth that [and the transaction is null]. Where there is a point of difference, it is a case in which he said, "Fifty....," and the silk is worth fifty.

D.   *Rabbah said, "It is not necessary to perform an act of Valuation in advance, since, after all, it is worthy fifty."*

E.   *R. Joseph said, "It is necessary to perform an act of Valuation in advance, since a woman is not necessarily an expert in the value of the silk, she will not depend on that, without an expert evaluation."*

F.   *There are those who say, even in a case in which the transaction was for any piddling value there is a dispute.*

G.   R. Joseph said, "The equivalent of cash must be treated like cash itself: Just as a cash transaction must involve an articulated sum, [8A] so cash equivalent must involve an articulated sum."

III.29 A.   *Said R. Joseph, "How do I know it? Because it has been taught on Tannaite authority:*

B.   "'If there be yet many years, according to them he shall give back the price of his redemption out of the money with which he was acquired' (Lev. 25:51) – he may be acquired by money, not by produce or utensils.

C.   *[Joseph continues,]* "Now what is the meaning of 'produce or utensils'? Should I say that there is no possibility of acquiring title through a transaction symbolized by these in any way at all? But Scripture has said, 'He shall return the price of his redemption' (Lev. 25:51), which serves to encompass what a cash equivalent as much as actual cash. And if these are of insufficient value to add up to a penny, then why make reference in particular to produce or utensils, when the same is the rule governing ready cash? So does it not mean that they are worth a penny,* but, since they do not add up to an articulated sum, they do not serve that purpose."

D. *And the other party?*

E. *This is the sense of the matter:* He is acquired under the torah governing cash, but he is not acquired under the torah governing produce and utensils. *And what might that involve? Barter.* [Freedman: Whatever is given for a slave, whether money or cash equivalents, must be given in money; produce and utensils can be given in that way, but not as barter, in exchange for the slave, for barter can acquire only movables, but human beings rank as real estate.]

F. *Well, then, from the perspective of R. Nahman, who has said, "Produce cannot effect a barter" [though a utensil can], what is to be said?*

G. *Rather, in point of fact, these objects [produce, utensils] are worth at least a penny, and as to your question, then why make reference in particular to produce or utensils, when the same is the rule governing ready cash? The intent of the Tannaite framer is to make the point in the form of a statement, it goes without saying, thus: It is not necessary to make that point in respect to cash, for if it is worth a penny, the transaction is valid, and if not, it is not valid, but even with regard to produce and utensils, where I might argue, since the benefit from these is close at hand, the slave permits himself to be acquired — so we are informed that that is not the case.*

H. *Said R. Joseph, "How do I know it? Because it has been taught on Tannaite authority:*

I. "[If someone said,] 'This calf is for the redemption of my firstborn son,' 'This cloak is for the redemption of my firstborn son,' he has said nothing whatsoever. '...This calf, worth five selas, is for the redemption of my son,' 'This cloak, worth five selas, is for the redemption of my son' – his son is redeemed [T. Bekh. 6:13].

J. *[Joseph continues,] "Now what is the meaning of redemption? Should I say that the calf or cloak is not worth five selas? Then does he have the power to make such a decision [when that is what is owing]? So isn't it a case in which that is so even though they are worth the stated sum, but since there is no fixed value assigned to them that is made articulate, they are not acceptable?"*

K. *Not at all. In point of fact it is a case in which they do not have the requisite value, but it is for example a case in which the priest accepted the object as full value for the redemption, as in the case of R. Kahana, who took a scarf in exchange for the redemption of the firstborn, saying to the father, "To me it's worth five selas."*

L. *Said R. Ashi, "Well, we make that rule only with someone such as R. Kahana, who is an eminent authority and needs a scarf for his head, but not of everybody in general."*

M. *That is like Mar bar R. Ashi, who bought a scarf from the mother of Rabbah of Kubi worth ten zuz for thirteen.*

III.30 A. *Said R. Eleazar, "[If the man said,] 'Be betrothed to me for a maneh,' but he gave her a denar, lo, this woman is betrothed, and he has to make up the full amount that he has promised. Why is that the rule? Since he referred to a maneh but gave her only a denar, it is as though he* had said to her, '...on the stipulation....,' and said R. Huna said Rab, 'Whoever uses the language, "on the stipulation that...," is as though he says, "...as of now."' [Freedman: Thus it is as though he said, 'Be betrothed to me immediately for a denar, on condition that I gave you a maneh later.']"

B.   *An objection was raised:* [If the man said,] "Be betrothed to me for a maneh," and he was continuing to count out the money, and one of the parties wanted to retract, even up to the final denar, he or she has every right to do so.

C.   *Here with what situation do we deal? It is one in which he said, "...For this particular maneh...."*

D.   *Lo, since the concluding clause makes reference to the language, "...For this particular maneh," it must follow that the introductory clause speaks of a case in which he made reference to a maneh without further specification. For the concluding clause goes as follows in the Tannaite formulation:* If he said to her, "Be betrothed to me for this maneh," and it turns out to be a deficient maneh coin, lacking a denar in value, or a denar of copper, she is not betrothed. If it was just a debased denar, she is betrothed, but he has to exchange it for a good one.

E.   *Not at all, the opening clause and the concluding one both deal with a case in which he said, "With this maneh," and the sense is to spell out the transaction and its meaning thus:* If one of the parties wanted to retract, even up to the final denar, he or she has every right to do so. How so? For example, if he said to her, "Be betrothed to me for this maneh." *And that, in point of fact, stands to reason. For if you should imagine that the opening clause deals with a case in which he has not specified the maneh, if in the case in which he has referred to a maneh without further clarification, there is no valid betrothal, if he made reference to "this maneh," can there be any question?*

F.   *If that's all you've got to say, then it is hardly a done deal; for the second clause may serve to clarify the first, so that you shouldn't maintain, the first clause deals with a case in which he said "this maneh," but if he did not specify the maneh, it would be a valid betrothal; so the second clause makes specific reference to his saying, "this maneh," from which it follows that the first case refers to an unspecified money, and yet even here the betrothal is null.*

G.   *R. Ashi said, "A case in which he is counting out the money it is difference, because in that case her intent concerns the whole of the sum."*

III.31 A.   *As to this a denar of copper, with what sort of a case do we deal? If she knew about its character, well, then she was informed and accepted it!*

B.   *Not at all, the specific reference is required to deal with a case in which he gave it to her at night, or she found it among other coins.*

III.32 A.   *As to this a debased denar, with what sort of a case do we deal? If it is not in circulation, then isn't it in the same class as a copper denar?*

B.   *Said R. Pappa, "It would be one that circulates but only with difficulty."*

III.33 A.   Said R. Nahman, "If he said to her, 'Be betrothed to me with a maneh,' and he gave her a pledge for it, she is not betrothed. [8B] There is no maneh here, there is no pledge here." [Freedman: She neither received the maneh nor did he actually give her a pledge, since that has to be returned.]

B.   *Raba objected to R. Nahman,* "If he betrothed her with a pledge, she is betrothed."

C.   *That refers to a pledge belonging to a third party, in accord with what R. Isaac said, for said R. Isaac,* "How on the basis of Scripture do we know that the creditor acquires title to the pledge [while it is in his possession and so is responsible for any accident that occurs]? Scripture states, 'In any case you shall deliver the pledge again when the sun goes down...and it shall be righteousness for you' (Deut. 24:13). Now if he doesn't have title to the object, whence the righteousness? This proves that the creditor takes the title to the pledge." [Freedman: It is legally his while in his possession, therefore he may validly offer it for a token of betrothal.]

III.34 A. *The sons of R. Huna bar Abin bought a female slave for copper coins. They didn't have the coins in hand, so they gave as a pledge a silver ingot. The slave's value increased. They came before R. Ammi. He said to them, "There are here neither coins nor an ingot" [and the transaction can be cancelled].*

III.35 A. *Our rabbis have taught on Tannaite authority:*

B.   **"Be betrothed to me with a maneh," and she took it and threw it into the sea or fire or anywhere where it is lost – she is not betrothed [T. Qid. 2:8A-C].**

III.36 A. *So if she threw it down before him, is it a valid betrothal? Lo, in so doing, she says to him, "You take it, I don't want it."*

B.   *The formulation means to say, it is not necessary to say..., thus: It is not necessary to say that if she throw it back before him, this is not a valid betrothal, but if she threw it into the sea or into the fire, I might have supposed that, since she now is liable for the money, she has most certainly allowed herself to be betrothed, and the reason that she did what she did is that she was thinking, "I'll test him to see whether he is temperamental or not." So we are informed that that is not the case.*

III.37 A. *Our rabbis have taught on Tannaite authority:*

B.   **"Be betrothed to me with this maneh" –**

C.   **"Give it to my father or your father" –**

D.   **she is not betrothed.**

E.   **"...On condition that they accept it for me" –**

F.   **she is betrothed [T. Qid. 2:8D-E].**

III.38 A. *The Tannaite formulation has made reference to "father" to show you the full extent of the application of the rule of the first clause [even then she is not betrothed], and the usage of "your father" shows how far we go in the second clause [that she is then betrothed].*

III.39 A. **"Be betrothed to me with a maneh" –**

B.   **"Give them to Mr. So-and-so" –**

C.   **she is not betrothed .**

D.   **"...On condition that Mr. So-and-so accept the money for me," she is betrothed [T. Qid. D-G].**

III.40 A. *And it was necessary to specify both cases. For if we had been informed of the cases of her referring to her father or his father, it would be in such a case in which if she said, "On condition that they receive them for me," she would have accomplished a valid betrothal, for she would have relied on them, assuming that they would carry out her commission. But that would not be the case when she merely made reference to Mr. So-and-so.*

And had we been informed of her referring to Mr. So-and-so, it would be in this case in particular that the rule would apply, for if she said, "Give them to Mr. So-and-so," she would not be betrothed, for she would not have known the man well enough to give her the money as a gift. But as for her referring to her father or his father, with whom she is closely related, one might have supposed that her intent was to make a gift of the money to them. So both cases are required.

III.41 A. Our rabbis have taught on Tannaite authority:
        B. "Be betrothed to me for this maneh" –
        C. "Put it on a rock" –
        D. she is not betrothed.
        E. But if the rock belonged to her, she is betrothed.

III.42 A. *R. Bibi raised this question: "If the rock belonged to the two of them, what is the law?"*
        B. *That question stands.*

III.43 A. "Be betrothed for this loaf of bread" –
        B. "Give it to a dog" –
        C. she is not betrothed.
        D. But if the dog belonged to her, she is betrothed.

III.44 A. *R. Mari raised this question: "If the dog was running after her, what is the law? In exchange for the benefit that she gets in being saved from the dog, she has determined to assign to him title over herself? Or perhaps she has the power to say, 'By the law of the Torah, you were obligated to save us?'"*
        B. *That question stands.*

III.45 A. "Be betrothed to me for this loaf of bread" –
        B. "Give it to that poor man" –
        C. she is not betrothed, even if it was a poor man who depended on her.

III.46 A. *How come?*
        B. *She can say to the man, "Just as I have an obligation to him, so you have an obligation to him."*

III.47 A. *There was someone who was selling* [9A] *glass beads. A woman came to him. She said to him, "Give me one string."*
        B. *He said to her, "If I give it to you, will you become betrothed to me?"*
        C. *She said to him, "Give it to me, do."*
        D. *Said R. Hama, "Any case in which someone said, 'Give it to me, do,' means absolutely nothing."*

III.48 A. *There was someone who was drinking wine in a wine shop. A woman came. She said to me, "Give me a cup."*
        B. *He said to her, "If I give it to you, will you be betrothed to me?"*
        C. *She said to him, "Oh, let me have a drink."*
        D. *Said R. Hama, "Any case in which someone said, 'Oh, let me have a drink,' means absolutely nothing."*

III.49 A. *There was someone who was throwing down dates from a date palm. A woman came along and said to him, "Throw me down two."*
        B. *He said to her, "If I throw them down to you, will you become betrothed to me?"*
        C. *She said to him, "Oh, throw them down to me."*
        D. *Said R. Zebid, "Every usage such as, 'Oh, throw them down to me,' is null."*

III.50 A. *The question was raised: "What if she said, 'give me,' 'let me drink,' or 'throw them down'?"*

B. Said Rabina, "She is betrothed."

C. *R. Sama bar Raqata said, "By the king's crown, she's not betrothed."*

D. *And the decided law is, she's not betrothed.*

E. *and the decided law is, silk doesn't have to be evaluated.*

F. *And the decided law is in accord with R. Eleazar.*

G. *And the decided law is in accord with Raba as stated by R. Nahman.*

IV.1 A. [a **writ:**] *Our rabbis have taught on Tannaite authority:*

B. A writ: How so?

C. If one wrote on a parchment or on a potsherd, even though they themselves were of no intrinsic value, "Lo, your daughter is betrothed to me," "Your daughter is engaged to me," "Your daughter is a wife for me" – lo, this woman is betrothed.

D. *Objected R. Zira bar Mammel, "Lo, this writ is not comparable to a writ of purchase, for there, the seller writes, 'My field is sold to me,' while here, it* is the prospective husband who writes, 'Your daughter is consecrated to me.'"

E. *Said Raba, "There the formulation derives from the expression of Scripture, and here the formulation derives from the expression of Scripture. In reference to that other matter it is written, 'And he sell some of his possessions' (Lev. 25:25), so it is on the seller that the All-Merciful has made the matter depend. Here it is written, 'When a man takes a woman' (Deut. 24:1), so it is on the husband that Scripture had made the matter depend."*

F. *But in that other contest, it is also written, "Men shall buy fields for money" (Jer. 32:44).*

G. *Read the letters as though they bore vowels to yield, "Men shall transmit" [that is, sell].*

H. *Well, then, if you read the word to yield "transmit," because it is written "And he sell," then here, too, read "If a man be taken," since it is written, "I gave my daughter to this man for a wife" (Deut. 22:16)!*

I. *Rather said Raba, "What we have is a law by decree, and our rabbis have then found support for the law in verses of Scripture. Or, if you prefer, I shall say, there, too, it is also written, 'So I took the deed of the purchase' (Jer. 32:11)."* [Freedman: This shows that Jeremiah, the purchaser, received the deed, which must have been drawn up by the vendor.]

IV.2 A. Said Raba said R. Nahman, "If one wrote on a piece of paper or a sherd, even though these were not worth a penny, 'Your daughter is consecrated to me,' 'Your daughter is betrothed to me,' 'Your daughter is mine as a wife,' whether this is effected through her father or through herself, she is betrothed by the father's consent. That is the case if she had not reached maturity. If one wrote for her on a piece of paper or a sherd, even though these were not worth a penny, 'You are consecrated to me,' 'You are betrothed to me,' 'You are mine as a wife,' whether this is effected through her father or through herself, she is betrothed by her own consent."

IV.3 A. R. Simeon b. Laqish raised the question, "As to a deed of betrothal that was not written for the purpose of betrothing this particular woman, what is the law? *Do we treat as comparable the formation of a marriage and its dissolution, so that, [9B] just as in the case of its disolution, we require that the writ of divorce be written for the particular purpose of divorcing this woman, so in the case of the formation of the marriage, we require the writ of betrothal to be written for the particular purpose of betrothing this woman? Or do we treat as comparable the several modes for effecting a betrothal: Just as the betrothal by a monetary token need not be accomplished by a token prepared for her sake in particular, so betrothal by a deed does not have to be through a deed prepared for this particular woman?"*

B. *After he raised the question, he went and solved it: "We do indeed treat as comparable the formation of a marriage and its dissolution. For said Scripture, 'And when she has gone forth...she may be another man's wife' (Deut. 24:1)."*

IV.4   A. *It has been stated:*

B. If someone wrote a deed of betrothal in her name but without her knowledge and consent –

C. *Rabbah and Rabina say, "She is betrothed."*

D. *R. Pappa and R. Sherabayya say, "She is not betrothed."*

E. *Said R. Pappa, "I shall state their scriptural foundations and I shall state mine. I shall state their reason: It is written, 'And when she has gone forth...she may be another man's wife' (Deut. 24:1). Scripture treats as comparable the betrothal and the divorce: Just as the writ of divorce must be written for the purpose of divorcing this particular written yet without her knowledge and consent, so the writ of betrothal must be written for her own sake, and without her consent. And I shall state the scriptural foundation of my position: 'And when she has gone forth...she may be another man's wife' (Deut. 24:1). This treats betrothal as comparable to divorce: Just as in the divorce, the knowledge of the giver is required [the husband has obviously to concur], so in betrothal the giver's knowledge is essential [and it is the woman who gives herself]."*

F. *An objection was raised:* **They write the documents of betrothal and marriage only with the knowledge and consent of both parties [M. B.B. 10:4A].** *Doesn't this mean literally, documents of betrothal and marriage?*

G. *No, it means deeds of apportionment [designating how much the families are giving to the son and daughter], in accord with what R. Giddal said R. said, for said R. Giddal said Rab, "'How much are you going to give to your son?' 'Thus and so.' "How much are you going to give to your daughter?" 'Thus and so.' If they then arose and declared the formula of sanctification, they have effected transfer of the right of ownership. These statements represent matters in which the right of ownership is transferred verbally."*

V.1   A. **Or sexual intercourse:**

B. *What is the scriptural source of this rule?*

C. *Said R. Abbahu said R. Yohanan, "Said Scripture, 'If a man be found lying with a woman who had intercourse with a husband' (Deut. 22:22) – this teaches that he became her husband through an act of sexual relations."*

D. Said R. Zira to R. Abbahu, and some say, R. Simeon b. Laqish to R. Yohanan, "Is then what Rabbi taught unsatisfactory, namely, '"And has intercourse with her" (Deut. 24:1) – this teaches that he became her husband through an act of sexual relations'?"

E. *If I had to derive proof from that verse, I might have supposed that he first has to betroth her [with a monetary token] and only then have sexual relations with her. So we are informed that that is not the case.*

F. *Objected R. Abba bar Mammel, "If so, then in the case of the betrothed maiden, where Scripture decrees stoning as the death penalty should she commit adultery, how can we find a concrete case in which that would be the upshot? If he first betrothed her and then had sexual relations, she is in the classification of a woman who has had sexual relations [and stoning is the death penalty for a virgin alone]; if he betrothed her but did not have sexual relations with her, then it is on this hypothesis null anyhow!"*

G. *Rabbis stated the solution to this conundrum before Abbayye: "You would find such a case if* the prospective groom had sexual relations with her through the anus."

H. *Said to them Abbayye, "But in point of fact, even Rabbi and rabbis conduct their dispute only with regard to an outsider; but as to the husband, all concur that if* the prospective groom had sexual relations with her through the anus, she is classified as one who has had sexual relations."

I. *What is the pertinent passage? As has been taught on Tannaite authority:*

J. **It ten men had intercourse with her and she remained yet a virgin, all of them are put to death by stoning.**

K. **Rabbi says, "The first is put to death by stoning, and the others by strangulation"** [T. San. 10:9C-D].

L. *Said R. Nahman bar Isaac, "You would find such a case, for instance, if he betrothed her with a writ. Since a writ is wholly sufficient to sever the marital bond, it also is sufficient fully to effect it."* [Freedman: Yet it might be that money betrothal must be followed by sexual relations.]

M. And as to the clause, "And has intercourse with her" (Deut. 24:1), *how does R. Yohanan make use of that item?*

N. *He requires it to show the following:* A wife is acquired by sexual relations, but a Hebrew slave girl is not acquired by sexual relations. *For it might have entered your mind to maintain that the contrary may be inferred by an argument a fortiori from the case of the levirate wife:* If a levirate wife, who is not acquired by a money payment is acquired through an act of sexual relations, this woman, who is acquired by a money payment, surely should be acquired by an act of sexual relations!

O. [But the verse is not required for that purpose, for one may well respond:] What characterizes the levirate wife is that she is already subject to the bond to the husband [which obviously does not pertain to the slave girl].

P. *Well, it might have entered your mind to maintain:* since it is written, "If he take another wife" (Ex. 21:10) [in addition to the slave girl] – just as the other is acquired by intercourse, so a Hebrew slave girl would be acquired through an act of sexual relations. *So by this verse we are informed to the contrary.*

Q. *And how does Rabbi deal with this theoretical proposition?*

R. *If it is so [that verse yields only the proposition that sexual relations is a medium of betrothal], Scripture should have written,* "And he have sexual relations." *Why say,* "And he have sexual relations with her"? *That yields both points.*

S. *And from the perspective of Raba, who said,* "Bar Ahina explained to me, "'When a man takes a woman and has sexual relations with her'" (Deut. 24:1) — a betrothal that can be followed by sexual relations is valid, but a betrothal that cannot be followed by sexual relations is not valid,'" *what is to be said?*

T. *If that were the sole point, Scripture could have written,* "Or has sexual relations with her." *Why,* "And has sexual relations with her"? *This yields all the pertinent points.*

U. *And how does Rabbi deal with the phrase,* "Who had intercourse with a husband"?

V. *He uses it to teach the following proposition:* A husband's act of anal intercourse renders her a woman who is no longer a virgin, but a third party's action does not.

W. *Well, now, is that Rabbi's position? Hasn't it been taught on Tannaite authority:*

X. **If ten men had intercourse with her and she remained yet a virgin, all of them are put to death by stoning.**

Y. **Rabbi says, "The first is put to death by stoning, and the others by strangulation"** [T. San. 10:9C-D].

Z. [10A] Said R. Zira, "Rabbi concedes that, in regard to the extrajudicial sanction, all have to pay the fine. *And how come this is different from the death penalty [in which case Rabbi classifies her as a virgin]? That is differentiated by Scripture itself:* 'Then the man alone that lay with her shall die' (Deut. 22:25)."

AA. *And rabbis — how do they deal with the word* "alone"?

BB. *They require it in line with that which has been taught on Tannaite authority:*

CC. "'Then they shall both of them die' (Deut. 22:22) means that a penalty is imposed only when the two of them are equal," the words of R. Josiah.

DD. R. Jonathan says, "'Then the man only that lay with her shall die' (Deut. 22:25)."

EE. *And whence does R. Yohanan derive this thesis?*

FF. *If it were so, Scripture should have said,* "Who has had intercourse with a man." *Why say,* "Who had had intercourse with a husband"? *That is to yield both matters.*

V.2 A. *The question was raised:* Is it the beginning of the act of intercourse that effects the acquisition of the woman, or the end of the act of sexual relations that does? *The practical difference would derive from a case in which* he performed the initial stage of sexual relations, then she put out her hand and accepted a token of betrothal from someone else; *or the case of whether a high priest may acquire a virgin through an act of sexual relations. What is the rule?*

B. Said Amemar in the name of Raba, "Whoever has sexual relations is thinking about the completion of the act of sexual relations [not only the commencement of the act]."

V.3   A.   *The question was raised:* Does sexual relations effect a consummated marriage or merely a betrothal? *The practical difference would pertain to the question of* whether he inherits her estate, contracts uncleanness to bury her [if he is a priest], and abrogates her vows. *If you maintain that* sexual relations effect a consummated marriage, then he inherits her estate, contracts uncleanness to bury her [if he is a priest], and abrogates her vows. *If you maintain that* sexual relations effect only betrothal, then he does not inherits her estate, contract uncleanness to bury her [if he is a priest], and abrogate her vows. *What is the rule?*

    B.   Said Abbayye, "The father retains control of his daughter [younger than twelve and a half] as to effecting any of the tokens of betrothal: Money, document, or sexual intercourse. And he retains control of what she finds, of the fruit of her labor, and of abrogating her vows. And he receives her writ of divorce [from a betrothal]. But he does not dispose of the return [on property received by the girl from her mother] during her lifetime. When she is married, the husband exceeds the father, for he disposes of the return [on property received by the girl from her mother] during her lifetime. But he is liable to maintain her, and to ransom her, and to bury her [M. Ket. 4:4]. *Now there is a clear reference to sexual relations, and yet the Tannaite formulation also qualifies the matter,* When she is married."

    C.   *But the clause,* When she is married, *may refer to other matters.*

    D.   *Said Raba, "Come and take note:* A girl three years and one day old is betrothed by intercourse. And if a levir has had intercourse with her, he has acquired her. And they are liable on her account because of the law [prohibiting intercourse with] a married woman. And she imparts uncleanness to him who has intercourse with her [when she is menstruating] [10B] to convey uncleanness to the lower as to the upper layer. [If] she was married to a priest, she eats heave-offering. [If] one of those who are unfit [for marriage] has intercourse with her, he has rendered her unfit to marry into the priesthood. [If one of all those who are forbidden in the Torah to have intercourse with her did so, they are put to death on her account. But she is free of responsibility. If she is younger than that age, intercourse with her is like putting a finger in the eye] [M. Nid. 5:4]. *Now there is a clear reference to sexual relations, and yet the Tannaite formulation also qualifies the matter,* When she is married."

    E.   *This is the sense of the passage: If this intercourse mentioned at the outset is with a priest, then she may eat priestly rations.*

    F.   *Come and take note:* It is the fact that Yohanan b. Bag Bag sent word to R. Judah b. Beterah in Nisibis, "I heard in your regard that you maintain, an Israelite woman who is betrothed to a priest may eat priestly rations." He replied, "And don't you concur? I have it on good authority in your regard that you are an expert in the innermost chambers of the Torah, knowing how to compose an argument a fortiori. So don't you know the following: 'If a Canaanite slave girl, upon whom an act of sexual relations does not confer the right to eat priestly rations, may eat priestly rations by reason of a money purchase of ownership to her, this one, upon whom an act of sexual relations does confer the right to eat priestly rations, surely should be permitted to eat priestly rations by means of the transfer of a token of betrothal!' But what can I do? For lo, sages have ruled: An Israelite girl betrothed to a priest may not eat priestly rations until she enters the marriage canopy." *Now how are we to understand the case here? If it is sexual relations after the marriage canopy and a betrothal through a monetary token followed by a marriage canopy, in both cases there is obviously no doubt that she may eat priestly rations. If it is intercourse with the marriage canopy or money without, then here there are two operative analogies, there, only one [and how can the rule governing money without a marriage canopy be deduced from the rules governing intercourse with]? So the passage surely must speak to both intercourse and money payment without a marriage canopy. If you maintain that intercourse brings about the consummated marriage, well and good; it is self-evident that sexual relations has a greater effect than money; but if you maintain that it effects only the betrothal, then what makes him certain in the one case and doubtful in the other?*

G.   *Said R. Nahman bar Isaac, "In point of fact, I shall explain the matter to you to refer to sexual relations accompanied by the marriage canopy or monetary token without. And as to your objection, here there are two operative analogies, there, only one [and how can the rule governing money without a marriage canopy be deduced from the rules governing intercourse with]? still there is an argument a fortiori that remains entirely valid. And this is what he sent to him by way of reply:* If a Canaanite slave girl, upon whom an act of sexual relations does not confer the right to eat priestly rations, even via the marriage canopy, may eat priestly rations by reason of a money purchase of ownership to her – without the intrusion of the rite of the marriage canopy, this one, upon whom an act of sexual relations does confer the right to eat priestly rations by means of the marriage canopy, surely should be permitted to eat priestly rations by means of the transfer of a token of betrothal – without the intrusion of the rite of the marriage canopy! But what can I do? For lo, sages have ruled: An Israelite girl betrothed to a priest may not eat priestly rations until she enters the marriage canopy. That is on account of what Ulla said ['By the law of the Torah, a girl of Israelite caste who was betrothed to a priest is permitted to eat priestly rations: "But if a priest buy any soul, the purchase of his money..." (Lev. 22:11) – *and this one also falls into the class of* "purchased of his money." And what is the reason that they have said that she may not eat priestly rations? Lest a cup of wine in the status of priestly rations be mixed for her in her father's house and she share it with her brother or sister who are not in the priestly caste']."

H.   *And Ben Bag Bag [doesn't he accept the argument a fortiori]?*

I.   *In the acquisition of the gentile slave girl, the man has left out nothing in acquiring her [once he pays the money, she is his], but her, he has left out part of the process of acquiring her [for only after the marriage canopy does he inherit her and so forth].*

J.   *Rabina said, "On the basis of the law of the Torah, [Ben Bag Bag] was quite certain that she may eat priestly rations, but it was only with respect to the position of rabbinical law that he sent word to him claiming that she is forbidden to do so, and this is the character of his inquiry:* 'I have heard in your regard that you maintain, an Israelite woman betrothed to a priest may eat priestly rations, thus disregarding the possibility of nullification' [for example, through discovery of an invalidating cause to nullify the betrothal; this then has no bearing on the question of status conferred by intercourse, since all concur that a betrothed girl may eat priestly rations so far as the law of the Torah is concerned (Freedman)]. And he sent word back, 'And don't you take the same position? I have it on good authority in your regard that you are an expert in the innermost chambers of the Torah, knowing how to compose an argument a fortiori. So don't you know the following: If a Canaanite slave girl, upon whom an act of sexual relations does not confer the right to eat priestly rations, may eat priestly rations by reason of a money purchase of ownership to her, *and we don't take account of the possibility of nullification of the betrothal* – this one, upon whom an act of sexual relations does confer the right to eat priestly rations, surely should be permitted to eat priestly rations by means of the transfer of a token of betrothal – *and we shouldn't take account of the possibility of nullification of the betrothal.* But what can I do? For lo, sages have ruled: An Israelite girl betrothed to a priest may not eat priestly rations [11A] until she enters the marriage canopy, on account of what Ulla said ["By the law of the Torah, a girl of Israelite caste who was betrothed to a priest is permitted to eat priestly rations: 'But if a priest buy any soul, the purchase of his money...' (Lev. 22:11) – *and this one also falls into the class of* 'purchased of his money.' And what is the reason that they have said that she may not eat priestly rations? Lest a cup of wine in the status of priestly rations be mixed for her in her father's house and she share it with her brother or sister who are not in the priestly caste"].'"

K. And Ben Bag Bag?

L. *He does not concede that a possibility of invalidating the transaction can take place in the sale of slaves. For if these were defects that were visible, then he has seen them and accepted them; if it was on account of defects that were concealed, what difference does it make to him? He wants the slave for work, and it wouldn't matter to him. If the slave turns out to be a thief or a rogue, he still belongs to the purchaser [since most slaves are that way anyhow]. So what can you say, that he turned out to be an thug or an outlaw? These would be known defects.*

M. *Now since both parties concur that a betrothed woman may not eat priestly rations, what's at issue?*

N. At issue is a case in which the husband accepted the body defects; or the father handed her over to the husband's messengers to be taken to her husband's house; or if the father's messengers were en route with the husband's. [In the first case, ben Bag Bag lets her eat priestly rations; in Judah b. Batera's view, she cannot do so, by reason of Ulla's explanation; in the second, Ulla's consideration no longer pertains, there being no family around, but there can be nullification; and the third is governed by the same rule (Freedman).]

VI.1   A.   **Through money: The House of Shammai say, "For a denar or what is worth a denar":**

       B.   *What is the operative consideration in the mind of the House of Shammai?*

       C.   Said R. Zira, "For a woman is particular about herself and is not going to allow herself to become betrothed for less than a denar."

       D.   *Said to him Abbayye, "Well, then what about the daughters of R. Yannai, who were so particular about themselves that they would not become betrothed for less than a tubful of denarii! If she should put out her hand and accept a coin from a stranger as a token of betrothal, is she then betrothed?!"*

       E.   He said to him, "Well, if she put out her hand and accepted the token, I don't take that position. I speak of a case in which he conducts the betrothal at night [so doesn't know what she got] or if she appointed an agent."

       F.   *R. Joseph said, "The operative consideration in the mind of the House of Shammai accords with what R. Judah said R. Assi said, for* said R. Judah said R. Assi, "Whenever 'money' is mentioned in the Torah, what is meant is Tyrian coinage; when rabbis speak of money, they refer to the coinage that circulates in the provinces. [The betrothal token is Scriptural, so it must be a valuable coin, not a copper coin, hence a denar.]"

VI.2   A.   *Reverting to the body of the foregoing:* Said R. Judah said R. Assi, "Whenever 'money' is mentioned in the Torah, what is meant is Tyrian coinage; when rabbis speak of money, they refer to the coinage that circulates in the provinces."

       B.   *Is this a ubiquitous principle?* Lo, there is the case of a claim, concerning which Scripture states, "If a man shall deliver to his neighbor money or utensils to keep" (Ex. 22:6), *and yet we have learned in the Mishnah:* **The oath imposed by judges [is required if] the claim is [at least] two pieces of silver, and the concession [on the part of the defendant is that he owes] at least a penny's [perutah's]worth [M. Shebu. 6:1A].**

       C.   *There the governing analogy is utensils:* Just as utensils are two, so the coins must be two, just as money speaks of what has intrinsic worth, so utensils speaks of something that is of worth.

       D.   Lo, there is the case of a second tithe, concerning which Scripture states, "And you shall turn it into money and bind up the money in your hand," *and yet we have learned in the Mishnah:* **One who exchanges a [silver] sela [sanctified as] second tithe [for other coins] in Jerusalem – The House of Shammai say, "The whole sela [he receives must consist] of [copper] coins." And the House of Hillel say, "[The sela he receives may consist] of one sheqel of silver [coins] and one sheqel of [copper] coins." The disputants before the sages say, "The sela may consist] of three silver denars and [one] denar of [copper] coins." R. Aqiba says, "[The sela may consist] of three silver denars and a quarter [of the fourth denar must consist of] [copper] coins." R. Tarfon says, "[The fourth denar may consist of] four aspers of silver [equal to four-fifths of the denar's value and the remaining asper must be of copper]." Shammai says, "Let him deposit it in a shop and consume its value [in produce]" [M. M.S. 2:9].**

E. Reference to "money" is inclusionary.

F. What about what has been consecrated, concerning which it is written, "Then he shall give the money and it shall be confirmed in his ownership," in which regard Samuel said, "If what has been consecrated is worth a maneh and it is redeemed with what is equivalent in worth to a penny, it is validly redeemed"?

G. *In that case, we deduce the meaning of "money" from the sense of the word when it is used in reference to tithes.*

H. Lo, there is the case of a token of betrothal given to a woman, concerning which Scripture states, "When a man takes a wife and marries her," and we have deduced the meaning of "take" from the transaction of the field of Ephron, *and yet we have learned in the Mishnah:* And the House of Hillel say, "For a perutah or what is worth a perutah"! *Is the upshot, then, that we shall have to concede R. Assi has made his ruling in accord with the position of the House of Shammai?*

I. *Rather, if such a statement was made, this is how it was made:* Said R. Judah said R. Assi, "Whenever 'money' in a fixed amount is mentioned in the Torah, what is meant is Tyrian coinage; when rabbis speak of money, they refer to the coinage that circulates in the provinces."

J. *Well, then, what does he tell us that we don't already know!? We have a Tannaite statement as follows:* The five selas for redeeming the firstborn son are in Tyrian coinage. (1) The thirty for the slave (Ex. 21:32), and (2) the fifty to be paid by the rapist and seducer (Ex. 22:15-16, Deut. 22:28-29), and (3) the hundred to be paid by the gossip (Deut. 22:19) – all are to be paid in the value of sheqels of the sanctuary, in Tyrian coinage. And everything which is to be redeemed [is redeemed] in silver or its equivalent, except for sheqel dues [M. Bekh. 8:7]!

K. *It is necessary to make that statement to cover the rule,* when rabbis speak of money, they refer to the coinage that circulates in the provinces, *which we have not learned in the Mishnah. For we have learned in the Mishnah,* he who boxes the ear of his fellow pays him a sela [M. B.Q. 8:6A]. *You should not suppose that the sela under discussion is four zuz, but it is half a zuz, for people call half a zuz a sela.*

VI.3 A. R. Simeon b. Laqish says, "*The operative consideration behind the ruling of the House of Shammai is in accord with Hezekiah, for said Hezekiah, 'Said Scripture, "Then shall he let her be redeemed" (Ex. 21:8) – this teaches that she deducts from her redemption money and goes out free.' Now if you maintain that the master gives her a denar [when he buys her, which would be the counterpart to the token of betrothal], then there is no problem; but if you say it was a mere penny, then what deduction can be made from a penny?*"

B. But maybe this is the sense of what the All-Merciful has meant to say: in a case in which he gave her a denar, there is a deduction made until a penny is left; but if he gave her a penny, there is no deduction made at all?

C. [12A] *Don't let it enter your mind. For it is comparable to the act of designating a Hebrew handmaid [for betrothal, once the Hebrew slave girl has been purchased; there is no further token of betrothal required]: Just as,* in the case of such a designation, even though the master can designate her or refrain from doing so, as he prefers, where he doesn't designate her for marriage, the sale is invalid, so here, too, where we cannot make such a deduction, the sale is invalid. And the House of Shammai derive the rule governing the betrothal of a woman from the rule governing the Hebrew slave girl. Just as a Hebrew slave girl cannot be acquired for a penny, so a woman cannot be betrothed for a penny.

D. Well why not say half a denar or two pennies?

E. Once the penny was excluded as a measure, the matter was set at a denar.

VI.4 A. Raba said, "This is the operative consideration for the position of the House of Shammai: So that Israelite women won't be treated as ownerless property."

VII.1 A. **And the House of Hillel say, "For a perutah or what is worth a perutah":**

B. R. Joseph considered ruling, "A penny, of any sort [however debased]."

C. Said to him Abbayye, "But lo, there is a Tannaite clarification of this matter in so many words: **And how much is a perutah? One eighth of an Italian issar.** And should you say, that ruling addresses the time of Moses, while at the present time, it is as generally valued, lo, when R. Dimi came, he said, 'R. Simai estimated the value in his time to determine how much a penny is, and determined, an eighth of an Italian issar,' and when Rabin came, he said, 'R. Dosetai, R. Yannai, and R. Oshayya estimated how much a penny is worth, and determined, a sixth of an Italian issar.'"

D. Said R. Joseph to him, "If so, then, that is in line with the following Tannaite statement: Go and estimate, how many pennies are there in two selas? More than 2000. Now, since there are not even 2,000, can the Tannaite call it more than 2,000?"

E. Said to them a certain sage, "I have the Tannaite formulation as, near two thousand."

F. One way or the other, it is only 1,536.

G. Since it goes beyond half [which would be a thousand], it is classified as "close to 2,000."

VII.2 A. Reverting to the body of the foregoing: When R. Dimi came, he said, "R. Simai estimated the value in his time to determine how much a penny is, and determined, an eighth of an Italian issar," and when Rabin came, he said, "R. Dosetai, R. Yannai, and R. Oshayya estimated how much a penny is worth, and determined, a sixth of an Italian issar."

B. Said Abbayye to R. Dimi, "May we then propose that you and Rabin differ in the same way as the following Tannaite authority, as has been taught on Tannaite authority:

C. [Following Tosefta's version:] "A perutah [translated above: Penny] of which they have spoken is one out of eight pennies [perutot] to an issar; an issar is one twenty-fourth of a denar; six silver maahs are a denar; a silver maah is two pondions; a pondion is two issars; an issar is two mismasin; a mismas is two quntronin; a quntron is two pennies [perutot].

D. "Rabban Simeon b. Gamaliel says, 'The perutah of which they have spoken is one of six pennies [perutot] to the issar; there are three hadrasin to a maah; two hannassin to a hadrash; two shemanin to a hannas; two pennies [perutot] to a shemen' [T. B.B. 5:11-12].

E.   *"So may we then say that the one authority concurs with the initial Tannaite authority, and Rabin accords with Rabban Simeon b. Gamaliel?"*

F.   *He said to him, "Whether in accord with my view of that of Rabin, we concur with the initial Tannaite statement here, and there is nonetheless no contradiction; in the one case, the issar bears full value, in the other, it had depreciated. In the one case the issar bears full value, twenty-four being the equivalent to a zuz; in the other case it had depreciated, thirty-two for a zuz."*

VII.3   A.   Said Samuel, "If one betrothed a woman with a date, even if a kor of dates were at a denar, she is deemed betrothed, *for we take account of the possibility that in Media it may be worth a penny."*

B.   *But lo, we have learned in the Mishnah:* **And the House of Hillel say, "For a perutah or what is worth a perutah"**!

C.   *No problem, the one speaks of a betrothal that is beyond all doubt, the other, a betrothal that is subject to doubt.*

VII.4   A.   *There was someone who betrothed a woman with a bundle of tow cotton [Freedman]. In session before Rab, R. Shimi bar Hiyya examined the question: "If it contains the value of a penny, she would be betrothed, if not, not."*

B.   *...If not, not? But didn't Samuel say, "For we take account of the possibility that in Media it may be worth a penny"?*

C.   *No problem, the one speaks of a betrothal that is beyond all doubt, the other, a betrothal that is subject to doubt.*

VII.5   A.   *There was someone who betrothed a woman with a black marble stone. In session, R. Hisda estimated its value: "If it contains the value of a penny, she would be betrothed, if not, not."*

B.   *...If not, not? But didn't Samuel say, "for we take account of the possibility that in Media it may be worth a penny"?*

C.   *R. Hisda does not view matters as does Samuel.*

D.   *Said his mother to him, "But lo, on that day on which he betrothed her, it was worth a penny."*

E.   *He said to her, "You don't have the power to prohibit her from marrying the other fellow [to whom in the interval she had been betrothed]. [12B] For isn't this parallel to the case of Judith, wife of R. Hiyya? She suffered terrible pains in childbirth [and didn't want more children]. She said to him, 'Mother told me, "Your father accepted a token of betrothal on your behalf from someone else when you were a child."' He said to her, 'Your mother doesn't have the power to forbid you to me.'"*

F.   *Said rabbis to R. Hisda, "Why not! Lo, there are witnesses in Idit who know as fact that, on that day, it was worth a penny."*

G.   *"Well, anyhow, they're not here with us now! Isn't that in line with what R. Hanina said, for said R. Hanina, 'Her witnesses are in the north, but she is nonetheless forbidden.'"*

H.   *Abbayye and Raba do not concur with that view of R. Hisda:* "If rabbis made a lenient ruling in the context of a captive woman [to which Hanina's statement referred], in which case the woman was humiliated in captivity of kidnappers, should we make an equivalently lenient ruling in the case of a married woman?"

I. *Members of that family remained in Sura, and rabbis kept away from them, not because they concurred with the position of Samuel, but because they concurred with the view of Abbayye and Raba.*

VII.6 A. *There was someone who in the marketplace betrothed a woman with a myrtle branch. R. Aha bar Huna sent word to R. Joseph, "In such a case, what is the ruling?"*

B. *He sent back, "Flog him in accord with the position of Rab, but require him to issue a writ of divorce in accord with the position of Samuel."*

C. *For Rab would flog someone who betrothed through an act of sexual relations, and one whom betrothed in the marketplace, and one who betrothed without prior negotiation, one who nullified a writ of divorce, one who called into question the validity of a divorce, one who offended an agent of the rabbis, one who permitted a rabbinical ban of ostracism to remain upon him for thirty days without coming to the court to ask for its removal, and a son-in-law who lived in his father-in-law's house [prior to the consummation of the marriage].*

D. *If he actually lives there but not if he merely goes by there? And lo, there was someone who merely passed by the doorway of his father-in-law's house, and R. Sheshet ordered him flogged!*

E. *That man was suspected of illicit relations with his mother-in-law.*

F. *The Nehardeans said, "In none of these cases did Rab order a flogging except in the case of the ones who betrothed through an act of sexual relations or did so without prior negotiations."*

G. *There are those who say, "Even in the case of preliminary negotiation, on account of the possibility of licentiousness."*

VII.7 A. *There was someone who in the marketplace betrothed a woman with a mat made of myrtle twigs. They said to him, "But it's not worth a penny!"*

B. *He said to them, "Let her be betrothed for the four zuz that it contains [wrapped up in the mat]."*

C. *She took the mat and shut up.*

D. *Said Raba, "You have then a case of* silence following receipt of funds, *and that kind of silence is null."*

E. *Said Raba, "How do I know it? Because it has been taught on Tannaite authority:*

F. **"'Take this sela as a bailment,' and then he said to her, 'Be betrothed to me with it' – if this was at the moment that he handed over the money, she is betrothed; if it was afterward, if she wanted, she is betrothed, but if she didn't want, she is not betrothed [T. Qid. 2:7A-D].**

G. *"Now what is the meaning of* if she wanted, *and what is the meaning of* if she didn't want? *Shall we say that the meaning of,* if she wanted, *is, she said yes, and the meaning of* if she didn't want *is, she said no? Then it would follow that the first clause bears the meaning, [13A] even if she said no, it is a valid act of betrothal. But why should that be the case? Lo, she has said no! Rather, is not the meaning of,* if she wanted, *she said yes, and would not the language,* if she didn't want, *mean, she remained silent? Then it would follow,* silence following receipt of funds is null."

H. *The following challenge was raised at Pum Nahara in the name of R. Huna b. R. Joshua, "But are the cases truly comparable? In that other case, the man handed over the money under the torah that governs bailments, and she reasoned, 'If I throw it away and it is broken, I am liable for it.' But here he handed it over under the torah of betrothals, and if it were the fact that she didn't concur, she should throw the money away."*

I.   *R. Ahai objected, "So are all women such experts in the law? Here, too, she could have thought, 'If I throw it away and it is broken, I am liable for it.'"*

J.   *R. Aha bar Rab sent word to Rabina, "So in such a case, what's the law?"*

K.   *He sent word to him, "We have heard no objection such as what R. Huna b. R. Joshua has raised, but you, who have heard it, have to pay full attention to it."*

VII.8   A.   *There was a woman who was selling silk skeins [Freedman]. Someone came along and grabbed a piece of silk from her. She said to him, "Give it back to me."*

B.   *He said to her, "If I give it back to you, will you be betrothed to me?"*

C.   *She took it from him and shut up.*

D.   *And said R. Nahman, "She has every right to claim, 'Yes, I took it, but I took what was mine!'"*

E.   *Raba objected to R. Nahman,* "If someone betrothed a woman with stolen property, or with what was gained by violence or by theft, or if he grabbed a sela from her hand and betrothed her with it, she is betrothed *[T. Qid. 4:5A-C]."*

F.   *"In that case, it was a situation in which there was negotiation about marriage."*

G.   *"And how do you know that we differentiate between a case in which there had been negotiation on marriage and one in which there had not? As it has been taught on Tannaite authority:* If he said to her, 'Take this sela, which I owe you,' and then he said to her, 'Be betrothed to me with it,' if this was at the moment that he handed over the money, if she wanted, she is betrothed, and if she didn't want, she is not betrothed. If this was after the handing over of the money, even if she wanted, she is not betrothed. *Now what is the meaning of* if she wanted, *and what is the meaning of* if she didn't want? *Shall we say that the meaning of,* if she wanted, *is, she said yes, and the meaning of* if she didn't want *is, she said no? Then it would follow that if she kept silent, it would have been a valid betrothal? Then the Tannaite formulation should be simply,* she is betrothed, *without further specification, just as in the prior instance. So we must say, the language,* if she wanted, *means, she said yes, and the language,* if she wanted, *means, she kept silent. And the Tannaite rule is,* she is not betrothed. *How come? She has every right to claim, 'Yes, I took it, but I took what was mine!' Nonetheless, there is a problem in connection with the language,* with stolen property, or with what was gained by violence or by theft and betrothed her with it, she is betrothed. *So doesn't it follow that the one speaks of a case in which there had been prior negotiations about marriage, the other of a case in which there had been none?"*

VII.9   A.   *When R. Assi died, rabbis assembled to collect his traditions. Said one of the rabbis, R. Jacob by name, "This is what R. Assi said R. Mani said, 'Just as a woman may not be acquired with less than a penny, so real estate cannot be acquired for less than a penny.'"*

B. *They said to him, "But hasn't it been taught on Tannaite authority:* Even though a woman may not be acquired with less than a penny, real estate can be acquired for less than a penny?"

C. *He said to them, "When that Tannaite ruling was set forth, it had to do with barter, for it has been taught on Tannaite authority:* Transfer of title may take place with a utensil even though the utensil is not worth a penny."

VII.10 A. *Further, in session they said, "Lo, in regard to what* R. Judah said Samuel said, 'Whoever doesn't know the essentials of writs of divorce and betrothals should not get involved in them,' said R. Assi said R. Yohanan, 'And such folk are more of a problem to the world than the generation of the flood, for it has been stated, "By swearing, lying, killing, stealing, and committing adultery, they spread forth and blood touches blood"' (Hos. 4:2)."

B. *How does that verse bear the alleged implication?*

C. *It is in line with the way in which R. Joseph interpreted the verse in his translation, "They beget children by their neighbors' wives, piling evil upon evil."*

D. [Reverting to A:] "And it is written, 'Therefore shall the land mourn and everyone who dwells therein shall language, with the beasts of the field and the fowl of heaven, yes the fish of the sea also shall be taken away' (Hos. 4:3). By contrast, with respect to the generation of the flood, there was no decree against the fish of the sea: 'Of all that was in the dry land died' (Gen. 7:22) – but not the fish in the sea; here even the fish in the sea are covered."

E. *But might one say that that penalty was inflicted only when all of the sins listed were committed [not only adultery]?*

F. *Don't imagine it! For it is written, "For because of swearing the land mourns" (Jer. 23:10) [a single crime suffices (Freedman)].*

G. *Well, maybe swearing stands on its own terms, and the others combined on theirs?*

H. [13B] Is it written, "and they spread forth"? What is written is, "they spread forth."

VII.11 A. *Further, in session they said, "Lo, in regard to what we have learned in the Mishnah,* **The woman who brought her sin-offering, and died – let the heirs bring her burnt-offering. [If she brought] her burnt-offering and died, the heirs do not bring her sin-offering [M. Qid. 2:5/O-Q),** and, in which regard, said R. Judah said Samuel, 'That rule applies to a case in which she had designated the offering while she was yet alive, but not otherwise,' *therefore taking the view that the obligation incurred by a debt is not based on the law of the Torah* [Freedman: if a man borrows money, we do not say that his property is automatically mortgaged for its repayment, so that in the event of his death, his heirs are liable on the law of the Torah, since they inherit mortgaged property unless the debtor explicitly mortgages his goods in a bond; here, too, the woman is under an obligation to God to bring a sacrifice, yet, since she did not designate an animal for it, no obligation lies on the heirs] – said R. Assi said R. Yohanan, 'That rule applies even though she had not designated the offering while she was yet alive, but not otherwise,' *therefore taking the view that the obligation incurred by a debt is based on* the law of the Torah – *in that context, lo, the dispute was set forth in another connection [and hardly required repetition].*

B. *"For Rab and Samuel both say, 'A debt attested only orally cannot be collected from the heirs or the purchasers of the indentured property,' and both R. Yohanan and R. Simeon b. Laqish say, 'A debt attested only orally can be collected from the heirs or the purchasers of the indentured property.'"*

C. *Well, as a matter of fact, both versions of the dispute had to be set forth. For if it had been stated in the latter case only, I should have supposed that it is only in that case that Samuel took the position that he did, because it is not a debt the type of which is set forth in the Torah, but in the other case, I might have said that he concurs with R. Yohanan and R. Simeon b. Laqish. And if it had been stated in the former case only, I should have supposed that it is only in that case that R. Yohanan took the position that he did, because a class of debt that is known in Scripture is equivalent to one that is written out in a bond, but in the latter case, I might have supposed that he concurs with Samuel. So both versions of the dispute had to be set forth.*

D. Said R. Pappa, "The decided law is, 'A loan that is only verbal is collected from an estate but may not be collected from purchasers [of the property from the now-deceased testator].

E. "It is collected from an estate, *since the indenture derives from the Torah,* but it may not be collected from purchasers [of the property from the now-deceased testator], *since it will not be widely known [so the purchasers cannot protect themselves]."*

VIII.1 A. **And she acquires herself through a writ of divorce or through the husband's death:**

B. *Well, there is no problem identifying the source for the rule concerning divorce, since it is written,* "And he shall write for her a writ of divorce" (Deut. 24:1). *But as to the husband's death, how do we know it?*

C. *It is a matter of reasoning:* He binds her [to himself, forbidden her to all other men] so he can free her.

D. *Well, what about the case of consanguineous relations, from whom he forbids her, but for whom he cannot release her [even after he dies]?*

E. *Rather, since the All-Merciful has said,* a levirate widow without children is forbidden, it must follow that, lo, if she has children [after the husband's death] she is permitted [to remarry].

F. *Well, maybe, if she has no children, she is forbidden to everybody but forbidden to the levir, and if she has children, she is forbidden to everybody without exception?*

G. *Rather, since Scripture has said that a widow is forbidden to marry a high priest, lo, she is permitted to marry an ordinary priest [and any other man].*

H. *Well, maybe, she is forbidden by a negative commandment to a high priest but to everyone else by a positive commandment?*

I. *So what's this alleged positive commandment doing here? If her husband's death matters, she should be wholly free to remarry, but if not, let her stay as she was.* [Freedman: As a married woman, she is forbidden to others by a negative commandment, there are no grounds for supposing that her husband's death leaves the prohibition but changes its nature.]

J. *Well, how come not? The husband's death can remove her from liability to the death penalty and place her under the prohibition involved in an affirmative commandment. It would then be comparable to the case of animals that have been consecrated but then rendered unfit for sacrifice. Before they were unfit, they would be subject to sacrilege and not sheared or worked with; when redeemed, they are no longer subject to the laws of sacrilege, but they still are not to be sheared or worked with.*

K. Rather, Scripture said, "What man is there...his house, lest he die in battle and another man take her" (Deut. 20:7).

L. *Objected R. Shisha b. R. Idi, "But might I then say, who is 'another man'? It is the levir."*

M. Said R. Ashi, "There are two replies in this matter. *The first is, the levir is not classified as 'another.' Furthermore, it is written, 'And if the latter husband hate her and write her a writ of divorce...or if the latter husband die...' (Deut. 24:3) – so death is treated as wholly comparable to a writ of divorce; just as the writ of divorce leaves her completely free, so death leaves her completely free."*

IX.1 A. **The deceased childless brother's widow is acquired through an act of sexual relations:**

B. *How do we know that she is acquired by an act of sexual relations?*

C. Said Scripture, [14A] "Her husband's brother shall go in to her and take her to him as a wife" (Deut. 25:5).

D. *Might I say that she is his wife in every regard [so that she can be acquired by money or a deed]?*

E. *Don't let it enter your mind, for it has been taught on Tannaite authority:* Might one suppose that a money payment or a writ serve to complete the bond to her, as much as sexual relations does? Scripture says, "Her husband's brother shall go in to her and take her to him as a wife" (Deut. 25:5) – sexual relations complete the relationship to her, but a money payment or a writ do not do so.

F. *Might I say, what is the meaning of* take her to him as a wife? *Even against her will he enters into levirate marriage with her?*

G. *If so, Scripture should have said, "and take her...." Why say, "and take her to wife? It bears both meanings just now under discussion.*

X.1 A. **And acquires [freedom for] herself through a rite of removing the shoe:**

B. *How do we know it?*

C. Said Scripture, "And his name shall be called in Israel, the house of him who has had his shoe removed" (Deut. 25:12) – once his shoe has been removed by her, she is permitted for all Israel.

D. *Is this the purpose of the word "Israel" in this context? Isn't it required in line with that which R. Samuel bar Judah taught as a Tannaite statement: "'In Israel' (Deut. 25:7) means that the rite of removing the shoe must be done in front of a court of Israelites by birth, not a court of proselytes"?*

E. *There are two references in context to "in Israel."*

F. *Nonetheless, it is required in line with that which has been taught on Tannaite authority:* Said R. Judah, "Once we were in session before R. Tarfon, and a levirate woman came to perform the rite of removing the shoe, and he said to us, 'All of you respond: "The man who has had his shoe removed"' (Deut. 25:10)."

G. *That is derived from the formulation,* "and his name shall be called" [with "in Israel" free for its own purpose].

XI.1   A. **And through the levir's death:**

B. *How do we know it?*

C. It derives from an argument a fortiori: If a married woman, who, if she commits adultery, is put to death through strangulation, is released by the death of the husband, a levirate widow, who is forbidden merely by a negative commandment [from marrying someone else] all the more so should be freed by the death of the levir!

D. But what distinguishes a married woman is that she goes forth with a writ of divorce. Will you say the same of this woman, who does not go forth with a writ of divorce?

E. But she, too, goes forth with the rite of removing the shoe [which is comparable to a writ of divorce].

F. Rather: What is special about the married woman is that the one who forbids her to other men also frees her [which is not the case with the levirate widow, since she is forbidden to others because of her childless deceased husband, but that the death of the levir frees her has yet to be proved].

G. *Said R. Ashi, "Lo, here, too, he who forbids her also frees her: The levir forbids her, the levir frees her"* [since if there were no levir, her husband's death alone would have freed her, so he really is responsible (Freedman)].

XI.2   A. A married woman also should be freed through the rite of removing the shoe, by reason of an argument a fortiori based on the levirate widow, namely: If a levirate wife, who is not freed by a divorce, is freed by the rite of removing the shoe, then this one [the levirate wife] who is freed by divorce surely should be freed by a rite of removing the shoe. Thus we are informed that that is not the case. Said Scripture, "Then he shall writ her a writ of divorce" (Deut. 24:1) – through a writ he divorces her, but he doesn't divorce her in any other way.

B. Then a levirate widow should go forth through a writ of divorce, by reason of an argument a fortiori, namely: If a married woman, who does not go forth through the rite of removing the shoe, goes forth through a writ of divorce, this one, who does go forth through the rite of removing the shoe, surely should go forth with a writ of divorce. So Scripture says to the contrary, "Thus it shall be done" (Deut. 25:9) – *this is the only possible way, and in any circumstance in which there is a clear indication of what is indispensable, an argument a fortiori is not composed.*

C. Then what about the case of the Day of Atonement, in connection with which there is clear scriptural reference to "lot" and "statute" (Lev. 16:9) [and "statute" is a sign of an indispensable detail], *and it has been taught on Tannaite authority:* "And Aaron shall present the goat upon which the lot fell for the Lord and make it a sin-offering" (Lev. 16:9) – the lot is what designates the goat as a sin-offering, and mere designation of the classification of the goat is not what turns it into a sin-offering, nor does the priest designate it as a sin-offering. For one might have argued to the contrary: Is it not a matter of logic? If in a case in which the lot does not consecrate an offering for a particular purpose, the designation does consecrate the offering for a particular purpose, in a case in which the lot does consecrate the offering for a particular purpose, is it not a matter of logic that the designation for a given purpose serves also to designate what is offered for a given purpose? For that reason Scripture states, "And Aaron shall present the goat upon which the lot fell for the Lord and make it a sin-offering" (Lev. 16:9) – the lot is what designates the goat as a sin-offering, and mere designation of the classification of the goat is not what turns it into a sin-offering. *So the operative consideration is that Scripture is what excludes that possibility. Then if it were not for that, we should have composed an argument a fortiori, even though the word "statute" is written in that correction!*

D.   [There is another reason altogether, namely,] said Scripture, "Then he shall write her a writ of divorce" (Deut. 24:1), for her, not for a levirate widow.

E.   *But might one say, "for her," meaning, for her in particular?*

F.   *There are two Scripture references to "for her."*

G.   *Nonetheless, they are needed for another purpose, one reference to, "for her," means, for her sake in particular, and the other reference to "her" meaning,* but not for her and another woman.

H.   Rather, said Scripture, "The house of him that has had a shoe removed" – *a shoe alone permits her to remarry, nothing else.*

I.   *Well, is that the purpose served by the reference to shoe? Isn't it necessary in line with that which has been taught on Tannaite authority:?*

J.   *"...Pull the sandal off his foot":*

K.   I know only that the rule speaks of a sandal belonging to him. How on the basis of Scripture do I know that it is all right if the sandal belongs to someone else?

L.   Scripture says, "pull the sandal" – under any circumstances.

M.   If so, why does Scripture say, "his sandal"?

N.   It excludes the case of a large shoe, in which one cannot actually walk, or a small one, which does not cover the larger part of his foot, [14B] or a slipper lacking a heel. [In such instances the act of removing the shoe is null]. [Sifré Deut. CCXCI:II.2].

O.   *If so, Scripture should have said merely "shoe." Why "the shoe"? To yield both propositions.*

I.1 presents an exegetical question for clarifying the formulation of the commencement of the Mishnah tractate. Nos. 2-4, 5-6 follow suit. II.1+2-3, 4-5 work on the problem of the scriptural origins of the Mishnah's rule. III.1-2, 3, 4-5 go through the same exercise. No. 6, with its talmud at Nos. 7-8, and No. 9, with its talmud at Nos. 10-12, then move on to a Tannaite complement to the Mishnah paragraph. Nos. 13+14-17 then extend the discussion of the foregoing set of entries in more general terms. Nos. 18-19 proceed to a variety of important theoretical questions, well within the framework of the foregoing. Nos.

20-25 present a sequence of systematic theoretical problems in the name of a single individual. There follow further theoretical questions along the same lines, Nos. 26-27. Then comes a case, No. 28 which yields a further theoretical problem, extending beyond the range of our particular topic. No. 29 extends the foregoing. No. 30, with a talmud at Nos. 31-2, resumes the analysis of theoretical questions pertinent to the protracted thematic appendix at hand. No. 33 proceeds with another, related theoretical problem. No. 34 illustrates the foregoing. No. 35, with a talmud at No. 36, then No. 37, with its talmud at No. 38, No. 39, with a talmud at No. 40, No. 41, analyzed by No. 42, No. 43, analyzed by No. 44, No. 45, analyzed at No. 46, in a coherent pattern and following a cogent program, all provide Tannaite complements to the same general theme as has been under discussion. Them come a set of cases, Nos. 47-50. **IV.1** starts back at the starting point, with the exposition of the Mishnah's rule. No. 2 then expands on the same theme. Nos. 3-4 raise secondary questions of refinement of the now-established facts. **V.1** finds the scriptural basis for the Mishnah's rule. Nos. 2, 3 proceed to theoretical questions, clarifying the fact given by the Mishnah rule. **VI.1**, with a footnote at No. 2, supplies an explanation of the Mishnah statement. Nos. 3, 4 continue the inquiry of No. 1. **VII.1**, with a footnote at No. 2, continues the exposition of the rule of the Mishnah. Nos. 3+4-8, 9+10-11 then move on to the elaboration and extension of the Mishnah's rule. **VIII.1, IX.1, X.1, XI.1+2** ask about the sources of the rule of the Mishnah, whether scriptural, whether logical. The former is preferred.

III. The Forms of the Two Talmuds in Comparison and Contrast

The comparison of forms is undertaken through parallel columns, the Yerushalmi's forms on the left, the Bavli's on the right. Differentiating entries between form and intellectual program leaves much intersection and overlap, the distinction between form and analytical, exegetical, or theoretical agenda being difficult to draw with clarity. For this first go-around I have chosen to err on the side of repetition.

1:1 I A-B Gloss of the Mishnah sentence.	1:1 I.1 What differentiates the language of the present Mishnah passage from that of an adjacent one, which is form-
1:1 I C-F Citation of Mishnah + how on the basis of Scripture do we know that fact?	ulated in a different way?
1:1 I G-L Conclusion & speculative question. I have the following proposition, how on the basis of Scripture do I	1:1 I.2 As above.
	1:1 I.3-4 Continuation of foregoing.
	1:1 I.5-6 What exclusionary

know that that is not so?

1:1 II Citation of Scripture based fact, this is a matter of logic, why do we require Scripture to make that point?

1:1 III It is possible to prove through an argument based on hierarchical classification that a proposition is so.

1:1 IV A-D Up to now we have proved X, what about X's counterpart & opposite + scriptural demonstration.

1:1 IV E-FF Dialectical exchange between two contradictory opinions.

1:1 V We have learned + proposition of unit IV, how about + further proposition generated in line with the foregoing.

1:1 I VI A-C Citation of a clause of the Mishnah plus paraphrase, setting forth proposition: X, but as to Y..., with further expanion along the same lines.

1:1 I VI H-BB Question and continuous argument answer.

1:1 VII Citation of Mishnah passage that intersects with and contradicts the rule before us. Harmonization.

1:1 VIII Same as above.

1:1 IX Citation of Mishnah clause plus gloss joined by a question.

1:1 X Citation of Mishnah clause plus "that is in line with this verse of Scripture."

1:1 XI Citation and systematic gloss of components

purpose is served by the wording...?

1:1 II.1 Citation of Mishnah clause + what is scriptural source of this rule?

1:1 II.2 Does the cited verse have to serve that purpose? Doesn't it serve this purpose?

1:1 II.3-4 It was necessary for Scripture to provide a verse for each purpose, because.

1:1 II.5 Tannaite composition to prove the point of the Mishnah; free-standing and inserted whole.

1:1 III.1 Same form as above.

1:1 III.2-3 As above.

1:1 III.4-5 Said X + free-standing statement, proposition of law that advances the theoretical inquiry.

1:1 III.6-7 Tannaite complement: citation of the Mishnah rule + how so + illustrative case.

1:1 III.8 Said X + free-standing statement, proposition of law that advances the theoretical inquiry.

1:1 III.9+10-16 Tannaite rule followed by a talmud, that is, secondary analytical inquiry into the problem introduced by that rule.

1:1 III.17-18 Free-standing statement of a rule, followed by secondary analysis, "it is obvious that...but what if...."

1:1 III.19 Said X + free-standing statement, proposition of law that advances the theoretical inquiry.

1:1 III.20, 21 As above.

of a verse of Scripture that stands behind Mishnah rule.

1:1 XII Question addressed to Mishnah clause, yielding a proposition for testing.

1:1 XIII Proposition plus secondary question.

1:1 III.22 Theoretical problem: X raised this question.

1:1 III.23-27 As above.

1:1 III.28 Case: there was a certain man who....

1:1 III.29 Said X, how do I know +.

1:1 III.30+31, 32 Said X + theoretical proposition.

1:1 III.33 As above.

1:1 III.34 Illustrative case.

1:1 III.35 Tannaite proposition.

1:1 III.36 Talmud to the foregoing.

1:1 III.37-8 Same pattern as above.

1:1 III.39-40 Same pattern as above [*And it was necessary to specify both cases...*].

1:1 III.41-42 Tannaite proposition + talmud.

1:1 III.43-44 As above.

1:1 III.45-46 As above.

1:1 III.47-49 Illustrative cases: There was someone who was.

1:1 III.50 Speculative question.

1:1 IV.1 Mishnah clause cited and glossed.

1:1 IV.2 Said + plus declarative sentence.

1:1 IV.3 X raised the question.

1:1 IV.4 It has been stated plus proposition plus dispute.

1:1 V.1 What is the scriptural basis for the Mishnah's rule.

1:1 V.2 The question was raised + theoretical issue, statement of practical consequences.

1:1 V.3 As above.

1:1 VI.1 *What is the operative consideration* behind a position taken in the Mishnah rule.

1:1 VI.2 Citation of and gloss on the foregoing.

1:1 VI. 3, 4 Continue No. 1.

1:1 VII.1 Citation of Mishnah clause plus X considered ruling....

1:1 VII.2 Citation of and gloss on the foregoing.

1:1 VII.3 Said X plus proposition.

1:1 VII.4-8 Illustrative cases.

1:1 VII.9-11 When X died..., plus citation of rulings in a given name and analysis thereof. Continued at Nos. 10-11.

1:1 VIII.1 Source in Mishnah, phrased slightly differently from the norm.

1:1 IX.1 Citation of Mishnah rule + how do we know that + said Scripture.

1:1 X.1 As above.

1:1 XI.1 Citation of Mishnah rule + how do we know it + it derives from + argument of comparison and contrast. No. 2 continues the foregoing.

When we compare the forms of the two Talmuds, we find in the second Talmud everything that is in the first, but important formal constructions lacking in the first as well. That is to say, on the left hand column we find the gloss form, the citation of a Mishnah clause with the question, "how do we know it," the proposal of the demonstration on the basis of an argument a fortiori, resting on hierarchical classification, in place of a Scripture proof, the dialectical exchange between two propositions, the paraphrase of the Mishnah leading to an exclusionary question: X but as to Y?, and so on. If I had to characterize the formal quality of the Yerushalmi, it would be simple: citation and gloss of

Mishnah statements and secondary developments along some few, paramount lines.

Where does the Bavli differ?

First, we begin with a sizable inquiry into the language of the Mishnah passage, and this linguistic criticism bears no counterpart in the Yerushalmi. The study of the wording of the Mishnah is worked out at some length. Then we take up the familiar program, citation of a Mishnah clause and inquiry into its scriptural foundations.

But this yields a second interesting difference, namely, the secondary development: Does the verse have to serve this purpose? And this is completed by "it was necessary" to have a verse for each of two or more parallel cases.

Third in sequence and certainly unique to the Bavli of our sample is the form, said X + theoretical inquiry.

Fourth, and all the same lines, we find "X raised this question." Fourth, sequences of cases are adduced for analysis or for mere reenforcement of a point.

Fifth, one of the Bavli's most interesting compositions is made up of a citation of a Tannaite statement (often marked with a TN-formula) followed by what I call "a talmud," which is to say, a secondary, systematic critical inquiry. In other words, for the Bavli, the Mishnah is not the sole received document to undergo the analysis of applied logic and practical reason; Tannaite statements now found, also, in the Tosefta, as well as others so marked but collected in no compilation now in our hands, also are treated in the same way. Mishnah analysis therefore overspreads the whole of the corpus classified as Tannaite. The sequence of 1:1 III.35-50 forms a wonderful example of this remarkable exercise.

It follows that there are important points of formal differentiation between the two Talmuds. In common their authorships read and gloss the Mishnah and ask for scriptural bases for Mishnah rules. But the Bavli proves far more Talmudic than the Yerushalmi, not because of its vastly greater dimensions, but because of a quality of mind. And that point of difference in no way emerges from an analysis of the formal traits.

IV. The Intellectual Programs of the Two Talmuds in Comparison and Contrast

Here we ask about each Talmud's generative questions and how they are answered: the intellectual program brought to the Mishnah and the consequent results, stated in general terms. Not surprisingly, we go over much the same ground as in the prior comparison.

1:1 I Clarification of the limitation of the Mishnah rule.	1:1 I.1 Comparison of the formulation of this Mishnah

1:1 I C-T How on the basis of Scripture do we know that fact? How on the basis of Scripture do we know that a false proposition is false? This set links two distinct questions, the one of scriptural origin, the other, the application of the rule to a given circumstance.

1:1 II How on the basis of applied logic do we know the facts just now adduced on the strength of Scripture?

1:1 III It is possible on the basis of applied logic to prove the proposition, but in fact that possibility is null.

1:1 IV A-D Scripture shows what the Mishnah law maintains, how now do we know the law for a category of persons to which the Mishnah rule does not pertain + scriptural evidence to that effect.

1:1 I E-FF Contrast between two statements that bear contradictory implications, set forth and resolved.

1:1 I V We have learned plus the proposition of unit IV – how about the further proposition, generated in line with the foregoing? This continues the prior interest in complementary questions concerning the category not treated by the Mishnah; secondary speculation.

1:1 VI A-C Continuation of secondary expanion of the Mishnah rule: X not Y.

rule with a parallel one, explaining the difference in wording. The word of the Mishnah analyzed.

1:1 I.2-4 The same problem considered, with new data.

1:1 I.5-6 The implications as to law of the wording of the Mishnah rule: What exclusionary purpose is served by this wording?

1:1 II.1-2+3 Scriptural foundations for the Mishnah rule; distinct verses are required for each case, which might be differentiated so that a single verse would not suffice for all cases.

1:1 II.4 Cited verse refers to such and such, but what is the case?

1:1 II.5 Tannaite proof of the proposition that the Mishnah rule presents, with stress on why reasoning alone is insufficient.

1:1 III.1-2 Same as above.

1:1 III.3 Even though monothetic taxi indicators fail, perhaps polythetic taxonomy succeeds: possibility considered and rejected.

1:1 III.4-5 Fresh proposition, which expands by applying the principle of the Mishnah to a new theoretical problem. This goes over the ground of No. 3: polythetic taxonomy and its limitations; only Scripture is reliable.

1:1 III.6-7 Case illustration of the rule of the Mishnah.

1:1 VI H-BB speculative question, dialectically carried forth.

1:1 I VII intersecting Mishnah rule cited, contrasted, harmonized.

1:1 VIII Same as above.

1:1 IX Gloss of Mishnah clause.

1:1 IX A-B, C-D Scriptural support for a detail of the Mishnah; Scripture and reason make the same point.

1:1 IX Eff. Further Tannaite materials that amplify the facts under discussion.

1:1 X Citation of Scripture demonstrates the facts of the Mishnah; this yields a secondary question, "that proves...but what about...."

1:1 XI Systematic exegesis of a verse of Scripture relevant to the Mishnah rule. (See below.)

1:1 XII Secondary question based on the rule of the Mishnah.

1:1 XIII Theoretical question deriving from an established fact.

1:1 III.8 Proposition of law that expands the principle of the Mishnah to a new theoretical problem.

1:1 III.9-12: Tannaite rule, with a talmud, first dealing with the formulation of the rule, then asking a theoretical question that carries the rule forward, following by further theoretical problems attached to the initial statement. Then, No. 13, the theoretical situation to which reference has been made.

1:1 III.13 Clarification of foregoing: With what situation do we deal?

1:1 III.14-15 Footnote to the foregoing.

1:1 III.16 The decided law.

1:1 III.17 It is obvious that...but if...what is the law?

1:1 III.18 If he said...what is the law? Conflict of possibly applicable principles.

1:1 III.19 Said X plus a proposed proposition.

1:1 III.20 Same as above.

1:1 III.21 Same as above.

1:1 III.22 X raised the following theoretical question.

1:1 III.23 Said X + theoretical proposition, with a secondary debate.

1:1 III.24 X raised the following theoretical question.

1:1 III.25 As above.

1:1 III.26 As above.

1:1 III.27 As above.

1:1 III.28 Case in point.

1:1 III.29 How do I know + restatement of the proposition of the foregoing.

1:1 III.30 Said X + proposition.

1:1 III.31, 32 Gloss of the foregoing.

1:1 III. 33 Said X + proposition.

1:1 III.34 Case illustrative of foregoing.

1:1 III.35-36 Tannaite rule; secondary implications thereof explored.

1:1 III.37-38 Same pattern as above.

1:1 III.39-40 As above. *And it was necessary to specify both cases. For if we had been informed of....*

1:1 III.41-2 Tannaite rule plus talmud.

1:1 III.43-4 As above.

1:1 III.45-6 As above.

1:1 III.47, 48, 49 Illustrative cases.

1:1 III.50 Secondary theoretical question.

1:1 IV.1 Mishnah clause cited, then explained in terms of a concrete illustrative situation.

1:1 IV.2 Said + plus theoretical rule.

1:1 IV.3 X raised this question.

1:1 IV.4 It has been stated + dispute on a theoretical case.

1:1 V.1 Citation of the Mishnah clause + what is the scriptural source of this rule?

1:1 V.2 The question was raised.

1:1 V.3 As above.

1:1 VI.1 Mishnah clause

cited + *What is the operative consideration...*, continued at Nos. 3, 4.

1:1 VI.2 Footnote to the foregoing.

1:1 VII.1 X considered ruling.

1:1 VII.2 Footnote to the foregoing.

1:1 VII.3 Said + proposition resting on a premise contradictory to the Mishnah's.

1:1 VII.4-8 Cases illustrative of the foregoing problem.

1:1 VII.9 Comparison of our rule with parallel rule on other topics. Continued at Nos. 10-11.

1:1 VIII.1 Secondary expansion of the rule, based on theoretical considerations and appeal to Scripture.

1:1 IX.1 How on the basis of Scripture do we know the Mishnah rule?

1:1 X.1 As above.

1:1 XI.1 How do we know the rule of the Mishnah + argument of applied reason based on hierarchical classification.

1:1 XI.1 Building on the result of the foregoing, a logical argument moving to a fresh problem.

The Yerushalmi's intellectual program corresponds to its formal plan: clarification of the Mishnah's statements through episodic, ad hoc gloss, on the one side, inquiry into the Mishnah's scriptural foundations, on the other. The latter initiative draws in its wake an interest in whether applied logic may do the work of Scripture. The program as a whole leads us to ask secondary questions, for example, if we know the rule for A, what about the opposite of A? what about classes of things or persons comparable to A but differentiated in some subordinate trait? A third important problem for the authors and compilers of the Yerushalmi draws attention to disharmony in statements of the law or their premises, and a labor of harmonization is invariably provoked when contradictions emerge, either on the surface or in the substrate of thought. A fourth interest (minor in our sample) is in the systematic exegesis of a verse of Scripture; this ordinarily focuses upon a verse of Scripture pertinent to a Mishnah statement. Theoretical questions are few and far between.

The Bavli's authorships and compilers concur on all these points of interest. They proceed along lines of their own. Specifically, the Bavli's interest is in the wording of the Mishnah, a correct reading in its own terms; in the Mishnah's word choices; in the implications for the law of one word choice over some other. So what we might now call "Mishnah criticism" forms an important point at which the Bavli differs from the Yerushalmi.

Second, they will want to subject a Tannaite statement to a Talmudic inquiry, even when said statement is not located in the Mishnah or the Tosefta. This is a systematic program and yields its own formal arrangements, as we have already noticed.

Third, the authors of the Bavli's compositions and framers of its sustained composites will entertain free-standing proposals, statements of the law pertinent in theme to what is under discussion but fresh in conception or problematic, for example, a case simply not addressed within the framework of the Mishnah rule or some other rule bearing a Tannaite classification. The fixed form, said X + generalization of a law followed by a sustained talmud, bespeaks an intellectual program of enormous ambition: to join in legislation through the inquiry into the practical implications of established theory, on the one side, or through the speculative analysis of secondary amplifications of said established theory, on the other. The two forms of speculation correspond, and, along with them, there is the third: the address to a theoretical question, formulated as such. B. 1:1 III.19-21 and 1:1 III.22 seem to me to differ only in form but in no material way.

A fourth intellectual inquiry characteristic of the Bavli but not the Yerushalmi is the interest in composition, proportion, and balance expressed in the language: *it was necessary...*, always in Aramaic. These inquiries may explain why we require three or more statements in diverse cases of what appears to be a single principle; or they will tell us why two or more verses of Scripture are required to make the same point; or in some other way they will defend the integrity of a prior composition or even composite.

So my hypothesis maintains that the Bavli's authorships and framers have formulated a talmud that undertakes intellectual tasks beyond the ambition of those of the Yerushalmi. The differences between the Talmuds then adumbrate a more profound point of departure, taken by the second Talmud's writers, in the definition of the work of applied reason and practical logic brought to the form of writing. Since, as a matter of fact, the two Talmuds share in common a huge store of statements, made by the very same authorities about the very same subjects, the differences between them pertain wholly to the analytical program of the second of the two Talmuds – that program and its intellectual consequences.

V. Comparison of B 1:1 IX.1 and Y's Counterpart

Given the impressive formal differences between the two Talmuds, the second being so much larger and better articulated than the first, the case can be that the second Talmud differs in quantity, and that difference then shades over into quality of mind. That is to say, the Bavli's differences might appear to derive from the sheer volume of the second Talmud, which vastly exceeds the first in size. So the two Talmuds, it may be thought, pursue pretty much the same intellectual program in response to their shared task of Mishnah exegesis; but the Yerushalmi is intellectually economical, the Bavli prolix; the Yerushalmi's authors may be thought inferior in acumen to the Bavli's truly brilliant minds – and the difference is one of form and circumstance, not substance.

To address that issue, I have selected a passage in which both Talmuds deal with the same matter, but the second Talmud addresses it in a succinct way. Here we cannot claim that the one Talmud differs from the other only in length, and, it will readily be clear, the difference also has nothing to do with acumen. The framers of the Yerushalmi here do what the framers of the Bavli do in a variety of other passages. I compare the treatment of the Mishnah's statement, cited at the head, that the levirate widow is acquired as fully married through an act of sexual relations. Both Talmuds want to know how Scripture says so.

Yerushalmi 1:1 IX		Bavli 1:1 IX.1		
[XI.A]	[With regard to M. 1:1 **The deceased childless brother's widow is acquired through an act of sexual relations,** we turn to the exegesis of Deut. 25: 5: "Her husband's brother shall go in to her, and take her as his wife, and perform the duty of a husband's brother to her."] "Her husband's	IX.1	A.	The deceased childless brother's widow is acquired through an act of sexual relations:
			B.	*How do we know that she is acquired by an act of sexual relations?*
			C.	Said Scripture, **[14A]** "Her husband's brother shall go in to her and take her to him as a wife" (Deut. 25:5).
			D.	*Might I say that she is*

brother shall go in to her"– this is the act of sexual relations.

[B] "And he shall take her as his wife– this refers to the act of bespeaking [that is, he says to her, "Behold you are sanctified to me]." [For the levirate marriage, bespeaking is the equivalent to an act of betrothal in an ordinary marriage.]

[C] May one say that, just as the act of sexual relations completes the transaction of acquiring her as a wife, so the act of bespeaking [by itself] also will accomplish the thing [so that the levir inherits his brother's property]?

[D] Scripture states, "[Take her as his wife] and perform the duty of a husband's brother to her" [meaning, even after he has taken her as his wife through betrothal, he remains in the status of the husband's brother and must have sexual relations and does not accomplish the marriage merely by an act of betrothal].

[E] The entire passage, therefore, indicates that, as to the levir, the act of sexual relations completes acquisition of the widow as his wife, and mere bespeaking does not complete the acquisition of the woman as his wife.

his wife in every regard [so that she can be acquired by money or a deed]?

E. *Don't let it enter your mind, for it has been taught on Tannaite authority:* Might one suppose that a money payment or a writ serve to complete the bond to her, as much as sexual relations does? Scripture says, "Her husband's brother shall go in to her and take her to him as a wife" (Deut. 25:5) – sexual relations complete the relationship to her, but a money payment or a writ do not do so.

F. *Might I say, what is the meaning of* take her to him as a wife? *Even against her will he enters into levirate marriage with her?*

G. *If so, Scripture should have said,* "and take her...." *Why say,* "and take her to wife? *It bears both meanings just now under discussion.*

[F] If so, what value is there in the act of bespeaking at all?

[G] It serves to betroth her, as against the claim of the other brothers.

[H] R. Simeon says, "Bespeaking either fully effects acquisition or does not." [Thus the foregoing position is rejected.]

[I] What is the scriptural basis for R. Simeon's position?

[J] "Her husband's brother shall go in to her"– this refers to an act of sexual relations.

[K] "And take her as a wife"– this refers to an act of bespeaking.

[L] [So the two are comparable, with the result that] just as an act of sexual relations effects complete possession of her as his wife, so does the act of bespeaking completely effect her acquisition as his wife.

[M] Or "Her husband's brother shall go in to her" and lo, "He takes her as a wife," with the result that the act of bespeaking has no standing in her regard at all.

[N] R. Eleazar b. Arakh said, "The act of bespeaking effects a complete acquisition in the case of the childless brother's widow."

[O] What is the scriptural basis for R. Eleazar b. Arakh's position?

[P] "and take her as his wife"– lo, it is tantamount to the act of betrothing a woman.

[Q] Just as in the case of betrothing a woman, one effects total possession, so in the case of a deceased childless brother's widow, also the act of bespeaking [which is the parallel, as explained above] effects total possession.

[R] What is "bespeaking"?

[S] If the brother says, "Lo, you are sanctified to me by money," or "by something worth money" [T. Yeb. 2: 1].

The Yerushalmi adduces its proof from Scripture, then conducts a sustained analysis of the proof text, element by element, at B, with a contrary proposition at C and a decisive prooftext at D. This is followed by a secondary question, if the act of sexual relations serves, then why bother with the prior rite of a declaration on the levir's part that he intends to enter into levirate marriage ("bespeaking")? This yields a secondary point, at which Simeon rejects the theory that has governed until now, that bespeaking is a preliminary but does not consummate the marriage; prooftexts are adduced for the two positions; and then, N, yet another authority takes the position that Simeon has announced. So we deal with two points. First, sexual relations effects levirate marriage; second, bespeaking is or is not preliminary, does or does not fully effect levirate marriage on its own.

The Bavli has its own program, and it involves not the secondary issue of bespeaking, but the consequent issue of whether or not the levirate marriage is equivalent in legal effect to a natural marriage, so that other media of acquisition, besides sexual relations, serve. That is rejected, on the strength of a reading of Scripture; that reading is challenged; and the wording of Scripture is adduced in evidence in behalf of the proposed reading.

What we see here is that, where the two Talmuds ask the same question, each pursues its own speculative path. The difference between the one and the other is not in size, nor in acumen. The Talmuds are different in some other way, which this comparison has not uncovered.

VI. Where the Differences Are Not to Be Located. The Next Step

The comparison of form yields nothing of consequence and leads us to repeat in two charts what may be stated in one. The difference is in intellectual program – not in prolixity of expression. And yet – comparing the two Talmuds' treatment of the same problem tells us that on the surface there is no material difference between them in the intellectual acumen and acuity of the authors of the second Talmud's compositions and the framers of its composites.[2]

But the numerous free-standing compositions, said X + hypothetical rule or theory, or the question was raised + theoretical problem with secondary reasons for two opposed positions, really do take a fundamental role in the Bavli and none in the Yerushalmi in our sample. So while the framers of the Bavli do not seem to be smarter than those of the Yerushalmi, they do emerge as more ambitious, capable of feats of speculation rarely found in the Yerushalmi and still more rarely spelled out when they are found. The Yerushalmi seems more closely governed by the assignment of exegesis of the Mishnah and its law, the Bavli, the additional work of speculation on the law in its own terms, not solely or mainly in terms defined by the Mishnah's (and related collections') formulations thereof.

We may therefore propose as a hypothesis that the Bavli differs from the Yerushalmi in the intellectual ambition of its authors, who appear to place a higher value than their predecessors on intellectual speculation. That would account for the provision of sustained talmuds for Tannaite statements other than those in the Mishnah, for the exceptionally subtle exercises in speculation, either proposed hypotheses subjected to sustained criticism, or theoretical questions answered through sustained speculation, and even the refinement of the "it is necessary" constructions. My experience in translating twenty-seven tractates of the Bavli's thirty-seven, and twenty-nine of the Yerushalmi's thirty-nine, certainly confirms that hypothesis.

But it is not a very useful hypothesis, since merely knowing that an authorship writes up a document that expresses vaulting ambition to formulate and solve speculative problems tells us nothing very important about that authorship, other than that it was more imaginative and intellectually freer than its predecessors. That fact (if it is a fact) then tells us a rather trivial detail, a historical accident, that a given set of writers

---

[2]The importance of that distinction is spelled out in *Making the Classics in Judaism: The Three Stages of Literary Formation* (Atlanta, 1990: Scholars Press for Brown Judaic Studies); and *The Rules of Composition of the Talmud of Babylonia. The Cogency of the Bavli's Composite* (Atlanta, 1991: Scholars Press for South Florida Studies in the History of Judaism).

included some better minds than another set; or (given my explicit rejection of that formulation) that a given set of writers attempted feats that equally gifted earlier minds neglected. Those adventitious facts tell us nothing of consequence for the study of the religious system and world represented in one writing or another. What does is an examination of where the differences lay not in form but in substance. And for that work, a systematic study of not forms or program of exegesis but the heuristic morphology thereof is now required – that, and one other thing, the classification of the consequent results. Let us move onward through our tractate's opening chapter.

2

Mishnah-Tractate Qiddushin 1:2 in the Yerushalmi and the Bavli

1:2

A. A Hebrew slave is acquired through money and a writ.

B. And he acquires himself through the passage of years, by the Jubilee Year, and by deduction from the purchase price [redeeming himself at this outstanding value (Lev. 25:50-51)].

C. The Hebrew slave girl has an advantage over him.

D. For she acquires herself [in addition] through the appearance of tokens [of puberty].

E. The slave whose ear is pierced is acquired through an act of piercing the ear (Ex. 21:5).

F. And he acquires himself by the Jubilee and by the death of the master.

I. The Talmud of the Land of Israel to M. Qiddushin 1:2

[I.A] It is written: "If your brother, a Hebrew man, or a Hebrew woman, is sold to you, he shall serve you six years, and in the Seventh Year you shall let him go free from you" (Deut. 15:12).

[B] Scripture treats in the same context a Hebrew man and woman.

[C] Just as the Hebrew woman is acquired through money or a writ, so a Hebrew man is acquired through money or a writ.

[D] The proposition that that is through money poses no problems, for it is said, "She shall go out for nothing, without payment of money" (Ex. 21:11).

[E] But whence do we know that that applies also to a writ?

[F] We derive the rule for the Hebrew woman servant from a free woman, and the rule for a Hebrew man servant derives from that for a Hebrew woman servant.

[G] It turns out that what derives from one proposition serves to teach the rule for another.

[H] To this point we have proved the proposition in accord with R. Aqiba, who indeed concurs that what derives from one proposition may then serve to teach the rule for another.

[I]   But as to R. Ishmael, who does not concur that what derives from
      one proposition may then serve to teach the rule for another, [how
      do we prove that a Hebrew manservant is acquired through a writ]?

[J]   The following Tannaite teaching is available: R. Ishmael teaches in
      regard to this statement, "Freedom has not been given to her" (Lev.
      19:20), "You shall let him go free from you" (Deut. 15:12). [The latter
      is interpreted in the light of the former.]

[K]   Now in all [other] contexts R. Ishmael does not concur that what
      derives from one proposition may then serve to teach the rule for
      another, and yet here [at J] he does indeed hold that view.

[L]   It [that is, the teaching at J] was taught in the name of a sage. "How
      does R. Ishmael prove [that a writ is applicable to the Hebrew
      manservant]?

[M]   "'Sending forth' is stated at Deut. 15:2, and also 'sending' is stated
      at Deut. 24:1.

[N]   "Just as 'sending forth' stated in regard to a divorce means that it is
      done through a writ, so the 'sending forth' stated in regard to the
      slave means that it is done through a writ."

[O]   [But the issue is not the same.] The two cases are dissimilar. For in
      the case of the divorce of the woman, the writ serves to give her full
      possession of herself. But here the writ serves to give possession of
      the Hebrew slave to others. [The proposition is to prove that a
      Hebrew man is acquired through a writ, and that has not been
      proved.]

[P]   Said R. Mattenaiah, "The use of the language of sale will prove the
      case. ['If your brother... is sold to you' (Deut. 15:12); 'If your brother
      becomes poor and sells part of his property' (Lev. 25:25).] Just as
      'sale' stated in the latter case involves use of a writ, so the language
      of 'sale' used here involves use of a writ."

[Q]   Or, perhaps may one argue, just as in the case of a field acquisition
      may be made through usucaption, so in the case of the slave, it may
      be through usucaption?

[R]   [There is a better mode of proof of the besought proposition.] Said
      R. Hiyya bar Ada, "A Hebrew man and a Hebrew woman are
      subject to one and the same law."

[II.A] Through money. ["If there are still many years according to them
      he shall refund out of] the price paid for him [the price for his
      redemption]" (Lev. 25:51).

[B]   Through the payment of money he is redeemed [from the owner, in
      line with the cited verse], and he is not redeemed through handing
      over grain or goods.

[C]   In all other contexts you treat what is worth money as tantamount
      to ready cash, but here you do not treat what is worth money as
      tantamount to ready cash.

[D]   Said R. Abba Meri, "The present case is to be treated differently, for
      Scripture itself twice mentioned 'price' (Lev. 25:51)."

[E]   Said R. Hiyya bar Abba, "Abba will concur that, if the slave sought
      to deduct from the purchase price, he may do so and go forth free
      even by means of paying grain or goods."

[F]   Said R. Yudan, father of R. Mattenaiah, "What you have stated [at
      A-D] applies to a case in which one has not estimated their value

[grain, goods], but if one has estimated their value, they are deemed tantamount to money."

[III.A] **Through a writ:** Said R. Abbahu, "This is by means of a writ covering the money that has been paid over. Lo, it is not to be with a writ of gift [of himself to the master], lest the slave retract his gift of himself to the master."

[B] But if that is the case, then perhaps even in the case of a writ covering money that has been paid over, the slave has the power to retract.

[C] [What was said at A was actually,] "Perhaps a year of famine may come, and the master may retract [on the purchase]." [Consequently, a writ of sale covering funds paid over must be made out, to prevent the master from retracting at will.]

[IV.A] The language of sale is this: "I, Mr. So-and-so, have sold my daughter to Mr. Such-and-such."

[B] The language of betrothal is this: "I, Mr. So-and-so, have betrothed my daughter to Mr. Such-and-such."

[C] R. Haggai raised the question before R. Yosé: "[If] one reversed the language and said, 'I, Mr. So-and-so, have purchased the daughter of Mr. Such-and-such,' 'I, Mr. So-and-so, have betrothed the daughter of Mr. Such-and-such,' [what is the law]?"

[D] He said to him, "That means nothing. But if he used the language of sale for the language of betrothal, or the language of betrothal for the language of sale, he has done nothing whatever."

[V.A] It is written: "When you buy a Hebrew slave, he shall serve six years, and in the seventh he shall go out free, for nothing" (Ex. 2:1).

[B] Is it possible to suppose that he goes forth at the end of the sixth year?

[C] Scripture says, "And in the seventh he shall go out free."

[D] Is it possible to suppose that he will go forth at the end of the Seventh Year?

[E] Scripture says, "Six years shall he serve."

[F] How then is this to be?

[G] He works all six years and goes forth at the beginning of the seventh.

[H] And as to this reference to the Seventh Year, he goes out at the Seventh Year of his own sale, not at the Seventh Year [the year of release] of the world at large.

[I] You say that he goes forth at the Seventh Year of his own sale. But perhaps it is at the Seventh Year of the world at large?

[J] When Scripture states, "He shall serve for six years," lo, six full years of service are specified.

[K] How then am I to interpret "And in the seventh he shall go out"?

[L] He goes forth in the Seventh Year of his own sale, but not in the Seventh Year of the world at large.

[M] Might I say the very opposite [that Scripture really does refer to the Seventh Year, the year of release, and not the Seventh Year of the man's personal status as a slave]?

[N] R. Zeira in the name of R. Huna, "'And in the Seventh Year' is written."

[O] [As a separate argument for the same basic proposition,] said R. Huna, "If you maintain that it is the Seventh Year at large [and not the Seventh Year of service of the individual slave], then when the Jubilee Year comes along, what sort of slave is it going to release, [since all of them will be free in accord with the previous seven years of release, every Seventh Year]."

[P] Said R. Yohanan bar Mareh, "That is in accord with the position of him who said, 'The Jubilee Year does not count among the years of the septennate' [but is in addition to them, thus it is the fiftieth year of the cycle].

[Q] "But in accord with the position of him who said, 'The Jubilee Year does count among the years of the septennate' [serving as the first year of the coming seven-year cycle], there are times in which the Jubilee Year will come in the middle of the years of the septennate, [in which case the question raised at O is a valid one, since there will be slaves to free]."

[R] The rabbis of Caesarea moreover point out, "Even in accord with the one who said, 'The Jubilee Year does not count among the years of the septennate,' we can still answer the argument [at O]. For the Seventh Year will serve to free ordinary slaves, and the Jubilee Year will serve to free slaves who have had their ears pierced and so remained permanently with their masters."

[VI.A] How do I know that one is freed in the Seventh Year even though he has not worked all six years?

[B] Scripture says, "And in the Seventh Year he shall go out free, for nothing."

[C] Is it possible to suppose that that applies even to a case in which he fled?

[D] Scripture says, "Six years he shall work."

[E] Why do you encompass this one [who fell ill, for he, too, is freed] and exclude that one [who fled]?

[F] After Scripture used encompassing language, it used exclusive language. Accordingly, I encompass this one [who fell ill] who remains in his domain and exclude that one who is not in the owner's domain."

[G] R. Bun bar Hiyya said R. Hoshaiah raised the question: "I see no problem in the case of one who was ill and later fled, that he serves out the required six years.

[H] "But if he fled and afterward he fell ill [what is the rule]? [Do we say that since he fled at the outset he must make up the years? Or perhaps he may claim that even if he were with the master, he would not have been able to work.]"

[I] Said R. Hiyya bar Ada, "Let us derive the answer from the following:

[J] "She who rebels against her husband by declining to have sexual relations with him] – they deduct from her marriage contract seven denars a week [M. Ket. 5:7].

[K] "They write for him a writ of rebellion as a charge against her marriage contract.

[L] "In this regard R. Hiyya taught, '[Even in the case of] a menstruating woman, a sick woman, a betrothed girl, and a deceased childless brother's widow – they write for him a writ of rebellion as a charge against her marriage contract.'

[M] "Now how do we interpret this matter? If it was a case in which she rebelled against him [refusing to have sexual relations], and she is already in her menstrual period, it is the Torah that has required her to rebel against him.

[N] "But thus must we interpret the matter: It is a case in which she rebelled against him [refusing to have sexual relations] before her menstrual period had begun.

[O] "Now [the argument continues], when in fact she comes to her menstrual period, she is no longer in a position to rebel, and yet you say that [nonetheless] he writes such a writ of rebellion against her marriage contract.

[P] "Here, too, [by analogy], if the slave fled [when he was well] and afterward fell ill [as at O], he still must make up the years he has not served.

[Q] "For the master has the right to say to him, 'If you had been with me, you would not have gotten sick.'"

[R] Said R. Hinena, "Even in regard to the first case [in which the slave got sick, then fled], the same ruling applies. If the slave got sick and then fled, he must complete the six years, for the master has the right to say to him, 'If you had been with me, you would have been healed more rapidly.'"

[VII.A] **And he acquires himself through the passage of years** [by the Jubilee Year, or by deduction from the purchase price, redeeming himself at his outstanding value]. [This is in line with Lev. 25:50-52: "He shall reckon with him who bought him from the year when he sold himself to him until the year of Jubilee, and the price of his release shall be according to the number of years; the time he was with his owner shall be rated as the time of a hired servant. If there are still many years, according to them he shall refund out of the price paid for him the price for his redemption. If there remain but a few years until the year of Jubilee, he shall make a reckoning with him; according to the years of service due from him he shall refund the money for his redemption."]

[B] There is a Tannaite authority who teaches: "He may be sold for less than six years, but he may not be sold for more than six years."

[C] There is a Tannaite authority who teaches: "He may not be sold either for [59b] less than six years or for more than six years."

[D] Said R. Jeremiah, "The reason for the former Tannaite authority's view is that there are times that he is sold two or three years before the Jubilee Year, and the Jubilee Year comes along and removes him [from the domain of the master] willy-nilly."

[E] By the Jubilee Year: As it is written, "He shall be released in the year of the Jubilee" (Lev. 25:54).

[F] Or by deduction from the purchase price: As it is written, "If there are still many years, according to them he shall refund out of the price paid for him the price for his redemption. If there remain but a few years until the year of Jubilee, he shall make a reckoning with him; according to the years of service due from him he shall refund the money for his redemption" (Lev. 25:51-52).

[G]   Now do we not know that if there are many years, there are not a few remaining, and if there are few, there are not many? [Why does the same proposition require repetition?]

[H]   Said R. Hila, "There are times that the money owing on the years remaining is greater than the value of the man as a slave, and there are times that the money owing for the years remaining is less than the value of the man as a slave.

[I]   "If the man was sold at the rate of a maneh [a hundred zuz] per year of service, and he has increased in value, so that lo, he now is worth two hundred zuz per year of service, how do you know that he reckons with him only at the rate of a maneh per year of service [as yet remaining]?

[J]   "Scripture states, 'Out of the money that he was bought for.'

[K]   "How do you know that if the man was sold at the rate of two hundred zuz per year of service, and he fell in value, and now is worth a maneh, how do you know that he reckons with him only at the rate of a maneh per year of service [as yet remaining]?

[L]   "Scripture states, 'According to his years of service due from him he shall refund the money for his redemption.'

[M]   'We have thus derived the rule in the case of an Israelite sold to a gentile that, when he is redeemed, he has the upper hand."

[N]   How do we learn that in the case of one sold to an Israelite, when he is redeemed, he also has the upper hand?

[O]   The word "hired servant" is used in both contexts [sold to an Israelite: Lev. 25:40; to a gentile: Lev. 25:53], serving the purpose of establishing a common rule for both.

[P]   Just as the use of the word "hired servant" stated in the context of gentile ownership means that, when he is redeemed, he has the upper hand, so the use of the word "hired servant" in the Israelite setting means that when he is redeemed, he has the upper hand.

[Q]   Rabbi says, "Why does Scripture repeat the word 'He will redeem him' three times? It is to encompass all acts of redemption, requiring that each of them follow the same procedures, [thus proving that when the slave is redeemed from an Israelite he also has the upper hand]."

[VIII.A]   "And if he is not redeemed by these [means, then he shall be released in the year of Jubilee, he and his children with him]" (Lev. 25:54).

[B]   R. Yosé the Galilean says, "By these [relatives (Lev. 25:49ff.] it is for freedom, or [if he is redeemed] by anyone else it is for subjugation [purchased for further service]."

[C]   R. Aqiba says, "By these [relatives] it is for subjugation, or by any one else it is for freedom."

[D]   [What is at issue in this dispute?] R. Abbahu in the name of R. Yohanan: "Now both of them interpret a single verse of Scripture: 'And if he is not redeemed by these' –

[E]   "R. Yosé the Galilean interprets the verse, 'And if he is not redeemed by these [relatives] but by others, then he remains in service [to the master until the Jubilee] and then goes free.

[F] "R. Aqiba interprets the verse, 'But if he is not redeemed by [himself]' but by relatives he serves out the years until the Jubilee and then goes free."

[G] But as to the opinion of sages [in the same matter], R. Yosa in the name of R. Yohanan: "Whether he is redeemed by these [relatives] or by others, it is for freedom."

[H] And so, too, has it been taught: "Or if his hand should turn up [sufficient funds], he will be redeemed" (Lev. 25:9) –

[I] "If his own hand turns up sufficient means for his redemption": Just as if his own hand turns up sufficient means, [he is freed and does not serve others], so if the hand of others [turns up sufficient means for his redemption], it is for his own benefit [and not so that he may then be subjugated to them].

[J] [Now to explain the position of those who say that he is redeemed in order to complete the term of service:] R. Jacob bar Aha in the name of R. Yohanan, "In the view of him who says, 'It is to subjugation,' [it is so that] he completes the original term of service and then goes forth [but does not serve another six years]."

[K] And has it not been taught: If after he has been redeemed [he is resubjugated], lo, it is as if he is sold to him? He is subjugated [for the six-year term of service] and then goes forth.

[L] R. Abba Meri said, "The proper reading here is not that he is subjugated [for the whole term of six years] and then goes free, but rather, 'He completes the original term of service and then goes free.'"

[M] If his relatives wanted to redeem him from the first purchaser, they have that right.

[N] [If he is redeemed from the first purchaser and] the relatives wanted to redeem him from the redeemer, they do not have that right.

[O] R. Yosa in the name of R. Yohanan, "That statement accords with the view of him who said, 'by these [relatives]' means that he is redeemed for freedom, but by any other person he is taken over into a new term of service. "

[IX.A] Samuel bar Abba raised the question before R. Yosa, "Here [in regard to redeeming the slave] it is written, 'He shall reckon with him...from the year when he sold himself to him until the year of Jubilee' (Lev. 25:50) and [in regard to redeeming an inherited field that one has consecrated, it is written, 'Then the priest] shall reckon [the money value for it according to the years that remain until the year of Jubilee, and a deduction shall be made from your Valuation]' (Lev. 27:23).

[B] "Now here [in the case of redeeming a slave] you take account of months as well as years, when he goes forth [so that if it is the middle of the year, half of the year is deemed to count as part of the term of service, but when the field is assessed by the priest, only whole years are taken into account (cf. M. Ar. 7:1)]. [What is the difference?]"

[C] He said to him, "The present case is different, for the Torah has treated the slave in the context of the hired hand. Just as the latter reckons months and completes his term of service, so this one also reckons months as well as years and completes his term of service."

[X.A] **[The Hebrew slave girl has an advantage over him. For she acquires herself in addition through the appearance of tokens of puberty (M. 1:1C-D):]** "She shall go out for nothing, without payment of money" (Ex. 21:11).

[B] "For nothing" – refers to the time of pubescence.

[C] "Without payment of money" – refers to the tokens of maturity.

[D] And why should the law not refer to only one of them?

[E] If it had referred to only one of them, I might have maintained, "If she goes forth through the appearance of the signs of puberty, all the more so will she go forth at the time of pubescence."

[F] If so, I would have maintained, the time of pubescence is the only time at which she goes forth, and not the time at which she produces signs of puberty.

[G] Now logic would suggest as follows: Since she leaves the domain of the father and leaves the domain of the master, just as from the domain of the father she goes forth only when she has produced the signs of puberty, also from the domain of the master should go forth only when she produces signs of puberty.

[H] On that account it was necessary to state:

[I] "For nothing" – refers to the time of pubescence.

[J] "Without a payment of money" – refers to the signs of puberty.

[K] And perhaps matters are just the opposite [so that "she will go forth for nothing" refers to the period of twelve and a bit more in which she is a girl, and "without a payment" refers to the time at which she has reached puberty]?

[L] R. Tanhuma in the name of R. Huna: "'Without money' – in any context in which the father receives money, the master does not receive money."

[XI.A] "[If she does not please her master,] who has designated her for himself, then he shall let her be redeemed" (Ex. 21:8).

[B] "This teaches that he may not designate her for himself unless there is sufficient time left in the day for redeeming her. [That is, the labor on this very last day of her term of service must still be worth at least a perutah, so that she could be designated to him by means of the deduction of that amount of money.]

[C] "[The consequence is that] in the remaining labor to be done by her there must be a value of a perutah, so that in the deduction applying to her, there will be a value of a perutah," the words of R. Yosé b. R. Judah.

[D] And sages say, "He may designate her all day long, down to the very last rays of the sun."

[E] Said R. Hiyya bar Ada, "All concur in the case of [redeeming] a Hebrew slave that this may be done only so long as there remains the sum of a perutah [to be worked off]. [If such a sum is yet owing, he may be redeemed therefrom. Otherwise the process does not apply.]"

[F] Well did R. Yosé b. R. Judah rule [that betrothal takes place only if there is sufficient time left in the day for labor of a value of a perutah to be remitted by the owner, thus constituting the sum owing to the girl for her betrothal].

[G] What is the reason of the rabbis? [For what constitutes the sum of betrothal, on the strength of which the owner designates the girl as his betrothed?] There is no issue of money, nor is there an issue of the value of her labor [at the end of that last day]. So with what does the owner designate her [and betroth her]?

[H] Said R. Zeira. "He designates her by a mere oral declaration, [which suffices]."

[I] R. Hoshaiah taught. "How does he designate her? He says to her before two witnesses, 'Lo, you are designated unto me [as my betrothed].'"

[J] [We turn to the principle at issue at B-D.] In the opinion of R. Yosé b. R. Judah it is only at the end of the transaction that [whatever] money [is left over from the period of service] is given to her for the purposes or designation [as his betrothed].

[K] In the opinion of the rabbis from the very beginning of the transaction [when the girl was sold by her father to the owner], the money was handed over tor the purposes of designation [and hence betrothal]. [That is why, so far as they are concerned, whether or not there is sufficient time left in the day for her to work off a perutah, which is forgiven her in exchange for the designation as betrothed, the rabbis deem her betrothed. The betrothal money was paid out as the original price for the girl.]

[L] What is the practical difference between the two?

[M] It is ownership of the fruits of her labor.

[N] The one who said that at the end the money is given over to her for the purposes of designation, [that is, R. Yosé b. R. Judah,] maintains that the usufruct of her labor belongs to the master [and not to her father]. [She is deemed married like any other woman.]

[O] The one who said that from the very outset the money is given over to her for the purposes of designation maintains that the usufruct of her labor belongs to her father. [If the master designates her at the end of the six years, it does not matter, since the original sum paid to the father covered the money owing for the designation as the betrothed of the master. Whatever work she does after the six years are over produces benefit to the father, since she is not deemed normally wed to the master. She returns to the domain of the father and is not deemed wed to the master. The effect of the designation is to betroth her, not to effect a complete marital bond.]

[P] Even in accord with the one who said that from the very outset the money is given over to her for the purposes of designation, the usufruct of her labor belongs to her husband. [Why?] [Because] he is in the status of one who says to a woman, "Lo, you are betrothed to me on condition that the usufruct of your labor belongs to me [even while you are merely betrothed to me, not in a fully consummated union]. [Consequently, even in this position one may maintain the same position as is given to one in the contrary view.]

[Q] If the master was married to her sister [in which case he was not permitted to marry her as well], and the sister died,

[R] the one who said that only at the end is the money given over to her for the purposes of designation [betrothal] will maintain that she requires the payment of another sum of money [to accomplish the designation as the master's betrothed, since in any event she was not suitable to marry him while the sister was alive, so no funds have been transferred for this purpose].

[S] [But] in the view of the one who said that from the very outset the money is given over to her for the purposes of designation, she does not have to be given another sum of money, [because we deem the money originally paid over to serve retroactively as the betrothal payment].

[T] [No, that proposition is rejected:] Even in accord with the one who said that from the very outset the money is given over to her for the purposes of designation, she still has to be given another sum of money, [because we certainly do not deem the money originally paid over to serve retroactively as the betrothal payment].

[U] Why? Because all parties concur that a betrothal is not valid in the case of a prohibited connection. [That is, if while the sister is yet alive the master should betroth the girl, the betrothal is null, since while the sister is alive there is no possibility of betrothing her; hence there is also no possibility of a retroactive interpretation of the money originally paid as having served for purposes of designation as the master's betrothed.]

[V] Does R. Yosé b. R. Judah maintain the view that this act of designation that takes place here [at the end of the six years of labor, in which there is yet enough time for the girl to perform a perutah's worth of labor, as explained above] enjoys the status of a betrothal as authorized by the laws of the Torah?

[W] Said R. Abun "R. Yosé b. R. Judah is of the same view as R. Simeon b. Eleazar, as we have learned in the following."

[X] He who says to a woman, "Lo, you are betrothed to me through my bailment that you have in your hand,"

[Y] [if] she went off and found that it had been stolen or had gotten lost,

[Z] if there was left in her possession something worth a perutah,

[AA] she is betrothed, and if not, she is not betrothed.

[BB] [But if it concerned] a loan, even though there was something worth a perutah left in her possession, she is not betrothed.

[CC] R. Simeon b. Eleazar says in the name of R. Meir, "A loan is equivalent to a bailment. If there remained in her hand something worth a perutah, she is betrothed. And if not, she is not betrothed" [T. Qid . 3:1].

[DD] Just as R. Simeon b. Eleazar treats a loan as equivalent to a bailment, so R. Yosé b. R. Judah treats funds paid for the girl for purposes of designation as equivalent to a loan.

[XII.A] "If he designates her for his son, [he shall deal with her as a daughter]" (Ex. 21:9).

[B] He designates her for his son, but he does not designate her for his brother.

[C] And let him be free to designate her for his brother, on the basis of the following argument a fortiori:

[D] Now if in the case of the son, who does not stand in his stead for purposes of the rite of removing the shoe or for levirate marriage, lo, he designates her for him,

[E]   his brother, who does stand in his stead for purposes of the rite of removing the shoe and for levirate marriage – is it not logical that he should be free to designate her for him?

[F]   No. If you have stated the rule in regard to the son, who stands in his stead in regard to a field received as an inheritance [M. Arakh. 7:2], will you say the same of his brother, who does not stand in his stead in regard to a field received as an inheritance?

[G]   Since he does not stand in his stead in that regard, it is not logical that he should be free to designate her for him.

[H]   Scripture states, "And if he designates her for his son," meaning, for his son he designates her, and he may not designate her for his brother.

[I]   "And if he designates her for his son" – and he may not designate her for his son's son.

[J]   Samuel bar Abba raised the question before R. Zeira: "In the law dealing with inheritances you treat the son of the son as equivalent to the son. But here you do not treat the son of the son as equivalent to the son."

[K]   R. Zeira said, "To whoever can explain this matter to me, I shall give a glass of spiced wine!"

[L]   R. Nahum answered, "Lo, [59c] in connection with inheritances, you treat the brother as equivalent to the son, and all other relatives as equivalent to the son, and so, likewise, you treat the son of the son as equivalent to the son.

[M]   "But here, in a case in which you have not treated the brother as equivalent to the son, and all other relatives as equivalent to the son, there is hardly much reason to treat the son of the son as equivalent to the son."

[N]   The rabbis of Caesarea objected: "Lo, in the matter of the priest's becoming unclean for a deceased relative, you have treated a brother as equivalent to the son, and all other relatives [listed, for whom the priest may become unclean with corpse uncleanness required in burying the deceased] likewise are treated as equivalent to the son. But you do not treat the son of the son as equivalent to the son."

[O]   They said, "There goes the cup of spiced wine" [since Zeira now did not owe it to Nahum].

[XIII.A]   "If he designates her for his son" (Ex. 21:9) –

[B]   It must be with the son's knowledge and consent.

[C]   Said R. Yohanan, "There is no requirement here for the son's knowledge and consent."

[D]   Said R. Jacob bar Aha, "There is indeed a requirement here for the son's knowledge and consent, along the lines of the position of R. Yosé b. R. Judah. [The money the father got at the outset was for selling the girl, not for purposes of betrothing her. It follows that if there is to be a betrothal it comes later on, hence with the girl's agreement. Likewise, if the father wishes to betroth her to his son, it must be with the son's agreement.]"

[E]   Said R. Samuel b. bar Abedoma, "Even if you say that this is in accord with the view of R. Yosé b. R. Judah, there is no need for advance knowledge and consent, "For cannot the son be a minor [who has no legal right of knowledge and consent, since the verse simply says 'son' with no qualifications (following Pené Moshe)]."

[XIV.A] "If he designates her for his son" (Ex. 21:9) – it must be with the son's knowledge and consent.

[B] R. Yohanan said, "He designates her, whether for his adult son or his minor son, whether with his knowledge and consent or not with his knowledge and consent."

[C] R. Simeon b. Laqish said, "He designates her only for his adult son, for it must be done with the son's knowledge and consent [and a minor legally has neither]."

[D] [Both views will be tested against the following:] A son who is nine years and one day old [who is married to a woman and dies] turns [that woman] into a widow [so far as her being prohibited to marry] a high priest; or [if he divorces his wife or performs the rite of removing the shoe with his sister-in-law], he turns [that woman] into a divorcée or a woman who has removed the shoe [so far as her being prohibited to marry] an ordinary priest [is concerned]. [Consequently, he is deemed for the present purposes to be a husband.]

[E] Now so far as R. Yohanan is concerned, who interprets that statement to apply to a case in which the father has designated a slave girl as the betrothed for his son, there is no problem.

[F] We deal here with an act of designation in which the son has a right of acquisition in the woman. Consequently, under the stated conditions, on his account the woman may be deemed a widow so far as marriage to a high priest is concerned, or a divorcée or a woman who has carried out the rite of removing the shoe so far as being married to an ordinary priest is concerned.

[G] As to the view of R. Simeon b. Laqish, will he interpret the matter to speak of a case in which the son was married [in an ordinary way]? Then the woman should be exempt from the status of a woman who has performed the rite of removing the shoe and from the requirement of levirate marriage. For have we not learned the following: If a nine-year-old married a woman and died [without children], lo, this woman is exempt [from levirate marriage, since the marriage of a nine-year-old is null. So Yohanan can interpret the cited passage, but by Simeon b. Laqish, who maintains that there is no possibility of designating the slave girl as the wife of a minor, how is the passage to be interpreted?].

[H] Said R. Abin, "The view of R. Simeon b. Laqish accords with the position of R. Yosé b. R. Judah [in the following dispute]:

[I] For so it has been taught:

[J] A son nine years and one day old up to twelve years and one day old who produced two pubic hairs or two hairs under the arm, lo, this [set of hairs] is deemed nothing but a mole [and he is not regarded as mature].

[K] R. Yosé b. R. Judah says, "Lo, these are regarded as valid signs of puberty, and he is deemed an adult."

[L] R. Jacob b. R. Bun in the name of R. Yosé b. Haninah [explaining Yosé's position]: "And that applies when the signs appeared at a time appropriate for producing signs of puberty [in the twelfth year]."

[M] R. Yosé raised the question: "If the signs of puberty appeared during such a period, is he deemed an adult retroactively or only from now on."

[N] R. Abun: "It is obvious that it is retroactively that he is treated as an adult, all the more so from now on."

[O] [The reason this was obvious to Abun is] that he interpreted this statement of R. Simeon b. Laqish in accord with the position of R. Yosé b. R. Judah. [That is, Simeon b. Laqish accords with Yosé b. R. Judah and maintains that a boy nine years and one day old who dies turns his wife into a widow so far as marriage to a high priest is concerned. We have then a case in which the signs of puberty appeared at a later age; retroactively he is deemed to be an adult. Accordingly, it is obvious that Simeon b. Laqish and Yosé will regard the puberty signs as retroactively effective. As to explaining D, Simeon b. Laqish does so in this wise].

[P] And why does R. Yosé not interpret the matter of R. Simeon b. Laqish in accord with the position of R. Yosé b. R. Judah?

[Q] Said R. Mana, "Because he was troubled by this problem. R. Yosé wanted to know, if the puberty signs appeared at the right time, whether retroactively he is deemed to be an adult, or only from now on. Now in this case, it poses no problem as to his turning his wife into a widow, but how can he turn her into a divorcée [for a minor may not give a writ of divorce]?" One may interpret the case to be one in which he had sexual relations and gave her a writ of divorce, or gave one when he became an adult.

[R] "In the case of her becoming a widow who has removed the shoe on his account, interpret the case in which he had sexual relations with his wife, then died, and his brother had performed the rite of removing the shoe with his widow. So on account of his brother, she entered the status of a woman with whom the rite of removing the shoe had been performed.

[S] "If that is the case, then why not invoke the same rule in the case of a boy less than nine years old [who later had intercourse and divorced his wife]?"

[T] Said R. Samuel b. Abodema, "And that is indeed correct. [It does apply.] But since [the Tannaite authority] wished to phrase the entire set of statements to concern a nine-year-old, he treated this particular case also in terms of a nine-year-old."

[U] R. Judah bar Pazzi in the name of R. Joshua b. Levi, "R. Yosé b. R. Judah derived the facts from Ahaz, for it has been taught: Ahaz fathered a son at the age of nine; Haran at the age of six; Caleb at the age of ten."

[V] And this is in accord with him who maintains that Caleb son of Hesron is the same as Caleb the son of Yefuneh [cf. B. San. 69a].

[XV.A] "If the father of the girl sold her to this one [in line with Ex. 21:7-11] and betrothed her to someone else, the father has ridiculed the master, [for what he has done is valid in both cases,]" the words of R. Yosé b. R. Judah.

[B]   And the sages say, "The father has not ridiculed the master [who has every right to designate the girl as his betrothed, despite the father's deed with the other party]. [Sages maintain that by selling the girl he has accepted betrothal money, and consequently his betrothal to another party was null.]"

[C]   [The theory of Yosé b. R. Judah is this:] The master is in the position of one who says to a woman, "Lo, you are betrothed to me after thirty days." Now if someone says to a woman, "Lo, you are betrothed to me after thirty days," and someone else came along and betrothed her during the thirty days, is it possible that she is not betrothed to the second party? [Obviously not. She certainly is betrothed to the second party, for there is no intervening rite of betrothal.]

[D]   [The theory of rabbis is this:] If he said to her, "Lo, you are betrothed to me from this point, effective in thirty days," and someone else came along and betrothed her during the period of thirty days, is it possible that she is not betrothed to the two of them [by reason of doubt]? [Obviously not. She is betrothed and yet prohibited to both parties by reason of doubt.]

[E]   [Now the betrothal effected by the master's designation of the girl to be his wife] is already [effective] whenever he wishes [to consummate the marriage]. [Accordingly, it is parallel to the case outlined just now, betrothal on condition. For the rabbis maintain that the money originally paid over also serves as betrothal money.]

[F]   All concur, to be sure, that if the father actually had married the girl off, he has ridiculed the master, [who can do nothing about it].

[XVI.A]   "When a man sells his daughter as a slave" (Ex. 21:7) –

[B]   "Solely as a slave. This teaches that he has the right to sell her to the master and to stipulate with him that it is on condition that he not have the right to designate her as his betrothed," the words of R. Meir.

[C]   And sages say, "In so stating, he has done nothing whatever, for he has made a stipulation contrary to what is written in the Torah, and whoever stipulates contrary to what is written in the Torah – what he has stipulated is null."

[D]   Now does R. Meir not concur that whoever stipulates contrary to what is written in the Torah – what he has stipulated is null?

[E]   He maintains that one's stipulation is null if it is not possible for him to carry it out without actually violating the rules of the Torah. But in the present case it is possible for him to carry it out in the end. [For the owner is not obligated by the Torah to designate the girl as his betrothed at all. Meir thus maintains that such a stipulation is valid. So this one has every possibility of carrying out the stipulation in the end without violating the Torah.]

[F]   And do rabbis [vis-à-vis Meir] not maintain that a stipulation is valid if it is possible for him to carry it out in the end without violating the Torah?

[G]   They concur that a stipulation is valid [if it is contrary to the Torah] so long as it is possible for him to carry it out in the end without violating the Torah. [But that is the case in which the stipulation deals with] a monetary matter, [while the present stipulation deals with] a matter covering the person herself.

[H] Now lo, it is taught: "A man marries a woman and stipulates with her that it is on condition that he not have the obligation to provide for her food, clothing, or marital rights" (Ex. 21:10).

[I] Now that poses no problem as to food or clothing. But marital rights do affect the body [the person herself].

[J] Said R. Hiyya bar Ada, "Interpret the passage to speak of a minor girl."

[K] As to the Tannaite authority who maintains that the stipulation is null, how does he interpret the reference to selling her for a slave girl?

[L] He maintains that the father] may sell her if she is a widow to a high priest, and if she is a divorcée or a woman who has undergone the rite of removing the shoe to an ordinary priest, [and the purpose of the specification "for a slave" is to indicate that that is permitted].

[M] And how does the other Tannaite authority interpret the specification "for a slave," [since he holds, as we shall see, that a man may not sell his daughter as a slave girl after he has sold her for marriage, since from that view, one may not interpret the matter to apply to selling the girl as a widow to a high priest, for, in this Tannaite authority's view, once she was married and widowed, the father may not sell her anyway]?

[N] Said R. Yosé b. R. Bun, "Interpret the statement to apply to a case in which the girl was widowed out of the status of merely being betrothed."

[O] But has it not been taught [in a passage that can speak only of the status of betrothal, not of a fully consummated marriage]: "A man may sell his daughter for marriage [and if she became widowed or divorced] he may do so again [provided she is still a minor]." Similarly, he may sell her as a slave girl, [and if she was a minor when receiving her freedom through the end of the six year period or the Jubilee Year or her master's death] he may do so again. He may sell her for a slave girl, [and if she became free] he may sell her for marriage. However, he may not sell her as a slave girl after he had already sold her for marriage.

[P] Said R. Yohanan, "There are two opinions. The one who holds that the passage refers to the father's selling her only as a slave girl, and that our case refers to a widow sold to a high priest [and consequently she cannot marry the high priest], maintains that the father may sell her as a slave girl after she has been married [and, as we see, widowed after being merely betrothed].

[Q] "The one who holds that the passage does not speak of a widow's being sold to a high priest also does not concur that the father has the right to sell the girl as a slave girl after she has been married."

[R] Then how does this second party interpret the language of Scripture, "as a slave girl"?

[S] Said R. Mattenaiah, "Interpret the passage to a case in which he was married to her sister. [Scripture thus indicates that the father may sell the girl to a man who already has married the girl's sister, since he sells her as a slave girl and not for the purpose of designation as the master's betrothed.]"

[T] R. Simeon b. Yohai taught, "Just as the father may not sell the girl as a slave girl after she has been married, so he may not sell her as a slave girl after she already has been sold as a slave girl."

[U] What is the scriptural basis for the position of R. Simeon b. Yohai?

[V] "Since he has dealt faithlessly with her" (Ex. 21:8).

[W] One time he has the opportunity to deal faithlessly with her, and he does not have the opportunity to deal faithlessly with her a second time.

[X] How do rabbis [who do not concur with Simeon's position] interpret this prooftext as adduced in evidence by Simeon b. Yohai, "since he has dealt faithlessly with her"?

[Y] Once [the master] has spread his cloak over her [and had sexual relations with her], the father has no further domain over her.

[XVII.A] R. Simeon b. Laqish raised the question before R. Yohanan: "A Hebrew slave girl should go forth if she is wed [to someone other than the master, going forth at that point from the domain of the master].

[B] "This position is based upon an argument a fortiori.

[C] "Now if the appearance of the signs of puberty, which do not remove her from the domain of the father, lo, do remove her from the domain of the master, the fact that she is married, which does remove her from the domain of the father – is it not a matter of logic that it should also remove her from the domain of the master?"

[D] He said to him, "I know only what the Mishnah states: The Hebrew slave girl has an advantage over him, for she acquires herself through the appearance of tokens of puberty [M. 1:2C-D] – [that and no more]."

[XVIII.A] Bar Pedaiah said, "A Hebrew slave girl goes forth at the death of her master."

[B] What is the scriptural basis for that view?

[C] "And to your bondwoman you shall do likewise" (Deut. 15:17).

[D] And it is written, "He shall be your bondman forever" (Deut. 15:17).

[E] Scripture thereby links the rule covering the Hebrew slave girl to the slave whose ear is pierced.

[F] Just as the slave whose ear is pierced goes free at the death of his master, so the Hebrew slave girl goes free at the death of her master.

[G] And this teaching of Bar Pedaiah accords with what the following Tannaite authority taught, for it has been taught:

[H] A Hebrew slave boy serves the son and does not serve the daughter. A Hebrew slave girl serves neither the daughter nor the son [following QE].

[I] There is a Tannaite authority who teaches, "Whether it is a Hebrew slave girl or a Hebrew slave boy, they do not serve either the son or the daughter [but go free at the death of the master]."

[J] How does that Tannaite authority interpret the language of Scripture, "And to your bondwoman you shall do likewise" (Deut. 15:17)?

[K] He interprets that language to apply to the matter of sending forth the slave well supplied ["And when you let him go free from you, you shall not let him go empty-handed; you shall furnish him liberally out of your flock, out of your threshing floor, and out of your winepress," (Deut. 15:13). That is, when the slave girl goes forth, she, too, should be liberally supplied by the master.]

[L] For it has been taught: These are the ones whom one supplies liberally when they go forth:

[M] He who goes forth at the end of his years of service and at the Jubilee, and the Hebrew slave girl who acquires possession of herself through the appearance of puberty signs.

[N] But he who goes forth by deducting [what is owing] or at the death of the master – they do not supply these liberally.

[XIX.A] It is written, "And his master shall bring him to the judges, and he shall bring him to the door or the doorpost" (Ex. 21:6).

[B] How is this possible?

[C] The slave who was sold by a court is subject to the statement, "And his master will bring him to the judges."

[D] And the one who sells himself is subject to the statement, "And he shall bring him to the door."

[E] R. Ami raised the question: "It is self-evident that, as to the one who is sold by a court, the court writes out [59d] his writ for him.

[F] "But as to the one who sells himself, who writes out the writ for him?" [This question is not answered.]

[XX.A] It is written, "It shall not seem hard to you, when you let him go free from you; for at half the cost of a hired servant he has served you six years" (Deut. 15:18).

[B] A hired hand works by day but does not work by night.

[C] A Hebrew slave works by day and by night.

[D] It is written, "He shall not rule with harshness over him in your sight" (Lev. 5:53), and yet you say this?

[E] R. Ami in the name of R. Yohanan: "His master marries off a Canaanite woman to him, so he turns out to work by day and by night [fathering children for the master by night]."

[F] R. Ba bar Mamel raised the question before R. Ami: "But take note: What if he purchased a priest? [He then could not marry a Canaanite woman.]"

[G] He said to him. "And is an Israelite not released from the general prohibition [against such marriages]? [Likewise a priest in these circumstances is no different.]" When R. Ba bar Mamel heard this, he retracted.

[XXI.A] R. Judah b. R. Bun interpreted this word: "The lobe of the ear is pierced so that, should the slave be a priest, he is not invalidated for service.

[B] R. Meir says, "He was pierced at the gristle [cartilage forming the ear]."

[C] On this basis R. Meir did say, "A priest is not to have his ear pierced [as a slave], lest he thereby be blemished and so be invalidated for the Temple service."

[D] But why should that be a problem? Let the gristle be pierced with a hole less than the size of a yetch, [which will not be a blemish].

[E] Perhaps it may become a hole the size of a yetch [and so blemish the priest].

[F] So let him be pierced with a hole the size of a yetch, [and what difference does that make]?

[G] The Torah has said, "And he shall return to his property" (Lev. 25:27) – that means, he must return whole [and not blemished].

[H] Now would he have his ear pierced, unless he had a wife and children [and, it follows, that that applies even to a priest, who is also given a Canaanite woman].

[XXII.A] "With an awl" (Ex. 21:6): I know that one may use only an awl. How do I know that it may be done with a wooden prick, thorn, or shard of glass?

[B] Scripture says, "And he will pierce" [by whatever means].

[C] Up to this point [we have answered the question] in accord with R. Aqiba['s mode of exegesis]. How does R. Ishmael answer the same question?

[D] R. Ishmael taught: "In three places the practical law supersedes the biblical text, and in one the legitimate interpretation of the text [ignoring the rules of interpretation].

[E] "The Torah has said, 'in a book' (Deut. 24:1), and the practical law says that on anything that is uprooted from the ground [a writ of divorce may be written].

[F] "The Torah has said, 'With dirt' [the blood is to be covered up] (Lev. 17:13), but the practical law requires that it be done with anything in which seeds will grow.

[G] "The Torah has said, 'With an awl,' but the practical law permits use of a wooden prick, thorn, or shard of glass.

[H] "And in one place the legitimate interpretation of the text:

[I] "[R. Ishmael taught] 'And it shall be on the seventh day he shall shave all his hair (Lev. 14:9)' – a generalization; 'of his head and his beard and his eyebrows' – a particularization; 'even all his hair he shall shave off' – generalization. Where there is a general proposition followed by a particular specification and again followed by a general proposition, only what is like the particulars is included.

[J] "This then tells you, 'Just as the particularization refers explicitly to a place on the body on which hair is gathered together and is visible, so I know only that every place on the body where hair is gathered together and is visible is to be shaved off.

[K] But the law rules: 'He should shave him as [smooth as] a gourd.'"

[XXIII.A] "With an awl": Just as an awl is made of metal so anything made of metal [will serve].

[B] Rabbi says, "This refers to a large spit."

[C] R. Yosé b. R. Judah says, "This refers to a chisel."

[D] "And he shall bring him to the door" (Ex. 21:6). Is it possible to suppose that that is the case even if the door is lying [on the ground]?

[E] "Scripture says, 'Or to the doorpost' (Ex. 21:6).

[F] "Just as the doorpost is standing, so the door must be standing.

[G] "It is a matter of shame to the slave and a matter of shame to a family."

[XXIV.A] It was taught: R. Eliezer b. Jacob says, "Why is it that he is brought to the door? It is because it is through [blood placed over the lintel on the] door that [the Israelites] went forth from slavery to freedom."

[B] His disciples asked Rabban Yohanan b. Zakkai, "Why is it that this slave has his ear pierced, rather than any other of his limbs?"

[C] He said to them, "The ear, which heard from Mount Sinai, 'You will have no other gods before me' (Ex. 20:3), and yet this one broke off the yoke of the kingdom of Heaven and accepted upon itself the yoke of flesh and blood –

[D] "the ear which heard before Mount Sinai, 'For to me the people of Israel are slaves, they are my slaves whom I brought forth out of the land of Egypt: I am the Lord your God' (Lev. 25:55), yet this one went and got another master for himself –

[E] "therefore let the ear come and be pierced, for it has not observed the things it heard."

[XXV.A] "His ear" [(Ex. 21:6) is stated here, and] "his ear" [is stated elsewhere (Lev. 14:14)] –

[B] just as "his ear" stated later on refers to the right ear, so "his ear" stated here is the right ear.

[C] "But if, saying, the slave says..." (Ex. 21:5). Two speeches are under discussion, one at the end of the sixth year of service, the other at the beginning of the Seventh Year –

[D] one at the end of the sixth year of service, while he is still in his period of service, and one at the beginning of the Seventh Year – [the phrase] "I will not go out free" [supposes that he could if he wishes, and that occurs only at the beginning of the Seventh Year].

[E] "I love my master, my wife, and my children" (Ex. 21:5). This teaches that he does not have his ear pierced before he has a wife and children, and before his master has a wife and children,

[F] before he has come to love his master, and his master to love him,

[G] before the master's possessions are greatly blessed on his account, as it is said, "Since he fares well with you" (Deut. 15:16).

[XXVI.A] And he acquires ownership of himself at the Jubilee [M. 1:2F]: As it is written, "He shall be released in the year of the Jubilee, he and his children with him" (Lev. 25:54),

[B] or at the death of the master: As it is written, "And he shall be your bondman forever" (Deut. 15:16) – for the "ever" of the master.

Following the pattern familiar from the discussion of Y. 1:1, we begin with an extensive exercise in proving the Mishnah's propositions on the basis of Scripture. Unit I carries out that exercise. Units II and III then provide a gloss to the Mishnah's language, again out of Scripture. Unit IV proceeds to discuss the language used in a writ. Unit V turns to the exposition of Scripture, relevant to, but not required by, the Mishnah. Unit VI carries forward that same range of interests. Its problem is entirely unrelated to the Mishnah. Units VII-IX proceed to the redemption of the male slave, and unit X to the female one. The main point of unit VII is to take up the matter of setting the purchase price for redemption. This is defined to the slave's maximum advantage. Unit VIII goes on to the matter of the slave's family s redeeming him. The principal issue is whether he must then serve out the original term. Unit IX, finally, provides an exegesis of verses relevant to the entire procedure. Unit X then goes on to the next clause of the Mishnah, now on the freeing of the Hebrew slave girl through her reaching sexual maturity. Units XI-XIV take up the slave girl who is to go free because the master does not designate her for himself (Ex. 28:8). This matter is allowed to follow its own program of inquiry rather than the Mishnah's. The exegesis of the pertinent verses occupies the center of attention. Unit XI expresses the dispute over the character of the money originally paid by the master to the girl's father. One position is that at the very outset that money has the character of payment for betrothal. The other is that only at the end, once it is so characterized, is that money deemed payment or betrothal. It is not assumed to be such until it is explicitly specified that the money is meant to betroth the girl. The operative language here is "designate," but for all intents and purposes what is meant is betrothal. Unit XII takes up the somewhat simpler issue of whether the master may designate her for someone else besides himself or his son. Units XIII and XIV continue this same inquiry. Unit XV completes the exposition of the views of Yosé b. R. Judah and sages, a construction leaving no obscure points. Unit XVI goes on to the Scripture's specification that the father sells the daughter as a slave girl. The issue is raised about what stipulations the father may make in that regard, and the familiar conundrum about stipulating against the requirements of the Torah is once more addressed. Unit XVII deals with M. 1:2C-D, and unit XVIII adds to the Mishnah another occasion on which the slave girl goes free. Units XIX-XXVI all take up M. 1:2E-F, the slave whose ear is pierced and who serves for life. Once more the principal point of interest is the exegesis of the relevant Scriptures.

II. The Talmud of Babylonia to M. Qiddushin 1:2

1:2

A. A Hebrew slave is acquired through money and a writ.
B. And he acquires himself through the passage of years, by the Jubilee Year, and by deduction from the purchase price [redeeming himself at this outstanding value (Lev. 25:50-51)].
C. The Hebrew slave girl has an advantage over him.
D. For she acquires herself [in addition] through the appearance of tokens [of puberty].
E. The slave whose ear is pierced is acquired through an act of piercing the ear (Ex. 21:5).
F. And he acquires himself by the Jubilee and by the death of the master.

I.1   A.   **A Hebrew slave is acquired through money and a writ:**

B.   *How do we know this?*

C.   Said Scripture, "He shall give back the price of his redemption out of the money that he was bought for" (Lev. 25:51).

D.   So we have found the source of the rule governing a Hebrew slave sold to a gentile, since the only way of acquiring him is by money. How do we know that the same rule applies to one sold to an Israelite?

E.   Said Scripture, "Then he shall let her be redeemed" (Ex. 21:8) – this teaches that she deducts part of her redemption money and goes free.

F.   So we have found the rule governing the Hebrew slave girl, since she is betrothed with a money payment, she is acquired with a money payment. How do we know of it a Hebrew slave boy?

G.   Said Scripture, "If your brother, a Hebrew man or a Hebrew woman, is sold to you and serves you six years" (Deut. 15:12) – Scripture treats as comparable the Hebrew slave boy and the Hebrew slave girl.

H.   So we have found the rule governing those sold by a court, since they are sold willy-nilly. If they have sold themselves, how do we know that that is the case?

I.   We derive the parallel between the one and the other because of the use of the word "hired hand" [Lev. 25:39: One who sells himself; one sold by a court, Deut. 15:12ff.; the same word appears in both cases, so the same method of purchase applies to both (Freedman)].

J.   *Well, that poses no problems to him who accepts the consequences drawn from the verbal analogy established by the use of the word "hired hand," but for him who denies that analogy and its consequences, what is to be said?*

K.   Said Scripture, "And if a stranger or sojourner with you gets rich" (Lev. 25:47) – thus adding to the discussion that is just prior, teaching rules governing what is prior on the basis of rules that govern in what is to follow. [The "and" links Lev. 25:47-55, one who sells himself to a non-Jew, to Lev. 25:39-46, one who sells himself to a Jew; just as the purchase in the one case is carried out by money, so is that of the other (Freedman)].

I.2   A.   *And who is the Tannaite authority who declines to establish a verbal analogy based on the recurrent usage of the word "hired hand" in the several passages?*

B.   *It is the Tannaite authority behind the following, which has been taught on Tannaite authority:*

C.   He who sells himself may be sold for six years or more than six years; if it is by a court, he may be sold for six years only.

D.   He who sells himself may not have his ear bored as a mark of perpetual slavery; if sold by the court, he may have his ear bored.

E.   He who sells himself has no severance pay coming to him; if he is sold by a court, he has severance pay coming to him.

F.   To him who sells himself, the master cannot assign a Canaanite slave girl; if sold by a court, the master can give him a Canaanite slave girl.

G. R. Eleazar says, "Neither one nor the other may be sold for more than six years; both may have the ear bored; to both severance pay is given; to both the master may assign a Canaanite slave girl."

H. *Isn't this what is at stake: The initial Tannaite authority does not establish a verbal analogy based on the appearance of "hired hand" in both passages, while R. Eleazar does establish a verbal analogy based on the occurrence of "hired hand" in both passages?*

I. *Said R. Tabyumi in the name of Abbayye, "All parties concur that we do establish a verbal analogy based on the appearance in both passages of 'hired hand.' And here, this is what is the operative consideration behind the position of the initial Tannaite authority, who has said,* He who sells himself may be sold for six years or more than six years? *Scripture has stated a limitation in the context of one sold by a court:* 'And he shall serve you six years' *(Deut. 15:12), meaning, he but not one who sells himself."*

J. *And the other party?*

K. "And he shall serve you" – not your heir.

L. *And the other party?*

M. *There is another* "serve you" *in context [at Deut. 15:18].*

N. *And the other party?*

O. *That is written to tell you that* the master must be prepared to give severance pay.

I.3 A. *And what is the scriptural foundation for the position of the initial Tannaite authority, who has said,* He who sells himself may not have his ear bored as a mark of perpetual slavery; if sold by the court, he may have his ear bored?

B. *Because the All-Merciful has already imposed a limitation in the context of one sold by a court, namely:* "And his master shall bore his ear through with an awl" *(Ex. 21:6) – his ear, but not the ear of the one who has sold himself.*

C. [15A] *And the other party?*

D. *That comes for the purpose of establishing a verbal analogy, for it has been taught on Tannaite authority:*

E. R. Eliezer says, "How on the basis of Scripture do we know that the boring of the ear of the Hebrew slave (Ex. 21:5) must be the right ear? Here we find a reference to 'ear,' and elsewhere, the same word is used [at Lev. 14:14]. Just as in the latter case, the right ear is meant, so here, too, the right ear is meant."

F. *And the other party?*

G. *If so, Scripture should have said merely,* "ear." *Why* "his ear"?

H. *And the other party?*

I. *That is required to make the point,* "his ear" not "her ear."

J. *And the other party?*

K. *That point derives from the statement,* "But if the slave shall plainly say..." *(Ex. 21:5) – the slave boy, not the slave girl.*

L. *And the other party?*

M. *That verse is required to make the point,* he must make the statement while he is still a slave.

N. *And the other party?*

O. *That fact derives from the use of the language* "the slave," *rather than simply,* "slave."

P.   *And the other party?*

Q.   *He draws no such conclusion from the use of the language* "the slave," rather than simply, "slave."

I.4   A.   *And what is the scriptural basis for the position of the initial Tannaite authority, who has said,* He who sells himself has no severance pay coming to him; if he is sold by a court, he has severance pay coming to him?

B.   *The All-Merciful expressed an exclusionary clause in regard to one sold by a court, namely,* "You shall furnish him liberally": (Deut. 15:14) – him, but not one who sells himself.

C.   *And the other party?*

D.   *That verse is required to make the point,* "You shall furnish him liberally" (Deut. 15:14): Him, but not his heir.

E.   *But why not provide for his heirs? For Scripture has classified him as a hired hand:* Just as the wages of a hired hand belong to his heirs, so here, too, his wages belong to his heirs!

F.   *Rather: Him – and not his creditor. [And it is necessary to make that point, for] since we concur in general with R. Nathan, as it has been taught on Tannaite authority:* R. Nathan says, "How on the basis of Scripture do we know that if someone claims a maneh from someone else, and the other party claims the same amount of money from a third party, the money is collected from the third party and paid out directly to the original claimant? 'And give it to him against whom he has trespassed' (Num. 5:7)," *the word* "him" *in the present case serves to exclude that rule here.*

G.   *And the other party?*

H.   *Otherwise, too, we do in point of fact differ from R. Nathan.*

I.5   A.   *And what is the scriptural basis for the position of the initial Tannaite authority, who has said,* To him who sells himself, the master cannot assign a Canaanite slave girl; if sold by a court, the master can give him a Canaanite slave girl?

B.   *The All-Merciful expressed an exclusionary clause in regard to one sold by a court, namely,* "If his master give him a wife" (Ex. 21:4) – him, but not one who sells himself.

C.   *And the other party?*

D.   "Him" – even against his will.

E.   *And the other party?*

F.   *He derives that rule from the phrase,* "For to the double of the hire of a hired servant has he served you" (Deut. 15:18), *for it has been taught on Tannaite authority:* "For to the double of the hire of a hired servant has he served you" (Deut. 15:18) – a hired hand works only by day, but a Hebrew slave works by day and night.

G.   Well, now can you really imagine that a Hebrew slave works day and night? But has not Scripture stated, "Because he is well off with you" (Deut. 15:16), meaning, he has to be right there with you in eat and drink [eating what you eat and living like you], and said R. Isaac, "On this basis it is the rule that his master gives him a Canaanite slave girl."

H.   *And the other party?*

I.   *If I had to derive the rule from that passage, I might have supposed that that is the case only with his full knowledge and consent, but if it is against his will, I might have thought that that is not so. So we are informed that that is not the case.*

I.6   A.   *And who is the Tannaite authority who declines to establish a verbal analogy based on the recurrent usage of the word "hired hand" in the several passages?*

B.   *It is the Tannaite authority behind the following, which has been taught on Tannaite authority:*

C.   "And go back to his own family, and return to the possession of his fathers":

D.   Said R. Eliezer b. R. Jacob, "Concerning what classification of slave does Scripture speak?

E.   "If it concerns a slave who has had his ear pierced to the doorjamb with an awl, lo, that classification has already been covered.

F.   "If it concerns the one who has sold himself, lo, that one has already been covered.

G.   "Lo, Scripture speaks only of one who has sold himself for one or two years prior to the Jubilee.

H.   "The Jubilee in his case frees him" [Sifra CCLVI:I.12 Parashat Behar Pereq 7].

I.   *Now if it should enter your mind that R. Eliezer b. Jacob accepts the verbal analogy based on the recurrent usage of the word "hired hand" in the several passages, what need do I have for this verse and its exegesis? Let him derive the point from the verbal analogy.*

J.   *Said R., Nahman bar Isaac, "In point of fact he does accept the verbal analogy involving the hired hand. But nonetheless, the proof we required as given here. For it might have entered your mind to suppose that it is one who sells himself alone who is subject to the law, for he has done no prohibited deed, but if the court has sold the man, in which case it is because he has done a prohibited deed, I might have supposed that we impose an extrajudicial penalty on him and deny him the present advantage. So we are informed that that is not so."*

I.7   A.   The master has said: "If it concerns a slave who has had his ear pierced to the doorjamb with an awl, lo, that classification has already been covered": *Where?*

B.   *It is as has been taught on Tannaite authority:*

C.   "When each of you shall return to his property and each of you shall return to his family":

D.   Said R. Eliezer b. Jacob, "Concerning what classification of slave does Scripture speak here?

E.   "If it concerns a [Hebrew slave] sold for six years, that of course has already been dealt with. And if it concerns a person sold for a year or two, that of course has already been dealt with.

F.   "The passage therefore addresses only the case of the slave who before the Jubilee has had his ear pierced to the doorjamb so as to serve in perpetuity.

G.   "The Jubilee serves to release him" [Sifra CCXLVIII:I.1 Parashat Behar Pereq 2].

H.   *How so?*

I. Said Raba bar Shila, "Said Scripture, 'And you shall return, every man' (Lev. 25:10) – now what is the rule that applies to a man but not to a woman? You have to say, it is the boring of the ear."

J. *Now it was necessary for Scripture to deal with the case of the court's selling him, and it was necessary for Scripture to deal with the one whose ear has been bored. For had we been informed of the case of the one whom the court has sold, that might have been because his term had not yet expired, but as for him whose ear was bored, since his term had expired, I might have said that we impose an extrajudicial penalty on him. And if we had been informed of the case of the one whose ear was pierced, that might have been because he had already worked for six years, but as to the one who was sold by the court, who has not yet served for six years, I might have maintained that he is not set free. So it was necessary for Scripture to make both points explicit.*

K. *And it was further necessary for Scripture to state both "and you shall return" and also "and he shall serve forever." For if the All-Merciful had said only "and he shall serve forever," I might have supposed that that is meant literally. So the All-Merciful found it necessary to state also* "and you shall return." *And if the All-Merciful had said only* "and you shall return," *I might have supposed that that is the case when he has not served for six years, but in a case in which he has served for six years, then his latter phase of service should not be subject to a more stringent rule than his former:* Just as the first phase of service, when he was sold, was for six years, so his last phase of service should be for only six years; so "forever" informs us, for ever to the end of the Jubilee.

I.8 A. *And who is the Tannaite authority who declines to establish a verbal analogy based on the recurrent usage of the word "hired hand" in the several passages?*

B. *It is Rabbi, for it has been taught on Tannaite authority:*

C. [15B] "And if he be not redeemed by these" (Lev. 25:54) –

D. Rabbi says, "Through these he is redeemed, but not by the passage of six years. For is not the contrary not plausible, namely, if he who cannot be redeemed by these [a Hebrew slave sold to a Jew, who cannot be redeemed by relatives], can be redeemed through the passage of six years, then this one, who can be redeemed by these, surely should be redeemed through working for six years! So it was necessary to say, 'And if he be not redeemed by these' – through these he is redeemed, but not by the passage of six years."

E. *Now if it should enter your mind that Rabbi agrees to establish a verbal analogy based on the recurrent usage of the word 'hired hand' in the several passages, then why does he say, if he who cannot be redeemed by these? Why not deduce the comparable law from the verbal analogy established by the repeated use of "hired hand"?*

F. *Said R. Nahman bar Isaac, "In point of fact, he does agree to establish a verbal analogy based on the recurrent usage of the word "hired hand" in the several passages. But the case at hand is exceptional, since Scripture has said, 'One of his brothers shall redeem him' (Lev. 25:48) – but not another" [a slave sold to a Jew (Freedman)].*

I.9 A. *And who is the Tannaite authority who differs from Rabbi?*

B. *It is R. Yosé the Galilean and R. Aqiba, for it has been taught on Tannaite authority:*

C.   "And if he be not redeemed by these" (Lev. 25:54) –

D.   R. Yosé the Galilean says, "'By these' persons for emancipation, but by anybody else for further subjugation [until the Jubilee]. [If anyone other than the listed relatives redeems him, it is for continued slavery.]"

E.   R. Aqiba says, "'By these persons' for further subjugation [until the Jubilee], but by anybody else for emancipation" [Sifra CCLXIX:I.1 Parashat Behar Pereq 9].

F.   *What is the scriptural basis for the position of R. Yosé the Galilean?*

G.   Said Scripture, "And if he be not redeemed by these" – but by a stranger – "then he shall go out in the year of Jubilee."

H.   And R. Aqiba?

I.   "And if he be not redeemed by these" – by any but these – "then he shall go out in the year of Jubilee."

J.   And R. Yosé the Galilean?

K.   *Is the language, "by any but these"?*

L.   *Rather, they differ on the following verse:* "Or his uncle, or his uncle's son, may redeem him" (Lev. 25:59) – this speaks of redemption by a relative. "Or if he gets rich" (Lev. 25:39) – this speaks of redeeming oneself. "And he shall be redeemed" (Lev. 25:49) – this speaks of redemption by strangers.

M.   *R. Yosé the Galilean takes the view that the verse is read in the context of what precedes, which join redemption by relatives with redemption of oneself:* Just as when one redeems oneself, it is for freedom, so if relatives do so, it has the same result.

N.   *And R. Aqiba maintains that a verse of Scripture is read in the context of what follows, which joins the act of redemption by others to the redemption of oneself:* Just as redemption of himself leads to liberation, so redemption by outsiders yields freedom.

O.   *Well, then, why say "by these"?*

P.   *If the phrase, "by these," were not set forth, I might have supposed,* a verse of Scripture is read in the context of either what precedes or what follows, with the result that redemption of any kind yields freedom.

Q.   *If so, our problem comes home again. Rather, it must be that at issue between them is a matter of logic. R. Yosé the Galilean takes the view that it is logic that redemption carried out by others should yield slavery, for if you say it would yield liberation, people would refrain and not redeem him. But R. Aqiba finds more reasonable the view that redemption by relatives yields slavery. For if you say it yields freedom, then every day the man is going to go out and sell himself.*

I.10   A.   Said R. Hiyya bar Abba said R. Yohanan, "Well, then, that represents the view of R. Yosé the Galilean and R. Aqiba. But sages say, 'Redemption by any party at all yields liberation.'"

B.   *Who are "sages"?*

C.   *It is Rabbi, who utilizes "by these" for a different interpretation,* while the verse indeed is read in the context of either what precedes or what follows, with the result that redemption of any kind yields freedom.

D.   *Then how does Rabbi read the verse,* "Then he shall go out in the year of Jubilee"?

E. *He requires it in line with that which has been taught on Tannaite authority:*

F. "Then he shall go forth in the Jubilee Year": [16A] Scripture speaks of a gentile who is subject to your authority.

G. Well, maybe it speaks of a gentile who is not subject to your authority?

H. How can you say so, for, if so, what can be done to him [Freedman: how can he be forced to provide facilities for redemption]?

I. You must say, therefore, Scripture speaks of a gentile who is subject to your authority.

II.1 A. **[A Hebrew slave is acquired through money] or a writ:**

B. *How on the basis of Scripture do we know that fact?*

C. Said Ulla, "Said Scripture, 'If he take him another wife' (Ex. 21:10) [in addition to the Hebrew slave girl] – Scripture thus treats the Hebrew slave girl as another wife: Just as another wife would be acquired by a writ, so a Hebrew slave girl is acquired through a writ."

D. *Well, that proof would clearly pose no problem to him who says, "The writ of a Hebrew slave girl – the master writes it," but from the perspective of him who says, "The father writes it," what is to be said? For it has been stated:*

E. The writ of a Hebrew slave girl – who writes it?

F. R. Huna said, "The master writes it."

G. R. Hisda said, "The father writes it."

H. *So the proposed derivation from Scripture poses no problems, but from the perspective of R. Hisda, what is to be said?*

I. Said R. Aha bar Jacob, "Said Scripture, 'She shall not go forth as slave boys do' (Ex. 21:7) [if the master blinds them or knocks out their teeth] – but she may be purchased in the manner in which slave boys are purchased. *And what might that way be? A writ.*"

J. *Well, why not say:* But she may be purchased in the manner in which slave boys are purchased. *And what might that way be? Usucaption?*

K. Said Scripture, "And you shall make [gentile slaves] an inheritance for your children after you" (Lev. 25:46) – they are acquired by usucaption, and slaves of no other classification are acquired by usucaption.

L. *Well, why not say:* They are acquired by a writ, and slaves of no other classification are acquired by a writ?

M. But isn't it written, "She shall not go forth as slave boys do" (Lev. 21:7)?

N. Well, then, how come you prefer the one reading rather than the other?

O. *It stands reason that a writ is encompassed as a medium of acquiring title,* since a writ serves to divorce an Israelite woman [Freedman: just as it is effective in one instance, so in another].

P. *To the contrary, usucaption should have been encompassed as a medium of acquiring title,* since it serves to effect acquisition of the property of an heirless proselyte.

Q. *But we don't find such a medium of acquisition relevant when it comes to matters of marital relationship. Or, if you prefer, I shall say that the language, "if he takes another" serves to make that very point*

[Freedman: "she shall not go out" teaches that she may be acquired by deed, as is implied by the analogy of "another"].

R.   *Now how does R. Huna deal with the clause,* "She shall not go forth as slave boys do" (Ex. 21:7) [if the master blinds them or knocks out their teeth]?

S.   *He requires that verse to indicate that* she does not go forth at the loss of the major limbs, as does a slave boy.

T.   And R. Hisda?

U.   *If so, Scripture should have said,* "She shall not go forth like slave boys." *Why say,* "She shall not go forth as slave boys do" (Ex. 21:7) [if the master blinds them or knocks out their teeth]? *That yields two points.*

III.1 A.   **And he acquires himself through the passage of years:**

   B.   *For it is written,* "Six years he shall serve, and in the seventh he shall go free for nothing" (Ex. 21:2).

IV.1 A.   **By the Jubilee Year:**

   B.   *For it is written,* "He shall serve with you into the year of Jubilee" (Lev. 25:40).

V.1 A.   **And by deduction from the purchase price [redeeming himself at this outstanding value]:**

   B.   Said Hezekiah, "For said Scripture, 'Then shall he let her be redeemed' (Ex. 21:8) – this teaches that she makes a deduction from her redemption money and goes out free."

V.2 A.   *A Tannaite statement:* And he acquires title to himself through money or a cash equivalent or through a writ.

   B.   *Now with respect to money, there is no difficulty, for it is written in so many words,* "He shall give back the price of his redemption out of the money he was bought for" (Lev. 25:51). *And as to a cash equivalent too:* "He shall give back the price of his redemption," *the All-Merciful has said, extended the law covering cash to a cash equivalent. But as to this writ, how is it to be imagined? Should we say that the slave writes a bond for the redemption money? Then it is tantamount to money. But if it is a writ of manumission, then why a deed? Let the master say to the slave in the presence of two witnesses of a court: "Go"?*

   C.   Said Raba, "That is to say, a Hebrew slave is owned by his master as to his very body, so a master who remitted the deduction – the deduction is not remitted."

VI.1 A.   **The Hebrew slave girl has an advantage over him. For she acquires herself [in addition] through the appearance of tokens [of puberty].**

   B.   Said R. Simeon b. Laqish, "A Hebrew slave girl has acquired from the domain of her master possession of herself [as a free woman] upon the death of her father. That is the result of an argument a fortiori: If the appearance of puberty signs, which do not free her from her father's authority, free her from the authority of her master, then death, which does free her from her father's authority [the father's heirs have no claim on her], surely should free her from her master's authority [whose heirs should not inherit her]!"

   C.   *Objected R. Oshayya,* "The Hebrew slave girl has an advantage over him. For she acquires herself [in addition] through the

appearance of tokens [of puberty]. *But if what he has said were so,
then the list should include reference to her father's death as well!"*

D. The Tannaite authority has listed some items and left out others.

E. Well, then, what else has he left out, if he has left out this item?

F. He leaves out reference to her master's death.

G. Well, if that is all he has left out, then he has left out nothing, since that
would pertain also to a male slave as well, it is omitted anyhow.

H. But why not include it?

I. The Tannaite framer of the passage has encompassed what is subject to a
fixed limit [the six years, the proportionate repayment of the purchase
price, the Jubilee], but what is not subject to a fixed limit he does not
include in his Tannaite rule.

J. But lo, there is the matter of puberty signs, which are not subject to a fixed
limit, but the Tannaite framer of the passage has covered them too.

K. Said R. Safra, "They have no fixed limit above, but they are subject
to a fixed limit [16B] below. *For it has been taught on Tannaite
authority:* A boy aged nine who produced two puberty hairs – these
are classified as a mere mole; from the age of nine years to twelve
years and one day, they are classified as a mere mole. R. Yosé b. R.
Judah says, 'They are classified as a mark of puberty.' From
thirteen years and one day onward, all parties concur that they are
classified as a mark of puberty."

L. *Objected R. Sheshet,* "R. Simeon says, 'Four are given severance pay,
three in the case of males, three in the case of females. And you
cannot say there are four in the case of the male, because puberty
signs are not effective in the case of a male, and you cannot say
there is boring of the ear in the case of the female.' *Now if what R.
Simeon b. Laqish has said were valid* ['A Hebrew slave girl has
acquired from the domain of her master possession of herself as a
free woman upon the death of her father'], *then the death of the father
also should be included here. And should you say, the Tannaite authority
has listed some items and left out others, lo, he has said matters explicitly
in terms of four items! And if you should say, the Tannaite framer of the
passage has encompassed what is subject to a fixed limit [the six years, the
proportionate repayment of the purchase price, the Jubilee], but he has left
off what is not subject to a fixed limit, lo, there is the matter of puberty
signs, which are not subject to a fixed limit, and he has encompassed them
in the Tannaite statement. And should you say, here as a matter of fact he,
too, accords with R. Safra, well, then, there is the matter of the death of the
master, which is not subject to a fixed definition as to time, and yet the
Tannaite framer has included it. So what are the four items to which
reference is made?"*

M. [1] Years, [2] Jubilee, [3] Jubilee for the one whose ear was bored,
and [4] the Hebrew slave girl freed by puberty signs. *And that
stands to reason, since the concluding clause goes on to say,* and you
cannot say there are four in the case of the male, because puberty
signs are not effective in the case of a male, and you cannot say
there is boring of the ear in the case of the female. *But if it were the
case [that the master's death is covered], then you would have four items
for the woman. So that's decisive proof.*

N. Objected R. Amram, "And these are the ones that get severance pay: Slaves freed by the passage of six years of service, the Jubilee, the master's death, and the Hebrew slave girl freed by the advent of puberty signs. *And if the stated proposition were valid, the father's death also should be on the list. And should you say, the Tannaite authority has listed some items and left out others, lo, he has said,* and these are the ones [which is exclusionary, these – no others]. *And if you should say, the Tannaite framer of the passage has encompassed what is subject to a fixed limit [the six years, the proportionate repayment of the purchase price, the Jubilee], but he has left off what is not subject to a fixed limit, lo, there is the matter of puberty signs, which are not subject to a fixed limit, and he has encompassed them in the Tannaite statement. And should you say, here as a matter of fact he, too, accords with R. Safra, well, then, there is the matter of the death of the master. So isn't this a refutation of R. Simeon b. Laqish's position?"*

O. *Sure is.*

P. *But lo, R. Simeon b. Laqish has set forth an argument a fortiori!*

Q. *It's a flawed argument a fortiori, along these lines:* The distinguishing trait of puberty signs is that they mark a change in the body of the girl, but will you say the same of the death of the father, by which the body of the girl is left unaffected?

VI.2 A. *One Tannaite version states,* The severance pay [the gifts given at the end of six years] of a Hebrew slave boy belongs to himself and that of a Hebrew slave girl belongs to herself. *Another Tannaite version states,* The severance pay [the gifts given at the end of six years] of a Hebrew slave girl and things that she finds belong to her father, and her master has a claim only to a fee for loss of time [taken up by finding the lost object]. *Is it not the case that the one speaks of a girl who goes forth by reason of the advent of puberty signs [in which case the severance pay goes to the father], the other liberated at the death of the father?*

B. *Not at all, both speak of freedom by reason of puberty signs, but there is still no conflict, in the one case, the father is alive, in the other, not.*

C. *There is no problem with the statement,* The severance pay [the gifts given at the end of six years] of a Hebrew slave girl belongs to herself, *for it serves to exclude any assignment to her brothers, as has been taught on Tannaite authority:* "And you make them an inheritance for your children after you" (Lev. 25:46, speaking of Canaanite slaves) – them you leave to your sons, and your daughters you do not leave to your sons. This states that a man does not leave title to his daughter as an inheritance to his son. *But as to the statement,* The severance pay [the gifts given at the end of six years] of a Hebrew slave boy belongs to himself, *surely that is obvious! Who else should get it?*

D. *Said R. Joseph, "I see hear a molehill made into a mountain. [This is all redundant.]"*

E. Abbayye said, "This is what R. Sheshet said: 'Who is the authority behind this unattributed statement? It is Totai. For it has been taught on Tannaite authority: Totai says, "'You shall furnish him' (Deut. 15:14) – him, not his creditor'" [and that is the point of the statement at hand]."

VI.3   A.   *Reverting to the body of the foregoing:* And these are the ones that get severance pay: Slaves freed by the passage of six years of service, the Jubilee, the master's death, and the Hebrew slave girl freed by the advent of puberty signs. But one who runs away or who is freed by deduction from the purchase price don't get severance pay.

    B.   R. Meir says, "A runaway doesn't get severance pay, but he who is freed by deduction from the purchase price does get severance pay."

    C.   R. Simeon says, "Four are given severance pay, three in the case of males, three in the case of females. And you cannot say there are four in the case of the male, because puberty signs are not effective in the case of a male, and you cannot say there is boring of the ear in the case of the female."

    D.   *What is the source of these rulings?*

    E.   *It is in line with that which our rabbis have taught on Tannaite authority:*

    F.   Is it possible to suppose that a gift is provided only to those who go forth after six years of work? How on the basis of Scripture do we know that one who goes forth on the occasion of the jubilee, or on the death of the owner, or a female slave who goes forth on the appearance of puberty signs [also gets a liberal gift]?

    G.   Scripture says, "When you set him free," "When you do set him free."

    H.   Is it possible to suppose that a runaway and one who goes out through a deduction get it? Scripture states, "When you do set him free," meaning, to him whom you set free you give a gift, and you do not give a gift to him who is set free on his own account [Sifré Deut. CXIX:I.1].

    I.   R. Meir says, "A runaway doesn't get severance pay, since his liberation is not on your account, but he who is freed by deduction from the purchase price does get severance pay, for his liberation is on your account."

VI.4   A.   *A runaway?! But he has to serve out his term of service. For it has been taught on Tannaite authority:* How on the basis of Scripture do we know that a runaway has to complete his term of service? Scripture states, "Six years he shall serve" (Ex. 21:2).

    B.   [17A] Might one suppose that that is so even if he got sick?

    C.   Scripture says, "And in the Seventh Year he shall go out free."

    D.   *Said R. Sheshet, "Here with what situation do we deal? With a slave that ran away and the Jubilee Year came into force for him. What might you have thought? Since the Jubilee Year is what has sent him forth, we classify the case as one in which you are the one who has sent him forth, and we do not impose a judicial penalty on him but rather we give him severance pay? So we are informed that that is not the case."*

VI.5   A.   A master has said: "Might one suppose that that is so even if he got sick? Scripture says, 'And in the Seventh Year he shall go out free – even if he were sick all six years'":

    B.   *But has it not been taught on Tannaite authority:* If he was sick for three years and worked for three years, he doesn't have to make up the lost time. If he was sick all six years, he is obligated to make up the time?

    C.   Said R. Sheshet, "It is a case in which he could still do needlework."

D.   *Lo, there is an internal contradiction. You have said,* If he was sick for three years and worked for three years, he doesn't have to make up the lost time. Lo, if it were four, he would have to make up the time. *Then note the concluding clause:* If he was sick all six years, he is obligated to make up the time. Lo, if it were four, he would not have to make up the time!

E.   *This is the sense of the matter:* If he was sick for four years, he is treated as though he were sick all six, and he does have to make up the time.

VI.6 A.   *Our rabbis have taught on Tannaite authority:*

B.   How much do they give in severance pay?

C.   "Five selas worth of each kind mentioned in Scripture [Deut. 15:14: 'Out of your flock and out of your threshing floor and out of your winepress'], that is, fifteen in all," the words of R. Meir.

D.   R. Judah says, "Thirty, as in the thirty paid for a gentile slave" (Ex. 21:32).

E.   R. Simeon says, "Fifty, as in the fifty for Valuations" (Lev. 27:3).

VI.7 A.   The master has said, "'Five selas worth of each kind mentioned in Scripture [Deut. 15:14: "out of your flock and out of your threshing floor and out of your winepress"], that is, fifteen in all,' the words of R. Meir."

B.   [With reference to "that is, fifteen in all," we ask:] *Well, then, is it R. Meir's intention to inform us how to count?*

C.   *What he proposes to tell us is that he may not diminish the total, but if he gives less of one classification and more of another, we have no objection.*

D.   *What is the scriptural basis for R. Meir's conclusion?*

E.   *He forms a verbal analogy on the basis of the occurrence of the word "empty-handed" here and with reference to the firstborn [Deut. 15:13: "You shall not let him go empty-handed"; Ex. 34:20: "All the first born of your sons you shall redeem, none shall appear before me empty-handed"]. Just as in that case, five selas is the fixed sum, so here, too, five selas is the fixed sum.*

F.   *Might one say then, there must be five selas worth of each item?*

G.   *If the word "empty-handed" had been written at the end of the verse, it might be as you say; but since the word "empty-handed" is written at the outset, the word "empty-handed" pertains to "flock," "threshing floor," and "winepress," item by item.*

H.   *Why not derive the meaning of the word "empty-handed" from the verbal analogy deriving from the burnt-offering brought at one's appearance on the pilgrim festival [and much less than five selas is required there]?*

I.   Said Scripture, "As the Lord your God has blessed you you shall give to him" (Deut. 15:14).

VI.8 A.   R. Judah says, "Thirty, as in the thirty paid for a gentile slave" (Ex. 21:32):

B.   *What is the scriptural basis for the position of R. Judah?*

C.   *He establishes a verbal authority on the basis of the occurrence of the word "giving" here and in the case of the slave. Just as in that case, thirty selas is involved, so here, too, thirty selas is involved.*

D.   *Why not establish the verbal analogy with the common use of the word giving with reference to severance pay and Valuations, with the result:*

Just as in that case, fifty selas is involved, so here, too, fifty selas is involved.

E. *First of all, if you hold onto a great deal, you hold nothing, but if you hold onto a little, you will hold onto it, and, furthermore, you should establish the verbal analogy on the basis of passages that speak in particular of slaves.*

VI.9 A. R. Simeon says, "Fifty, as in the fifty for Valuations" (Lev. 27:3).

B. *What is the scriptural basis for the position of R. Simeon?*

C. *He establishes a verbal authority on the basis of the occurrence of the word "giving" here and in the case of Valuations.* Just as in that case, fifty selas is involved, so here, too, fifty selas is involved.

D. *Might one say it may be the least sum that will serve for a Valuation [which is five sheqels, Lev. 27:6]?*

E. "...As the Lord your God has blessed you" (Deut. 15:14).

F. *And why not establish a verbal authority on the basis of the occurrence of the word "giving" here and in the case of the slave.* Just as in that case, thirty selas is involved, so here, too, thirty selas is involved, *for, after all, first, if you hold onto a great deal, you hold nothing, but if you hold onto a little, you will hold onto it, and, furthermore, you should establish the verbal analogy on the basis of passages that speak in particular of slaves?*

G. *R. Simeon draws his verbal analogy on the basis of the recurrent word "poverty" [Lev. 25:39 for the slave, Lev. 27:8 for the Valuation].*

VI.10 A. *Well, now, from R. Meir's perspective, we can understand why Scripture states, "out of your flock and out of your threshing floor and out of your winepress" (Deut. 15:14). But from R. Judah's and R. Simeon's viewpoint, why are these items – flock and threshing floor and winepress – required?*

B. *These are required in line with that which has been taught on Tannaite authority:*

C. "...Of the flock, threshing floor, and vat":

D. Might one suppose that one furnishes a gift solely from the flock, threshing floor, and vat in particular? How on the basis of Scripture do I know to encompass every sort of thing?

E. Scripture says, "Furnish him... with whatever the Lord your God has blessed you, you shall give to him," which serves to encompass every sort of thing.

F. If so, why is it said, "...of the flock, threshing floor, and vat"?

G. "Just as the flock, threshing floor, and vat are characterized by being worthy of blessing, so is excluded a payment of cash, which is not the occasion for a blessing": The words of R. Simeon.

H. R. Eliezer b. Jacob says, "What is excluded are mules, which do not produce offspring" [Sifré Deut. CXIX:II.3].

VI.11 A. And R. Simeon?

B. *Mules themselves can increase in value.*

C. And R. Eliezer b. Jacob?

D. *One can do business with ready cash.*

VI.12 A. *And it was necessary for all of these items to be made articulate. For if the All-Merciful had made reference to the flock, I might have thought that the law applies to animate creatures but not to what grows from the soil. So the All-Merciful has written, "threshing floor." And if the Scripture had made reference only to threshing floor, I might have thought that the gift may be what grows from the soil but not animate creatures. So Scripture wrote, "flock."*

B. *What need do I have for a reference to the vat?*

C. [17B] *In the view of one master, it serves to exclude ready cash, of the other, mules.*

VI.13 A. *Our rabbis have taught on Tannaite authority:*

B. *"Furnishing him, you shall furnish him liberally" (Deut. 15:14):*

C. I know only that if the household of the master has been blessed on account of the slave, that one must give a present. How do I know that even if the household of the master was not blessed on account of the slave, a gift must be given?

D. Scripture says, "Furnishing him, you shall furnish him liberally" (Deut. 15:14) – under all circumstances.

E. R. Eleazar b. Azariah says, "If the household has been blessed for the sake of the slave, a present must be given, but if not, then the present need not be made" [Sifré Deut. CXIX:III.1].

F. *Then what is the sense of "Furnishing him"?*

G. In this case Scripture used language in an ordinary way.

VI.14 A. *Our rabbis have taught on Tannaite authority:*

B. The Hebrew slave boy serves the son but doesn't serve the daughter. The Hebrew slave girl serves neither the son nor the daughter. The slave whose ear has been bored and the slave that is sold to a gentile serves neither the son nor the daughter.

VI.15 A. The master has said, "The Hebrew slave boy serves the son but doesn't serve the daughter":

B. *What is the source for that ruling?*

C. *It is in line with that which has been taught on Tannaite authority:*

D. "[If a fellow Hebrew, man or woman, is sold to you,] he shall serve you six years":

E. ["You,"] and also your son. [The Hebrew slave remains the possession of the son, if the father dies within the six-year spell.]

F. Might one think that the same rule applies to the heir [other than the son]?

G. Scripture says, "Six years he shall serve you."

H. What is it that moved you to include the son but to exclude any other heir?

I. I include the son because the son takes the father's place in [Hammer:] designating [the Hebrew bondwoman as his wife], and in recovering for his family an ancestral field that has been alienated.

J. But I exclude any other heir, because any other heir does not take the father's place in [Hammer:] designating [the Hebrew bondwoman as his wife], and in recovering for his family an ancestral field that has been alienated [CXVIII:IV.1] [given in Sifré Deut.'s wording].

K. But to the contrary: I should encompass the brother, who takes the place of the deceased childless brother for a levirate marriage! Is there a levirate marriage except where there is no offspring? If there is an offspring, there is no levirate marriage.

    L.   *Then the operative consideration is that there is this refutation, but otherwise, would the brother be preferable?*

    M.   *Why not infer the opposite: Here where there is a son, there are two points in his favor, there, only one?*

    N.   *The consideration of the son in regard to the field of inheritance is also inferred from this same refutation, namely: Is there a levirate marriage except where there is no son?*

VI.16   A.   The Hebrew slave girl serves neither the son nor the daughter.

    B.   *What is the source for that ruling?*

    C.   Said R. Peda, "Said Scripture, 'And if he say to you, I will not go out from you...then you shall take an awl and thrust it through his ear...and also to your slave girl you shall do likewise' (Deut. 15:16-17). In this way Scripture has treated her as comparable to him whose ear is bored: Just as the latter serves neither the son nor the daughter, so the former serves neither the son nor the daughter."

    D.   *Well, is that the purpose that is served by this verse? It surely is required in line with that which have been taught on Tannaite authority:*

    E.   **"Do the same with your female slave":**

    F.   **That refers to providing a generous gift when she leaves.**

    G.   **What about piercing her ear to the door?**

    H.   **Scripture says, "But should he say to you...," the slave, not the slave girl [Sifré Deut. CXXI.V.3].**

    I.   How then do I deal with the clause, "and also to your female slave do the same"?

    J.   It is in regard to the severance pay.

    K.   *If so, Scripture should have said, "and also to your slave girl likewise," why add, "you shall do"? It makes both points.*

VI.17   A.   The slave whose ear has been bored and the slave that is sold to a gentile serves neither the son nor the daughter.

    B.   The slave whose ear has been bored: "And his master shall bore his ear through with an awl, and he shall serve him forever" (Ex. 21:6) – him but not his son or daughter.

    C.   And the slave that is sold to a gentile serves neither the son nor the daughter: *What is the source for that ruling?*

    D.   Said Hezekiah, "Said Scripture, 'And he shall reckon with his purchaser' (Lev. 25:50) – but not with his purchaser's heirs."

VI.18   A.   Said Raba, "By the law of the Torah, a gentile may inherit his father's estate, as it is said, 'And he shall reckon with his purchaser,' but not with his purchaser's heirs, *which proves that he has heirs. A proselyte's inheriting from a gentile is not based on the law of the Torah but only on the rulings of scribes. For we have learned in the Mishnah: A proselyte and a gentile who inherited [the property of] their father, [who was] a gentile – he [the proselyte brother] may say to him [the gentile brother], 'You take the idols and I [will take] the coins; you [take] the libation wine and I [will take] the produce.' And if [he said this] after it [the property] came into his possession, this [arrangement] is forbidden [M. Dem. 6:9A-E]. Now if it should enter your mind that it is by the law of the Torah that the proselyte inherits his gentile father's estate, then even if the goods have not yet come into his possession, when he takes the money or produce, he is taking something in exchange for an idol* [which would be forbidden, since the inheritance is automatically of a half-share of everything, whether he has taken possession or not (Freedman)]. *So it follows that it is by rabbinical law, a preventive measure enacted by rabbis to take account of the threat that he may return to his wickedness."*

B. *So, too, it has been taught on Tannaite authority:* Under what circumstances? In a case of inheritance. But in a case of mere partnership, such an arrangement is forbidden [and the proselyte may not derive benefit from an idol or libation wine].

C. [Raba continues,] "A gentile inherits the estate of a proselyte, or a proselyte inherits the estate of a proselyte, neither by the law of the Torah nor by the law of the scribes. *For it has been taught on Tannaite authority:* A man who borrows money from a proselyte whose children converted with him must not return the money to the children [who are not his heirs], and if he does, sages are not pleased with him."

D. *But it also has been taught on Tannaite authority,* and if he does, sages are pleased with him!

E. *No problem,* the former refers to a case in which his conception and birth were not in a circumstance of sanctification, **[18A]** the latter, a case in which his conception was not in conditions of sanctification, but his birth was in conditions of sanctification.

F. R. Hiyya bar Abin said R. Yohanan said, "A gentile inherits his father's estate by the law of the Torah, as it is written, 'Because I have given Mount Seir to Esau for an inheritance' (Deut. 2:5)."

G. *But perhaps the case of an Israelite apostate is exceptional?*

H. *Rather, proof derives from the following:* "Because I have given to the children of Lot Ar as an inheritance" (Deut. 2:9).

I. *And how come R. Hiyya bar Abin does not rule as does Raba?*

J. *Is it written,* "And he shall reckon with his purchaser but not his purchasers heirs"?

K. *And how come Raba does not rule as does R. Hiyya bar Abin?*

L. *Because the honor owing to Abraham makes the situation exceptional.*

VI.19 A. *Our rabbis have taught on Tannaite authority:*

B. "...A fellow Hebrew, man or woman":

C. Rules pertain to the Hebrew male that do not pertain to the Hebrew female,

D. and rules pertain to the Hebrew female that do not pertain to the Hebrew male:

E. Rules pertain to the Hebrew male: For a Hebrew male goes forth through the passage of years and at the Jubilee and through the deduction of the years yet to be served by the payment of money and through the death of the master, none of which applies to the Hebrew female slave.

F. A Hebrew female slave goes forth when she produces puberty signs, she may not be sold to third parties, she may be redeemed even against her wishes, none of which applies to the Hebrew male slave.

G. Lo, since it is the fact, therefore, that rules pertain to the Hebrew male that do not pertain to the Hebrew female, and rules pertain to the Hebrew female that do not pertain to the Hebrew male, it is necessary to make explicit both the Hebrew man and the Hebrew woman [Sifré Deut. CXVIII:III.2].

VI.20 A. The master has said: "Rules pertain to the Hebrew male that do not pertain to the Hebrew female":

B. *By way of contradiction:* The Hebrew slave girl has an advantage over him. For she acquires herself [in addition] through the appearance of tokens [of puberty]!

C. Said R. Sheshet, "For instance, if he designated her as his wife" [in which case these signs would not apply].

D. *If he designated her as his wife? Obviously! She would require a writ of divorce in that case!*

E. *What might you imagine? In her instance the rules pertaining to a Hebrew slave girl are not suspended? So we are informed that that is not the case.*

F. *If so, then how come she goes forth through the advent of the tokens of puberty?*

G. *This is the sense of the matter:* If he did not designate her for marriage, then she would go forth by the advent of the tokens of puberty as well.

VI.21 A. She may not be sold to third parties: *So does that imply that a slave boy may be sold to third parties? But has it not been taught on Tannaite authority:*

B. "If he have nothing, then he shall be sold for his theft" (Ex. 22:2) – but not for paying the double indemnity [that is owing by a thief, Ex. 22:3].

C. "If he have nothing, then he shall be sold for his theft" (Ex. 22:2) – but not for paying the indemnity brought on him by testimony of his that has been shown part of a conspiracy of perjury.

D. "If he have nothing, then he shall be sold for his theft" (Ex. 22:2) – once he has been sold one time, you are not again permitted to sell him. [There can be no sale to third parties.]

E. *Said Raba, "No problem,* the one speaks of a single act of theft, the other of multiple acts of theft."

F. *Said to him Abbayye, "'...For his theft...' bears the sense of any number of thefts."*

G. *Rather, said Abbayye, "No problem,* the one speaks of a single individual, the other of two or more."

VI.22 A. *Our rabbis have taught on Tannaite authority:*

B. If the theft was worth a thousand zuz and the thief is worth only five hundred, he is sold and resold. If his theft was worth five hundred zuz and he was worth a thousand, he is not sold at all.

C. R. Eliezer says, "If his theft was worth his sale price, he is sold, and if not, he is not sold."

VI.23 A. *Said Raba, "In this matter R. Eliezer got the better of rabbis, for what difference does it make whether what he stole is worth five hundred and he is worth a thousand, in which case he is not sold? It is because Scripture says, 'then he shall be sold,' meaning, all of him, not half. Well, here, too, Scripture says, 'he shall be sold for his theft,' but not for half of his theft."*

VI.24 A. She may be redeemed even against her wishes, none of which applies to the Hebrew male slave:

B.   *Raba considered interpreting, "...Against the wishes of the master."*

C.   *Said to him Abbayye, "What would be the case? That a bond is written for the master covering her value? But then why does he have to accept the bond? The guy's holding a pearl in his hand, shall we give him a sherd?"*

D.   *Rather, said Abbayye, "The meaning can only be, against the father's will, because of the embarrassment of the family."*

E.   *If so, then same should apply to the Hebrew slave – let the members of his family be forced to redeem him because of the embarrassment of his family.*

F.   *But he may just go and sell himself again, and here, too, the father will just go and sell her again!*

G.   *But hasn't it been taught as part of the Tannaite statement at hand:* **She may not be sold to third parties?** *[So that can't happen]. And who is the authority? It is R. Simeon, for it has been taught on Tannaite authority: A man may sell his daughter into marriage, then do the same for bondage, then do the same for marriage after bondage, but he may not sell her into bondage after she has been married. R. Simeon says, "Just as he may not sell his daughter into bondage after marriage, so a man may not sell his daughter into bondage after he has sold her into bondage."*

H.   *This involves the dispute of the following Tannaite statements, as has been taught on Tannaite authority:*

I.   *"To sell her unto a strange people he shall have no power, since he has dealt deceitfully with her" (Ex. 21:8):*

J.   *[18B] "Since he spread his cloth over her [reading the letters that yield 'dealt deceitfully' as though they bore the vowels to yield 'his cloth'], he may not again sell her," the words of R. Aqiba.*

K.   *R. Eliezer says, "'...since he has dealt deceitfully with her' (Ex. 21:8) – he may not again sell her."*

L.   What is at issue here?   R. Eliezer rejects the view that the reading supplied by the vowels dictates the sense of Scripture, R. Aqiba affirms the view that the reading supplied by the vowels dictates the sense of Scripture, R. Simeon both maintains and denies the view that the reading supplied by the vowels dictates the sense of Scripture.

VI.25   A.   *Rabbah bar Abbuha raised this question:* "Does designating the slave girl for marriage effect the status of a fully consummated marriage or does it bring about the status of betrothal? *The upshot is the familiar issue of* whether or not he inherits her estate, contracts uncleanness to bury her if he is a priest and she dies, and abrogates her vows. *What is the law?"*

B.   *Come and take note:* "Since he spread his cloth over her [reading the letters that yield 'dealt deceitfully' as though they bore the vowels to yield 'his cloth'], he may not again sell her" – *so what he can't do is sell her, but lo, he may designate her for marriage. Now, if you maintain that the designation effects a consummated marriage, then, once she has married, her father has no more power over here. So must it not follow that the designation effects only a betrothal?"*

C.   *Said R. Nahman bar Isaac,* "Here the issue concerns a betrothal in general [not only the slave girl's being designated by her master for marriage to himself or his son], and this is the sense of the statement: Since the father has handed her over to one who accepts liability to provide for 'her food, clothing, and conjugal rights' (Ex. 21:10) [and so betrothed her], he may not sell her again."

D. *Come and take note:* The father may not sell her to relatives [who because of consanguinity cannot designate her as a wife]. In the name of R. Eliezer, they have said, "He may sell her to relatives." But both sides concur that, if she is a widow, he may nonetheless sell her to a high priest, and, if she is a divorcée or a woman who has executed the rite of removing the shoe, he may sell her to an ordinary priest." *Now as to the widow, what sort of a situation confronts us? Shall we say that she accepted a betrothal in her own behalf? Then can she be classified as a widow?* [Freedman: Not at all, her actions are null, as would be the case of any other minor.] *So it must mean that her father has betrothed her. But can he have sold his daughter for bondage after she was married? And lo,* a man may not sell his daughter into bondage after she has been married, *and in that connection said R. Amram said R. Isaac, "Here we deal with a case of designation, within the theory of R. Yosé b. R. Judah, who has said, 'The original money for her was not given for betrothal.'"* [The money paid for the slave girl is not for betrothal; when the girl is designated for marriage, it is via the work she owes him, not the money he has given; therefore the father can resell her after the master's death, and it is not regarded as bondage after betrothal, since he didn't accept the original money as betrothal money (Freedman).] *Now, if you take the position that the designation has effected a consummated marriage, then, once she is married, her father has no longer got any authority over her?*

E. *Yes, but, what's the sense of "it effects a betrothal" or of "and both agree"? For lo, a man may not sell his daughter into bondage after she has been married! Rather, what do you have to say? An act of betrothal done by her is different from one done by her father?* [Freedman: When her father receives a token of betrothal on her behalf, he loses his authority to sell her later on; but when she gets it, for example, through her labor, meaning, renunciation of the work she owes, her father still has the right to sell her.] *But then, even if you maintain that designation effects a fully consummated marriage, her own arrangement of the fully consummated marriage still will differ in effect from her father's.*

F. *But how are the matters parallel? True enough, the act of betrothal that she undertakes will produce a different result from the act of betrothal that her father undertakes, but will there be any difference between an act of consummated marriage done by her and one done by her father?*

G. *[19A] And from the perspective of R. Nahman bar Isaac, who said even from the viewpoint of R. Yosé b. R. Judah, "The original money for her was not given for betrothal," how are you going to explain the matter?*

H. *It will be in accord with R. Eliezer, who has said, "It is for a condition of subjugation after another condition of subjugation that he cannot sell her, but he can sell her for subjugation after marriage."*

VI.26 A. *R. Simeon b. Laqish raised this question:* "What is the law on designating the slave girl for his minor son? 'His son' (Ex. 21:9) *is what Scripture has said, meaning, his son of any classification? Or perhaps, 'his son' comparable to him, meaning, just as he is an adult, so his son must be an adult?"*

B. *Said R. Zira, "Come and take note:* ['And the man who commits adultery with another man's wife, even he who commits adultery with his neighbor's wife, the adulterer and the adulteress shall surely be put to death' (Lev. 20:10)]. 'A man' – excluding a minor. '...Who commits adultery with another man's wife' – excluding the wife of a minor. Now if you say that he can designate [her for a minor], then you find the possibility of a matrimonial bond in the case of a minor."

C. *So what's the upshot? That he can't designate her for a minor son? Then why should Scripture exclude that possibility? Rather, on this basis, solve the problem to indicate that he can designate her for a minor [since that's the only way a minor male can be legally married]!*

D. *Said R. Ashi, "In this case we deal with a levir who is nine years and a day old who has sexual relations with his levirate bride, in which case, on the basis of the law of the Torah, she is a suitable wife for him. Now what might you have said? Since on the strength of the law of the Torah, she is a suitable wife for him, and his act of sexual relations is valid, then he who has sexual relations with her is liable on the count of doing so with a married woman? So we are informed to the contrary."*

E. *So what's the upshot of the matter?*

F. *Come and take note:* Said R. Yannai, "The designation of the slave girl for a wife can take place only with an adult male; the designation of a slave girl for a wife may take place only with full knowledge and consent of the man," [which solves Simeon b. Laqish's problem].

G. *Two items?*

H. *The sense of the matter is what is set forth, that is, how come* the designation of the slave girl for a wife can take place only with an adult male? *It is because* the designation of a slave girl for a wife may take place only with full knowledge and consent of the man.

I. *But why not say, what is the meaning of* full knowledge and consent? It must be full knowledge and consent of the woman!

J. *For Abbayye b. R. Abbahu repeated as a Tannaite statement: "'If she does not please her master, who has not espoused her'* – this teaches that he has to inform her that he plans to designate her." He is the one who repeated it, and he is the one who explained it: "It refers to the betrothal effected by designation, *and accords with the position of R. Yosé b. R. Judah,* who said, 'The original money for her was not given for betrothal.'"

K. *R. Nahman bar Isaac said, "You may even maintain that the money was given for betrothal, but this case is exception, for the All-Merciful has said, 'designate' [meaning, designate with full knowledge and consent]."*

VI.27 A. *What is the source for the position of R. Yosé b. R. Judah?*

B. *It is in line with that which has been taught on Tannaite authority:*

C. "If she does not please her master, who has espoused her to himself, then he shall let her be redeemed" – there must be enough time in the day to allow redeeming her. [Freedman: If her master wishes to designate her on the very last day of her servitude, her labor still owing must be worth at least a penny, so that she could be redeemed from the work; otherwise he cannot designate her.] On the strength of that fact, said R. Yosé b. R. Judah, "If there is enough time left on that last day for her to work for him to the value of a penny, she is betrothed, and if not, she is not betrothed." *Therefore he takes the position that* the original money for her was not given for betrothal.

D. *R. Nahman bar Isaac said, "You may even maintain that* the original money for her was given for betrothal, *but this case is different, for said the All-Merciful, 'then he shall let her be redeemed.'"*

VI.28 A. Said Raba said R. Nahman, "A man may say to his minor daughter, 'Go, accept your own token of betrothal.' *This is on the basis of what R. Yosé b. R. Judah has said. For didn't he say that* the original money for her was not given for betrothal? *But when the master leaves her only a penny's worth of her labor, that serves for a token of betrothal, so here, too, it is no different."*

VI.29 A. And said Raba said R. Nahman, "He who betroths a woman through transfer of a debt on which there is a pledge – she is betrothed. *This is on the basis of what R. Yosé b. R. Judah has said. For didn't he say that* the original money for her was not given for betrothal? [19B] *But this work represents a loan, for which she herself is pledge, when the master leaves her only a penny's worth of her labor, that serves for a token of betrothal, so here, too, it is no different."*

VI.30 A. *Our rabbis have taught on Tannaite authority:*

B. How is the religious duty of designating the slave girl carried out?

C. The master says to her in the presence of two valid witnesses, "Lo, you are consecrated to me," "Lo, you are betrothed to me,"

D. – even at the end of six years, even near sunset at the end of that time.

E. And he then deals with her in the custom of a matrimonial bond and he does not deal with her in the custom of servitude.

F. R. Yosé b. R. Judah says, "If there is enough time left on that last day for her to work for him to the value of a penny, she is betrothed, and if not, she is not betrothed."

G. This matter may be compared to one who says to a woman, "Be betrothed to me as from now, after thirty days have gone by," and someone else comes along and betroths her within the thirty days. So far as the law of designation is concerned, she is betrothed to the first party.

VI.31 A. *Now whose position is served by this parable? Should we say the parable pertains to the position of R. Yosé b. R. Judah? Lo,* if there is enough time left on that last day for her to work for him to the value of a penny, she is betrothed, and if not, she is not betrothed! [Freedman: This proves that the betrothal commences not at the beginning of her servitude but only at the last moment; here, too, the betrothal commences at the end of thirty days, and therefore if another man betroths her in the meantime, she is betrothed to the second.]

B. *Said R. Aha b. Raba, "The parable serves to illustrate the position of rabbis."*

C. *Yeah, so what else is new?*

D. *What might you otherwise have supposed? The master didn't say, "As from now"?* [Freedman: Therefore in the analogous case, even if he says, "You are betrothed after...," and another does so within the thirty days, she is betrothed to the first.] *So we are informed that that consideration does not come into play.*

VI.32 A. *It has further been taught on Tannaite authority:*

B. "He who sells his daughter and went and accepted betrothal for her with a second party has treated the master shabbily, and she is betrothed to the second party," the words of R. Yosé b. R. Judah.

C. But sages say, "If he wants to designate her as a wife for himself or for a daughter, he may do so."

D. This matter may be compared to one who says to a woman, "Be betrothed to me after thirty days have gone by," and someone else comes along and betroths her within the thirty days. So far as the law of designation is concerned, she is betrothed to the second party.

VI.33 A. *Now whose position is served by this parable? Should we say the parable serves the position of rabbis? Lo, rabbis maintain, "If he wants to designate her as a wife for himself or for a daughter, he may do so." Said R. Aha b. Raba, "The parable serves to illustrate the position of rabbis."*

B. *Yeah, so what else is new?*

C. *What might you otherwise have supposed? Lo, he did not say to her, "After thirty days"? So we are informed that that is not the operative consideration.* [Freedman: Her master did not say he would designate her after a certain period, therefore the second man's betrothal is valid; but if he said, "Be betrothed after...," I might have thought she is betrothed to him, and the second man's betrothal is null. Now, since Scripture empowered him to designate her through purchase, it is as though he had said he would subsequently designate here; the cases are analogous.]

VI.34 A. *It has further been taught on Tannaite authority:*

B. "He who sells his daughter and agreed that it was on condition that her master not designate her as a wife for himself or his son, the stipulation is valid," the words of R. Meir.

C. And sages say, "If he wanted to designate her as a wife for himself or his son, he may do so, since he has made a stipulation contrary to what is written in the Torah, and any stipulation in violation of what is written in the Torah is null."

VI.35 A. *Well, then, from R. Meir's perspective, is his stipulation valid? And hasn't it been taught on Tannaite authority:*

B. "He who says to a woman, 'Lo, you are betrothed to me on the stipulation that you have no claim upon me for provision of food, clothing, and sex' – lo, she is betrothed, and his stipulation is null," the words of R. Meir.

C. And R. Judah says, "With respect to property matters [food, clothing], his stipulation is valid."

D. *Said Hezekiah, "This case is exceptional, for Scripture has said, '...And if a man sell his daughter to be a slave girl' (Ex. 21:7) – there are occasions on which he may sell her only to be a slave girl alone."*

E. *And as to rabbis, how do they deal with this statement, "And if a man sell his daughter to be a slave girl" (Ex. 21:7)?*

F. *They require it in line with that which has been taught on Tannaite authority:*

G. "And if a man sell his daughter to be a slave girl" (Ex. 21:7) – this teaches that he may sell her to those who are invalid to marry her [for example, a mamzer].

H. But does that fact not follow merely from a logical argument, namely, if he can betroth her to unfit persons, can't he sell her to unfit persons?

I. But what makes it possible for him to betroth her to unfit persons is that a man may betroth his daughter when she is in the status of pubescent, but can he sell her to unfit persons, since he cannot sell his daughter when she is pubescent? Therefore it is required to prove that point from Scripture's explicit statement, "He may sell her to those who are invalid to marry her [for example, a mamzer]," which teaches that he may sell her to those who are invalid to marry her [for example, a mamzer].

J. R. Eliezer says, "If the purpose is to indicate that he may sell her to those who are invalid to marry her [for example, a mamzer], lo, that is already indicated by the verse, 'If she displease her master so that he has not espoused her,' meaning, she was displeasing in regard to an entirely valid matrimonial bond. So what is the point of the verse, 'And if a man sell his daughter to be a slave girl' (Ex. 21:7)? This teaches that he may sell her [20A] to relatives."

K. But does that fact not follow merely from a logical argument, namely, if he can betroth her to unfit persons, can't he sell her to relatives?

L. What makes it possible for him to sell her to unfit persons is that, if he wanted to designate her as a wife, he may do so, but can he sell her to relatives, who, if one of them wished to designate her as a wife, may not do so? So it was necessary for Scripture to say, "He may sell her to those who are invalid to marry her [for example, a mamzer]," which teaches that he may sell her to relatives.

M. And R. Meir?

N. *That he may sell her to unfit persons is a proposition he derives from the same verse used by R. Eliezer for that proposition, and as to selling her to relatives, he concurs with rabbis, who take the position that* he may not sell her to relatives.

VI.36 A. *One Tannaite statement holds:* He may not sell her to relatives, *and another Tannaite statement,* he may sell her to his father, but he may not sell her to his son, *and yet another Tannaite statement,* he may not sell her either to his father or to his son.

B. *Now there is no problem understanding the position,* he may not sell her either to his father or to his son, *since this would accord with rabbis. But in accord with what authority is the position,* he may sell her to his father, but he may not sell her to his son? *This is neither in accord with rabbis nor with R. Eliezer?*

C. *In point of fact is is in accord with rabbis, for rabbis concede in a case in which there is a possibility of designating her as a wife* [the father for the son, who may be her uncle; but the son cannot betroth her for himself nor designate her for his son (Freedman)].

VI.37 A. *Our rabbis have taught on Tannaite authority:*

B.   "If he came in by himself, he shall go out by himself" (Ex. 21:3) – he comes in with his body whole and undamaged, and he goes out in the same condition.

C.   R. Eliezer b. Jacob says, "He comes in single, he goes out single."

VI.38 A.   *What is the meaning of the phrase,* he comes in with his body whole and undamaged, and he goes out in the same condition?

B.   Said Raba, "This is to say that he is not freed through loss of his major limbs, as a gentile slave is."

C.   *Said to him Abbayye, "That proposition derives from the language, 'She shall not go out as slave boys do' (Ex. 21:7)."*

D.   *"If I had to rely on that verse, I should have thought that he has to pay him, at least, the value of his eye, at which point he also frees him. So we are informed that that is not the case."*

VI.39 A.   *What is the meaning of the phrase,* he comes in single, he goes out single?

B.   *Said R. Nahman bar Isaac, "This is the sense of the statement:* If a Hebrew slave does not have a wife and children, his master cannot give him a Canaanite slave girl. If he does have a wife and children, his master may give him a Canaanite slave girl."

VI.40 A.   *Our rabbis have taught on Tannaite authority:*

B.   If a person was sold as a slave for a maneh and increased in value so that he was then worth two hundred zuz, how do we know that they reckon with his value only at the rate of a maneh?

C.   As it is said, "He shall give back the price of his redemption out of the money that he was bought for" (Lev. 25:51).

D.   If he was sold for two hundred zuz and lost value and was priced at a maneh, how do we know that we reckon his worth only at a maneh?

E.   As it is said, "According to his years shall he give back the price of his redemption" (Lev. 25:52).

F.   Now I know thus far that that is the rule for a Hebrew slave who is sold to an idolator, and who is redeemed [by his family], for his hand is on the top. How do I know that the same rule applies to an Israelite [who owns a Hebrew slave who is up for redemption]?

G.   Scripture states, "A hired servant" in two different contexts [Lev. 25:40, a slave sold to an Israelite, and Lev. 25:50, a slave sold to an idolator], serving therefore to establish an analogy between them [and to invoke for the one the rules that govern the case of the other. The lenient ruling for the slave governs the redemption of the field].

VI.41 A.   Said Abbayye, "Lo, I am equivalent to Ben Azzai in the marketplaces of Tiberias [who challenged all comers to ask him hard questions]." [Abbayye is challenged, B, G-V, and replies at C-F, then W + Y-BB.]

B.   *One of the rabbis [taking up the challenge] said to Abbayye, "There is the possibility of interpreting [the verses referring to the redemption of the Hebrew slave] in a lenient way [favoring the redemption and making it easy] and in a strict way. Why do you choose to do so in a lenient way? I might propose that they should be interpreted in a strict way."*

C.   *"Let not the thought enter your mind, for the All-Merciful was lenient to [the Hebrew slave]. For it has been taught on Tannaite authority:*

D. "'Because he fares well with you' (Deut. 15:16). He must be with you [and at your status] in food and in drink, so that you may not eat a piece of fine bread while he eats a piece of coarse bread, you may not drink vintage wine while he drinks new wine, you may not sleep on a soft bed while he sleeps on the ground.

E. "On this basis it is said that he who buys a Hebrew slave is like one who buys a master for himself."

F. *"But might one not say, that pertains to what has to do with eating and drinking, so as not to distress him, but, so far as redemption, we should impose a strict rule on him, along the lines of what R. Yosé b. R. Hanina said?"*

G. For it has been taught on Tannaite authority: R. Yosé bar Hanina says, "Come and see how harsh is the dust kicked up in connection with the laws of the Seventh Year. [Even if one violates only derivative rules, the result is severe.] If a person trades in produce grown in the Seventh Year, in the end he will have to sell his movables, as it is said, 'In this year of Jubilee you shall return, every man to his possession' (Lev. 25:13), and it is said, 'If you sell anything to your neighbor or buy anything from your neighbor's hand' (Lev. 25:14). [The two verses are juxtaposed to indicate that if a person does the one, he will be punished by the other, so for selling or buying produce of the Seventh Year, he will have to sell his property, in this case], movables, something acquired from hand to hand.

H. "If the person does not perceive [what he has done], in the end he will have to sell his fields, as it is said, 'If your brother becomes poor and has to sell some of his possessions' (Lev. 25:25).

I. "It is not brought home to him, so in the end he will have to sell his house, as it is said, 'And if a man sells a dwelling house in a walled city' (Lev. 25:29)" [T. Arakhin 5:9].

J. *What is the difference between the two cases, in that, in the former instance, it says, "If the person does not perceive," and in the latter, "It is not brought home to him"?*

K. *The answer accords with what R. Huna said.*

L. *For R. Huna said, "Once a person has committed a transgression and done it again, it is permitted to him."*

M. "It is permitted to him" *do you say?*

N. *Rather, I should say,* "It is transformed for him so that it appears to be permitted."

O. [Continuing I:] "It is not brought home to him so in the end he will sell his daughter, as it is said, 'And if a man sells his daughter to be a maidservant' (Ex. 21:7).

P. *[Abbayye continues:] "And even though the matter of one's selling his daughter is not mentioned in the present context, it would be better for a person to sell his daughter and not to borrow on usurious rates, for in the case of his daughter, what is owing gradually diminishes [as she works off the debt], while in the present instance, the debt grows and grows.*

Q. "Then it is not brought home to him, so in the end he will sell himself into slavery, as it is said, 'And if your brother becomes poor with you and sells himself to you' (Lev. 25:39).

R. "And not to you, but to a proselyte, as it is said, 'To the proselyte' (Lev. 25:47).

S. "And not to a sincere proselyte but to a resident alien, as it is said, 'To a resident alien' (Lev. 25:47).

T. "'A proselyte's family' refers to an idolator.

U. "When Scripture further states, 'Or to the stock,' [20B] it refers to one who sells himself to become a servant of the idol itself.'

V. *He [Abbayye, A] replied, "But Scripture restores him [to his status]."*

W. *And a member of the household of R. Ishmael repeated as a Tannaite statement,* "Since this one has gone and sold himself to an idol, [one might have thought], 'Let us throw a stone after the fallen.' Scripture therefore has said, 'After he is sold, he shall be redeemed, one of his brothers shall redeem him' (Lev. 25:48)."

X. *Might I maintain that "He shall be redeemed" means that, while he is not to be permitted to be absorbed among the idolators, as to the matter of redeeming him, we should impose a strict ruling?*

Y. *Said R. Nahman bar Isaac,* "It is written, 'If there be yet increases in the years' (Lev. 25:51) and 'If there remain but little in the years' (Lev. 25:51). Now are there years that are prolonged and years that are shortened? [Surely not.] Rather, if his value should be increased, then 'out of the money that he was bought for' he shall be redeemed, and if his value diminishes, then 'in accord with the remaining years.'"

Z. *And might I propose a different reading, namely, where he has worked two years and four remain, let him pay the four years at the rate of* "the money that he was bought for," *and if he had worked for four years, with two remaining, then let him repay two years* "according to his year"?

AA. "If that were the case, then Scripture should have stated, 'If there be yet many years.' *Why does it say,* 'in years'? *It means, as stated above,* if his value should be increased, [then his redemption shall be paid] 'out of the money that he was bought for,' and if his value decreased, then the basis of the fee for redemption will be] 'according to his remaining years.'"

BB. *Said R. Joseph,* "R. Nahman has interpreted these verses as if from Sinai.

VI.42 A. *R. Huna bar Hinena asked R. Sheshet,* "A Hebrew slave sold to a gentile – may he be redeemed by halves, or may he not redeemed by halves? Do we derive the meaning of 'his redemption' by analogy to the rule governing redeeming a field of possession, namely, just as a field of possession cannot be redeemed by halves, so he cannot be redeemed by halves? *Or maybe we invoke that analogy to produce a lenient rule but not to produce a strict rule?*"

B. *He said to him,* "Didn't you say in that context, he is sold whole but not by halves? So here, too, he is redeemed whole but not by halves."

C. *Said Abbayye,* "If you find grounds for maintaining, he may redeemed by halves, *then you turn out to produce a ruling that is lenient for him and also strict for him. The leniency is, if the gentile bought him for a hundred zuz and then the slave paid back fifty, which is half his value, and then he went up in value and was worth at two hundred, if you say, he can be half-redeemed, he pays him another hundred and goes out a free man;*

but if you say, he cannot be half-redeemed, then he has to pay him a
hundred and fifty."

D. *But you said, "If he increased in value, he is redeemed out of the
money that he was bought for"!*

E. *That would refer to a case in which he was valuable when he was bought
then lost value then gained value.*

F. *"And also strict for him: If he bought him for two hundred, and the slave
paid back a hundred, which was half his value, and then went down in
value to a hundred – if you say he can be half-redeemed, he has to pay him
fifty and go free; but if you say he cannot be redeemed by halves, then the
hundred was merely a bailment held by the master, and the slave gives that
to him and goes free."*

VI.43 A. *R. Huna bar Hinena asked R. Sheshet,* "He who sells a house in a
walled city – is the house redeemed by halves or is it not redeemed
by halves? Do we derive the meaning of 'his redemption' by
analogy to the rule governing redeeming a field of possession,
namely, just as a field of possession cannot be redeemed by halves,
so he cannot be redeemed by halves? *Or maybe where Scripture made
that point explicit, it stands, but where not, it is not made explicit and so is
null?"*

B. He said to him, "We derive the answer from the exegesis of R.
Simeon that one may borrow and redeem and redeem by halves.
For it has been taught on Tannaite authority: '"And if a man shall
sanctify to the Lord part of the field of his possession, and if he that
sanctified the field will indeed redeem it" (Lev. 25:52) – this teaches
that one may borrow and redeem and redeem by halves. Said R.
Simeon, "What is the reason? The reason is that we find in the case
of one who sells a field of possession that he enjoys certain
advantages. That is, if the Jubilee Year comes and the field has not
been redeemed, it automatically reverts to the owner at the Jubilee
Year. On the other hand, for that very reason, he suffers the
disadvantages that he may not borrow to redeem the field and he
may not redeem the field in halves. But [the opposite
considerations apply to] one who sanctifies a field of possession.
For, on the one side, he suffers a disadvantage in that, if the Jubilee
Year comes and the field has not been redeemed, it automatically
goes forth to the ownership of the priests. So, by contrast, he is
given an advantage, in that he may borrow in order to redeem the
field and he may redeem it in halves."' *Lo, one who sells a house in a
walled city, too* – since he suffers the disadvantage in that, if a
complete year goes by and the field is not redeemed, it is
permanently alienated; but he gains the advantage that he can
borrow and redeem and redeem by halves."

C. *An objection was raised:* "And if he will indeed redeem it" – this
teaches that he can borrow and redeem and redeem by halves. For
one might have supposed that logic dictates the opposite
conclusion, namely: If one who sells a field of possession, who
enjoys the advantage that, if the Jubilee comes and the field has not
been redeemed, it reverts to its original owner in the Jubilee, but
who suffers the disadvantage that he may not borrow money and
redeem it and redeem it by halves, then he who sanctifies a field,

who suffers the disadvantage that, if the Jubilee comes and he has not redeemed the field, the field goes out to the ownership of the priests at the Jubilee, surely it follows that he does not enjoy the advantage such that he can borrow and redeem or redeem by halves [but has not got that right].

D.   But as for the one who sells a field of possession, the reason is that the advantage he enjoys is not so strong, for he cannot redeem the field forthwith. But will you say the same of one who sanctifies a field, who enjoys a considerable advantage, in that he can redeem the field forthwith?

E.   Let the one who sells a house in a walled city prove the contrary, since his advantage is sufficiently puissant that he can redeem the field forthwith – and yet he can't borrow and redeem the field or redeem the field by halves.

F.   *There is no problem,* [21A] *the one represents the view of rabbis, the other, R. Simeon.* [Freedman: Sheshet's answer having been deduced from Simeon's statement; Simeon holds that the reason of a scriptural law must be sought, and when found it may modify the rule and provide a basis for other laws; rabbis disagree; Simeon argues that the disabilities require compensating privileges and finds this embodied in the laws of sanctification of a field of possession, from which the same principles are applied to analogous cases; rabbis argue that when Scripture impairs one's privileges in one direction, they are weakened in all a fortiori, the sanctification of an inherited field being explicitly excepted by Scripture.]

G.   *One Tannaite statement holds:* He who sells a house in a walled city may borrow and redeem and redeem by halves. *One Tannaite statement holds:* He who sells a house in a walled city may not borrow and redeem and redeem by halves.

H.   *There is no problem, the latter represents the view of rabbis, the former, R. Simeon.*

VI.44   A.   *Said R. Aha b. Raba to R. Ashi, "One may raise the following objection:* What characterizes the one who sells a house in a walled city is that he is at a disadvantage since he can never redeem it again [after the first year has passed, Lev. 25:30]. But can you say the same of one who consecrates a field, who has the power to redeem the field at any time?"

B.   *Said R. Aha the Elder to R. Ashi, "Because one can say, let the argument run full circle, and invoke a proof on the basis of shared traits among otherwise different classes, namely:* One who sells a field of possession will prove the contrary, for his power is such that he can redeem the field at any time in the future, but he may not borrow and redeem the field or redeem the field by halves. But what characterizes the one who sells a field of possession is that he is at a disadvantage in regard to redeeming the field immediately. Then one who sells a house in the walled cities will prove the contrary – and so we go around in circle. The definitive trait of the one is not the same as the definitive trait of the other, but what characterizes them all in common is that they may be redeemed, one may not borrow and redeem, and one may redeem them all by halves. So I introduce the case of one who sanctifies a field, which may be redeemed, but one may now borrow and redeem or redeem by halves."

C. *Said Mar Zutra b. R. Mari to Rabina, "One may raise the following objection:* What they have in common is that the owner is at a disadvantage, in that they cannot be redeemed in the second year [after the act; one who sells an inherited field can redeem it only from the third year, the seller of a house in a walled city can't redeem it after the first year has passed]. But then will you say the same of one who sanctifies a field, who has the power, after all, to redeem the field in the second year?"

D. *Said to him Rabina, "It is because one may say:* A Hebrew slave sold to a gentile will prove the contrary, for he has the advantage of being redeemed in the second year, but he may not borrow and redeem himself, nor may he be redeemed by halves."

VI.45 A. *R. Huna bar Hinena asked this question of R. Sheshet:* "He who sells a house in a walled city – may the house by redeemed by relatives or may the house not be redeemed by relatives? Do we draw a verbal analogy based on the appearance of 'his redemption' both here and with regard to a field of possession: Just as a field of possession may not be redeemed by halves but may be redeemed by relatives, *so the same would apply here, namely,* this, too, may not be redeemed by halves but may be redeemed by relatives. *Or maybe, when the word 'redemption' is stated by Scripture, it serves to establish an analogy with respect to redeeming the field by halves, but it is not stated by Scripture with regard to redemption by relatives?"*

B. He said to him, "It may not be redeemed by relatives."

C. *An objection was raised:* "'And in all the land of your possession you shall effect a redemption for the land' (Lev. 25:24) – that serves to encompass houses and Hebrew slaves [relatives may redeem these]. *Doesn't this refer to houses in walled cities?"*

D. *No, it refers to houses in villages.*

E. *But Scripture explicitly refers to houses in villages:* "They shall be reckoned with the fields of the country" (Lev. 25:31).

F. *That verse serves to impose as an obligation the duty of redemption by relatives, in line with the position of R. Eliezer, for it has been stated on Tannaite authority:* "'If your brother become poor and sell some of his possessions, then shall his kinsman that is next to him come and shall redeem that which his brother has sold' (Lev. 25:25) – that is an option.

G. "You say it is an option, but maybe it's an obligation? Scripture states, 'And if a man has no kinsman' (Lev. 25:26). Now is it conceivable that there can be an Israelite who has no [kinsmen to serve as] redeemers? Rather, this refers to one who has such but whose kinsmen doesn't want to repurchase it, showing he has the option to do so," the words of R. Joshua.

H. R. Eliezer says, "'If your brother become poor and sell some of his possessions, then shall his kinsman that is next to him come and shall redeem that which his brother has sold' (Lev. 25:25) – that is an obligation.

I.   "You say it is an obligation, but maybe it's only an option? Scripture states, 'And in all... you shall effect a redemption' (Lev. 25:26) – thus Scripture establishes it as an obligation."

J.   *Rabbis said to R. Ashi, and some say, Rabina to R. Ashi, "There is no problem for one who maintains that it serves to encompass houses in walled cities, that is in line with Scripture's statement, 'in all.' But from the perspective of the one who says that it encompasses houses in villages, what is the meaning of 'in all'?"*

K.   *That's a problem.*

L.   *Objected Abbayye, "Why does the clause, 'he shall redeem him' occur three times [at Lev. 25:48, 49, 52]? It serves to encompass all instances of redemption, indicating that they are to be redeemed in this manner [encompassing redemption by relatives]. Doesn't this mean houses in walled cities and Hebrew slaves?"*

M.   No, it refers to houses in villages and fields of possession.

N.   *But Scripture explicitly covers the matter of houses in villages and fields of possession, in the language, "They shall be reckoned with the fields of the country"!*

O.   *It is in line with what R. Nahman bar Isaac said, "It is to indicate that the closer the relation, the greater his priority." Here, too, it is to indicate, the closer the relation, the greater his priority.* [Freedman: It is in the same order of priority as the kinsmen enumerated at Lev. 25:48, 49.]

VI.46 A.   *In what connection is this statement of R. Nahman bar Isaac made?*

B.   *It is in connection with the question that was raised: "A Hebrew slave sold to an Israelite – is he redeemed by relatives or is he not redeemed by relatives? With respect to Rabbi that is not an issue, for he has said, 'Through these he is redeemed, but not by the passage of six years.' Therefore he cannot be redeemed. Our question addresses the view of rabbis. What is the law? Do we establish a verbal analogy on the strength of the recurrent use of the word 'hired hand,' and we do not derive a lesson from the language, 'One of his brothers may redeem him' (Lev. 25:38)? Or perhaps, 'he may redeem him,' means, him but no one else [a Hebrew slave sold to an Israelite]?"*

C.   *Come and take note: "In all... you shall effect a redemption' – this encompasses houses and Hebrew slaves." Doesn't that mean houses in a walled city and Hebrew slaves sold to Israelites?*

D.   No, it means a Hebrew slave sold to a gentile.

E.   *A Hebrew slave sold to a gentile is covered by an explicit statement of Scripture, "or his uncle or his uncle's son may redeem him" (Lev. 25:49) –* [21B] *that serves to make doing so obligatory, and even from the perspective of R. Joshua.*

F.   *Come and take note: "Why does the clause, 'he shall redeem him' occur three times [at Lev. 25:48, 49, 52]? It serves to encompass all instances of redemption, indicating that they are to be redeemed in this manner [encompassing redemption by relatives]. Doesn't this mean houses in walled cities and Hebrew slaves sold to Israelites?"*

G.   No, it refers to houses in villages and fields of possession

H.   *But Scripture makes explicit reference to the matter of the field of possession: "They shall be reckoned with the fields of the country"!*

I. Said R. Nahman bar Isaac, "It is to indicate that the closer the relation, the greater his priority."

VII.1 A. **The slave whose ear is pierced is acquired through an act of piercing the ear (Ex. 21:5):**

B. *For it is written, "Then his master shall bore his ear through with an awl" (Ex. 21:6).*

VIII.1 A. **And he acquires himself by the Jubilee or by the death of the master:**

B. *For it is written, "and he shall serve him" but not his son or daughter;*

C. *"forever" – until the "forever" of the Jubilee.*

VIII.2 A. *Our rabbis have taught on Tannaite authority:*

B. "'An awl' (Deut. 15:17):

C. "I know only that an awl is sufficient for boring the ear of the slave. How do I know that sufficient also would be a prick, thorn, borer, or stylus?

D. "Scripture states, 'Then you shall take' (Deut. 15:12) – including everything that can be taken in hand," the words of R. Yosé b. R. Judah.

E. Rabbi says, "Since the verse says, 'an awl,' we draw the conclusion that the awl is made only of metal, and so anything that is used must be metal.

F. "Another matter: 'You shall take an awl' – teaches that a big awl is meant."

G. Said R. Eleazar, "R. Yudan b. Rabbi would expound as follows: 'When they pierce the ear, they do it only through the earlobe.'

H. "Sages say, 'A Hebrew slave of the priestly caste is not subjected to the boring of the ear, because that thereby blemishes him.'"

I. *Now if you hold that the boring is done only through the earlobe, then the Hebrew slave of the priestly caste cannot be blemished thereby, since we bore only through the top part of the ear [and in any event, boring makes a blemish, and Yosé takes the view that even a needle's point, a smaller hole than a lentil's size, constitutes maiming]!*

VIII.3 A. *What is at issue here?*

B. *Rabbi invokes the categories of an encompassing rule followed by an exclusionary particularization:*

C. "You shall take" is an encompassing rule; "an awl" is an exclusionary particularization; "through his ear into the door" reverts and gives an encompassing rule. So where you have an encompassing rule, an exclusionary particularization, and another encompassing rule, you cover under the encompassing rule only what bears the traits of the exclusionary particularization; just as the exclusionary particularization states explicitly that the object must be of metal, so must anything used for the purpose be of metal.

D. *R. Yosé b. R. Judah interprets the categories of scriptural evidences of inclusionary and exclusionary usages:*

E. "You shall take" is inclusionary; "an awl" is exclusionary; "through his ear into the door" reverts and forms an inclusionary statement. Where you have an inclusionary, an exclusionary, and an inclusionary statement, the upshot is to encompass all things.

F. *So what is excluded? An ointment.*

VIII.4 A. The master has said: "'You shall take an awl' – teaches that a big awl is meant":

B. *On what basis?*

C. It is in line with what Raba said, "'Therefore the children of Israel don't eat the sinew of the hip that is on the hollow of the thigh' (Gen. 32:33) – the right thigh; here, too, 'the awl,' means, the most special of awls."

VIII.5 A. Said R. Eleazar, "R. Yudan b. Rabbi would expound as follows: 'When they pierce the ear, they do it only through the earlobe.' Sages say, 'A Hebrew slave of the priestly caste is not subjected to the boring of the ear, because that thereby blemishes him'":

B. So let him be blemished!

C. Said Rabbah b. R. Shila, "Said Scripture, 'And he shall return to his own family' (Lev. 25:41) – to his family's presumptive rights."

VIII.6 A. *The question was raised:* "A Hebrew slave who is a priest – what is the law as to his master's giving him a Canaanite slave girl? *Is this an anomaly, in which case there is no distinguishing priests from Israelites? Or perhaps priests are exceptional, since* Scripture imposes additional religious duties on them?"

B. Rab said, "It is permitted."

C. And Samuel said, "It is forbidden."

D. *Said R. Nahman to R. Anan, "When you were at the household of Master Samuel, you wasted your time playing chess. Why didn't you reply to him on the basis of the following:* Sages say, 'A Hebrew slave of the priestly caste is not subjected to the boring of the ear, because that thereby blemishes him'? *Now if you say his master can't give him a gentile slave girl, the law that a Hebrew slave who is a priest is not bored simply follows that we require that the slave be able to say, 'I love my master, my wife, and my children' and that is not possible here [cf. Ex. 21:5]."*

E. *Nothing more is to be said.*

VIII.7 A. *The question was raised:* "A priest – what is the law as to his taking 'a woman of goodly form' (Deut. 21:11)? *Is this an anomaly, in which case there is no distinguishing priests from Israelites? Or perhaps priests are exceptional, since* Scripture imposes additional religious duties on them?"

B. Rab said, "It is permitted."

C. And Samuel said, "It is forbidden."

D. *With respect to the first act of sexual relations, all parties concur that it is permitted, for* the Torah spoke only with reference to the human desire to do evil. *There there is a disagreement, it concerns* a second and later act of sexual relations.

E. Rab said, "It is permitted."

F. And Samuel said, "It is forbidden."

G. Rab said, "It is permitted, *for once it is permitted, it remains so.*"

H. And Samuel said, "It is forbidden, *for she is a proselyte, and a proselyte is not a worthy bride of a priest.*"

I. There are those who say that with respect to the second act of sexual relations all parties concur that it is permitted, since she is a proselyte. Where there is a disagreement, it concerns the first act of sexual relations.

J.   Rab said, "It is permitted, *for* the Torah spoke only with reference to the human desire to do evil. "

K.   And Samuel said, "It is forbidden, *for in any case in which one can invoke the verse,* 'Then you shall bring her home to your house' (Deut. 21:12), *we also invoke the verse,* 'And see among the captives' (Deut. 21:11), *but in any case in which one cannot invoke the verse,* 'Then you shall bring her home to your house' (Deut. 21:12), *we also do not invoke the verse,* 'And see among the captives' (Deut. 21:11)."

VIII.8 A.   *Our rabbis have taught on Tannaite authority:*

B.   ["When you take the field against your enemies, and the Lord your God delivers them into your power, and you take some of them captive, and you see among the captives a beautiful woman and you desire her and would take her to wife, you shall bring her into your house, and she shall trim her hair, pare her nails, and discard her captive's garb. She shall spend a month's time in your house lamenting her father and mother. After that you may come to her and possess her, and she shall be your wife. Then, should you no longer want her, you must release her outright. You must not sell her for money; since you had your will of her, you must not enslave her" (Deut. 21:10-14)].

C.   "...And you see among the captives":

D.   At the time of the taking of the captives.

E.   "...A [beautiful] woman":

F.   Even a married woman [Sifré Deut. CCXI:II.1-2].

G.   "...A [beautiful] woman":

H.   The Torah spoke only with reference to the human desire to do evil. It is better for the Israelites to eat meat of [22A] beasts about to die but properly slaughtered than the meat of dying animals that have perished on their own without slaughter.

I.   "And you desire" – even if she's not pretty.

J.   "Her" – but not her and her girlfriend [the soldiers get one each].

K.   "...And would take her to wife": – you have marriage rights over her.

L.   "...For yourself to wife": – that is so that you may not say, "Lo, this one is for father," "Lo, this one is for my brother" [Sifré Deut. CCXI:II.4].

M.   "And you shall bring her home" – this teaches that he must not molest her in battle.

VIII.9 A.   *Our rabbis have taught on Tannaite authority:*

B.   "But should he say to you, 'I do not want to leave you,' [for he loves you and your household and is happy with you, you shall take an awl and put it through his ear into the door, and he shall become your slave in perpetuity. Do the same with your female slave. When you do set him free, do not feel aggrieved, for in the six years he has given you double the service of a hired man. Moreover, the Lord your God will bless you in all you do]" (Deut. 15:12-17):

C.   Is it possible to suppose that this may take place one time only?

D.   Scripture says, "But should he say to you, 'I do not want to leave you,'" – unless he says so and repeats it.

E.   If he said so during the six years, but did not say so at the end of the six years, lo, this one does not have his ear pierced to the doorpost,

F.   for it is said, "I do not want to leave you" – which applies only if said at the time of his leaving.

G.   If he said so at the end of the six years, but did not say so during the six years, lo, this one does not have his ear pierced to the doorpost,

H.   for it is said, "But if the slave should say to you...,"

I.   that is, while he is yet a slave [Sifré Deut. CXXI.I.1-3].

VIII.10 A.   The master has said, "If he made the statement at the beginning of the sixth year but not at the end, he is not bored, for it is said, 'I will not go out free'" [so he has to make the statement when he is about to leave].

B.   *But we derive the law from the passage*, "I will not go out free," *why not derive the rule from the fact that he has to say*, "I love my master, my wife, and my children," *which condition is not met? Furthermore*, "If he says it at the end of the sixth year but not at the beginning, he is not bored, for it is said, 'the slave...'": *Isn't he then a slave at the end of the sixth year?*

C.   Said Raba, "The meaning is, 'at the beginning of the last penny's worthy of service, and at the end of the same.'"

VIII.11 A.   *Our rabbis have taught on Tannaite authority:*

B.   If he has a wife and children, and his master does not have a wife and children, lo, this one does not have his ear pieced to the doorpost,

C.   as it is said, "...For he loves you and your household and is happy with you." [Sifré Deut. CXXI:II.2].

D.   If his master has a wife and children and he doesn't have a wife and children, he is not bored, as it is said, "I love my master, my wife, and my children."

E.   "...For he loves you and your household and is happy with you":

F.   Since it is said, "I have loved my master" (Ex. 21:5), do I not know that "he loves you and your household and is happy with you"?

G.   On this basis, you may rule:

H.   If the slave loved the master, but the master did not love the slave,

I.   if he was beloved of his master, but he did not love his master –

J.   lo, this one does not have his ear pieced to the doorpost, as it is said, "...For he loves you and your household and is happy with you" [Sifré Deut. CXXI:II.1].

K.   "...Is happy with you":

L.   Lo, if he was sick, or his master was, lo, this one does not have his ear pieced to the doorpost [Sifré Deut. CXXI:III].

VIII.12 A.   *R. Bibi bar Abbayye raised this question:* "If both of them are sick, what is the law? *We require* 'with thee' *which pertains, or maybe we require* 'because he is well with thee,' *which doesn't pertain?*"

B.   *The question stands.*

VIII.13 A.   *Our rabbis have taught on Tannaite authority:*

B.   "Because he fares well with you" (Deut. 15:16). He must be with you [and at your status] in food and in drink, so that you may not eat a piece of fine bread while he eats a piece of coarse bread, you may not drink vintage wine while he drinks new wine, you may not sleep on a soft bed while he sleeps on the ground.

C. On this basis it is said that he who buys a Hebrew slave is like one who buys a master for himself.

VIII.14 A. *Our rabbis have taught on Tannaite authority:*

B. "Then he shall go out from you, he and his children with him" (Lev. 25:41):

C. Said R. Simeon, "If he was sold, were his sons and daughters sold? But on the basis of this verse, it is the fact that his master is obligated for food for his children."

D. Along these same lines:

E. "If he is married, then his wife shall go out with him" (Ex. 21:3):

F. Said R. Simeon, "If he was sold, was his wife sold? But on the basis of this verse, it is the fact that his master is obligated for food for his wife."

VIII.15 A. *And both items were required. For had we been told the fact concerning his children, it is because they are not able to work for a living, but as to a wife, who can work for her living, I might say, "Well, then, let her earn her keep." If we had the rule only concerning the wife, that might be because it is inappropriate for her to go begging, but as for the children, who may appropriately go begging, I might have thought that that is not the case. So both items were necessary.*

VIII.16 A. *Our rabbis have taught on Tannaite authority:*

B. [22B] If Scripture had said, "...his ear on the door," I might have thought, then let a hole be bored against his ear through the door. So it is only the door, but not his ear.

C. "Not his ear"?! But it's written, "And his master shall bore his ear through with an awl" (Ex. 21:6).

D. Rather, I might have said, the ear is bored outside and then placed on the door, and a hole bored through the door opposite his ear. Therefore it is said, "and you shall thrust it through his ear into the door." How? The boring goes on until the door is reached.

VIII.17 A. "The door":

B. May I then infer that that is so whether it is removed from the hinges or not?

C. Scripture states, "unto the door or unto the doorpost" (Ex. 21:6): Just as the doorpost must be standing in place, so the door must be standing in place.

VIII.18 A. Rabban Yohanan ben Zakkai would expound this verse in the manner of a *homer* exegesis: "How come the ear was singled out of all the limbs of the body? Said the Holy One, blessed be He, 'The ear, which heard my voice at Mount Sinai at the moment that I said, "For to me the children of Israel are slaves, they are my slaves" (Lev. 25:55), nonetheless went and acquired a master for itself. So let it be pierced.'"

B. R. Simeon b. Rabbi would expound this verse of Scripture in the manner of a *homer* exegesis: "How come the door and doorpost were singled out from all other parts of the house? Said the Holy One, blessed be He, 'The door and the doorpost, which were witnesses in Egypt when I passed over the lintel and the doorposts and proclaimed, "For to me the children of Israel are slaves, they are my slaves" (Lev. 25:55), not servants of servants, now I brought them forth from slavery to freedom; yet this man has gone and acquired a master for himself – let him be bored before them in particular.'"

I.1+2-6+7-10 commence with attention to the scriptural source for the Mishnah's law. II.1, III.1, IV.1, V.1-2 all do the same, but with less elaboration. The sustained composite at VI.1-2, with a long thematic appendix at Nos. 3-5, 6+7-13, 14+15-18 utilizes a clause of our Mishnah paragraph to work out a problem of its own. None of this is put together as Mishnah commentary; the whole is worked out in its own terms and parachuted down for the reason given. Only at VI.19, with its talmud at Nos. 20-21, and a Tannaite complement at No. 22, with its talmud at No. 23, and further talmud at Nos. 24-25, do we regain the Mishnah sentence that is under discussion, there complemented with a Tannaite formulation. The string of theoretical problems that extend from the original tangential discussion of the designation of a slave girl for marriage continues at No. 26, with a footnote at Nos. 27+28-29. Nos. 30+31, 32+33, 34+35-36, 37+38-39, 40+41, continue with a Tannaite formulation this sizable appendix on a tangential topic. Nos. 42-43+44, 45 with its footnote at 46, pursue the same general theme, though the strung-out character of the composite is entirely self-evident. Clearly, a rather formidable talmud had taken shape around the themes expounded here, and the whole was then preserved as a huge appendix to a rather modest discussion of a Mishnah statement. VII.1, VIII.1 find a source for the Mishnah's rule. VIII.2, with a talmud at Nos. 3+4-5, with what is now the usual thematic appendix at Nos. 6-8, then addresses the topic of the Mishnah's rule. Another well composed set, Nos. 9-18, forms an appropriate, and sizable, sizable composite on the theme of our Mishnah topic. So the rather considerable corpus of materials for VIII.1 really does amplify the theme at hand in a relevant manner.

III. The Exegetical Programs of Yerushalmi and of the Bavli Compared

Our task is now to compare the two Talmuds' fundamental programs, not merely in form as we did for M. Qid. 1:1, but for the basic intellectual program that each Talmud brings to its reading of the Mishnah paragraph. For this purpose we pay more attention to the substance of passages than we did in the earlier reading, what I called the heuristic morphology. The result is astonishing. We could not differentiate the two Talmuds in their forms. But we shall now see that we can scarcely treat them as comparable in their heuristic morphology: they have nothing in common. The Bavli is different simply because it is different: it draws upon a corpus of compositions and composites that differs beginning to end from the Yerushalmi's corpus of compositions and composites. Where for our pericope the two Talmuds intersect, it is at the Mishnah's topic; but that topic does not then tell the Bavli's framers to study the issues that engaged the Yerushalmi's framers. They have their own interests, which they pursue in their own way: a different Talmud, produced in a different place by different people.

1:2 I How on the basis of Scripture do we know that the Hebrew male slave is acquired as the Mishnah maintains? Underlying issue: correct hermeneutics. Does what derive from one proposition serve to teach the rule for another?

1:2 II **Through money:** money, not goods.

1:2 III **Through a writ:** writ covering money that has been paid over, not writ of gift.

1:2 IV Language of sale, of betrothal.

1:2 V When in the seven year cycle does the Hebrew slave go forth, end of sixth or end of Seventh Year?

1:2 VI How do I know that one is freed in the Seventh Year even though he has not worked all six years?

1:2 VII A-D **And he acquires himself through the passage of years etc.:** he may be sold for less than six years but not for more than six vs. not.

1:2 VII E prooftext for Mishnah detail.

1:2 VII F prooftext for Mishnah detail.

1:2 VIII exegesis of prooftext.

1:2 IX Exegesis of prooftexts & harmonization thereof.

1:2 X **Hebrew slave girl has**

1:2 I.1 How do we know this + verse of Scripture.

1:2 I.2 Who is the Tannaite authority behind one of the foregoing demonstrations.

1:2 I.3 What is the scriptural foundation for the position of the initial Tannaite authority, who has said....

1:2 I.4 What is the scriptural foundation for the position of the initial Tannaite authority, who has said....

1:2 I.5 What is the scriptural foundation for the position of the initial Tannaite authority, who has said....

1:2 I.6 Who is the Tannaite authority who declines to establish....

1:2 I.7 Footnote to the foregoing.

1:2 I.8 Who is the Tannaite authority who declines to establish....

1:2 I.9 Who is the Tannaite authority who differs from....

1:2 I.10 That represents...but who are....

1:2 II.1 How on the basis of Scripture do we know that fact?

1:2 III.1 For it is written.

1:2 IV.1 For it is written.

1:2 V.1 For said Scripture.

1:2 V.2 Tannaite statement plus its talmud.

an advantage + prooftext, exegesis of prooftext.

1:2 XI Exegesis of prooftext.

1:2 XII Exegesis of prooftext.

1:2 XIII Exegesis of prooftext.

1:2 XIV Exegesis of prooftext.

1:2 XV Exegesis of prooftext.

1:2 XVI Exegesis of prooftext

1:2 XVII Simeon b. Laqish raised the question to Yohanan: A Hebrew slave girl should go forth if she marries someone other than the master, on an argument a fortiori.

1:2 XVIII Hebrew slave girl goes forth at death of master + prooftext.

1:2 XIX Prooftext and clarification.

1:2 XX As above.

1:2 XXI Piercing lobe of ear, where and exceptions to rule (priests).

1:2 XXII Exegesis of prooftext on ear piercing.

1:2 XXIII As above.

1:2 XXIV Why the door?

1:2 XXV right ear; other exegeses of operative verses.

1:2 VI.1 Said X + theoretical statement: Hebrew slave girl acquires possession of herself as a free woman on death of her father; theoretical inquiry into that proposition, which adds to the Mishnah an additional advantage of the Hebrew slave girl. Contrast to Y. 1:2 X.

1:2 VI.2 Contrast and harmonization of Tannaite statements.

1:2 VI.3 Footnote to the foregoing.

1:2 VI.4 Continuation of footnote.

1:2 VI.5 Citation and gloss of a sentence in the footnote.

1:2 VI.6 Tanniate statement on how much is severance pay.

1:2 VI.7 Gloss of sentence in foregoing.

1:2 VI.8-12 Continuation of gloss. Ending with "and it was necessary."

1:2 VI.13 Tannaite statement on Deut. 15:14.

1:2 VI.14 Tannaite statement.

1:2 VI.15 Talmud to foregoing, source of ruling.

1:2 VI.16 Hebrew slave girl doesn't serve son or daughter of master + Scriptural source for that proposition.

1:2 VI.17 Slave whose ear has been bored etc. serves neither son nor daughter + prooftexts.

1:2 VI.18 Said Raba, by the law of the Torah, a gentile may inherit his father's estate.

1:2 VI.19 Tannaite rule: rules pertain to Hebrew male slave

that don't pertain to female and vice versa.

1:2 VI.20-24 Talmud to foregoing.

1:2 VI.25 Rabbah bar Abbuha raised this question: Does designating the slave girl for marriage effect the status of a fully consummated marriage or does it bring about the status of betrothal?

1:2 VI.26 Simeon b. Laqish raised this question: What is the law on designating the slave girl for his minor son?

1:2 VI.27 Footnote to foregoing.

1:2 VI.28-29 Two theoretical proposals based on foregoing.

1:2 VI.30+31 Tannaite rule: How is duty of designating the slave girl as a bride carried out? + talmud.

1:2 VI.32+33 Tannaite rule: he who slaves his daughter and went and accepted ebrothal for her with another party has treated the first party poorly and she is betrothed to the second. + gloss as to authority behind a detail of the foregoing.

1:2 VI.34-5 Tannaite rule contiguous to foregoing + secondary talmud.

1:2 V.36 Contrast and harmonization of two Tannaite statements on the topic now under discussion, sale of slave girl.

1:2 VI.37-39 Tannaite rule + talmuds, interpreting Ex. 21:3.

1:2 VI.40 Tannaite rule: If a

person was sold as a slave for a maneh and went up [in value, how do we know he is valued only at a maneh?

1:2 VI.41 Various possibilities of interpreting verses on redemption of Hebrew slave – topic contiguous to foregoing, but treated autonomously.

1:2 VI.42 Huna asked Sheshet: A Hebrew slave sold to a gentile – may he be redeemed by halves?

1:2 VI.43-44 Huna asked Sheshet: He who sells a house in a walled city – is the house redeemed by halves or not?

1:2 VI.45+46 Huna asked Sheshet: He who sells a house in a walled city – may the house be redeemed by relatives? + footnote.

1:2 VII.1 **Slave whose ear is pierced +** for it is written.

1:2 VIII.1 **And he acquires +** for it is written.

1:2 VIII.2+3, 4, 5 Tannaite statement on awl (Deut. 15:17) + Yosé b. R. Judah + what is at issue here? That is, generalization on conflict of exegetical principles; footnote glosses.

1:2 VIII.6 Question was raised: Hebrew slave who is a priest – what is law on master's giving him a Canaanite slave girl? Is this an anaomaly or are priests excepted from the law + Rab, Samuel dispute.

1:2 VIII.7 Question was raised: priest – what is the law as to his taking a woman of goodly form, Deut. 21:11 – formulated as before.

1:2 VIII.8 Tannaite statement on woman of goodly form, tacked on to foregoing.

1:2 VIII.9-11+12 Sif. Deut. on Deut. 15:12-17 + secondary theoretical question.

1:2 VIII.13 Tannaite statement on Deut. 15:15.

1:2 VIII.14+15 Complementary Tannaite statement on Lev. 25:41 + "both items necessary."

1:2:VIII.16 Tannaite statement on verses of Scripture on boring the ear to the door.

1:2 VIII.17 Continuation of foregoing.

1-2 VIII.18 Free-standing exegesis: how was ear singled out of all the limbs of the body.

If I had to characterize the Yerushalmi's interest in the Mishnah paragraph before us, I should say that it is principally in the prooftexts that undergird the Mishnah's rule – that, and the secondary exegesis of those same texts. True, at some points there is analysis of the Mishnah rule and its language, secondary problems being generated in those connections as well. But if we eliminated the treatment of relevant Scripture, we should have no sustained commentary to the Mishnah paragraph, and, in sheer volume, very little talmud. That is what is to be said about the Yerushalmi and its program: remarkably coherent, but (compared to what was to come) disappointingly thin. If we had never seen the Bavli, we should not know what a real talmud is.

That simple observation begins from the opening composite, which is really a composition. For Bavli 1:2 I:1-10 form a completely unitary composition, which to be sure draws upon available materials, as indicated, and which systematically investigates the theories as to Scripture exegesis and Mishnah exegesis of diverse authorities. While in general covering the same Mishnah paragraph, the composition is simply incomparable to the Yerushalmi's treatment. Its topical program is dictated by the Mishnah and what is clearly the exegetical sine qua non of Mishnah reading: the scriptural basis. From that point on, such considerations as governing principles of hermeneutics, recourse to various authorities who take various positions on said principles, consistency of position of said authorities, balanced proofs afforded to all cited authorities, indications of how each authority deals with the proofs of the other – these enormous issues are sorted out and worked out in such a way as to create the massive and sustained discourse before us. I find I.1-10 simply an amazing formulation, on account of its coherence and thoroughness. The Bavli compares to the Yerushalmi only in its superficial, definitive traits: same base text, the Mishnah, and some of the same generative questions. But from that point forward, the Bavli simply goes its own way. Its material is different from that of the Yerushalmi because it is different. From that point on, our survey repeatedly produces a single result: the Bavli is different because all of its materials are different. It intersects with the Yerushalmi at the Mishnah and at a few points in which prior Tannaite formulations accessible to the authors of compositions or framers of composites in both documents are utilized; but wherever the same sayings occur, with the exception of the provision of prooftexts for Mishnah rules, the discussion of the Bavli goes its own way.

To drive this point home, let us now repeat the contrast between Yerushalmi and Bavli where both treat the same problem. Here we shall see a good illustration of what it means to say, the Bavli is different because it's different.

Yerushalmi 1:2	Bavli 1:2
[X.A.] [The Hebrew slave girl has an advantage over him. For she acquires herself in addition through the appearance of tokens of puberty (M. 1:1C-D):] "She shall go out for nothing, without payment of money" (Ex. 21:11).	VI.1 A. The Hebrew slave girl has an advantage over him. For she acquires herself [in addition] through the appearance of tokens [of puberty].
[B] "For nothing" – refers to the time of pubescence.	B. Said R. Simeon b. Laqish, "A Hebrew slave girl has acquired from the domain of her master possession of herself [as a free woman] upon the death of her father. That is the result of an argument a fortiori: If the appearance of puberty signs, which do not free her from her father's authority, free her from the authority of her
[C] "Without payment of money" – refers to the tokens of maturity.	
[D] And why should the law not refer to only one of them?	
[E] If it had referred to only one of them, I might have main-	

tained, "If she goes forth through the appearance of the signs of puberty, all the more so will she go forth at the time of pubescence."

[F] If so, I would have maintained, the time of pubescence is the only time at which she goes forth, and not the time at which she produces signs of puberty.

[G] Now logic would suggest as follows: Since she leaves the domain of the father and leaves the domain of the master, just as from the domain of the father she goes forth only when she has produced the signs of puberty, also from the domain of the master she should go forth only when she produces signs of puberty.

[H] On that account it was necessary to state:

[I] "For nothing" – refers to the time of pubescence.

[J] "Without a payment of money" – refers to the signs of puberty.

[K] And perhaps matters are just the opposite [so that "she will go forth for nothing" refers to the period of twelve and a bit more in which she is a girl, and "without a payment" refers to the time at which she has reached puberty]?

[L] R. Tanhuma in the

master, then death, which does free her from her father's authority [the father's heirs have no claim on her], surely should free her from her master's authority [whose heirs should not inherit her]!"

C. *Objected R. Oshayya, "The Hebrew slave girl has an advantage over him. For she acquires herself [in addition] through the appearance of tokens [of puberty].* But if what he has said were so, then the list should include reference to her father's death as well!"

D. *The Tannaite authority has listed some items and left out others.*

E. *Well, then, what else has he left out, if he has left out this item?*

F. *He leaves out reference to her master's death.*

G. *Well, if that is all he has left out, then he has left out nothing, since that would pertain also to a male slave as well, it is omitted anyhow.*

H. *But why not include it?*

I. *The Tannaite framer of the passage has encompassed what is subject to a fixed limit [the six years, the proportionate repayment of the purchase price, the Jubilee], but what is not subject to a fixed limit he does not include in his Tannaite rule.*

J. *But lo, there is the matter of puberty signs, which are not subject to* name of R. Huna: "'Without money' – In any context in which the father receives money, the master does not receive money."

a fixed limit, but the Tannaite framer of the passage has covered them, too.

K. Said R. Safra, "They have no fixed limit above, but they are subject to a fixed limit [16B] below. *For it has been taught on Tannaite authority:* A boy aged nine who produced two puberty hairs – these are classified as a mere mole; from the age of nine years to twelve years and one day, they are classified as a mere mole. R. Yosé b. R. Judah says, 'They are classified as a mark of puberty.' From thirteen years and one day onward, all parties concur that they are classified as a mark of puberty."

L. *Objected R. Sheshet,* "R. Simeon says, 'Four are given severance pay, three in the case of males, three in the case of females. And you cannot say there are four in the case of the male, because puberty signs are not effective in the case of a male, and you cannot say there is boring of the ear in the case of the female.' *Now if what R. Simeon b. Laqish has said were valid* ['A Hebrew slave girl has acquired from the domain of her master possession of herself as a free woman upon the death of her father'], *then the death of the father also should be included here. And should you say, the Tannaite authority has listed some items and left out others, lo, he has said matters explicitly in terms of four items! And if you should say, the Tannaite framer of the passage has encompassed what is subject to a fixed limit [the six years, the proportionate repayment of the purchase price, the Jubilee], but he has left off what is not subject to a fixed limit, lo, there is the matter of puberty signs, which are not subject to a fixed limit, and he has encompassed them in the Tannaite statement. And should you say, here as a matter of fact he, too, accords with R. Safra, well, then, there is the matter of the death of the master, which is not subject to a fixed definition as to time, and yet the Tannaite framer has included it. So what are the four items to which reference is made?"*

M. [1] Years, [2] Jubilee, [3] Jubilee for the one whose ear was bored, and [4] the Hebrew slave girl freed by puberty signs. *And that stands to reason, since the concluding clause goes on to say,* and you cannot say there are four in the case of the male, because puberty signs are not effective in the case of a male, and you cannot say there is boring of the ear in the case of the female. *But if it were the case [that the master's death is covered], then you would have four items for the woman. So that's decisive proof.*

N. *Objected R. Amram,* "And these are the ones that get severance pay: Slaves freed by the passage of six years of service, the Jubilee, the master's death, and the Hebrew slave girl freed by the advent of puberty signs. *And if the stated proposition were valid, the father's death also should be on the list. And should you say, the Tannaite authority has listed some items and left out others,* lo, he has said, a n d these are the ones [which is exclusionary, these – no others]. *And if you should say, the Tannaite framer of the passage has encompassed what is subject to a fixed limit [the six years, the proportionate repayment of the purchase price, the Jubilee], but he has left off what is not subject to a fixed limit, lo, there is the matter of puberty signs, which are not subject to a fixed limit, and he has encompassed them in the Tannaite statement. And should you say, here as a matter of fact he, too, accords*

> with R. Safra, well, then,
> there is the matter of the
> death of the master. So
> isn't this a refutation of
> R. Simeon b. Laqish's
> position?"
>
> O. Sure is.
> P. But lo, R. Simeon b.
> Laqish has set forth an
> argument a fortiori!
> Q. It's a flawed argument a
> fortiori, along these
> lines: The distinguish-
> ing trait of puberty
> signs is that they mark
> a change in the body
> of the girl, but will
> you say the same of
> the death of the father,
> by which the body of
> the girl is left unaf-
> fected?

When I say, the Bavli is different because it is different, I refer to
phenomena typified by the foregoing. And it seems to me there is no
more accurate or elegant way of stating the difference between the two
Talmuds: they have in common most matters of form, but no matters of
intellectual substance.

Once the Yerushalmi cites our Mishnah sentence, it proceeds to its
prooftext, Ex. 21:11; spells out its implications, asks whether a prooftext
is required when the logic of hierarchical classification yielding an
argument a foretiori can have produced the same result [G], and shows
that that is not the case. So much for the problem at hand.

The Bavli's interest is in a theoretical problem, Simeon b. Laqish's,
which utilizes the Mishnah's fact for its own purposes. We note, of
course, that this Simeon belongs to the Land of Israel; the Bavli's framers
drew as they liked on sayings formulated in the other country's schools.
But what they did with those sayings accorded with their own modes of
thought about their own interests. These sayings are treated as a
sentence of the Mishnah is treated, that is to say, for whatever purpose
the Bavli's framers had in mind in general. For it is the simple fact that
the Mishnah sentence shared by both Talmuds in no way permits us to
predict the shape and program of the Bavli's composition's authors.

The fact of the Mishnah is inert, not an active ingredient in a
dialectical inquiry. This produces a sustained reading of the Mishnah
text as evidence for or against the proposition at hand, C-F. The
Mishnah's rule now is a passive ingredient, rather than the active and

determinative force behind the talmud composition at hand. It is hardly necessary to spell out the enormous differences from that point to the end. I simply repeat what I said at the beginning of this book: the Talmuds differ because they differ. The Bavli's voice is unique because, at its foundations, the Bavli is different from the Yerusahlmi. The two Talmuds differ because they differ, not in detail, but in origin. The Bavli's statement belongs to its compositions' authors and its composites' compilers and its penultimate and ultimate authorship – to them, to them alone, to them uniquely. The Bavli differs from the Yerushalmi because the framers of the Bavli drew upon their distinctive, local sources for compositions and composites, and the framers of the Yerushalmi drew upon their equivalently distinctive, local sources for compositions and composites.

Here is a fine instance of the facts of the matter: the two Talmuds treat the same Mishnah but only very rarely intersect other than at a given Mishnah paragraph. The reason is that the penultimate and ultimate framers of the two Talmuds utilized what they had in hand, and each document's framers drew upon a corpus of materials utterly different from that available to the other. Since the Bavli's framers produced their document, it is generally agreed, hundreds of years after the Yerushalmi's finished their work, we may conclude that, if they had access to the Yerushalmi's compositions and composites, they chose not to use them but preferred to make their own statement in their own way and for their own purpose. Where sayings are shared by the two Talmuds, they are episodic, ad hoc, singular; rarely do entire compositions make their way from the former to the latter document, and whole composites, never. Referring in common with the authors of the Yerushalmi's composites and even compositions to the same Scripture, Mishnah, Tosefta, Sifra, and the two Sifrés, the Bavli's authorship drew upon composites and compositions that differed, beginning to end and top to bottom, from the Yerushalmi's counterparts.

The question remains: Do the two Talmuds not share – at least – a single exegetical heritage? To answer that question, let us review what each has to say about Deut. 15:12ff.

[I.A] It is written: "If your brother, a Hebrew man, or a Hebrew woman, is sold to you, he shall serve you six years, and in the Seventh Year you shall let him go free from you" (Deut. 15:12).

I.1 A. A Hebrew slave is acquired through money and a writ:
B. *How do we know this?*
C. Said Scripture, "He shall give back the price of his redemption out of the money that he was bought

[B] Scripture treats in the same context a Hebrew man and woman.

[C] Just as the Hebrew woman is acquired through money or a writ, so a Hebrew man is acquired through money or a writ....

[I] But as to R. Ishmael, who does not concur that what derives from one proposition may then serve to teach the rule for another, [how do we prove that a Hebrew manservant is acquired through a writ]?

[J] The following Tannaite teaching is available: R. Ishmael teaches in regard to this statement, "Freedom has not been given to her" (Lev. 19:20), "You shall let him go free from you" (Deut. 15:12). [The latter is interpreted in the light of the former.]

[K] Now in all [other] contexts R. Ishmael does not concur that what derives from one proposition may then serve to teach the rule for another, and yet here [at J] he does indeed hold that view.

[L] It [that is, the teaching at J] was taught in the name of a sage. "How does R. Ishmael prove [that a writ is applicable to the Hebrew manservant]?

[M] "'Sending forth' is stated at Deut. 15:12,

for" (Lev. 25:51).

D. So we have found the source of the rule governing a Hebrew slave sold to a gentile, since the only way of acquiring him is by money. How do we know that the same rule applies to one sold to an Israelite?

E. Said Scripture, "Then he shall let her be redeemed" (Ex. 21:8) – this teaches that she deducts part of her redemption money and goes free.

F. So we have found the rule governing the Hebrew slave girl, since she is betrothed with a money payment, she is acquired with a money payment. How do we know of it a Hebrew slave boy?

G. Said Scripture, "If your brother, a Hebrew man or a Hebrew woman, is sold to you and serves you six years" (Deut. 15:12) – Scripture treats as comparable the Hebrew slave boy and the Hebrew slave girl.

H. So we have found the rule governing those sold by a court, since they are sold willy-nilly. If they have sold themselves, how do we know that that is the case?

I. We derive the parallel between the one and the other because of the use of the word and also 'sending' is stated at Deut. 24:1.

[N] "Just as 'sending forth' stated in regard to a divorce means that it is done through a writ, so the 'sending forth' stated in regard to the slave means that it is done through a writ."

[O] [But the issue is not the same.] The two cases are dissimilar. For in the case of the divorce of the woman, the writ serves to give her full possession of herself. But here the writ serves to give possession of the Hebrew slave to others. [The proposition is to prove that a Hebrew man is acquired through a writ, and that has not been proved.]

[P] Said R. Mattenaiah, "The use of the language of sale will prove the case. ['If your brother... is sold to you' (Deut. 15:12); 'If your brother be– comes poor and sells part of his property' (Lev. 25:25).] Just as 'sale' stated in the latter case involves use of a writ, so the language of 'sale' used here involves use of a writ."

"hired hand" [Lev. 25:39: One who sells himself; one sold by a court, Deut. 15:12ff.; the same word appears in both cases, so the same method of purchase applies to both (Freedman)].

J. *Well, that poses no problems to him who accepts the consequences drawn from the verbal analogy established by the use of the word "hired hand," but for him who denies that analogy and its consequences, what is to be said?*

K. Said Scripture, "And if a stranger or sojourner with you gets rich" (Lev. 25:47) – thus adding to the discussion that is just prior, teaching rules governing what is prior on the basis of rules that govern in what is to follow. [The "and" links Lev. 25:47-55, one who sells himself to a non-Jew, to Lev. 25:39-46, one who sells himself to a Jew; just as the purchase in the one case is carried out by money, so is that of the other (Freedman)].

I.2   A. *And who is the Tannaite authority who declines to establish a verbal analogy based on the recurrent usage of the word "hired hand" in the several passages?*

B. *It is the Tannaite authority behind the following, which has been taught on Tannaite authority:*

C. He who sells himself may be sold for six years or more than six years; if it is by a court, he may be sold for six years only.

D. He who sells himself may not have his ear bored as a mark of perpetual slavery; if sold by the court, he may have his ear bored.

E. He who sells himself has no severance pay coming to him; if he is sold by a court, he has severance pay coming to him.

F. To him who sells himself, the master cannot assign a Canaanite slave girl; if sold by a court, the master can give him a Canaanite slave girl.

G. R. Eleazar says, "Neither one nor the other may be sold for more than six years; both may have the ear bored; to both severance pay is given; to both the master may assign a Canaanite slave girl."

H. *Isn't this what is at stake: The initial Tannaite authority does not establish a verbal analogy based on the appearance of "hired hand" in both passages, while R. Eleazar does establish a verbal analogy based on the occurrence of "hired hand" in both passages?*

I. *Said R. Tabyumi in the name of Abbayye, "All*

parties concur that we do establish a verbal analogy based on the appearance in both passages of 'hired hand.' And here, this is what is the operative consideration behind the position of the initial Tannaite authority, who has said, He who sells himself may be sold for six years or more than six years? Scripture has stated a limitation in the context of one sold by a court: 'And he shall serve you six years' (Deut. 15:12), meaning, he but not one who sells himself."

J.   *And the other party?*

K.   "And he shall serve you" – not your heir.

L.   *And the other party?*

M.   *There is another* "serve you" in context [at Deut. 15:18].

N.   *And the other party?*

O.   *That is written to tell you that* the master must be prepared to give severance pay.

VIII.2 A.   *Our rabbis have taught on Tannaite authority:*

B.   "'An awl' (Deut. 15:17):

C.   "I know only that an awl is sufficient for boring the ear of the slave. How do I know that sufficient also would be a prick, thorn, borer, or stylus?

D.   "Scripture states, 'Then you shall take' (Deut. 15:12) – including everything that can be taken in hand," the words of R. Yosé b. R. Judah.

E. Rabbi says, "Since the verse says, 'an awl,' we draw the conclusion that the awl is made only of metal, and so anything that is used must be metal.

F. "Another matter: 'You shall take an awl' — teaches that a big awl is meant."

G. Said R. Eleazar, "R. Yudan b. Rabbi would expound as follows: 'When they pierce the ear, they do it only through the earlobe.'

H. "Sages say, 'A Hebrew slave of the priestly caste is not subjected to the boring of the ear, because that thereby blemishes him.'"

I. *Now if you hold that the boring is done only through the earlobe, then the Hebrew slave of the priestly caste cannot be blemished thereby, since we bore only through the top part of the ear [and in any event, boring makes a blemish, and Yosé takes the view that even a needle's point, a smaller hole than a lentil's size, constitutes maiming]!*

VIII.3 A. *What is at issue here?*

B. *Rabbi invokes the categories of an encompassing rule followed by an exclusionary particularization:*

C. "You shall take" is an encompassing rule; "an awl" is an exclusionary particularization; "through his ear into the door" reverts and gives an encompassing rule. So where you have an encompassing rule, an exclusionary particularization, and another encompassing rule, you cover under the encompassing rule only what bears the traits of the exclusionary particularization; just as the exclusionary particularization states explicitly that the object must be of metal, so must anything used for the purpose be of metal.

D. *R. Yosé b. R. Judah interprets the categories of scriptural evidences of inclusionary and exclusionary usages:*

E. "You shall take" is inclusionary; "an awl" is exclusionary;
"through his ear into the door" reverts and forms an inclusionary statement. Where you have an inclusionary, an exclusionary, and an inclusionary statement, the upshot is to encompass all things.

F. *So what is excluded? An ointment.*

VIII.4 A. The master has said: "'You shall take an awl' — teaches that a big awl is meant":

B. *On what basis?*

C. It is in line with what Raba said, "'Therefore the children of Israel don't eat the sinew of the hip that is on the hollow of the thigh' (Gen. 32:33) – the right thigh; here, too, 'the awl,' means, the most special of awls."

VIII.5 A. Said R. Eleazar, "R. Yudan b. Rabbi would expound as follows: 'When they pierce the ear, they do it only through the earlobe.' Sages say, 'A Hebrew slave of the priestly caste is not subjected to the boring of the ear, because that thereby blemishes him'":

B. So let him be blemished!

C. Said Rabbah b. R. Shila, "Said Scripture, 'And he shall return to his own family' (Lev. 25:41) – to his family's presumptive rights."

VIII.9 A. *Our rabbis have taught on Tannaite authority:*

B. "But should he say to you, 'I do not want to leave you,' [for he loves you and your household and is happy with you, you shall take an awl and put it through his ear into the door, and he shall become your slave in perpetuity. Do the same with your female slave. When you do set him free, do not feel aggrieved, for in the six years he has given you double the service of a hired man. Moreover, the Lord your God will bless you in all you do]" (Deut. 15:12-17):

C. Is it possible to suppose that this may take place one time only?

D. Scripture says, "But should he say to you, 'I do not want to leave you,'" – unless he says so and repeats it.

E. If he said so during the six years, but did not say so at the end of the six years, lo, this one does not have his ear pierced to the doorpost,

F. for it is said, "I do not want to leave you" – which applies only if said at the time of his leaving.

G. If he said so at the end of the six years, but did not say so during the six years, lo, this one does not have his ear pierced to the doorpost,

H. for it is said, "But if the slave should say to you...,"

I. that is, while he is yet a slave [Sifré Deut. CXXI.I.1-3].

VIII.10 A. The master has said, "If he made the statement at the beginning of the sixth year but not at the end, he is not bored, for it is said, 'I will not go out free'" [so he has to make the statement when he is about to leave].

B. *But we derive the law from the passage,* "I will not go out free," *why not derive the rule from the fact that he has to say,* "I love my master, my wife, and my children," *which is not*

> *met? Furthermore, "If*
> *he says it at the end*
> *of the sixth year but*
> *not at the beginning,*
> *he is not bored, for it*
> *is said, 'the slave...":*
> *Isn't he then a slave at*
> *the end of the sixth year?*
>
> C. Said Raba, "The
> meaning is, 'at the
> beginning of the last
> penny's worthy of
> service, and at the end
> of the same.'"

Here again, when it speaks of a verse read by the other Talmud in the same way, the Bavli's voice nonetheless is unique: it is different because it is different, and there is no negotiation of the difference. For while Deut. 15:12 serves both Talmuds in the same way: proving that the Hebrew male slave is subject to the same law as the Hebrew female slave, that fact, critical to the Yerushalmi's composition, is secondary to the focus of interest of the Bavli's. The Bavli's inquiry concerns a problem not dealt with in the Mishnah at all, namely, how we know that a Hebrew slave sold to an Israelite is subject to the same law as one sold to a gentile? With that problem in hand, we invoke the prooftext at hand. The point for our inquiry is not to be missed: where the Talmuds share the same prooftext and read it in the same way and with the same propositional consequence, still, the Bavli's interest in the matter is defined by its larger program, and that program differs radically and persistently from the Yerushalmi's. That the Bavli has its own hermeneutic is shown at I.2 in our sample, which asks a question that simply does not occur in the Yerushalmi, even when the same prooftext plays a role in both Talmuds. A second reading of Deut. 15:12 occurs at VIII.2, and that Tannaite reading plays no role in the Yerushalmi's presentation of the Mishnah pericope under discussion. No reasonable person would insist that the framers of the Yerushalmi never knew Rabbi's and Yosé b. R. Judah's dispute about the meaning of the reference to "an awl." After all, both are principal late Tannaite authorities in the Land of Israel itself!

But, when we consider the continuation of the matter, at VIII.3 – the dispute on the classification of the components of the verse – encompassing rule, exclusionary particularization, then encompassing rule, versus inclusionary and exclusionary usages – we realize that, whatever they inherited from the corpus of sayings of the Land of Israel's Tannaite masters, the Bavli's composition authors did whatever they liked; and what they liked was not to the taste of the Yerushalmi's composition authors. That is clear because the latter do not do what the former do. The provision then of a footnote, VIII.4, and a secondary expansion, at VIII.5, characterize the Bavli but never the Yerushalmi. So what is shared in common proves inert, and what is done with received facts by the Bavli's composition writers and composite makers is unique: the Bavli's voice is unique. That VIII.9-10 stand on their own simply underlines that conclusion. The Bavli is different because it's different. We now proceed to the same exercise for the remainder of the Mishnah pericopes of Mishnah-tractate Qiddushin Chapter One. Without a sustained probe of this and other chapters of the two Talmuds, we may entertain the proposition that the differences are local and topical. What we see in the next chapters is that they are not at all local. In Part Two of this monograph we find they are not local, and, indeed, the same differences divide the Bavli from every other, prior document of its canon, whether Sifra or Sifré to Deuteronomy, or Tosefta, when the framers of all those writings along with the Bavli address precisely the same topic.

So the topic decides nothing; throughout, what governs is the generative problematic. But to define that – that is a problem, and, as I have hinted in the preface, I do not think it can be solved within the framework of the Bavli read by itself. For we can identify the generative problematic of a writing only when we know what problem the framers of that writing wished to solve: what provoked their thought, what stimulated them to frame their thought in one way, rather than in some other, what held together and imparted proportion, coherence, and power, to the consequent writing. When we know the answers to those questions, which context may suggest, we can say what we think our authorship wanted to accomplish, not in general but in particular: its generative problematic, dictating what answers were to be found in connection with each and over topic.[1]

---

[1] I of course allude here to my projected continuation of this project of defining the Bavli, which I plan to undertake in the comparison of other documents that propose to solve the same problem, that is, documents that sum up and conclude, restate and recapitulate in a systematic and orderly way, an entire tradition. That accounts for my plan, expressed in the projected study, *The Bavli and the Denkart. A Comparison of the Systemic Statements of Judaism and Zoroastrianism.* I anticipate that other comparisons, e.g., *The Bavli and the Matigan-i Hazar Datastan,* may also be called for.

3

Mishnah-Tractate Qiddushin 1:3 in the Yerushalmi and the Bavli

1:3

A. A Canaanite slave is acquired through money, through a writ, or through usucaption.

B. "And he acquires himself through money paid by others or through a writ [of indebtedness] taken on by himself," the words of R. Meir.

C. And sages say, "By money paid by himself or by a writ taken on by others,

D. "on condition that the money belongs to others."

I. M. Qiddushin 1:3 in the Talmud of the Land of Israel

[I.A] It is written, "[As to Canaanite slaves] you may bequeath them to your sons after you, to inherit as a possession forever; you may make slaves of them" (Lev. 25:46).

[B] Acquisition of slaves thereby is treated under the same rubric as inherited real estate.

[C] Just as inherited real estate is acquired through money, writ, or usucaption so a Canaanite slave is acquired through money, writ, or usucaption.

[D] How do we know that inherited real estate itself is acquired through money, writ, or usucaption?

[E] It is written, "Fields will be bought for money, deeds will be signed and sealed and witnessed" (Jer. 32:44).

[F] "And signed and sealed and witnessed" – "signed and sealed" refers to witnesses to a writ; "witnessed" refers to witnesses to usucaption.

[G] Or perhaps these latter serve as witnesses to the writ?

[H] Since it already is written, "And signed and sealed," [which must mean a writ, the other witnesses are to usucaption].

[I] R. Yosa in the name of R. Mana, R. Tanhum, R. Abbahu in the name of R. Yohanan: "Real estate is not acquired for less than a perutah."

[J] What is the scriptural basis for that statement?

171

[K] "Fields will be bought for money" [and less than a perutah is not deemed money].

[L] Now [Yohanan] disputes what R. Haninah said: "All references to sheqels in the Torah are to selas; in the Prophets, to litras, and in the Writings to qintin." [Thus Jeremiah refers to twenty-five selas = a litra.]

[M] Said R. Judah bar Pazzi, "That is except for the sheqels of Ephron, which are qintin [a hundred selas]."

[N] What is the scriptural basis for this statement?

[O] "For the full price let him give it to me" (Gen. 23:9) [and "full price" implies the larger coin].

[P] But the cases are not similar. There [Jer. 32:4] it is written "money," but here it is written "sheqels."

[Q] They objected, "Lo, there is the case of the rapist [Deut. 22:28], and lo, in that case what is written is only 'money,' and do you say it refers to sheqels? [So there is a dispute even when 'money' stands by itself.]"

[II.A] [The statement that land is acquired only through usucaption] is not in accord with the view of R. Eliezer.

[B] For R. Eliezer said, "If one merely traversed the field, he has acquired it [without usucaption]."

[C] For it has been taught: "If one traversed a field lengthwise and breadthwise, he has acquired it up to the place in which he has walked," the words of R. Eliezer.

[D] And sages say, "He acquires it only once he effects possession through usucaption."

[E] All concur in the case of one who sells a path to his fellow, that once he has walked in it, he has acquired it.

[F] What is the scriptural basis for that position [of Eliezer]?

[G] "Arise, walk through the length and the breadth of the land, for I will give it to you" (Gen. 13:17).

[III.A] There are Mishnah rules that maintain slaves are equivalent to real estate; there are Mishnah passages that maintain they are equivalent to movables; and there are Mishnah passages that maintain they are neither like real estate nor like movables.

[B] A Mishnah passage that treats slaves as equivalent to real estate is what we have learned there:

[C] **Title by usucaption to houses, cisterns, trenches, vaults, dovecotes, bathhouses, olive presses, irrigated field, and slaves, [and whatever brings a regular return, is gained by usucaption during three complete years]** [M. B.B. 3:1].

[D] A Mishnah passage that treats slaves as not equivalent to real estate is in line with what we have learned there [following QE]:

[E] **How is usucaption [established in the case of] slaves?**

[F] **[If] he [the slave] tied on his [the master's] sandal, or loosened his sandal, or carried clothes after him to the bathhouse, lo, this is usucaption.**

[G] **[If] he lifted him up [the slave lifted the master up] –**

[H] **R. Simeon says, "You have no act of usucaption more effective than that!"** [T. Qid. 1:5].

[I] What rabbis have stated implies that slaves are equivalent to movables.

[J] For R. Yosé said in the name of rabbis, "No lien applies to one who makes a gift [unless it is made explicit]. They do not exact payment from a debtor's slaves as they do from his real estate. [That is, slaves cannot be treated as mortgaged for payment of a debt.]"

[K] Said R. Mana to R. Shimi, "Who are these rabbis?"

[L] He said to him, "They are R. Isaac and R. Imi."

[M] A widow seized a slave girl as payment for her marriage settlement. R. Isaac ruled, "Since she has seized her, she is properly seized, [and the action is valid]. [But that is not the case at the outset, and hence, in general, the slave is not equivalent to real estate.]"

[N] R. Imi took the slave away from her, for she thought that the slave belonged to her, and she was not hers [for the collection of her outstanding marriage settlement]. [The slave is in the status of movables, not real estate.]

[O] Slaves are not equivalent to real estate, for it has been taught: [If one sold] real estate and slaves to someone, when he has taken possession of the real estate, [he has not taken possession of the slaves].

[P] Now if you maintain that slaves are in the status of real estate, once the purchaser has taken possession of the real estate, he should be deemed to have taken possession of the slaves.

[Q] For R. Yosa in the name of R. Yohanan has said, "If someone had two fields, one in Judah and one in Galilee, and the purchaser took possession of this one in Judah, intending also to acquire ownership of that one in Galilee,

[R] "or if he took possession of that one in Galilee, [60a] intending to take possession of this one in Judah,

[S] "he has acquired possession thereof. [Consequently, by taking possession of one piece of real estate, one may take possession of all the real estate. But in the cited case, taking possession of real estate has no effect upon ownership of the slaves, which therefore are not equivalent to real estate.]"

[T] They are not equivalent to movables: If you say that slaves are equivalent to movables, once the purchaser has acquired possession of real estate, he should have acquired possession of the slaves [at O].

[IV.A] For we have learned there: **If one has to take an oath in regard to movables, the oath may be extended to real estate as well, [and movables are acquired along with real estate].**

[B] **Through money [paid by others] [M. 1:3B]:** R. Jeremiah said, "[It is money paid] by another party to his master."

[C] Lo, if it is money paid by his master to someone else, there is no [freedom for the slave]. [Meir's view is that it is a disadvantage to the slave to go out to freedom. If a third party gives money to the master, then by accepting the money the master makes the slave accept his freedom. The third party thus does not impose an unwanted disadvantage on the slave. But if the master should give money to others, he cannot on that account force the slave to leave his service.]

[D] [Differing from this view,] said R. Zeira, "Even if it is payment from his master to another party. For what this third party takes from the master is for the slave himself."

[E] R. Jeremiah raised the question before R. Zeira, "If someone said, 'Here is this money, on account of which your field should go forth to freedom,' [what is the ruling]? [That is, someone had a field on a mortgage from a borrower. A third party offered him money, here is money, so that the field may go into the hands of the borrower. This is without the borrower's knowledge.]"

[F] He said to him, "It has gone forth. [One may transfer a benefit to someone in the beneficiary's absence.]"

[G] "'That your field may go forth to the status of ownerless property'"?

[H] He said to him, "It has not gone forth."

[I] "What is the difference between this language and that?"

[J] "The use of the former language imputes ownership to some intelligent party [the borrower] aware of the transaction, but the use of the latter language does not impute ownership to some intelligent party aware of the transaction."

[K] "Take note of this: What if it was a deaf-mute?"

[L] He said to him, "It applies to a man [even a deaf-mute]."

[M] "Take note: What if it was a minor?"

[N] He said to him, "He will grow up."

[O] Said R. Yohanan, "That which R. Zeira [C] has said accords with the view of R. Simeon b. Eleazar, for it has been taught":

[P] **R. Simeon b. Eleazar said in the name of R. Meir, "Also: Through a writ of indebtedness taken by others. but not taken by himself" [vs. M. 1:3C] [T. Qid. 1:6]. [For the slave cannot make acquisition in his own behalf.]**

[Q] What is the meaning of the language, "Through a writ of indebtedness taken on by others, but not taken on by himself?"

[R] Is it not that his master gives a writ to others so that his slave will go forth to freedom?

[S] Here, too, his master gives money to others that his slave may go forth to freedom [C].

[V.A] **[One who is half-slave and half-free works for his master one day and for himself the next (M. Git. 4:5A).]** Said R. Abun, "This accords with Rabbi.

[B] "For Rabbi has said, 'A man emancipates half of his slave.'"

[C] And do rabbis not hold that a man emancipates half of his slave?

[D] They agree that that is the case when it is a slave owned by partners, but in the case of a slave wholly owned by one man, it is different. For it is as if he has passed a writ of emancipation from the right hand [of the slave] to the left [and that means nothing].

[E] In Rabbi's view is it not as if he has passed a writ of emancipation from his right hand to his left hand?

[F] He concurs in that principle. But here he effects acquisition through another's intervention.

[G] And do rabbis not concur that he acquires ownership of himself by means of another party?

[H] Rabbis maintain that he who is suitable to acquire for himself, [that is, a writ of emancipation,] is suitable for others to acquire in his behalf, and he who is not suitable to acquire in his own behalf is not suitable for others to acquire in his behalf.

[I] Rabbi says, "Even though it is not suitable for him to acquire in his own behalf, it is suitable for others to acquire in his behalf."

[VI.A] [If a slave] picked up a lost object and said, "It is with the stipulation that I acquire ownership of it, and not my master," [what is the law]?

[B] [Do we say,] despite his wishes, he and his master [hence, his master] acquire ownership of the object, or is it that he has acquired ownership and not his master?

[C] Let us derive the answer from the following case:

[D] **He who was prohibited by vow from imparting any benefit to his son-in-law, but who who wants to give his daughter some money says to her, 'Lo, this money is given to you as a gift, on condition that your husband has no right to it, but you dispose of it for your own personal use"** [M. Ned. 11:8].

[E] In this regard it was taught, "[He must say,] 'It is not yours [except for your personal use]. [You do not acquire ownership of this money, except what you actually use.]'"

[F] Said R. Zeira, "Who taught, [He must add,] 'And it is not yours'? It is R. Meir. For R. Meir treats the hand of the slave as the hand of the master."

[G] In the case of a gift [the law] is in accord with the view of R. Meir, that the hand of the wife is tantamount to the hand of the husband.

[H] But as regards a lost object, will the law accord with rabbis? [All the more so should the law accord with Meir, as at M. Ned.]

[I] Said R. Zeira before R. Mana, "The case [of M. Ned. 11:8] is different [from the present one], for it is a case in which she has made acquisition with the knowledge and consent of another party [namely, the father]."

[J] He said to him, "Is it not an argument a fortiori: Now if, in the cited case in which she has made acquisition with the knowledge and consent of another party, namely, her father, you maintain that when the woman makes acquisition her husband makes acquisition, here, in a case in which he makes acquisition in his own behalf [without third-party intervention], is it not all the more so the case that when the slave makes acquisition, his master should acquire the object? [That is, in the case of the slave, there is no question of the intervention of a donor, that is. the father. All the more so should the master enjoy ownership of whatever the slave finds.]"

[VII.A] [In listing the means by which a slave goes free], why do we not learn that he also goes free at the loss of limbs that do not grow back?

[B] Said R. Yohanan b. Mareh, "It is because there is a dispute about the matter.

[C] "Specifically, there is a Tannaite authority who teaches that [if he loses his limbs] he still requires a writ of emancipation from the master, and there is a Tannaite authority who teaches that, in that circumstance, he does not require a writ of emancipation from his master."

[VIII. A] It is self-evident that a slave receives a gift from someone else for someone else, from someone else for his master [who acquires the object as soon as it hits the hand of the slave], but not from his master for himself, [for whatever the master gives him remains the property of the master].

[B] But as to what comes from another party to the slave himself there is a dispute between R. Meir and sages.

[C] "If someone says to him, 'Here is some money for you, on condition that your master has no right to it,' once the slave has acquired possession of the money, the owner has acquired possession of it," the words of R. Meir.

[D] And sages say, "The slave acquires ownership of the money, and the master does not acquire the ownership of it."

[E] What is a problem is this: What about a gift from the master to a third party?

[F] Just as the slave acquires possession of an object from a third party in behalf of his master, so does the slave acquire ownership of the object from his master for a third party?

[G] Let us derive the answer from the following:

[H] He who borrowed a cow and the one who lent it sent it along with his son, slave, or messenger, or with the son, slave, or messenger of the borrower, and it died, the borrower is exempt. If the borrower had said to him, "Send it with your son," "your slave," "your messenger," the borrower is liable [M. B.M. 3:3].

[I] Does this [latter clause] not indicate that the slave made acquisition of the object from his master in behalf of the other party? [Indeed it does.]

[J] Said R. Eleazar, "Interpret the passage to speak only of a Hebrew slave, [in which case the question is not answered at all]."

[K] Said R. Yohanan, "Lo, you may as well interpret the passage to apply to a case in which it was a Canaanite slave. But interpret the passage to speak of a case in which the lender said to him, 'Open the gate for it, and it will follow along on its own.'

[L] "For we have learned that he who led a cow, or drew it, or called it and it came after him, is liable for what happens to the cow just as if he had borrowed it."

[M] R. Zeira derived from the following passage that the slave does not acquire ownership from his master in behalf of a third party: "'But one may not impart ownership of a meal of commingling by means of his minor son or daughter, or by means of his male or female Canaanite slaves, for their hand is tantamount to his hand.'

[N] "Does that not indicate that a slave cannot impart ownership from his master in behalf of a third party?"

[O] Interpret the cited statement to accord [solely] with the position of R. Meir, for R. Meir treats the hand of a slave as tantamount to the hand of his master.

[P] "And has it not been taught: 'He may impart ownership of a meal of commingling by means of his wife.' [It cannot therefore be R.

Meir,] for R. Meir treats the hand of a wife as equivalent to the hand of her husband.

[Q] R. Haninah in the name of R. Pinhas: "Interpret the matter in accord with the following Tannaite authority, who taught: One's wife does not redeem in his behalf produce in the status of second tithe. 'One's wife redeems on his behalf produce in the status of second tithe [without paying the added fifth],' according to the words of R. Simeon b. Eleazar in the name of R. Meir [T. M.S. 4:7D-E].

[R] "Now this Tannaite authority of the views of R. Meir treats the hand of the slave as the hand of his master, but not the hand of the wife as the hand of her husband, [so Meir may stand behind the cited law]."

[IX.A] R. Zeira and R. Hiyya in the name of R. Yohanan: "It appears that the slave should acquire ownership of a writ of emancipation [for his fellow slave], for he does have a right to a writ of emancipation.

[B] "But he should not acquire a writ of divorce of a woman [to deliver for her husband], for he is not subject to the laws of a writ of divorce of a woman."

[C] "If you say that the Tannaite teaching [that follows disputes this point at E, I shall answer that objection]:

[D] "'Lo, you are a slave, but your offspring is free' –

[E] "if she was pregnant, she makes acquisition of the writ of emancipation for the fetus"– [so how can she acquire the writ for the fetus?] – 'They have treated the fetus as one of her limbs, [and she may receive such a writ for herself, A]."

[F] R. Ba bar Hiyya in the name of R. Yohanan, "It appears that a slave may receive a writ of emancipation [for his fellow slave].

[G] "But not [if they belong to] the same [master] –

[H] "if you say that the Tannaite teaching has already made the same point –

[I] "'Lo, you are a slave, but your offspring is free,' if she was pregnant she acquires the writ of emancipation for her fetus –

[J] "they have treated the fetus as one of her limbs."

[X.A] "As to Madame So-and-so, my slave girl, I issue a writ to her, so that she could not be subjugated as a slave [after I die]"– [are the heirs bound by that statement]?

[B] R. Eleazar and S. Simeon b. Yaqim brought a case to R. Yohanan.

[C] He said, "He has not got the power to encumber his heirs."

[D] What is her children's status? They are slaves.

[E] What did he then allow her [in so stating]?

[F] The right to retain the usufruct of her own labor.

[XI.A] R. Abba and R. Yosé both maintain that [VIII.J-K] is the view of Rabbi.

[B] For Rabbi said, "A man may free half of his slave."

[C] If one wrote over all of his property to two of his slaves simultaneously, both of them go forth to freedom,

[D] and each of them has to free the other.

[E] R. Judah in the name of Samuel, R. Abbahu in the name of R. Yohanan, "That statement follows the view of Rabbi, for Rabbi has said, 'A man frees half of his slave.' [Each slave owns half of himself and half of the other.]"

[F] Said R. Zeira to R. Ba, "Does that not imply that a slave may acquire ownership of an object in behalf of a third party?"

[G] He said to him, "What are you thinking? It is that after they have acquired ownership of the property [including half of each other], they go forth to freedom?

[H] "But that is not so. It is simultaneously that the slaves and the property go forth to freedom."

[XII.A] "Lo, you are free, but your offspring is a slave" –

[B] "Her offspring is in the same status as she is," the words of R. Yosé the Galilean.

[C] And sages say, "He has not done a thing."

[D] Said R. Eleazar, "So did R. Hoshaiah, father of the Mishnah explain the matter [of C]: "Both of them are deemed to be free." [The language of A frees mother and child.]

[E] R. Imi in the name of R. Yohanan: "Both of them are regarded as slaves."

[F] In the opinion of R. Yohanan, it is understandable that there is a dispute [of Yosé and sages].

[G] But in the opinion of R. Eleazar, why should there be a dispute?

[H] But thus is the law to be taught:

[I] "His statement is valid," the words of R. Yosé the Galilean.

[J] And sages say, "He has accomplished nothing at all."

[K] What is the meaning of "He has accomplished nothing at all"?

[L] Said R. Eleazar, "Thus did R. Hoshaiah, father of the Mishnah, explain the matter: 'Both of them are free.'"

[M] R. Ami in the name of R. Yohanan: "Both of them are slaves."

[N] And it accords with Rabbi, for Rabbi has said, "A man frees half of his slave."

Unit I introduces the paramount theme of the discussion, the ambiguous status of the Canaanite slave: like real estate, like movables, like neither, like both. But the point is that the slave is in the status of real estate, for the stated reason. Unit II completes the clarification of the opening proposition. Unit III takes up the analogies applicable to the slave once more. Unit IV returns to the modes by which the Canaanite slave acquires himself, M. 1:3B, beginning with money. The main interest of unit IV is in whether a slave can acquire a writ or money so as to secure his own emancipation. The secondary issue is Meir's view that it is no advantage to a slave to go free. So the tertiary issue is, may this be done not in the presence of the slave, for example, by third parties, when in general people may secure advantages, but may not accept disadvantages, for a third party? The solution is at IV.O-R. Unit V takes up the possibility of acquiring half a slave, the other half remaining free, and the issue is the same as at unit IV, namely, how a slave may be freed in part. The problem is to describe the way ownership or acquisition is effected, and this Rabbi does. Unit VI carries forward the same problem, namely, how and whether a slave effects acquisition of anything, since whatever comes into his domain belongs forthwith to his master. Unit

VII raises and answers a simple question. Unit √III returns to the matter of whether, and how, a slave effects acquisition of an object, seeing that, in Meir's view, whatever falls into his hand belongs to his master anyway. Unit IX pursues a different side to the same problem, namely, a slave's acting in behalf of a third party. Since he may receive a writ of emancipation for himself, he also may receive one for someone else, but not a writ of divorce. IX.A-F gives us one version, IX.G-K a second. Unit X is distinct from the rest, a separate problem. Unit XI returns us to unit IX. How can the slave acquire the writ for the fetus? The answer is that a man may free half of his slave, and the foetus is half of the slave girl. Unit XII takes up the question of freeing a slave, again giving us two versions of a simple dispute.

II. M. Qiddushin 1:3 in the Talmud of Babylonia

1:3

A. A Canaanite slave is acquired through money, through a writ, or through usucaption.

B. "And he acquires himself through money paid by others or through a writ [of indebtedness] taken on by himself," the words of R. Meir.

C. And sages say, "By money paid by himself or by a writ taken on by others,

D. "on condition that the money belongs to others."

I.1 A. *How on the basis of Scripture do we know this fact?*

B. As it is written, "And you shall make them [gentile slaves] an inheritance for your children after you, to possess as an inheritance" (Lev. 25:46) – Scripture thus has treated them as comparable to a field of inheritance. Just as a field of inheritance is acquired through money, writ, or usucaption, so **a Canaanite slave is acquired through money, through a writ, or through usucaption.**

C. Might one then propose: Just as a field of inheritance reverts to its original owner at the Jubilee, so a Canaanite slave reverts to the original owner at the Jubilee?

D. Scripture states, "Of them shall you take your slaves forever" (Lev. 25:46).

I.2 A. *A Tannaite statement: Also through barter.*

B. *What about the Tannaite statement before us [which omits that medium of acquisition]?*

C. *He has specified those modes of acquisition that do not apply to movables; but what applies to movables [and also to slaves, in that same category] he does not specify in his Tannaite formulation.*

I.3 A. Said Samuel, "A Canaanite slave is acquired also through drawing. How so? If the purchaser grabs the slave and he goes with him, he acquires title to him; if he calls him and he goes to him, he does not acquire title to him."

B.   *What about the Tannaite statement before us [which omits that medium of acquisition]?*

C.   *There is no problem in explaining the omission of drawing, for he has specified those modes of acquisition that do not apply to movables; but what applies to movables [and also to slaves, in that same category] he does not specify in his Tannaite formulation. But as to that other Tannaite authority [the one cited at No. 2], should his formulation not encompass drawing?*

D.   *What he has encompassed in his Tannaite statement are modes of acquisitions that pertain to both real estate and movables, but drawing, which pertains to movables but not to real estate, he has not encompassed in his Tannaite formulation.*

I.4   A.   "How so? If the purchaser grabs the slave and he goes with him, he acquires title to him; if he calls him and he goes to him, he does not acquire title to him":

B.   *Well, now, he doesn't, does he? Then what about that which has been taught on Tannaite authority:*

C.   How is an animal acquired through the mode of handing over [delivery] [Slotki: harnessing, like drawing, is one of the modes of acquiring right of ownership; the buyer takes possession of the animal by performing some act that resembles harnessing, or, in the case of other objects, obtaining full delivery]? If the buyer takes hold of the hoof, hair, saddle, saddlebag that is upon it, bit in the mouth, or bell on the neck, he has acquired title. How is it done through drawing the object? If he calls the beast and it comes, or if he strikes it with a stick and it runs before him, he acquires title as soon as it has moved a foreleg and a hind leg.

D.   R. Ahi, and some say, R. Aha, says, "That takes place only if it has moved the full length of its body." [The four legs must be moved from their original position.]

E.   *Say: A beast moves on its master's will, a slave on his own.*

F.   Said R. Ashi, "A minor slave is classified as a beast."

I.5   A.   *Our rabbis have taught on Tannaite authority:*

B.   How is a slave acquired through an act of usucaption? If the slave fastened the shoe of the man or undid it, or if he carried his clothing after him to the bathhouse, or if he undressed him or washed him or anointed him or scraped him or dressed him or put on his shoes or lifted him up, the man acquires title to the slave.

C.   Said R. Simeon, "An act of usucaption of this kind should not be greater than an act of raising up, since raising up an object confers title under all circumstances."

I.6   A.   *What is the meaning of this statement?*

B.   Said R. Ashi, "[*This is the sense of his statement:*] If the slave lifted up his master, the master acquires title, but if the master lifts up the slave, the master does not acquire ownership of the slave. Said R. Simeon, 'An act of usucaption of this kind should not be greater than an act of raising up, since raising up an object confers title under all circumstances.'" [Simon: If the master lifts up the slave, this action also confers ownership.]

I.7   A.   *Now that you have said,* if the slave lifted up his master, the master acquires title," *then what about the following:* A Canaanite slave girl should be acquired through an act of sexual relations [since in that situation she lifts up the master]?

B.   *When we invoke the stated rule, it is in a case in which* the one party derives pleasure, but the other party suffers anguish. *But here,* this one enjoys it and so does that one.

C.   *Well, then, what about anal intercourse?*

D.   Said R. Ahai bar Ada of Aha, "Who's going to tell us that both of them don't get a kick out of it? And, furthermore, the language that Scripture uses is, 'You shall not lie with mankind with the lyings of a woman' (Lev. 18:22), in which case Scripture has treated as comparable anal and vaginal sexual relations."

I.8   A.   R. Judah the Hindu was a proselyte, so he had no heirs. *He fell ill. Mar Zutra came to inquire after his health. He saw that he was dying, so he said to his slave, "Take off my shoes and take them to my house for me" [so that when the proselyte died, the slave would be engaged in a service to him, and he would thereby acquire title through usucaption].*

B.   *There are those who say, the slave was an adult.*

C.   [23A] This one left for death and the other one [the slave] left to life.

D.   *Others say, he was a minor, and this did not accord with what Abba Saul said, for it has been taught on Tannaite authority:* A proselyte who died, and Israelites grabbed his property, and among them were slaves, whether adult or minor, the slaves have acquired title to themselves as free persons. Abba Saul says, "The adults have acquired title to themselves as free persons, but the minors – whoever takes hold of them has acquired title to them."

II.1   A.   **"And he acquires himself through money paid by others or through a writ [of indebtedness] taken on by himself," the words of R. Meir:**

B.   **Through money paid by others** – but not by money paid by the slave himself? *With what situation do we deal? Should we say,* without his knowledge and consent? *Then note: We have heard that* R. Meir holds, it is a disadvantage for the slave to go forth from the possession of his master to freedom, *and we have learned as a Tannaite statement in the Mishnah,* **For they act to the advantage of another person not in his presence, but they act to his disadvantage only in his presence [M. Git. 1:6F].** *So it is obvious that it is with the slave's knowledge and consent, and so we are informed that* it may be done through money paid by others – but not by money paid by the slave himself. *Then it follows that* there is no possibility for a slave to acquire title to anything without his owner's participation. *But then note what follows:* **Through a writ [of indebtedness] taken on by himself!** *So if it is taken on by himself, it is a valid medium of emancipation, but if it is taken on by others, it is not! Now if it is with his own knowledge and consent, then why cannot be validly done by third parties? And should you say, what is the meaning of,* **through a writ [of indebtedness] taken on by himself?** *It means,* even through a writ [of indebtedness] taken on by himself, *and so we are informed that* the advent of his writ of emancipation and his right to form a domain unto himself come about simultaneously, *lo, that is not how it has been taught as a Tannaite statement, for lo, it has been taught on Tannaite authority:* **"...By a writ undertaken on his own** account, but not one undertaken by others," the words of R. Meir [T. Qid. 1:6F].

C.   *Said Abbayye, "In point of fact, it is not with his knowledge and consent. But a slave acquired by reason of a monetary obligation [that he is unable to meet, on account of which he is sold into slavery] is exceptional, for, since the master acquires title to him willy-nilly, the master also transfers title back to him willy-nilly."*

D.   *If so, the same rule should pertain to a writ!*

E.   *This sort of deed stands by itself [with its own wording] and that kind of writ stands by itself.*

F.   *Well, then, here, too, this money stands by itself and that money stands by itself [since each is paid for its own purpose]!*

G.   *They have the same mint mark.*

H.   Raba said, "As to money, when the master receives it, it effects his liberation, but as for a deed, when others receive it, it effects his liberation."

III.1   A.   **And sages say, "By money paid by himself or by a writ taken on by others":**

B.   If the money is paid by himself, it liberates him, but if it is paid by others, it doesn't? *Now why should this be the case? Granting that this is without his knowledge and consent, in any event notice: We know that rabbis take the position that* it is to the slave's advantage to leave the master's domain for freedom, *and we have learned in the Mishnah,* **For they act to the advantage of another person not in his presence, but they act to his disadvantage only in his presence [M. Git. 1:6F].** *And should you say, what is the meaning of* **paid by himself?** *Also money paid by himself, and so we are informed that* here is every possibility for a slave to acquire title to anything without his owner's participation, *if so, note what follows:* **By a writ taken on by others** – not undertaken by him himself! *And yet it is an established fact for us that* he advent of his writ of emancipation and his right to form a domain unto himself come about simultaneously. *And should you say, what is the meaning of* **by a writ taken on by others?** *Also by a writ taken on by others, and so we are informed that* it is to the slave's advantage to leave the master's domain for freedom, *if so, then why not blend the whole and repeat the entire matter in a single statement, namely:* With money and with a writ, whether taken on by others or taken on by himself?

C.   *Rather, the sense must be:* With money, whether taken on by others or taken on by himself, or with a writ, if it is taken on by others, but not if it is taken on by the slave himself, *and the whole represents the position of R. Simeon b. Eleazar, for it has been taught on Tannaite authority:*

D.   **R. Simeon b. Eleazar says, "Also by a writ when taken on by others, but not when taken on by himself" [T. Qid. 1:6F].**

E.   There are three different opinions on the matter [Meir, money through others, without his knowledge, but not through his own agency, and by deed through his own agency but not that of others; Simeon b. Eleazar, both by money and deed, through the agency of others but not through his own; rabbis, both by money and by deed, through the agency of others and his own (Freedman)].

F. Said Rabbah, "What is the scriptural foundation for the position of R. Simeon b. Eleazar? He derives a verbal analogy on the basis of the same word, *to her*, that occurs with reference to a slave and a wife, namely, just as a woman is divorced only when the writ of divorce will be taken into a domain that does not belong to the husband, so a slave, too, is liberated only when the writ reaches a domain that is not his master's."

III.2 A. *Rabbah asked,* [23B] *"From the perspective of R. Simeon b. Eleazar, what is the law on a Canaanite slave's appointing a messenger to receive his writ of emancipation from the hand of his master? Since we derive a verbal analogy on the basis of the word 'to her' that appears both in his context and in that of a woman, he is in the status of a woman, or perhaps, as to a woman, since she has the power to receive her writ of divorce, an agent also can do so, but a slave, who has not got the power to receive his writ of emancipation, also has not got the power to appoint an agent?"*

B. *After he raised the question, he solved it:* "We do deduce the verbal analogy on the basis of the common word that joins the slave to the married woman, so he is in the status of a married woman."

C. *Then what about that which R. Huna b. R. Joshua said, namely:* "The priests serve as the agents the All-Merciful," *for if it should enter your mind that they are our slaves, is there something that we could not do, but they have the power to do in our behalf? Well, isn't there anything? Then what about the case of a slave, for he can't accept his writ of emancipation in his own behalf, but he can appoint someone as an agent to do so!*

D. *But the analogy is null.* For an Israelite has no relevant to the rules governing offerings at all, but a slave most certainly bears a relevant to writs of severance, *for it has been taught on Tannaite authority:* It is quite appropriate that a slave may accept a writ of emancipation in behalf of his fellow from the hand of the other's master, but not from his own.

IV.1 A. **On condition that the money belongs to others:**

B. *May we then say that this is what is at issue between sages and R. Meir: R. Meir takes the position that* the slave has no right of effecting title without his master's participation, and a woman has no right of effecting title without her husband's participation, *while rabbis maintain that* the slave has the right of effecting title without his master's participation, and a woman has the right of effecting title without her husband's participation?

C. *Said Rabbah said R. Sheshet,* "All parties concur that the slave has no right of effecting title without his master's participation, and a woman has no right of effecting title without her husband's participation. *And here with what case do we deal? It is one in which a stranger gave the slave a title to a maneh, with the stipulation,* 'This is on the stipulation that your master has no right to it.' *R. Meir maintains that, when the donor said to him,* 'Acquire title,' *the slave acquired title and so did the master, and the statement,* 'This is on the stipulation that your master has no right to it,' *is null. And rabbis maintain that once he said to him,* 'This is on the stipulation that your master has no right to it,' *the stipulation takes effect."*

D.   *And R. Eleazar said, "In any case such as this, all parties concur that what the slave acquires the master acquires. Here with what situation do we deal? With a case in which a third party gave him title to a maneh and* said to him, 'It is on the stipulation that with this money you go forth to freedom.' *R. Meir maintains that, when the donor said to him, 'Acquire title,' the slave acquired title and so did the master, and the statement,* 'This is on the stipulation that your master has no right to it,' *is null. And rabbis maintain that he did not accord title of it even to the slave, for he said to him,* 'It is on the stipulation that with this money you go forth to freedom.'"

E.   *Now there is a contrast between what R. Meir has said with another statement of R. Meir, and likewise between what rabbis have said and another statement of rabbis, for it has been taught on Tannaite authority:*

F.   [24A] **A woman may not redeem second tithe without adding a fifth to its value.**

G.   **R. Simeon b. Eleazar says in the name of R. Meir, "A woman does redeem second tithe without adding a fifth to its value"** [T. M.S. 4:7D-E]. [Freedman: When one redeems second tithe produce of his own and turns its value into ready cash, he adds a fifth to its value, but if he does the same for produce belonging to another, he does not have to do so unless the owner made him his agent to do so].

H.   *Now with what situation do we deal here? If we say that the money belongs to the husband and the produce in the status of second tithe likewise belongs to the husband, then the wife is just carrying out the commission of her husband [so she surely should have to pay the added fifth]! So it must be a case in which the money belongs to her and the produce in the status of second tithe belongs to her husband. But what Scripture has said, is,* "And if a man will redeem any of his tithe, then he shall add thereto the fifth party" (Lev. 27:31) – he but not his wife. *So it must be a case in which a third party has given the wife title to a maneh and said to her,* "It is on the stipulation that with it you redeem the produce in the status of second tithe." *So we infer that they hold contrary opinions [to the ones they announce with respect to the slave's freedom.]* [Freedman: The rights of a slave and a woman are similar: Either they can both acquire independently or they both cannot.]

I.   *Said Abbayye, "Big deal – so reverse the attributions."*

J.   *Raba said, "Under no circumstances reverse the attributions. Here we deal with produce in the status of second tithe that comes to the woman from her father's household as his heir. R. Meir is consistent with views expressed elsewhere, for he has said,* 'Tithe is property belonging to what has been sanctified,' *so that her husband does not acquire title to it. And rabbis are consistent with views expressed elsewhere, for they maintain,* 'Tithe is property belonging to the ordinary person,' *so that her husband does acquire title to it. Therefore she does indeed carry out the commission of her husband."*

IV.2 A.   *A Tannaite statement:* A gentile slave goes free through the loss of his eye, tooth, or major limbs that do not grow back [in line with Ex. 21:26-27].

B. *Now there is no problem understanding why that is so for the eye and tooth, since they are made explicit in Scripture, but on what basis do we know that that is the fact for the lost of the major limbs?*

C. *These are comparable to the tooth and eye:* Just as the loss of the tooth or eye represent blemishes that are exposed to sight and these do not grow back, so any blemishes that are exposed to sight and that are not going to grow back are covered by the same loss.

D. *But why not say:* The reference to "tooth" and "eye" constitute two rules that are redundant [Freedman: for the analogy could not be drawn if only one of them were mentioned], and whenever you have two verses that are redundant, they cannot be used to illuminate other cases.

E. *But both are required and they are not redundant, for if the All-Merciful had made reference only to the matter of the tooth, I might have supposed that even* [24B] *a milk tooth's loss would suffice; so the All-Merciful made reference to "eye" as well. And if the Merciful had made reference only to "eye," I would have supposed:* Just as the eye was created with the person himself, so that would apply to any such limb, *but the law would not cover the tooth, which grew in later on.*

F. *Well, why not say,* "And if a man smite" (Ex. 21:26-27) forms an encompassing generalization; "the tooth...the eye" form a particularization; in any case in which you have an encompassing generalization followed by a particularization, covered by the generalization is only what is contained in the particularization, with the result that the slave goes free for the loss of the tooth or the eye, *but nothing else.*

G. "He shall go free" forms another encompassing generalization, and wherever you have a sequence made up of an encompassing generalization, a particularization, and another encompassing generalization, you include under the rule what is similar to the particularization: Just as the particularization makes explicit that the slave goes free by reason of blemishes that are exposed to sight and these do not grow back, so any blemishes that are exposed to sight and that are not going to grow back are covered by the same loss and with the same outcome.

H. *Well, how about this:* Just as the particularization makes clear that a blemish that is exposed to sight, which causes the body part to cease to work, and which body part does not grow back, serves to liberate the slave, so any sort of blemish that is exposed to sight, which causes the body part to cease to work, and which body part does not grow back, serves to liberate the slave? *Then how come it has been taught on Tannaite authority:* If the owner pulled out the slave's beard and loosened his jaw, the slave is freed on that account?

I. "He shall let him go free" forms an extension of the law.

J. *Well, if it's an extension of the law, then even if he hit him on his hand and it withered but is going to get better, he also should go free. Then how come it has been taught on Tannaite authority:* If he hit him on his hand and it withered but is going to get better, he does not go free?

K. *If he did go free, then what's the point of tooth and eye?*

IV.3   A.   *Our rabbis have taught on Tannaite authority:*

        B.   "In all these cases, a slave goes forth to freedom, but he requires a writ of emancipation from his master," the words of R. Simeon.

        C.   R. Meir says, "He doesn't require one."

        D.   R. Eliezer says, "He requires one."

        E.   R. Tarfon says, "He doesn't require one."

        F.   R. Aqiba says, "He requires one."

        G.   Those who settle matters in the presence of sages say, "The position of R. Tarfon makes more sense in the case of a tooth or eye, since the Torah has itself assigned him freedom on these counts, but the position of R. Aqiba is more sensible in the case of other parts of the body, because the freedom that is assigned in those cases represents an extrajudicial penalty imposed by sages on the master."

        H.   It is an extrajudicial penalty? *But there are verses of Scripture that are interpreted here!*

        I.   Rather, "Since it is an exposition of sages."

IV.4   A.   *What is the scriptural basis for the position of R. Simeon?*

        B.   He derives the sense of "sending her" from the use of the same word in the case of a woman: Just as the woman is sent forth by a writ, so a slave is sent forth by a writ.

        C.   And R. Meir?

        D.   *If the words "to freedom" were included at the end of the verse in question, it would be as you say, but since it is written at the outset, "to freedom shall he send him away," the sense is, to begin with he is free.*

IV.5   A.   *Our rabbis have taught on Tannaite authority:*

        B.   If the master hit the slave on his eye and blinded him, on his ear and deafened him, the slave goes forth by that reason to freedom. If he hit an object that was opposite the slave's eye, and the slave cannot see, or opposite his ear, so that he cannot hear, the slave does not go forth on that account to freedom.

IV.6   A.   *Said R. Shemen to R. Ashi, "Does that bear the implication that noise is nothing? But didn't R. Ammi bar Ezekiel teach as a Tannaite statement:* A chicken that put its head into an empty glass jar and crowed and broke the jar – the owner pays full damages? And said R. Joseph, *'They say in the household of the master: A horse that neighed or an ass that brayed and broke utensils – the owner pays half-damages'!"*

        B.   *He said to him, "Man is exceptional, for, since he is self-aware, he frightens himself [and is responsible if he is frightened by noise], for it has been taught on Tannaite authority:* He who frightens his fellow to death is exempt under the laws of humanity but liable under the laws of Heaven. How so? If he blew on the ear and deafened him, he is exempt. If he seized him and tore him on the ear and deafened him, he is liable. [In the latter case he did a deed of consequence.] [cf. T. B.Q. 9:26]."

IV.7   A.   *Our rabbis have taught on Tannaite authority:*

        B.   If he hit his eye and impaired his eyesight, his tooth and loosened it, but he still can use them at this time, the slave does not go forth on their account to freedom, but if not, the slave does go forth on their account to freedom.

        C.   *It has further been taught on Tannaite authority:*

D. If the slave had poor eyesight but the master totally blinded him, or if his tooth was loose and the master knocked it out, then, if he could use them before times, the slave goes free on their account, but if not, the slave does not go free on their account.

IV.8 A. *And it was necessary to state both rules, for had we been informed of only the first rule, it might have been because to begin with the man had healthy vision and now he has weak vision, but in this case, since to begin with he had weak vision, I might have said that that is not the rule. And if we had been informed only of the second case, then it might have been because now he has totally blinded him, but in that case, in which he did not totally blind him, I might have said that the slave does not go free. So both were needed.*

IV.9 A. *Our rabbis have taught on Tannaite authority:*

B. Lo, if his master was a physician, and the slave told him to paint his eye with an ointment, and the master blinded him, or to drill his tooth and he knocked it out, the slave just grins at his master and walks out free.

C. Rabban Simeon b. Gamaliel says, "'...And he destroy it' (Ex. 21:26) – only if he intends to destroy it."

IV.10 A. *So how do rabbis deal with the clause, "...And he destroy it" (Ex. 21:26)?*

B. *They require it in line with that which has been taught on Tannaite authority:*

C. R. Eleazar says, "Lo, if the master stuck his hand into his slave girl's womb and blinded the foetus that was in her belly, he is exempt from punishment. How come? Scripture said, '...And he destroy it' (Ex. 21:26) – only if he intends to destroy it."

D. *And the other party?*

E. *That rule he derives from the language, "And he destroy it" instead of the language, "And he destroy."*

F. *And the other party?*

G. *He derives no lesson from the language, "And he destroy it" instead of the language, "And he destroy."*

IV.11 A. Said R. Sheshet, "If the slave's eye was blind and the master removed it, the slave goes forth to freedom on that account. How come? Because he now lacks a limb."

B. *And a Tannaite statement is repeated along these same lines:* Freedom from blemish and male gender are required in the case of animals for sacrifice, but not for fowl. Might one then suppose that if the wing was dried up, the foot cut off, the eye plucked out, the bird remains fit? Scripture said, "And if the burnt-offering be of fowl" (Lev. 1:14), but not all fowl.

IV.12 A. Said R. Hiyya bar Ashi said Rab, "If the slave had [25A] an extra finger and the master cut it off, the slave goes out free."

B. Said R. Huna, "But that is on condition that the extra finger counts along with the hand."

IV.13 A. *The elders of Nezonayya didn't come to the public sessions of R. Hisda. He said to R. Hamnuna, "Go, excommunicate them."*

B. *He went and said to him, "How come rabbis have not come to the session?"*

C.   *They said to him, "Why should we come? For when we ask him a question, he can't answer it for us."*

D.   *He said to them, "Well, have you ever asked me a question that I couldn't answer for you?"*

E.   *They asked him the following: "A slave whose master castrated him, what is the law on classifying this blemish? Is it tantamount to one that is visible to the eye or is it not?"*

F.   *He didn't know the answer.*

G.   *They said to him, "So what's your name?"*

H.   *He said to them, "Hamnuna."*

I.   *They said to him, "It's not Hamnuna but Qarnuna."*

J.   *He came before R. Hisda. He said to him "Well, they asked you a question that can be answered from the Mishnah, for we have learned in the Mishnah:* **Twenty-four tips of limbs in man which are not susceptible to uncleanness because of quick flesh: The tips of the joints of hands and feet, and the tips of the ears, and the tip of the nose, and the tip of the penis. And the tips of the breasts which are in the woman. R. Judah says, 'Also of the man.' R. Eliezer says, 'Also the warts and the wens are not susceptible to uncleanness because of quick flesh'** [M. Neg. 6:7]. *And a Tannaite statement in that connection:* And on account of the loss of all of these, a slave goes forth to freedom. Rabbi says, 'Also on account of castration.' Ben Azzai says, 'Also on account of the tongue.'"

IV.14 A.   The master has said: "Rabbi says, 'Also on account of castration'":

B.   *Castration of what? Should I have said castration of the penis? But that is the same as loss of the penis [to which reference is explicitly made]. So it must mean, castration of the testicles.*

IV.15 A.   Rabbi says, "Also on account of castration":

B.   *And doesn't Rabbi include in the last version removal of the tongue? And by way of contrast:* If a priest was sprinkling a man made unclean by corpse uncleanness with purification water, and a sprinkle hit his mouth – Rabbi says, "This constitutes a valid act of sprinkling." And sages say, "This does not constitute a valid act of sprinkling." *Now isn't this sprinkling on his tongue* [Freedman: so Rabbi regards the tongue as an exposed limb, contradicting his exclusion of the tongue in the case of a slave]?

C.   *No, it means on his lips.*

D.   *Well, if it means on his lips, then that is self-evidently the rule and it hardly needs to be spelled out!*

E.   *What might you otherwise have supposed, sometimes the lips are tightly pressed together? So we are informed that, one way or the other [they are regarded as exposed].*

F.   *But it has been taught on Tannaite authority:* "On his tongue," *and it further has been taught on Tannaite authority:* And that the greater part of the tongue has been removed. R. Judah says, "The greater part of the fore-tongue"!

G.   Rather, Rabbi says, "Castration, *and it is not necessary to say,* the tongue, too."

H.   Ben Azzai says, "The tongue but not castration."

I.   *And what is the point of saying "also"?*

J.   *It refers to the first clause.*

K.   *If so, then Ben Azzai's statement should have come first.*

L.   *The Tannaite framer of the passage heard Rabbi's statement and set it in place, then he heard Ben Azzai's statement and repeated it,* but the initial Tannaite formulation of the Mishnah paragraph did not move from the place assigned to it.

M.   Said Ulla, "All concur in regard to the tongue that, so far as issues of uncleanness are concerned, it is held to be exposed with respect to dead creeping things. *How come? The All-Merciful has said,* 'And whomsoever he who has a flux touches' (Lev. 15:11), *and this, too, can be touched.* With respect to immersion, however, it is tantamount to a concealed part of the body. *What is the scriptural basis? The All-Merciful has said,* 'And he shall bathe his flesh in water' (Lev. 15:13) – just as the flesh is exposed, so everything that has to be touched by the water must be exposed. They differ only with respect to sprinkling in particular. *Rabbi compares it to the matter of uncleanness, and sages invoke the analogy of immersion, and both parties differ with respect to this one verse of Scripture:* 'And the clean shall sprinkle upon the unclean' (Num. 19:19) – *Rabbi interprets the matter,* 'And the clean shall sprinkle upon the unclean on the third day and on the seventh day and purify him,' *and rabbis read,* 'And on the seventh day he shall purify him and he shall wash his clothes and bathe himself in water' [Freedman: hence sprinkling must be on the same part that needs immersion, excluding the tongue, which doesn't]."

N.   *So why don't rabbis make the comparison to the matter of uncleanness?*

O.   *We seek governing analogies for matters of cleanness from matters of cleanness.*

P.   And why shouldn't Rabbi invoke the analogy of immersion?

Q.   "And he shall wash his clothes" *closes the subject* [Freedman: therefore "shall purify" cannot be linked with "bathe himself"].

R.   *But does Rabbi really take the view that, with respect to immersion, the tongue is regarded as concealed?* But didn't Rabin bar R. Ada say R. Isaac said, "There is the case of the slave girl of Rabbi, who immersed, and when she came up out of the water, a bone that constituted interposition between her body and the water was found between her teeth, so Rabbi required her to immerse a second time"?

S.   *To be sure, we don't require that the water enter the spot, but we do require that there be the possibility of its entering, and that accords with what R. Zira said, for* said R. Zira, "In the case of whatever is suitable for mingling, actual mingling is not essential, and in the case of whatever is not suitable for mingling, actual mingling is indispensable." [Cashdan, *Menahot* 18B: In Zira's view the law before us is that mingling can be omitted so long as it is possible to do so if one wants, and the Mishnah's rule would mean that no oil at all was poured in.]

T.   *There is a conflict of Tannaite statements on the same matter:*

U.   "'That which has its stones bruised, crushed, torn, or cut' (Lev. 22:24) – all of them affect the testicles," the words of R. Judah.

V.   *"In the stones" but not in the penis? Rather: "Also in the stones,"* the words of R. Judah.

W.   R. Eliezer b. Jacob says, "All of them refers to defects in the penis."
X.   R. Yosé says, "'Bruised, crushed' also can refer to the testicles, but 'torn, or cut' can refer to the penis, but in the testicles do not constitute a blemish."

I.1 finds a scripture basis for the Mishnah's rule. Nos. 2-3+4 address a further Tannaite statement on the same topic. Then we have a Tannaite complement, tacked on to the foregoing for obvious reasons, at No. 5, with its talmud at Nos. 6, 7. No. 8 illustrates the foregoing. II.1 analyzes the language of the Mishnah sentence. III.1+2 follow suit. IV.1 Nos. 2-3+4, 5-6, 7-8, 9-10, 11-12, 13 then move on to a tangential theme, relevant to our topic but not to the particular rule at hand. Nos. 13+14-15 are added because of its general congruence to the foregoing, but, of course, we have moved from a supplement to an appendix.

III. The Exegetical Programs of Yerushalmi and of the Bavli Compared

We once more take up the comparison of the heuristic morphology of the one two Talmuds, with the Yerushalmi at the left, the Bavli at the right, as before.

1:3 I Comparison of the acquisition of slaves and the acquisition of real estate, based on a verse of Scripture, Lev. 25:46, yielding the rule that the Mishnah has presented. How do we know that inherited real estate is acquired through money writ or usucaption?

1:3 II Statement that land is acquired only through usucaption does not accord with Eliezer [footnote to the foregoing].

1:3 III There are Mishnah rules that maintain slaves are equivalent to real estate, others that maintain slaves are equivalent to movables, others that compare them neither to real estate nor to movables.

1:3 IV Gloss on M. 1:3B: money paid to the master. Issue

1:3 I.1 How on the basis of Scripture do we know this fact? Lev. 25:46 treats acquisition of slaves as equivalent to acquisition of a field of inheritance. Might one suppose that just as a field of inheritance reverts to the original owner at the Jubilee, so does the Canaanite slave? Scripture closes off that possibility. While the prooftext is the same as the Yerushalmi's, the issue that is raised – maybe the slave reverts – is different.

1:3 I.2 Slave may be acquired also through barter. This point is not raised in the Yerushalmi.

1:3 I.3 Slave may be acquired through drawing. This point is not raised in the Yerushalmi.

1:3 I.4 Continues foregoing.

of how the transfer takes place, secondary quesion of whether one may transfer a benefit to someone in the beneficiary's absence.

1:3 V Analysis of M. Git. 4:5A: one who is half-slave and half-free.

1:3 VI If a slave picked up a lost object, can he avoid giving it to the master? Intersects with M. Ned. 11:8. Basic point: hand of slave is equivalent to hand of master.

1:3 VII Why doesn't the Mishnah list also make the point that the slave goes free at loss of limbs?

1:3 VIII Meir and sages on status of a gift from a third party to the slave.

1:3 IX Slave should acquire ownership of writ of emancipation for a fellow slave, since he has right to a writ of emanciation, but he should not acquire a writ of divorce of a woman, since he is not subject to that law.

1:3 X Are heirs bound by a writ of emancipation issued to take effect upon the master's death?

1:3 XI Continuation of foregoing.

1:3 XII You are free but your offspring is a slave.

1:3 I.5 Tannaite rule: How is a slave acquired through an act of usucaption? Clarifies the Mishnah rule. This point is not raised in the Yerushalmi.

1:3 I.6 Continues foregoing.

1:3 I.7 Continues foregoing.

1:3 I.8 Case. No counterpart in the Yerushalmi to the problem addressed here.

1:3 II.1 Gloss of Meir's statement: Can someone act in behalf of a third party not in his presence? Intersects with M. Git. 1:6. The problem is the same as the Yerushalmi's, but the treatment is different, since Abbayye insists the case is not one in which it is not with his knowledge and consent. So the issue intersects, but it is treated entirely differently in the Bavli.

1:3 III.1 Clarification of Mishnah statement: with money – whether taken on by others or by himself; with a writ, if taken on by others but not by himself; this represents the position of Simeon b. Eleazar. In fact, there are three positions on this issue, Meir's, Simeon's, and rabbis'. This analysis does not have a counterpart in the Yerushalmi.

1:3 III.2 Continues the foregoing.

1:3 III.3 What is at issue in the Mishnah dispute? Meir – slave has no right to acquire title without master's participation and woman has no right without her husband's; rabbis – slave may do so, wife may do so.

1:3 IV.2 Tannaite complement: slave goes free through loss of major limbs. Why is that so in case of major limbs, since Scripture refers only to tooth and eye? The Yerushalmi does not know this problem.

1:3 IV.3 Tannaite statement: Does slave require a writ of emancipation if he goes forth because of loss of major limb? The Yerushalmi does not know this problem.

1:3 IV.4 Continuation of foregoing.

1:3 IV.5 If the master directly hit the slave etc., the slave is freed; if the injury was indirect, the slave doesn't go free. The Yerushalmi knows nothing of this problem.

1:3 IV.6 Continuation of foregoing.

1:3 IV.7 If the slave can still use his eyes etc., he is not freed.

1:3 IV.8 It was necessary to talk about the several possibilities just now listed.

1:3 IV.9 If the master was a physician and the slave told him to paint the eye and the master blinded him, the slave goes free.

1:3 IV.10 Continuation of foregoing.

1:3 IV.11 Secondary development of foregoing.

1:3 IV.12 Supplementary rule added to foregoing.

1:3 IV.13 Story that contains a supplementary rule for the foregoing.

1:3 IV.14 Footnote to the foregoing.

1:3 IV.15 Continuation of the footnote.

The two Talmuds intersect at a few points, as noted. Where they intersect, it is because of the contents of the Mishnah. It is on the issue of how the slave acquires ownership of himself, since what the slave acquires belongs automatically to the master, that the two Talmuds come closest together. But, as we see, while the issue is shared, the Bavli goes its own way. The question is the same, but the treatment of the question in the later Talmud is not continuous with the treatment of the same matter in the earlier one. And, still more interesting, the Bavli asks about matters that the Yerushalmi treats superficially or simply ignores, for instance, other modes of acquisition, on the one side, and the freeing of the slave through the loss of major limbs, on the other.

Not only so, but even where the same verse of Scripture figures, as at Y 1:3Y=B. 1:3 I.1, the discussions of the two Talmuds exhibit strikingly distinctive characters:

[I.A] It is written, "[As to Canaanite slaves] you may bequeath them to your sons after you, to inherit as a possession forever; you may make slaves of them" (Lev. 25: 46).	I.1 A. *How on the basis of Scripture do we know this fact?*
[B] Acquisition of slaves thereby is treated under the same rubric as inherited real estate.	B. As it is written, "And you shall make them [gentile slaves] an inheritance for your children after you, to possess as an inheritance" (Lev. 25:46) – Scripture thus has treated them as comparable to a field of inheritance. Just as a field of inheritance is acquired through money, writ, or usucaption, **so a Canaanite slave is acquired through money, through a writ, or through usucaption.**
[C] Just as inherited real estate is acquired through money, writ, or usucaption so a Canaanite slave is acquired through money, writ, or usucaption.	
[D] How do we know that inherited real estate itself is acquired through money, writ, or usucaption?	C. Might one then propose: Just as a field of inheritance reverts to its original owner at
[E] It is written, "Fields will be bought for	

money, deeds will be signed and sealed and witnessed" (Jer. 32:44).

[F] "And signed and sealed and witnessed"– "signed and sealed" refers to witnesses to a writ; "witnessed" refers to witnesses to usucaption.

[G] Or perhaps these latter serve as witnesses to the writ?

[H] Since it already is written, "And signed and sealed," [which must mean a writ, the other witnesses are to usucaption].

[I] R. Yosa in the name of R. Mana, R. Tanhum, R. Abbahu in the name of R. Yohanan: "Real estate is not acquired for less than a perutah."

[J] What is the scriptural basis for that statement?

[K] "Fields will be bought for money" [and less than a perutah is not deemed money].

[L] Now [Yohanan] disputes what R. Haninah said: "All references to sheqels in the Torah are to selas; in the Prophets, to litras, and in the Writings to qintin." [Thus Jeremiah refers to twenty-five selas = a litra.]

[M] Said R. Judah bar Pazzi, "That is except for the sheqels of Ephron, which are qintin [a hundred selas]."

the Jubilee, so a Canaanite slave reverts to the original owner at the Jubilee?

D. Scripture states, "Of them shall you take your slaves forever" (Lev. 25:46).

[N] What is the scriptural basis for this statement?

[O] "For the full price let him give it to me" (Gen. 23:9) [and "full price" implies the larger coin].

[P] But the cases are not similar. There [Jer. 32:4] it is written "money," but here it is written "sheqels."

[Q] They objected, "Lo, there is the case of the rapist [Deut. 22:28], and lo, in that case what is written is only 'money,' and do you say it refers to sheqels? [So there is a dispute even when 'money' stands by itself.]"

Here is a fine instance in which, dealing with the same problem and the same prooftext, the Bavli's framers go their own way, essentially indifferent to what the Yerushalmi's authors have done (whether or not they knew what they did). Nor can we say that the later authorities (merely) supplement what the earlier ones have done, since, after all, the Bavli is simply indifferent to the entire issue addressed in the prior Talmud. And the contrary is the case. We noted that the Yerushalmi asks about the omission of the loss of major limbs from the Mishnah's list. A glance back at the Bavli shows that that Talmud has taken over a huge exposition of that topic, with a broad range of secondary issues, fully exposed and carefully analyzed. So even when the framers of both Talmuds are puzzled by the Mishnah's omission, the later Talmud goes its own way, pursuing its own method, and its method is self-evidently different from that of the earlier Talmud.

This question of the difference in heuristic morphology may now be addressed head-on. Here is what the Yerushalmi and Bavli have to say about the loss of major limbs:

[VII.A] [In listing the means by which a slave goes free], why do we not learn that he also goes free at the loss of limbs that do not grow back?

[B] Said R. Yohanan b. Mareh, "It is because there is a dispute about the matter.

[C] "Specifically, there is a Tannaite authority who teaches that [if he loses his limbs] he still requires a writ of emancipation from the master, and there is a Tannaite authority who teaches that, in that circumstance, he does not require a writ of emancipation from his master."

IV.7 A. *Our rabbis have taught on Tannaite authority:*

B. If he hit his eye and impaired his eyesight, his tooth and loosened it, but he still can use them at this time, the slave does not go forth on their account to freedom, but if not, the slave does go forth on their account to freedom.

C. *It has further been taught on Tannaite authority:*

D. If the slave had poor eyesight but the master totally blinded him, or if his tooth was loose and the master knocked it out, then, if he could use them before times, the slave goes free on their account, but if not, the slave does not go free on their account.

IV.8 A. *And it was necessary to state both rules, for had we been informed of only the first rule, it might have been because to begin with the man had healthy vision and now he has weak vision, but in this case, since to begin with he had weak vision, I might have said that that is not the rule. And if we had been informed only of the second case, then it might have been because now he has totally blinded him, but in that case, in which he did not totally blind him, I might have said that the*

slave does not go free.
So both were needed.

IV.9 A. *Our rabbis have taught*
on Tannaite authority:

B. Lo, if his master was a physician, and the slave told him to paint his eye with an ointment, and the master blinded him, or to drill his tooth and he knocked it out, the slave just grins at his master and walks out free.

C. Rabban Simeon b. Gamaliel says, "'...And he destroy it' (Ex. 21:26) – only if he intends to destroy it."

IV.10 A. *So how do rabbis deal with the clause, "...And he destroy it" (Ex. 21:26)?*

B. *They require it in line with that which has been taught on Tannaite authority:*

C. R. Eleazar says, "Lo, if the master stuck his hand into his slave girl's womb and blinded the foetus that was in her belly, he is exempt from punishment. How come? Scripture said, '...And he destroy it' (Ex. 21:26) – only if he intends to destroy it."

D. *And the other party?*

E. *That rule he derives from the language, "And he destroy it" instead of the language, "And he destroy."*

F. *And the other party?*

G. *He derives no lesson from the language, "And he destroy it"*

*instead of the language,
"And he destroy."*

IV.11 A. Said R. Sheshet, "If the slave's eye was blind and the master removed it, the slave goes forth to freedom on that account. How come? Because he now lacks a limb."

B. *And a Tannaite statement is repeated along these same lines: Freedom from blemish and male gender are required in the case of animals for sacrifice, but not for fowl. Might one then suppose that if the wing was dried up, the foot cut off, the eye plucked out, the bird remains fit? Scripture said, "And if the burnt-offering be of fowl" (Lev. 1:14), but not all fowl.*

IV.12 A. Said R. Hiyya bar Ashi said Rab, "If the slave had [25A] an extra finger and the master cut it off, the slave goes out free."

B. Said R. Huna, "But that is on condition that the extra finger counts along with the hand."

IV.13 A. *The elders of Nezonayya didn't come to the public sessions of R. Hisda. He said to R. Hamnuna, "Go, excommunicate them."*

B. *He went and said to him, "How come rabbis have not come to the session?"*

C. *They said to him, "Why should we come? For*

when we ask him a question, he can't answer it for us."

D. *He said to them, "Well, have you ever asked me a question that I couldn't answer for you?"*

E. *They asked him the following:* "A slave whose master castrated him, what is the law on classifying this blemish? *Is it tantamount to one that is visible to the eye or is it not?"*

F. *He didn't know the answer.*

G. *They said to him, "So what's your name?"*

H. *He said to them, "Hamnuna."*

I. *They said to him, "It's not Hamnuna but Qarnuna."*

J. *He came before R. Hisda. He said to him "Well, they asked you a question that can be answered from the Mishnah, for we have learned in the Mishnah:* **Twenty-four tips of limbs in man which are not susceptible to uncleanness because of quick flesh: The tips of the joints of hands and feet, and the tips of the ears, and the tip of the nose, and the tip of the penis. And the tips of the breasts which are in the woman. R. Judah says, 'Also of the man.' R. Eliezer says, 'Also the warts and the wens are not susceptible to unclean-**

ness because of quick flesh' [M. Neg. 6:7]. *And a Tannaite statement in that connection:* And on account of the loss of all of these, a slave goes forth to freedom. Rabbi says, 'Also on account of castration.' Ben Azzai says, 'Also on account of the tongue.'"

IV.14 A. The master has said: "Rabbi says, 'Also on account of castration'":

B. *Castration of what? Should I have said castration of the penis? But that is the same as loss of the penis [to which reference is explicitly made]. So it must mean, castration of the testicles.*

IV.15 A. Rabbi says, "Also on account of castration":

B. *And doesn't Rabbi include in the last version removal of the tongue? And by way of contrast:* If a priest was sprinkling a man made unclean by corpse uncleanness with purification water, and a sprinkle hit his mouth – Rabbi says, "This constitutes a valid act of sprinkling." And sages say, "This does not constitute a valid act of sprinkling." *Now isn't this sprinkling on his tongue* [Freedman: so Rabbi regards the tongue as an exposed limb, contradicting his exclusion of the tongue in the case of a slave]?

C.   *No, it means on his lips.*
D.   *Well, if it means on his lips, then that is self-evidently the rule and it hardly needs to be spelled out!*
E.   *What might you otherwise have supposed, sometimes the lips are tightly pressed together? So we are informed that, one way or the other [they are regarded as exposed].*
F.   *But it has been taught on Tannaite authority:* "On his tongue," *and it further has been taught on Tannaite authority:* And that the greater part of the tongue has been removed. R. Judah says, "The greater part of the fore-tongue"!
G.   Rather, Rabbi says, "Castration, *and it is not necessary to say,* the tongue, too."
H.   Ben Azzai says, "The tongue but not castration."
I.   *And what is the point of saying* "also"?
J.   *It refers to the first clause.*
K.   *If so, then Ben Azzai's statement should have come first.*
L.   *The Tannaite framer of the passage heard Rabbi's statement and set it in place, then he heard Ben Azzai's statement and repeated it,* but the initial Tannaite formulation of the Mishnah paragraph did not move from the place assigned to it.

M.   Said Ulla, "All concur in regard to the tongue that, so far as issues of uncleanness are concerned, it is held to be exposed with respect to dead creeping things. *How come? The All-Merciful has said,* 'And whomsoever he who has a flux touches' (Lev. 15:11), *and this, too, can be touched.* With respect to immersion, however, it is tantamount to a concealed part of the body. *What is the scriptural basis? The All-Merciful has said,* 'And he shall bathe his flesh in water' (Lev. 15:13) – just as the flesh is exposed, so everything that has to be touched by the water must be exposed. They differ only with respect to sprinkling in particular. *Rabbi compares it to the matter of uncleanness, and sages invoke the analogy of immersion, and both parties differ with respect to this one verse of Scripture:* 'And the clean shall sprinkle upon the unclean' (Num. 19:19) – Rabbi interprets the matter, 'And the clean shall sprinkle upon the unclean on the third day and on the seventh day and purify him,' *and rabbis read,* 'And on the seventh day he shall purify him and he shall wash his clothes and bathe himself in water' [Freedman: hence sprinkling must be on the same part that needs immersion, excluding the tongue, which doesn't]."

N. *So why don't rabbis make the comparison to the matter of uncleanness?*

O. *We seek governing analogies for matters of cleanness from matters of cleanness.*

P. And why shouldn't Rabbi invoke the analogy of immersion?

Q. "And he shall wash his clothes" *closes the subject* [Freedman: therefore "shall purify" cannot be linked with "bathe himself"].

R. *But does Rabbi really take the view that, with respect to immersion, the tongue is regarded as concealed?* But didn't Rabin bar R. Ada say R. Isaac said, "There is the case of the slave girl of Rabbi, who immersed, and when she came up out of the water, a bone that constituted interposition between her body and the water was found between her teeth, so Rabbi required her to immerse a second time"?

S. *To be sure, we don't require that the water enter the spot, but we do require that there be the possibility of its entering, and that accords with what R. Zira said, for* said R.

Zira, "In the case of whatever is suitable for mingling, actual mingling is not essential, and in the case of whatever is not suitable for mingling, actual mingling is indispensable."

[Cashdan, *Menahot* 18B: In Zira's view the law before us is that mingling can be omitted so long as it is possible to do so if one wants, and the Mishnah's rule would mean that no oil at all was poured in.]

T.   *There is a conflict of Tannaite statements on the same matter:*

U.   "'That which has its stones bruised, crush-ed, torn, or cut' (Lev. 22:24) – all of them affect the testicles," the words of R. Judah.

V.   "In the stones" but not in the penis? Rather: "Also in the stones," the words of R. Judah.

W.   R. Eliezer b. Jacob says, "All of them refers to defects in the penis."

X.   R. Yosé says, "'Bruised, crushed' also can refer to the testicles, but 'torn, or cut' can refer to the penis, but in the testicles do not con-stitute a blemish."

With this, I rest my case: if the Bavli is a talmud, the Yerushalmi is something else. That is one way of putting it. But it is not the right way: things so profoundly alike are to be differentiated – because they are not so different that they cannot be differentiated.

In any event, of course, both are Talmuds – systematic analytical commentaries to the Mishnah. But as is clear, the Bavli has its own program, the shape and structure of which are replicated at every point. And the Yerushalmi has a program, too, a different one, and one that, clearly, the Bavli's framers did not find to be a suitable model for their work.

4

Mishnah-Tractate Qiddushin 1:4 in the Yerushalmi and the Bavli

1:4

A. "Large cattle are acquired through delivery, and small cattle through lifting up," the words of R. Meir and R. Eleazar.
B. And sages say, "Small cattle are acquired through an act of drawing."

I. Mishnah Qiddushin 1:4 in the Talmud of the Land of Israel

[I.A] R. Huna said, "Delivering a beast does not transfer ownership in regard to the estate of a proselyte."

[B] R. Hezekiah, R. Ba, R. Eleazar asked, "If one had ten camels tied one to the other, if one handed over to [the purchaser] the reins of one of them, [60b] has he acquired all of them, or has he acquired only that one that he handed over to him alone?"

[C] R. Hisda said, "If one said, 'Draw this beast to acquire ownership of it,' he has acquired ownership thereof.

[D] "'In order to acquire ownership of its offspring,' he has not acquired ownership of it. [Drawing the beast has no effect on the status of the offspring.]

[E] "'Of it and its offspring,' he has acquired them."

[F] [Replying to D:] He who says to his fellow, "Draw this beast so that you will acquire its burden," is it possible that he has not acquired ownership of it? [Likewise at D, he should effect acquisition.]

[G] Said R. Yosé, "That applies when the beast was not pregnant.

[H] "But if it was pregnant, they have treated [the offspring] as equivalent to a burden."

[I.A] [Y. A.Z. 5:10I] R. Abba, R. Huna in the name of Rab, "He who draws a skin of wine from his fellow [without having agreed on a price for it with him], and the skin was torn [so that the wine poured out] – the man does not owe him for it [because he had not made an agreement on its price, and therefore the purchaser had not come to a decision to acquire the skin, and the skin of wine did not yet pass into the domain of the prospective purchaser]."

207

[B]   Said R. Yosé b. R. Bun, "Therefore it was necessary to teach [this obvious rule, A, to indicate that,] even if the prospective purchaser should bring the skin into his own stall, [he is not liable should the skin break,] for his intention in doing so was only so that other people should not make acquisition of the skin. [But it still has not fallen into his domain. Until a price has been agreed upon, the skin does not belong to the prospective purchaser [just as is indicated at M. A.Z. 5:10A-B].]"

[C]   What is the law regarding the skin of wine's having [automatically] been acquired by him at the lowest price [prevailing in the market at that time, even though there has been no agreement on any price at all]? [Do we say that, if he could have gotten the wine for the lowest prevailing price, he would have accepted lt for that price? Or do we say that, since the skin of wine has not yet entered the prospective purchaser's domain, he is exempt of all liability for the wine?"

[D]   Said R. Haggai before R. Yosé, "The Mishnah itself has laid down the law that it is not [presumptively] acquired by the prospective purchaser for the lowest prevailing price.

[E]   "For we have learned there: **He who sells wine to a gentile and agreed on a price before he had measured the wine out – proceeds paid for it are permitted. If he had measured it out before he had fixed its price, proceeds paid for it are prohibited** [M. A.Z. 5:10A-C].

[F]   "Now if you maintain that one should regard [the wine] as [presumptively] acquired by the prospective purchaser at the lowest prevailing price, then even a case in which he measured it out before he agreed upon a price should be treated as equivalent to a case in which he had agreed to a price before he had measured out the wine [so that even in the case raised above, C], the proceeds should be permitted. [For what difference will it make whether a price has been agreed upon, if we maintain that there is a putative price, that is, the lowest prevailing price in the market, which the prospective purchaser is assumed to be willing to accept under all conditions?]"

[III.A] Samuel said, "He who picked up a chicken [to examine it for possible purchase], and it flew off – is he liable for it? [Do we hold the purchaser liable?]"

[B]   [In raising the question of liability, rather than requiring him to go and try to find the chicken again,] said R. Samuel bar Abodema, "That is applicable to Tyre and its surrounding towns or to Caesarea and its surrounding towns, [which are so large that we cannot expect someone to go looking for the chicken].

[C]   "But as to this area, it is the practice to go look for the lost object until it tires itself, and then he will find it and return it to the owner."

[IV.A]   R. Simeon b. Laqish in the name of R. Yannai, "He who sells a flock to his fellow – once he has handed over to him the bellwether, [the purchaser] has acquired ownership of it."

[B]   What is the meaning of bellwether?

- [C] Some say it is the staff, some say the shepherd's pipe, and some say it is the leaders of the flock.
- [D] R. Jacob bar Aha, R. Simeon b. Abba in the name of R. Joshua b. Levi, "He who sells a cistern to his fellow, once he has handed over to him the bucket [belonging to the cistern] – the purchaser has acquired ownership."
- [E] R. Ami in the name of R. Yohanan: "He who sells a house to his fellow, once he has piled up his possessions in it, [he has acquired it]."
- [F] R. Judah b. Pazzi raised the question: "If he handed over the key to him, what is the law?"
- [G] Said R. Zechariah, son-in-law of R. Levi, "It is a dispute between R. Simeon and sages.
- [H] "For we have learned there:
- [I] "He who gives over his key to an am haares – the house is clean, for he gave him only the charge of guarding the key [M . Toh. 10:1E-F]. It was taught [in this connection]: R. Simeon declares the house unclean [so it is giving over charge of the house]."
- [J] R. Abbahu in the name of R. Simeon b. Levi: "He who sells the tithes of his field to his fellow has done nothing whatever [since at the moment of sale the tithes are not yet in being and subject to sale].
- [K] "...The offspring of his slave girl to his fellow has done nothing.
- [L] "The fetus of his cow to his fellow has done nothing.
- [M] "The contained air space of a ruin to his fellow has done nothing.
- [N] "But he sells his field and leaves out of the sale its tithes, sells the slave girl and retains ownership of the offspring, sells his cow and retains ownership of its offspring, sells his ruin and retains ownership of its contained air space."
- [O] How is it possible for someone to sell the air space of his ruin [M] anyway?
- [P] Interpret the case to speak of one in which he says to him, "Remove something from this ruin so that you may acquire one-tenth of it" [for added space required by the purchaser, for example, for a balcony].
- [Q] And in the case of real estate, here [in the case of tithes], he says, "Remove something from the ground so that you may acquire one-tenth of what is in it."
- [V.A] R. Samuel, R. Zeira, R. Hiyya bar Ashi in the name of Rab: "An act of drawing a beast does not effect acquisition thereof in a courtyard that does not belong to both the buyer and the seller."
- [B] R. Hiyya taught this teaching, which differs [at D-E]: "In what circumstances have they ruled that movables are acquired through an act of drawing them?
- [C] "In the public domain, or in a courtyard that does not belong to the two of them.
- [D] "But if it is in the domain of the purchaser, once he has agreed to the purchase, he has acquired ownership.
- [E] "[If it is] in the domain of the seller, the purchaser has not effected acquisition until he raises the beast up off the ground or until he draws it and takes it outside the limits of the domain of the owners.

[F] "[If it is] in the domain of one in whose hands [movables] were left as a bailment, he has not made acquisition until he effects ownership of them, or until he hires a place for himself [in that property, in which he then acquires them]."

[VI.A] **And sages say, "Small cattle are acquired through an act of drawing" [M. 1:4B].**

[B] What is the scriptural basis for the position of the rabbis?

[C] "Draw and take a lamb for your families" (Ex. 12:3).

[D] This is in accord with that incident in which R. Judah set a question:

[E] "A large beast – how does it get acquired?"

[F] He said to him, "By being delivered."

[G] He said to him, "And does not the Mishnah explicitly state: Large cattle are acquired through delivery [M. 1:1A]?

[H] "But there is a Tannaite authority who teaches the matter in the reverse."

[VII.A] R. Judah asked R. Eleazar, "A firstborn son who was injured [with a death-causing injury] during thirty days after birth, [does the father owe the priest redemption money]?"

[B] He said to him, "It is as if it has died, and the owner [father] is exempt from paying the five selas owing for the son."

[C] R. Judah sent and asked R. Eleazar, "An afterbirth, part of which went forth on one day, and part on the next – [how are the two days counted in line with Lev. 12]?"

[D] He said to him, "If it is as to the blood of purifying, one should count from the former of the two days, and if it is for unclean blood, one begins counting from the latter of the two days."

[E] Said R. Mattenaiah, "That rule you state applies when the offspring did not come forth with it. But if the offspring came forth with it, whether it is as to the blood of purifying or as to blood of uncleanness, one begins counting only from the moment the offspring itself came out."

[F] R. Judah sent to R. Eleazar, "A bailiff who handed over his bailment to another bailiff, [what is the law if an accident should happen to the bailment]?"

[G] He said to him, "The first is liable."

[H] R. Yohanan said, "The first is liable."

[I] R. Simeon b. Laqish said, "The second is liable."

[J] [As at Y. Ket. 9:5:] There we have learned: He who rents a cow from his fellow, and then lent it to someone else, and the cow died of natural causes – let the one who rented it take an oath that it died of natural causes, and the one who borrowed it then pays compensation to the one who rented it, [not to the owner]. Said R. Yosé, "How should this one get to do business with the other one's cow? But the funds paid for the cow are to return to the owner" [M. B.Q. 3:2].

[K] R. Ila in the name of R. Yannai, "And that rule applies in a case in which, to begin with, he gave the man permission to lend the cow out, but if he did not give him permission to lend the cow – it is not in such a case that the rule applies."

[L] And so, too, did R. Hiyya teach:

[M] **One who borrows has no right to lend out,**

[N] and one who hires has no right to rent out,

[O] and one who borrows has no right to rent out,

[P] and one who hires has no right to lend out,

[Q] and the one with whom these things are left as a bailment has no right to leave them as a bailment with someone else,

[R] unless the householder [who owns the objects] has given him permission to do so [T. B.M. 3:1].

[S] And in all cases in which they changed the conditions of guardianship without the knowledge and consent of the owner, they are liable.

[T] But as to a borrower, even if he did not change the conditions agreed to by the owner, he is liable. [So why say, S, in all cases?]

[U] It is on this account that we have learned there:

[V] An unpaid bailee may stipulate that he will be exempt from having to take an oath, and a borrower that he will be exempt from having to pay restitution [M. B.M. 7:10F-H].

[W] [S] comes to say to you, "Even if [a borrower] made a stipulation that he will be exempt, he remains liable."

[X] If [at J = M. B.Q. 3:2] he sought to impose an oath on the borrower, must he take an oath in line with the following:

[Y] If he wrote to her, "I have no right to impose a vow or an oath on you," he has not got the right to impose an oath on her. But he does impose an oath upon her heirs and those who are her legal agents [M. Ket. 9:5].

[Z] That is to say that if he wished to impose an oath on the borrower [of M. B.Q. 3:2], he has the right to impose an oath on him [since he falls within his domain].

[AA] Then the rule covering that case [M. B.Q. 3:2] derives from the present case [M. Ket. 9:5], and the rule covering the present case derives from the rule covering that one.

[BB] The rule covering that case derives from the present case: If he wanted to impose an oath on the borrower, he may impose an oath on him. [but then he may not impose an oath on the one who rented the beast]. [That follows M. Ket.'s rule that he may impose an oath on the heirs but not on the woman herself.]

[CC] The rule covering the present case derives from the rule covering that one: If he wanted to impose an oath on the woman, he may not impose an oath on her.

[DD] Said R. Haninah, "You have no need to derive the rule covering that case [of M. B.Q. 3:2] from this one. [It is obvious that the woman may not be subjected to an oath, for the man himself has freed her from that obligation anyway. Why turn to the other cases to prove this obvious proposition?]

[EE] "Rather, there is a need to derive the rule covering the case [at M. Ket.] from this other. In regard to what R. Hila said in the name of R. Yannai, [K]: 'And that rule applies in a case in which, to begin with, he gave the man permission to lend the cow out, but if he did not give him permission to lend the cow, it is not in such a case that the rule applies.'

[FF] "Here, too, the man has given permission for the woman's sons to serve as guardians."

[GG] [Reverting to M. B.Q. 3:2 = J above:] Said R. Yosé, "The one who rents the beast has to pay the owner of the beast a fee so long as it is rented out to him, [even though the one who rents the beast has lent it to a third party]."

[HH] R. Zeira asked R. Abuna, "If the owner borrowed the beast [that they had rented out to this other party] and then it died, [do they have to pay the one who rented the beast out, in line with the sages' position at M. B.Q. 3:2]?"

[II] He said to him, "Indeed so do we rule, and even if the owner ate it."

[JJ] Said R. Yosé bar Abun, "If they ate it! But they ate what belongs to themselves!"

[KK] [Reverting to F-I, above,] R. Zeira raised the question before R. Yosa, "How do we decide such a case?"

[LL] He said to him, "[We follow the majority.] Here we have two against four [so the second party is liable, since Eleazar, Yohanan, Yannai, and Hiyya all maintain that is so]. [The borrower has no right to lend out the beast, so the original guardian is liable.] The law follows the majority."

[MM] He said to him, "We have only two against two, for R. Eleazar is the disciple of R. Hiyya the Great, and R. Yohanan is the disciple of R. Yannai."

[NN] R. Judah sent and asked R. Eleazar, "Brothers who divided their father's estate, and afterward one of them entered into levirate marriage with the deceased brother's widow [whose husband had been dead at the time of the division – do we maintain that the levir has abandoned his claim on the brother's share in the estate]? For does he retain his claim on his brother's share?]"

[OO] He said to him, "As they divide the entire property, so they divide the property of the deceased brother [equally, and the levir does not get the deceased brother's share]."

[PP] Ulla bar Ishmael said, "Who can understand the ruling of R. Eleazar, [which is not spelled out and explained]? For there is no difference even in a case in which they had divided the estate, and afterward one of them had entered into levirate marriage [60c]. [Here the levir certainly lays no claim to a larger share in the estate.] Nor would it matter if he had entered into levirate marriage and afterward divided the estate. In both cases all of them take an equal share in the estate of their father.

[QQ] [So why did he answer him without further specification?"

[RR] He said to him, "To the question he asked the other party answered, and not to any other question."

[SS] And why did he not ask the question [about the reverse order of events]?

[TT] It is in line with what R. Abina said in the name of R. Assi: "A firstborn son who took a share in his father's estate like an ordinary son – it may be assumed that he has given up his claim to a double portion. [Likewise the case would be obvious that if there were a general division of the estate, and then the levir entered into marriage, he did not wish to claim the share of the deceased brother at all.]"

[UU] R. Judah sent and asked R. Eleazar, "Brothers who divided their father's estate – [what do they include when they estimate the total value of the estate]? [Does this include their clothing and that of their families, already received from the father?]"

[VV] He said to him, "They divide [the value of] what is on them, but they do not divide the value of what is on their sons and daughters."

[WW] R. Imi says, "He who appraises his wife's garments brings that appraisal [of expensive garments provided for his wife] to the common pot and divides it up.

[XX] "He who makes jewelry for his wife – they do not put the value into the common pot and divide it up. [That is her own property, not part of the estate to be appraised.]

[YY] "That applies to what may be used on an ordinary day. But as to what is used on a festival, they bring the value into the common pot and divide it up."

[ZZ] R. Mana said, "Garments used for a festival are appraised, and the value is divided as part of the estate. Garments used for the Sabbath pose a problem."

[AAA] To R. Abin it was self-evident that, whether the garments were for a festival or for the Sabbath, they appraise their value and contribute it to the common pot and divide it up.

[BBB] R. Zeira asked before R. Mana, "As to those glass utensils, [what is the law about dividing them up among the heirs]?"

[CCC] He said to him, "You are known to have plenty of glass utensils."

[DDD] [Zeira] said to him, "They bring them and divide up their value as part of the estate."

[EEE] R. Judah sent and asked R. Eleazar, "What is the law as to collecting a debt from the debtor's slaves, as one does from his real estate?"

[FFF] He said to him, "They collect a debt from slaves as from real estate."

[GGG] R. Eleazar instructed the members of the house of R. Yannai to collect a debt from slaves as from real estate.

[HHH] R. Judah sent and asked R. Eleazar, "As to the thug, thief, and robber, [how are they forced to effect repayment]? [Does the owner have to accept the carcass or the broken shards of his original beast or object, or do the thief, robber and thug have to pay the value of these objects and keep the carcass or the broken shards?]"

[III] He said to him, "It is to be assumed that the owner does not have to be troubled with the dead beast."

[JJJ] And how do we know that the owner does not have to be troubled with the dead beast?

[KKK] Said R. Ba bar Mamel, "'If the beast is alive, he will pay back double indemnity' (Ex. 22:1). The meaning is, 'He pays a live beast, and not a dead beast.'"

[LLL] Now that applies to a case of thievery. What about a case of robbery?

[MMM] Said R. Abun, "'He shall restore what he took by robbery' (Lev. 6:4) – in its original condition."

The Talmud presents an anthology of materials on how movables pass from one person's domain to another's. Unit I takes up the issue of acquiring a number of beasts all at once. Unit II deals with purchase of movables, not beasts, and it belongs at Y. A.Z. 5:11, where it is explained in context. Unit III turns to acquiring a small animal by lifting it up and asks about one's liability when he lifts it up only to examine it. Unit IV specifies the point at which a transfer is definitively effected. Unit V deals with the location in which acquisition of a beast or movables is effected. Unit VI goes on to the exposition of the scriptural foundations of the Mishnah. I assume that the long sequence of questions and answers of unit VII is attached because it is deemed continuous with the question and answer of VI.D-H. The immense set of materials, bearing their own extensive discussions, requires no comment in the present context.

II. Mishnah Qiddushin 1:4 in the Talmud of Babylonia

I.1   A.   Rab expounded in Qimhunayya, "Large cattle are acquired through drawing the beast."

        B.   *Samuel came across the disciples of Rab. He said to them, "Did Rab say* that large beasts are acquired through drawing? *But we have learned as the Tannaite formulation, 'through delivery'! And Rab also said that it was through delivery."*

        C.   *So did Rab retract his opinion?*

        D.   *He made his ruling in accord with the Tannaite authority behind the following, which has been taught on Tannaite authority:* And sages say, "This and that [large, small beasts alike] are acquired through drawing." R. Simeon says, "This and that are acquired through lifting up the beast."

        E.   *Objected R. Joseph,* "Well, then, how in R. Simeon's opinion can an elephant be acquired [who can lift up the damn thing]!"

        F.   Said to him Abbayye, "Through a symbolic barter, *or also* by renting the place in which it is located [on which account the place belongs to the purchaser, along with its contents]."

        G.   R. Zira said, "The purchaser brings four utensils and puts them under the elephant's feet."

        H.   *That yields the proposition:* When the purchaser's utensils are in the domain of the seller and a commodity that has been purchased is put in them, the purchaser has acquired title to the commodity. [But that is not a settled question, so how can we be so sure?]

        I.   *Here with what situation do we deal? It is an alley [belonging to no private party]. [26A] Or also, it may involve bundles of twigs [of a height that serve to raise the elephant above the ground when he steps on them].*

I.1 works on the correct wording of our Mishnah rule.

III. The Exegetical Programs of Yerushalmi and of the Bavli Compared

Do we find shared compositions or composites? The following summary comparison answers that question.

1:4 I Transfer of ownership in the estate of a proselyte (who dies without heirs).

1:4 II Transfer of title does not take place until a price has been agreed upon.

1:4 III Is one who examines an object for possible purchase liable for it?

1:4 IV He who sells a flock to his fellow – transfer of title takes place with the handing over of the bellwether.

1:4 V Drawing a beast does not transfer title in a courtyard that belongs to neither buyer nor seller.

1:4 VI Scripture basis for position of sages at 1:4B.

1:4 VII A firstborn son who was injured during thirty days after birth – does father owe priest redemption money? An afterbirth, part of which went forth on one day, part on the next, how are these counted in line with Lev. 12? A bailiff who handed over his bailment to another bailiff, what is the law? etc. This composite continues VI.D-H – questions raised by Judah. The composite is a conglomeration joined by formal considerations and then worked out in its own terms.

1:4 I.1 Rab: Large cattle are acquired through drawing the beast. Samuel cites our Mishnah rule: through delivery. Harmonization through correction of the wording of the Mishnah rule.

Yerushalmi's rather well-crafted inquiry into the point at which ownership or title is transferred has no counterpart in the Bavli – but it also has little to do with our Mishnah paragraph. More to the point, Yerushalmi's vast composite, No. VII, has no counterpart in the Bavli. Here is yet another point at which the two Talmuds share the same Mishnah paragraph but nothing else: the Talmuds differ because they're different. The Yerushalmi, too, has its composites, and some of them compete even in size and complexity with the Bavli's. And the Bavli knows nothing of the Yerushalmi's composites.

5

Mishnah-Tractate Qiddushin 1:5 in the Yerushalmi and the Bavli

1:5

A. Property for which there is security is acquired through money, writ and usucaption.

B. And that for which there is no security is acquired only by an act of drawing [from one place to another].

C. Property for which there is no security is acquired along with property for which there is security through money, writ, and usucaption.

D. And property for which there is no security imposes the need for an oath on property for which there is security.

I. The Talmud of the Land of Israel to M. Qiddushin 1:5

[I.A] At first they would effect acquisition by removing the shoe, in accord with what is written, "Now this was the custom in former times in Israel [concerning redeeming and exchanging: To confirm a transaction the one drew off his sandal and gave it to the other, and this was the manner of attesting in Israel]" (Ruth 4:7).

[B] Who removed the shoe?

[C] There they say, [that] Rab and Levi [ruled on the matter].

[D] One said, "It was the purchaser," and the other said, "It was the seller."

[E] Now this disagreement accords with the dispute in the following:

[F] For it is taught: Boaz gave [the shoe] to the next of kin.

[G] R. Judah says, "The next of kin gave it to Boaz."

[H] Then they went and effected transfer of ownership through a rite of cutting off, [which took note of the alienation of an inherited property to an outsider].

[I] What is this rite of cutting off?

[J] When someone would sell an inherited property, his relatives would bring jugs and fill them with parched corn and nuts and break them before the children, and the children would collect the parched corn and nuts and say, "Mr. So-and-so has been cut off from his inherited property." When he would regain the property [for example, at the Jubilee or through prior redemption], they would perform the same rite and say, "Mr. So-and-so has gotten back to his inherited property."

[K] [This same rite was performed in another case of alienation, for] said R. Yosah b. R. Bun, "Also he who married a woman who was unworthy for his status – his relatives would bring jugs and fill them with parched corn and nuts and break them before the children, and the children would collect the parched corn and nuts and say, 'Mr. So-and-so is cut off from his family.' When he would divorce the woman, they would perform the same rite and say, 'Mr. So-and-so has gotten back to his family.'"

[L] They finally went and established that transfer of ownership would be effected through money, writ, or usucaption [M. 1:5A].

[II.A] With money: As it is written, "Fields will be bought for money, deeds will be signed and sealed and witnessed" (Jer. 32:44).

[B] "And signed and sealed and witnessed" – "signed and sealed" refers to witnesses to a writ; and "witnessed" refers to witnesses to usucaption.

[C] Or perhaps these latter serve as witnesses to the writ?

[D] Since it is already written, "And signed and sealed," [which must mean a writ, the other witnesses are to usucaption].

[E] R. Yosa in the name of R. Mana, R. Tanhum, R. Abbahu in the name of R. Yohanan: "Real estate is not acquired for less than a perutah."

[F] What is the scriptural basis for that statement?

[G] "Fields will be bought for money" [and less than a perutah is not deemed money].

[H] [Yohanan] disputes what R. Haninah said, "All references to sheqels in the Torah are to selas; in the Prophets, to litras; and in the Writings to qintrin." [Thus Jeremiah refers to twenty-five selas = a litra.]

[I] "That is, except for the sheqels of Ephron, [which are qintrin, a hundred selas]."

[J] What is the scriptural basis for this statement?

[K] "For the full price let him give it to me" (Gen. 23:9) [and "full price" implies the larger coin].

[L] But the cases are not similar. There (Jer. 32:44) it is written "money," but here it is written "sheqels."

[M] They objected, "Lo, there is the case of the rapist (Deut. 22:28), and lo, in that case what is written is only 'money,' and do you say it refers to sheqels? [So there is a dispute even when 'money' stands by itself.]"

[N] [The statement that land is acquired only through usucaption] is not in accord with the view of R. Eliezer.

[O] For R. Eliezer said, "If one merely traversed the field, he has acquired it [without usucaption]."

[P] For it has been taught, "If one traversed a field lengthwise and breadthwise, he has acquired it up to the place in which he has walked," the words of R. Eliezer.

[Q] And sages say, "He acquired it only once he effects possession through usucaption."

[R] All concur in the case of one who sells a path to his fellow, that once he has walked in it, he has acquired it.

[S] What is the scriptural basis for that position [of Eliezer]?

[T] "Arise, walk through the length and the breadth of the land, for I will give it to you" (Gen. 13:17).

[III.A] **Through a writ:** R. Jeremiah contemplated ruling, "This refers to a deed [of gift], [a writ] not on condition that money be paid over, but in the case of a writ on condition that money be paid over, the purchaser has not acquired the property until he has actually paid out the money."

[B] Both R. Jonah and R. Yosé say, "Even if he has not paid over the stated sum of money, the purchaser has acquired ownership of the field."

[C] The following Tannaite teaching supports the position of R. Yohanan and R. Yosé:

[D] If one has sold to the purchaser ten fields, once he has effected ownership through usucaption of one of them, [if the funds have been paid over], he has acquired ownership through usucaption of all of them. But if he had paid him the purchase price of only one of them, or if he wrote over to him the deed of only one of them, he has acquired ownership of only that field which he sold to him alone.

[E] Now is a deed of ownership written over without the payment of money?

[F] Now if you that is the case in which he paid over the money for all of the fields, note that we read, "The purchase price of only one of them."

[G] So it is either one way or the other [as Jonah and Yosé have said].

[IV.A] **Through money:** R. Ba contemplated ruling, "With money, on condition that he not write a deed of ownership, but if it is with money on condition that he write a deed of ownership, the purchaser acquires the field only when the seller writes out the deed of ownership."

[B] [As above,] R. Jonah and Yosé differ.

[C] The position of R. Ba accords with the position of Samuel, and the position of R. Huna [stated below] accords with the position of R. Yohanan.

[D] The position of R. Ba accords with the position of Samuel:

[E] Samuel asked R. Huna, "If one was slaughtering a beast and was occupied with some other matter, and so did not slaughter the beast as Holy Things, [what is the law?]"

[F] He said to him, "It is written, '[And when you sacrifice a sacrifice to the Lord, you shall sacrifice it] so that you may be accepted' (Lev. 22:29). This then excludes one who is busy with other things, [in which case the act of slaughter is null]."

[G] [Samuel again asked,] "If one wrote a deed of gift using the language of acquisition [or sale], [what is the law?]"

[H] He said to him, "He made him ride on two horses [he gave him a doubly strengthened document]."

[I] R. Ba stated that Samuel did not accept that decision [D].

[J]   What is the meaning of the language, "He made him ride on two white horses"?

[K]   They thought to rule, "He brings two crazy horses, and they set him on the two of them, so that one horse pulls in one direction, and the other goes in the other direction. The driver turns out to gain nothing. [This does no good at all for the document.]"

[L]   R. Yosé of Malehayya said, "It strengthens his position in two respects. First, there is a lien in the case of a sale, but no lien in the case of a gift, [so using the language of sale rather than gift is to the recipient's advantage].

[M]   "Second, in the case of a sale, the seller has not sold everything [since there are restrictions on what is automatically included in the sale of a house], while in the case of a gift, the giver gives all."

[N]   Now as to R. Huna, [who maintains that the intention is to improve the position], as R. Yohanan has said, we derive the rule from the following case:

[O]   When a certain man was dying, he said, "Let all my property be given to Mr. So-and-so." Then he went and said, "Let it be written over in a deed and given to him."

[P]   [The problem is whether the testator's intention is to give the property over only through a deed. But such a deed is invalid after the testator's death. So] R. Eleazar and R. Simeon b. Yaqim brought the case to R. Yohanan.

[Q]   He ruled, "If he made that statement in order to impart ownership to him, all concur that the donee has acquired ownership. If he made that statement in order to give him ownership through a deed, all concur that a man does not impart ownership through a deed after death. [What a dying man says is deemed done. Hence if the statement was merely to strengthen the donee's claim on the property, it was valid as soon as it was made. But if the statement was to do the whole transfer by deed, then as soon as the man died the instructions he gave on drawing up the deed are null.]"

[R]   Who will tell [us] what the statement meant?

[S]   Interpret the case to involve witnesses who knew the answer.

[T]   Then take note: What if there are no witnesses who know the man's intention?

[U]   In that case, said R. Yosé, "In all circumstances the field remains in the possession of its owner, and he who wishes to extract property from his fellow bears the burden of proof."

[V.A] How do we know that **property that does not serve as security is acquired along with property that serves as security through money, writ, or usucaption [M. 1:5C]**?

[B]   R. Yosé in the name of Hezekiah, both R. Jonah and R. Hananiah says in the name of Hezekiah: "It is written, 'Their father gave them great gifts, of silver, gold, and valuable possessions, together with fortified cities in Judah' (2 Chr. 21:3)."

[C]   That proof serves in a case in which the real estate and movables were in a single location.

[D]   If the real estate was in one place and the movables elsewhere, [how do we know that the same rule applies]?

[E] Said R. Bun b. Hiyya, "Let us derive the answer to that question from the following case."

[F] Said R. Eliezer, "Ma'aseh B: There was a man from Meron in Jerusalem, who had a great many movables, and he wanted to give them as a gift [60d]. They said to him, 'You are not able to do so, because you have no real property.' He went and bought a single rock near Jerusalem and said, 'The northern part of this [rock], and with it a hundred sheep and a hundred jugs of wine, are handed over to Mr. So-and-so. The southern part of this [rock], and with it a hundred sheep and a hundred jugs of wine, are handed over to Mr. Such-and-such. The eastern part of this [rock], and with it a hundred sheep and a hundred jugs of wine, are handed over to Mr. So-and-so.'

[G] "And sages confirmed what he had said" [T. B.B. 10:12F-G].

[H] Said R. Haninah before R. Mana, "Now was he not dying? [So this would be a special case.] For in all situations a person transfers ownership of property only in writing, and here it was permitted to do so even orally, in all situations;

[I] "and likewise: In all situations a person may not transfer ownership unless the real property and movables were in a single location, and here even with the real estate in one place and the property in another, he could transfer ownership. [But this, then, would be a special case.]"

[J] R. Mana said to him, "It does not accord only with the view of R. Eliezer. For does it make a difference to R. Eliezer whether he is dying or healthy? For the rule applied by R. Eliezer to a dying man is applied by rabbis to a healthy man."

[K] He said to him, "Indeed so. The rule applying to a dying man in the view of R. Eliezer is the same as the rule applied by rabbis to a healthy man."

[L] There we have learned: R. Aqiba says, "A plot of ground, however small, is subject to the laws of peah and first fruits; a prosbol may be written on its security, and along with it movables may be acquired by money, writ, or usucaption" [M. Pe. 3:6].

[M] A plot of ground, however small – what is it good for? [It is useless, and one certainly cannot pile up on a tiny plot all the movables one may transfer. Consequently, it is assumed by Aqiba that one may transfer movables along with property, even though the movables are not situated on the property.]

[N] Said R. Mattenaiah, "Interpret the rule to speak of a plot of ground on which there was a single stalk of corn, with a pearl hidden in it."

[VI.A] R. Yosa in the name of R. Yohanan: "If someone had two fields, one in Judah and one in Galilee, and the purchaser took possession of this one in Judah, intending also to acquire ownership of that one in Galilee,

[B] "or if he took possession of that one in Galilee, intending to take possession of this one in Judah,

[C] "he has acquired possession thereof.

[D] "But in the case of property belonging to a proselyte, he has not effected acquisition [of a second piece of land by taking ownership of the first], even if there is no boundary between the two pieces of land except a narrow path."

[E] R. Zeira asked before R. Yosa, "If one intended to acquire the land from a narrow path and below it, [what is the law?]" [This question is not answered.]

[F] R. Hisda said, "As to the property of a proselyte, if one took possession of the northern part on the stipulation that he also acquires possession of the southern part,

[G] "or of the southern part on condition that he acquires possession of the northern part,

[H] "but he had no intention of acquiring the land in the middle,

[I] "he has not made acquisition of the northern and southern parts of the property – until he also will have the intention of effecting ownership of the land in the middle."

[J] The following Tannaite teaching stands at variance with this statement of R. Hisda:

[K] "A proselyte who died, and the property of whom Israelites took over – he who seizes possession of real estate is liable for all the tithes owing therefrom]. He who seizes possession of what is harvested from the ground is exempt from obligation for all tithes. He who seizes possession of the unharvested crop is liable to provide the gifts of the gleanings, forgotten sheaf, and corner of the field for the poor but exempt from having to hand over the tithes [T. Pe. 2:10]."

[L] Now is there no air space intervening between one sheaf and another? [Now Hisda should say that if one has taken the standing crop it should be null, since he has no part of the real estate. Now in this case there is space between the sheaves. Therefore he should have obligations of gleaning, forgotten sheaf, and the corner of the field.]

[M] There we have learned the following rule: If one bought flax from his fellow, he has acquired possession of it only after he has moved it from one place to another. If it was still ungathered, and he harvested any of it at all, he has acquired possession of all of it [M. B.B. 5:7].

[N] Samuel ruled, "He has acquired only that stalk alone."

[O] And have we not learned, "If it was still ungathered, and he harvested any of it at all, he has acquired possession of all of it"?

[P] Said R. Yosé, "R. Abodema, the emigrée, interpreted the matter as follows: 'Samuel concurs in the case of the property of a proselyte [that one acquires only that stalk alone that one has plucked]. [But in ordinary transfers of a crop of flax, the rule is as given at M. He would be in agreement with Hisda that if there is a space between one sheaf and another, only the sheaf actually seized has been acquired.]'"

[VII.A] R. Yohanan raised the question, "As to movables, what is the law on their being acquired by being dragged [rather than being lifted up]?"

[B] Said R. Ba bar Mamel, "His question concerns hard hides, [which are difficult to lift up], but as to soft hides, one makes acquisition of them only after he raises them up."

[C] The following Tannaite teaching stands at variance with the position of R. Ba bar Mamel:

[D] "He who steals a man's purse and takes it out of private domain on the Sabbath is liable [to pay compensation, even though there is the rule that one is not liable both to the death penalty, for violating the Sabbath, and also to paying monetary compensation for the same felony]. The reason is that he had already established liability through his act of theft of the purse before he had violated the sanctity of the Sabbath [by removing the purse from private domain]. [By merely lifting up the purse, he effected acquisition thereof.]

[E] "But if he was dragging the purse and so removing it from private domain, he is exempt from paying compensation, for the penalty of death and the liability to pay compensation coincidentally apply to the felon."

[F] Lo, if the penalty of death and the liability to pay compensation had not coincidentally applied to him, he would have been liable [and that is because, as indicated, he would have effected acquisition merely through dragging the purse]. [This then differs from Ba b. Mamel's view that dragging effects acquisition only when the object is too heavy to lift.]

[G] Said R. Mattenaiah, "Interpret the rule to apply to a case of very heavy purses, which usually are dragged and not lifted up."

[VIII.A] [With reference to M. 1:5D:] Whence did they derive the law that an oath's applicability may be extended from the thing that precipitates it to yet other considerations?

[B] It is from the law of the accused wife:

[C] "Amen" [she says, I have not committed adultery with] this particular man, and "Amen," [I have not committed adultery with] any other man. [So the oath, precipitated in connection with the named lover, then is extended to cover all other lovers, so that she is claiming never to have committed adultery with anyone. even though the original oath was on account of the named man only] [M. Sot. 2:5C].

[D] That covers matters that are suitable to be subjected to the oath.

[E] What about matters that are not suitable to be subjected to an oath [being covered along with those that are]?

[F] Said R. Yosé b. R. Bun, "We derive the answer from the following: **'Amen that I have not gone aside while betrothed, married. awaiting levirate marriage, or wholly taken in levirate marriage'** [M. Sot. 2:5D]."

[G] Now are the betrothed woman and the one awaiting levirate marriage suitable to be subject to such an oath? [Clearly they are not.] Yet you say that they assign the oath to that status, and here, too, they assign the oath to cover other than the original and appropriate matters for which the oath has been called.

[H] ["Then the Lord make you an execration and an oath among your people" (Num. 5:21).] There is a Tannaite authority who teaches, "Just as the accused wife is subject to the execration and the oath, so all those who take an oath are subject to an execration and an oath."

[I]   And there is a Tannaite authority who teaches, "To this one applies the execration and the oath, and to all others who take an oath do not apply both the execration and the oath."

[J]   Now they proposed to state: "The one who holds that just as this one is subject to an execration and an oath, so all those who are subjected to oaths are subject to an execration and an oath" is reasonable, [since quite consistently, he will derive from the laws of the oath imposed on the accused wife all the details affecting those who take oaths in general].

[K]   But the one who said, "This one is subject to an execration and an oath, but to all others who take an oath do not apply both the execration and the oath," there is a problem. For from the laws of the accused wife such a person derives the rule of applying the oath to matters not originally covered by it, but from those laws he does not derive the rule that the execration and the oath apply [in general]. [So he is inconsistent.]

[L]   There is a Tannaite authority who teaches, "Just as the accused wife is subject to saying 'Amen, Amen' two times, so all those who take oaths are subject to saying 'Amen, Amen' two times."

[M]   Then there is a Tannaite authority who teaches, "The accused wife is subject to saying 'Amen, Amen,' two times, but all others who take an oath are not subject to saying 'Amen, Amen' two times."

[N]   Now they proposed to state, "The one who holds that just as this one is subject to saying 'Amen, Amen' two times, so all those who are subjected to oaths are subject to saying 'Amen, Amen' two times, is consistent with the view that we transfer the oath from one matter to some other matter, [for the reason given above].

[O]   "But the one who said, 'This one is subject to saying "Amen, Amen" two times, but all others who take an oath are not subject to saying "Amen, Amen" two times,' there is a problem.

[P]   "Have they not derived the rule about applying the oath to matters not originally covered by it from the accused wife? Now it appears that, so far as deriving the rule of applying the oath to matters no covered by it, they do so from the accused wife, but as to saying 'Amen, Amen,' two times, they do not derive that rule from the same analogy."

The Yerushalmi broadens the range of discourse to provide an account of theories on effecting ownership of movables in general. No point in the Mishnah is omitted; all are given ample clarification, even where it isn't needed. Units I and II go over scriptural statements. From III onward, we ask more general questions. Units III, IV, and V cite and investigate the Mishnah's laws. Unit V clarifies an ambiguity in the Mishnah. Unit VI continues the inquiry into acquiring property through various means. The special interest is acquiring the property of a proselyte, who has no legitimate heirs. At unit VII acquisition of movables once more is under discussion. Unit VIII discusses the scriptural basis for the procedure outlined in the Mishnah.

II. The Talmud of Babylonia to M. Qiddushin 1:5

I.1   A.   **Property for which there is security is acquired through money:**

        B.   *How on the basis of Scripture do we know that fact?*

        C.   Said Hezekiah, "Said Scripture, 'People will acquire fields with money' (Jer. 32:44)."

        D.   *But might one say, that is valid only unless there is a deed, since the verse goes on,* "And subscribe the deeds and attest them and call witnesses" *(Jer. 32:44)?*

        E.   *If the order of the language were such that* "acquire" *came at the end, it would be as you maintain; but since* "acquire" *appears at the beginning, the meaning is, money transfers title, the deed merely attests to that fact.*

I.2   A.   Rab, "This rule was repeated only in reference to a place in which they do not write out a deed, but in a place where they did write out a deed, money by itself does not effect transfer of title."

        B.   *But if the buyer stipulates [that either money or deed serves], that is the case.*

        C.   *For instance, that is as in the case of R. Idi bar Abin, when he bought land, he would say,* "If I want, I'll acquire it through transfer of cash, if I want, I'll acquire it through a deed. If I want, I'll acquire it through transfer of cash – and if you want to retract after I've paid, you can't. If I want, I'll acquire it through a deed, and if I want to retract, I can."

II.1   A.   **Writ:**

        B.   *How on the basis of Scripture do we know that fact?*

        C.   *Shall we say, because it is written,* "And subscribe the deeds and attest them and call witnesses" *(Jer. 32:44)? But haven't you already said, "The deed merely attests to that fact"? Rather, proof derives from the following:* "So I took the deed of purchase" *(Jer. 32:11).*

II.2   A.   Said Samuel, "This rule was repeated only in reference to a deed of gift, but as to a deed of sale, the transfer of title takes place only when the purchaser gives him the cash."

        B.   *Objected R. Hamnuna,* "'**Writ:** How so? If the seller wrote on a parchment or on a potsherd, themselves of no intrinsic value, "My field is sold to you, my field becomes your property," it is deemed to have been sold or given by deed'! [So the deed confers ownership, even prior to the transfer of funds.]*

        C.   *R. Hamnuna refuted his own allegation? For he added:* "That rule pertains to a case in which someone sold the field because it was really worthless" [the money therefore hardly matters, but this would not ordinarily be so (Simon)].

        D.   And R. Ashi said, "The seller really wanted to transfer the field as a gift and to give it over to him, and the reason he made the transfer in the form of a deed and in the language of a sale is so as to strengthen the hold of the donee to the title of the field."

III.1   A.   **And usucaption:**

        B.   *How on the basis of Scripture do we know that fact?*

        C.   Because it is written, "And dwell in the cities that you have taken" (Jer. 40:10) – how did you take them? By dwelling in them.

        D.   *A Tannaite authority of the household of R. Ishmael:* "And you shall possess it and dwell therein" (Deut. 11:31) – how shall you possess it? By dwelling therein.

IV.1   A.   And that for which there is no security [= movables] is acquired only by an act of drawing [from one place to another]:

        B.   *How on the basis of Scripture do we know that fact?*

        C.   It is written, "And if you sell anything to your neighbor or buy anything of your neighbor's hand" (Lev. 25:14) – this speaks of something that is acquired by passing from hand to hand [by drawing, that is, only movables].

        D.   *And from the viewpoint of R. Yohanan, who has said, "By the law of the Torah, the transfer of cash serves to transfer title," what is to be said?*

        E.   *The Tannaite authority here repeats the rule governing an ordinance deriving from rabbis.*

V.1   A.   Property for which there is no security is acquired along with property for which there is security through money, writ, and usucaption:

        B.   *How on the basis of Scripture do we know that fact?*

        C.   Said Hezekiah, "Said Scripture, 'And their father gave them gifts... with walled cities in Judah' (2 Chr. 21:3)." [Freedman: Thus they acquired the gifts, which were movables, in conjunction with the walled cities, that is, real estate.]

V.2   A.   *The question was raised: "Do the movables have to be heaped upon the land to be transferred, or is that not the case?"*

        B.   *Said R. Joseph, "Come and take note: R. Aqiba says, 'Any area of land, however minuscule, (1) is subject [to the laws of] peah, and [the laws of] first fruits [26B] (2) [may be used as security] for writing a prosbol [which states that the Sabbatical Year will not negate the obligation to repay a loan], (3) [and may be used as collateral] for purchasing movable property with money, a contract, or usucaption' [M. Pe. 3:6]. Now if you maintain that we require that the goods be piled up on the land, then what good is a very small piece of land?"*

        C.   *R. Samuel bar Bisna explained the matter in the presence of R. Joseph, "For instance, sticking a needle into it." [That would be acquired along with the land (Freedman).]*

        D.   *Said to him R. Joseph, "All you're doing is harassing us! Does the Tannaite authority go to so much trouble to give us a lesson about a needle?"*

        E.   *Said R. Ashi, "So whose going to tell us that he didn't suspend a pearl on the needle, worth a thousand zuz?"*

        F.   *Come and take note:* Said R. Eleazar, "There was a case of a certain man of Meron who was in Jerusalem, who had a large volume of movables that he wanted to give away. They told him that he had no remedy except to transfer title along with a piece of real estate. What did he do? He went and he bought a land no bigger than a sela coin near Jerusalem, and he said, 'The north of this property belongs to Mr. So-and-so, and along with it go a hundred sheep and a hundred barrels of wine.' [And the same for the other directions.] When he died, the court confirmed his instructions." *Now, if you maintain that we require that the goods be piled up on the land, then what good would land the size of a sela coin ever serve under such circumstances?*

G. *Well, do you really think that it was actually land no bigger than a sela coin? What is the meaning of "sela" here? A big area. And why was it called "a sela"? Because it was hard as a rock [and the word "sela" means rock as well as sela coin].*

H. *Come and take note:* Said R. Judah said Rabbi, "There was the case of a man in Jerusalem who got sick – that is in accord with R. Eliezer – and some say, he was healthy – and that is in accord with rabbis. Now he had movables in abundance that he wanted to give away as a gift. They said to him that he had no remedy except to buy some land. What did he do? He went and purchased land of the size of a quarter-qab in the area near Jerusalem, and he stated, 'A square handbreadth of this land goes to Mr. So-and-so, and with it a hundred sheep and a hundred barrels of wine,' and then he died. Sages confirmed his instructions." *Now, if you maintain that we require that the goods be piled up on the land, then what good would land the size of a quarter-qab ever serve under such circumstances?*

I. *Here with what situation do we deal? It is in fact one in which the transfer consisted of cash. And that is a reasonable supposition, for if you should imagine that the gift really involved a hundred sheep and a hundred barrels of wine in fact, why couldn't he transfer title to him through barter?*

J. *Well, what are you thinking then, that it was money? So why couldn't he transfer title to him for the money through an act of drawing? So the sense must be: The recipient was not there to do the drawing. And here, too, the reason is that the recipient was not there to go through the process of acquiring the title as specified.*

K. *Well, then, why not transfer title to him through a third party?*

L. *He didn't want to rely on a third party, fearing that he would take off and eat up the gift!*

M. *So what's the sense of the language,* he had no remedy...?

N. *This is the sense of the matter: Because he had no confidence in a third party,* under those circumstances he had no remedy except to transfer the goods along with a piece of real estate.

O. *Come and take note:* There was the case involving Rabban Gamaliel and the elders, traveling on a ship when the time for removal of the agricultural gifts had come, requiring their transfer to their proper recipients. Said Rabban Gamaliel, "The tenth I intend to measure out and designate as first tithe is given [27A] to Joshua [who is a Levite], and the place in which it is located is rented to him. The other tenth which I intend to remove and designate as poor man's tithe is given to Aqiba ben Joseph, who will make it available to the poor, and the place in which it is located is rented to him" [M. M.S. 5:9C]. *Now this surely proves that the goods must be heaped up on the real estate.*

P. *No, this case is exceptional, for he didn't want to put them to any trouble.*

Q. *Come and take note of what* Rabbah bar Isaac said Rab said, "There are two classifications of deeds. If someone says, 'Take possession of the field in behalf of Mr. So-and-so [as my gift to him], and also write a deed for him,' he may retract on the deed [Slotki: if the donor, having given instructions to the witnesses, desires to have no written confirmation of the gift, he may recall the deed at any time before it reaches the donee], but he may not retract on the gift of the land. If he says, 'Take possession of the field on condition that you write a deed for him,' he may retract both the deed and the field." And R. Hiyya bar Abin said R. Huna said, "There are three classifications of deeds, *the two that we have said just now, and the following:* If the seller prior to the sale went ahead and wrote a deed, [Slotki: being anxious to sell, and in order to expedite the transaction on obtaining the consent of the buyer, he requests a scribe to prepare the deed before he knows whether the person to whom he wishes to sell would consent to buy], in line with that which we have learned in the Mishnah: **They write a writ of sale to the seller, even though the buyer is not with him. But they do not write a writ of sale for the purchaser, unless the seller is with him [M. B.B. 10:3H-I].** Then, once the buyer has taken possession of the land, he acquires the deed as well, without regard to the location of the deed." *That proves that we do not require that the goods be piled up on the land.*

R. *The case of a deed is exceptional, since it has a bearing on the land itself.*

S. *But lo, in that regard there is a Tannaite statement:* And that is in line with what we have learned: **"Movable property may be acquired along with landed property through transfer of money, deed, and exercising a right of possession."**

T. *That is decisive proof.*

V.3   A. *The question was raised: "Do we require the explicit statement that the movables are acquired* by virtue of *the acquisition of the land, or do we not require such an explicit statement?"*

B. *Come and take note of the Tannaite formulation, using the word "all," but the Tannaite formulation of the transaction does not require use of the words "by virtue of...."*

C. *Well, from your viewpoint, is the language, "let him acquire it" stated as part of the Tannaite formulation [though we know that that has to be articulated]? Rather, the meaning is, he certainly must make use of the language, "let him acquire it," and here, too, he has to articulate the language, "by virtue of...."*

D. *And the decided law is, we do not require that* the movables be piled up on the real estate, *but we do require that the language be used,* "in virtue of...," *and* "let him acquire it."

V.4   A. *The question was raised:* "What if the field is transferred through sale, but the movables are transferred as a gift?" [Are the movables then transferred along with the real estate?]

B. *Come and take note:* **The tenth I intend to measure out and designate as first tithe is given to Joshua [who is a Levite], and the place in which it is located is rented to him.**

C. *That's decisive proof [the tithe was a gift, the place rented, which is like a sale].*

V.5   A. *The question was raised:* If the field went to one party and the movables to another, what is the rule?

B. *Come and take note:* **The other tenth which I intend to remove and designate as poor man's tithe is given to Aqiba ben Joseph, who will make it available to the poor, and the place in which it is located is rented to him.** *Now what is the meaning of "rented"? It is,* *rented for the tithe [so the locus was rented to* Aqiba, but the tenth was for the poor (Freedman)]. *If you prefer, I shall say: The case of R. Aqiba is exceptional, sense he was serving in the agency of the poor.*

V.6　A.　Said Raba, "The rule that movables are acquired along with land applies only if the purchaser had paid money for all of the movables. But if he had not paid money for them all, he acquires only the movables that are covered by his money."

　　　B.　*It has been taught on Tannaite authority in accord with the position of Raba:* **Greater is the power of a document than the power of money, and greater is the power of money than the power of a document.** [T.: For a document allows one to collect from indentured property, which is not the case with money.] **Greater is the power of money, for money serves for the redemption of things that have been given as Valuations and as herem to the sanctuary, things that have been sanctified, and second tithe, which is obviously not the case with a document [T. Ket. 2:1M-O].** [B.:] **Greater is the power of a document, for a document removes an Israelite woman from a marriage, which is not the case with money. And greater is the power of both of them than the power of usucaption, and greater is the power of usucaption than the power of both of them. Greater is the power of both of them, that both of them serve to acquire title to a Hebrew slave, which is not the case with usucaption. And greater is the power of usucaption, for usucaption serves if one has sold to the other ten fields in ten provinces, so that, once the purchaser has acquired one of them by usucaption, he has acquired all of them.** [27B] **Under what circumstances? If he gave him the cash price for all of them. But if he didn't give him the cash for all of them, he has acquired title to only what his money has paid for [T. Ket. 2:1P-S].**

V.7　A.　*That supports the position of Samuel, for* said Samuel, "If one has sold to the other ten fields in ten provinces, so that, once the purchaser has acquired one of them by usucaption, he has acquired all of them."

　　　B.　Said R. Aha b. R. Iqa, "You may know that that is the case, for if he had given him ten beasts tied by one cord and said to him, 'Acquire them,' wouldn't he acquire all of them?"

　　　C.　*He said to him, "But are the cases comparable? There the cord is in hand [tying all the beasts together,] but in the case of the land, there is no cord that binds them all in the hand of the purchaser!"*

　　　D.　*There are those who say,* said R. Aha b. R. Iqa, "You may know that he does not as a matter of fact acquire them all, for if he had given him ten beasts tied by one cord and said to him, 'Acquire them,' would he acquire all of them?"

　　　E.　*But are the cases comparable? There the beasts are distinct entities, but here, the earth forms a single block.*

VI.1　A.　**And property for which there is no security imposes the need for an oath on property for which there is security:**

　　　B.　Said Ulla, "How on the basis of the Torah do we derive the rule of the superimposed oath [by which, if one is required to take an oath on one count, he may be forced to extend the oath to other counts]? As it is said, 'And the woman shall say,"Amen, Amen",' *and we have learned in the Mishnah:* **To what does she say, 'Amen, Amen'?...'Amen that I have not gone aside while betrothed, married, awaiting levirate marriage, or wholly taken in Levirate marriage' [M. Sot. 2:5A-D].** *Now as this reference to her having been betrothed, what can it possibly mean? If we say that he expressed his warning of jealousy to her when she was betrothed, and then she went aside with the alleged lover, and is now made to drink the bitter water while still betrothed, then is a woman who has been merely betrothed required to undergo the ordeal of drinking the bitter water as a woman accused of adultery? Lo, we have learned in the Mishnah:* **A betrothed girl and a deceased childless brother's widow awaiting levirate marriage neither undergo the ordeal of drinking the bitter water nor receive a marriage contract, since it is written, 'When a wife, being subject to her husband, goes astray' (Num. 5:29) – excluding the betrothed girl and the deceased childless brother's widow awaiting levirate marriage [M. Sot. 4:1A-C].** *And if it is proposed that she was warned when betrothed, then went aside with the alleged lover, and now has to drink that she has been married, do the waters test her under these conditions? Has it not been taught on Tannaite authority:* 'And the man shall be free from iniquity, and the woman shall bear her iniquity' (Num. 5:31). [The sense of the foregoing verse of Scripture is that] when the man is free of transgression, the water puts his wife to the test, [and] if the man is not free of transgression, the water does not put his wife to the test? *Rather, the oath can be imposed [to cover the specified matter] only because it is superimposed."*

C. *Well, we have found that the superimposed oath pertains in the case of the wife accused of adultery, which involves a prohibition of a religious nature. But how do we know that it applies to monetary matters?*

D. *A Tannaite statement of the household of R. Ishmael:* "It is based on an argument a fortiori, namely: If an accused wife **[28A]** who has not been subjected to an oath on the evidence of one witness, nonetheless is subject to a superimposed oath, a monetary claim, which can be brought on the strength of a single witness so that an oath has to be taken, surely will be subject to an oath on which other matters are superimposed!"

E. *Well, we have found that the superimposed oath pertains in a case in which the claim is certain; what about one that is subject to doubt?*

F. *It has been taught on Tannaite authority:* R. Simeon b. Yohai says, "There is a statement concerning the taking of an oath outside of the Temple court [all oaths except the one taken by the accused wife are administered outside of the Temple court], and there is a statement covering the taking of an oath within the Temple court. Just as in the case of an oath taken inside the Temple court, the law has treated a case of doubt as equivalent to a case of certainty, so an oath that is imposed outside of the Temple court is such that the law has treated a case of doubt as equivalent to a case of certainty."

VI.2 A. Then to what extent is a superimposed oath carried?

B. Said R. Judah said Rab, "Even if he imposes the demand: 'Take an oath to me that you're not my slave.'"

C. *But in such a case we would excommunicate that character! For it has been taught on Tannaite authority:* He who calls his fellow a slave – let him be excommunicated. If he called him a mamzer, he is flogged with forty stripes. If he calls him wicked, he may take action against the slanderer's livelihood [cf. Freedman].

D.   Rather, said Raba, "'Swear to me that you were not sold to me as a Hebrew slave.'"

E.   *Well, that's a perfectly honorable claim – he owes him money [and is claiming his service in payment for the money, so why should that be regarded as a superimposed oath]?*

F.   *Raba is consistent with his views expressed elsewhere, for* said Raba, "A Hebrew slave is acquired as to his very body."

G.   *Well, if so, then what we have is nothing other than a claim as to real estate!*

H.   *What might you have supposed? Only in the case of land is it common for people to make a sale in secret, so if he had sold the land, it would not be broadly known, but as for a case such as this, if he had sold himself, it would have been known? So we are informed that that is not the case.*

I.1 finds a scriptural basis for the rule of the Mishnah, so, too, II.1, II.1, IV.1, V.1. I.2, and II.2-6 qualify the rule at hand. Nos. 6+7 then continues the tangential inquiry. VI.1-2 find a scriptural foundation for the Mishnah's fact and extend the amplification of that fact.

III. The Exegetical Programs of Yerushalmi and of the Bavli Compared

What happens when one Talmud has access to teachings of authorities prominent in the other Talmud's locale? As it happens, the Bavli very commonly cites authorities of the Land of Israel. The Yerushalmi may do the same, if somewhat less commonly, for authorities of Babylonia. Here at Y. 1:5 I, we have a secondary gloss in the names of the Babylonian authorities, Levi and Rab. The Bavli's counterpart, 1:5 I. know nothing either of the proof for the proposition of the Mishnah that the Yerushalmi has provided – the Bavli has its own proof – or the gloss on that proof provided by Babylonian authorities. So a different proof for the same proposition is set forth, though, it would seem, the Babylonian authorities had among them statements in the names of their own countrymen on the same problem. So we have a case in which the Yerushalmi makes use of sayings of sages of Babylonia, which are ignored by the Bavli's framers when commenting on the same passage, for the same purpose and with the same effect.

Let us now examine the entire program of the two Talmuds.

1:5 I At first they would effect acquisition by removing the shoe, in line with Ruth 4:7. Who removed the shoe? Rab and Levi. Then they effected it through a rite of cutting off

1:5 I.1 How on the basis of Scripture do we know that fact?

1:5 I.2 Rab: This rule, M. 1:5A, refers to a place in which they don't write out a deed, but where they do, payment of [when inherited property was sold outside of the family].

1:5 II With money: + prooftext.

1:5 III Through a writ: deed of gift, a writ not on condition that money be paid over; in the case of a writ that stipulates money be paid over, the acquisition takes place when the money has been paid.

1:5 IV Through money: same considerations as above.

1:5 I V How do we know the Mishnah rule at M. 1:5C + prooftext.

1:5 VI Continuation of problem of foregoing: if someone had two fields in different places and purchaser acquired title of one, intended to acquire title of the other as well, he has done so; but that would not apply to property of a proselyte.

1:5 VII As to movables, what is law on their being acquired by being dragged, not raised up?

1:5 VIII Scriptural source for M. 1:5D – from law of accused wife.

money by itself does not effect transfer of title.

1:5 II.1 How on the basis do we know that a writ serves + Jer. 32:44, 32:11.

1:5 II.2: Samuel: This rule pertains only to a deed of gift, but as to a deed of sale, transfer takes place only when the purchaser pays the case. Runs parallel to Y. 1:5 III.

1:5 III.1 How on the basis of Scripture do we know this + Jer. 40:10.

1:5 IV.1 How on the basis of Scripture do we know this + Lev. 25:14.

1:5 V.1 How on the basis of Scripture do we know this + 2 Chr. 21:3.

1:5 V.2 Theoretical question, parallel to Y. 1:5.VI: Do the movables have to be heaped upon the land to be transferred, or is that not the case?

1:5 V.3 Does an explicit statement have to be made to the effect in the case of 1:5 V.2?

1:5 V.4 Secondary problem on the same general theme.

1:5 V.5 Tertiary problem on the same general theme.

1:5 V.6 Qualification of the rule subject to analysis.

1:5 V 7 Foregoing intersects with another pertinent problem.

1:5 VI.1 How do we derive the rule of the superimposed oath + M. Sot. 2:5.

1:5 VI.2 Expansion of foregoing.

Here we have a fine opportunity to test the hypothesis contrary to mine: the two Talmuds interrelate in some important manner or aspect. Three substantial discussions go over the same issues in both Talmuds. Let us now compare those items in sequence:

[II.A] **With money:** As it is written, "Fields will be bought for money, deeds will be signed and sealed and witnessed" (Jer. 32:44).	I.1 A. **Property for which there is security is acquired through money:** B. *How on the basis of Scripture do we know that fact?*
[B] "And signed and sealed and witnessed" – "signed and sealed" refers to witnesses to a writ; and "witnessed" refers to witnesses to usucaption.	C. Said Hezekiah, "Said Scripture, 'People will acquire fields with money' (Jer. 32:44)."
[C] Or perhaps these latter serve as witnesses to the writ?	D. *But might one say, that is valid only unless there is a deed, since the verse goes on, "And subscribe the deeds and attest them and call witnesses" (Jer. 32:44)?*
[D] Since it is already written, "And signed and sealed," [which must mean a writ, the other witnesses are to usucaption].	E. *If the order of the language were such that "acquire" came at the end, it would be as you maintain; but since "acquire" appears at the beginning, the meaning is, money transfers title, the deed merely attests to that fact.*
[E] R. Yosa in the name of R. Mana, R. Tanhum, R. Abbahu in the name of R. Yohanan: "Real estate is not acquired for less than a perutah."	
[F] What is the scriptural basis for that statement?	I.2 A. Rab, "This rule was repeated only in reference to a place in which they do not write out a deed, but in a place where they did write out a deed, money by itself does not effect transfer of title."
[G] "Fields will be bought for money" [and less than a perutah is not deemed money].	B. *But if the buyer stipulates [that either money or deed serves], that is the case.*
[H] [Yohanan] disputes what R. Haninah said, "All references to sheqels in the Torah are to selas; in the Prophets, to litras; and in the Writings to qintrin." [Thus Jeremiah refers to twenty-	C. *For instance, that is as in the case of R. Idi bar*

five selas = a litra.]

[I]   "That is, except for the sheqels of Ephron, [which are qintrin, a hundred selas]."

[J]   What is the scriptural basis for this statement?

[K]   "For the full price let him give it to me" (Gen. 23:9) [and "full price" implies the larger coin].

[L]   But the cases are not similar. There [Jer. 32:44] it is written "money," but here it is written "sheqels."

[M]   They objected, "Lo, there is the case of the rapist [Deut. 22:28], and lo, in that case what is written is only 'money,' and do you say it refers to sheqels? [So there is a dispute even when 'money' stands by itself.]"

[N]   [The statement that land is acquired only through usucaption] is not in accord with the view of R. Eliezer.

[O]   For R. Eliezer said, "If one merely traversed the field, he has acquired it [without usucaption]."

[P]   For it has been taught, "If one traversed a field lengthwise and breadthwise, he has acquired it up to the place in which he has walked," the words of R. Eliezer.

[Q]   And sages say, "He acquired it only once he effects possession through usucaption."

Abin, when he bought land, he would say, "If I want, I'll acquire it through transfer of cash, if I want, I'll acquire it through a deed. If I want, I'll acquire it through transfer of cash – and if you want to retract after I've paid, you can't. If I want, I'll acquire it through a deed, and if I want to retract, I can."

[R] All concur in the case of one who sells a path to his fellow, that once he has walked in it, he has acquired it.

[S] What is the scriptural basis for that position [of Eliezer]?

[T] "Arise, walk through the length and the breadth of the land, for I will give it to you" (Gen. 13:17).

The same prooftext serves both Talmuds. But the secondary development in each case goes its own way. The Yerushalmi want to know to what the witnesses testify; the Bavli wants to know more about the proof at hand, asking a question that challenges the premise of the proof that has been adduced. The Bavli further qualifies the rule before us. I see no point at which the two compositions that are set in parallel columns intersect, beyond the opening lines. When I say, the two Talmuds differ because they are different, this is what I mean: they meet at the Mishnah, they may well have had access to a common store of prooftexts for Mishnah rules or propositions; but from that point, the framers of the composition and composite on the Bavli's side simply went their own way. They do not, in this context, even find important the questions that for the Yerushalmi's writers govern.

[III.A] **Through a writ:** R. Jeremiah contemplated ruling, "This refers to a deed [of gift], [a writ] not on condition that money be paid over, but in the case of a writ on condition that money be paid over, the purchaser has not acquired the property until he has actually paid out the money."

[B] Both R. Jonah and R. Yosé say, "Even if he has not paid over the stated sum of money, the purchaser has acquired ownership of the field."

II.2 A. Said Samuel, "This rule was repeated only in reference to a deed of gift, but as to a deed of sale, the transfer of title takes place only when the purchaser gives him the cash."

B. *Objected R. Hamnuna, "'Writ: How so? If the seller wrote on a parchment or on a potsherd, themselves of no intrinsic value, "My field is sold to you, my field becomes your property," it is deemed to have been sold or given by deed'! [So the deed confers ownership, even*

[C] The following Tannaite teaching supports the position of R. Yohanan and R. Yosé:

[D] If one has sold to the purchaser ten fields, once he has effected ownership through usucaption of one of them, [if the funds have been paid over], he has acquired ownership through usucaption of all of them. But if he had paid him the purchase price of only one of them, or if he wrote over to him the deed of only one of them, he has acquired ownership of only that field which he sold to him alone.

[E] Now is a deed of ownership written over without the payment of money?

[F] Now if you that is the case in which he paid over the money for all of the fields, note that we read, "The purchase price of only one of them."

[G] So it is either one way or the other [as Jonah and Yosé have said].

prior to the transfer of funds.]"

C. *R. Hamnuna refuted his own allegation? For he added:* "That rule pertains to a case in which someone sold the field because it was really worthless" [the money therefore hardly matters, but this would not ordinarily be so (Simon)].

D. And R. Ashi said, "The seller really wanted to transfer the field as a gift and to give it over to him, and the reason he made the transfer in the form of a deed and in the language of a sale is so as to strengthen the hold of the donee to the title of the field."

I see a difference between Jeremiah's and Samuel's statements only as to detail, but the main point is the same: if there is a stipulation that money is to be paid, transfer of title must be validated only when the money is actually handed over. Then the differences are quite striking, given the concurrence on the main point. The Yerushalmi at III.B has a contrary opinion; then appeals to a Tannaite rule for support; then concludes that the law can be only opposite the proposed rule, on the basis of the received tradition. The Bavli's argument appeals to the prooftext that has been adduced: the deed confers ownership, without regard to the transfer of funds; this is then refuted (that the same authority refutes himself is not surprising, given the remarkable standard of intellectual honesty that characterizes both Talmuds!). Then Ashi explains the situation. The result is the same – but the structure and morphology of the Bavli scarcely intersect with those of the Yerushalmi. Here is yet another case in which the two Talmuds wish to say the same thing, but the second Talmud does so in entire disregard for the first Talmud's formulation of matters. If I had to differentiate the two on the basis of the present instance, I would say, the Yerushalmi appeals to the authority of formulated rules, the Bavli, to the power of analysis of the case adduced in evidence, on the one side, and of distinctions and differentiations and operative considerations – applied reason, practical logic – on the other. The two passages' points are indistinguishable; the two passages do not intersect.

[V.A] How do we know that property that does not serve as security is acquired along with property that serves as security through money, writ, or usucaption [M. 1:5C]?

[B] R. Yosé in the name of Hezekiah, both R. Jonah and R. Hananiah says in the name of Hezekiah: "It is written, 'Their father gave them great gifts, of silver, gold, and valuable possessions, together with fortified cities in Judah' (2 Chr. 21:3)."

[C] That proof serves in a case in which the real estate and movables were in a single location.

[D] If the real estate was in one place and the movables elsewhere, [how do we know that the same rule applies]?

[E] Said R. Bun b. Hiyya, "Let us derive the answer to that question from the following

V.2 A. *The question was raised: "Do the movables have to be heaped upon the land to be transferred, or is that not the case?"*

B. *Said R. Joseph, "Come and take note:* R. Aqiba says, 'Any area of land, however minuscule, (1) is subject [to the laws of] peah, and [the laws of] first fruits [26B] (2) [may be used as security] for writing a prosbol [which states that the Sabbatical Year will not negate the obligation to repay a loan], (3) [and may be used as collateral] for purchasing movable property with money, a contract, or usucaption' [M. Pe. 3:6]. *Now if you maintain that we require that the goods be piled up on the land, then what good is a very small piece of land?"*

C. *R. Samuel bar Bisna explained the matter in the presence of R. Joseph, "For instance, sticking a needle into it."*

case."

[F] Said R. Eliezer, "Ma'aseh B: There was a man from Meron in Jerusalem, who had a great many movables, and he wanted to give them as a gift [60d]. They said to him, 'You are not able to do so, because you have no real property.' He went and bought a single rock near Jerusalem and said, 'The northern part of this [rock], and with it a hundred sheep and a hundred jugs of wine, are handed over to Mr. So-and-so. The southern part of this [rock], and with it a hundred sheep and a hundred jugs of wine, are handed over to Mr. Such-and-such. The eastern part of this [rock], and with it a hundred sheep and a hundred jugs of wine, are handed over to Mr. So-and-so.'

[G] "And sages confirmed what he had said" [T. B.B. 10:12F-G].

[H] Said R. Haninah before R. Mana, "Now was he not dying? [So this would be a special case.] For in all situations a person transfers ownership of property only in writing, and here it was permitted to do so even orally, in all situations;

[I] "and likewise: In all

[That would be acquired along with the land (Freedman).]

D. Said to him R. Joseph, "All you're doing is harassing us! Does the Tannaite authority go to so much trouble to give us a lesson about a needle?"

E. Said R. Ashi, "So whose going to tell us that he didn't suspend a pearl on the needle, worth a thousand zuz?"

F. Come and take note: Said R. Eleazar, "There was a case of a certain man of Meron who was in Jerusalem, who had a large volume of movables that he wanted to give away. They told him that he had no remedy except to transfer title along with a piece of real estate. What did he do? He went and he bought a land no bigger than a sela coin near Jerusalem, and he said, 'The north of this property belongs to Mr. So-and-so, and along with it go a hundred sheep and a hundred barrels of wine.' [And the same for the other directions.] When he died, the court confirmed his instructions." *Now, if you maintain that we require that the goods be piled up on the land, then what good would land the size of a sela coin ever serve under* situations a person may not transfer ownership unless the real property and movables were in a single location, and here even with the real estate in one place and the property in another, he could transfer ownership. [But this, then, would be a special case.]"

[J] R. Mana said to him, "It does not accord only with the view of R. Eliezer. For does it make a difference to R. Eliezer whether he is dying or healthy? For the rule applied by R. Eliezer to a dying man is applied by rabbis to a healthy man."

[K] He said to him, "Indeed so. The rule applying to a dying man in the view of R. Eliezer is the same as the rule applied by rabbis to a healthy man."

[L] There we have learned: R. Aqiba says, "A plot of ground, however small, is subject to the laws of peah and first fruits; a prosbol may be written on its security, and along with it movables may be acquired by money, writ, or usucaption" [M. Pe. 3:6].

[M] A plot of ground, however small – what is it good for? [It is useless, and one certainly cannot pile

such circumstances?

G. *Well, do you really think that it was actually land no bigger than a sela coin? What is the meaning of "sela" here? A big area. And why was it called "a sela"? Because it was hard as a rock [and the word "sela" means rock as well as sela coin].*

H. Come and take note: Said R. Judah said Rabbi, "There was the case of a man in Jerusalem who got sick – that is in accord with R. Eliezer – and some say, he was healthy – and that is in accord with rabbis. Now he had movables in abundance that he wanted to give away as a gift. They said to him that he had no remedy except to buy some land. What did he do? He went and purchased land of the size of a quarter-qab in the area near Jerusalem, and he stated, 'A square handbreadth of this and goes to Mr. So-and-so, and with it a hundred sheep and a hundred barrels of wine,' and then he died. Sages confirmed his instructions." *Now, if you maintain that we require that the goods be piled up on the land, then what good would land the size of a quarter-qab ever serve under such circumstances?*

up on a tiny plot all the movables one may transfer. Consequently, it is assumed by Aqiba that one may transfer movables along with property, even though the movables are not situated on the property.]

[N] Said R. Mattenaiah, "Interpret the rule to speak of a plot of ground on which there was a single stalk of corn, with a pearl hidden in it."

I.   *Here with what situation do we deal? It is in fact one in which the transfer consisted of cash. And that is a reasonable supposition, for if you should imagine that the gift really involved a hundred sheep and a hundred barrels of wine in fact, why couldn't he transfer title to him through barter?*

J.   *Well, what are you thinking then, that it was money? So why couldn't he transfer title to him for the money through an act of drawing? So the sense must be: The recipient was not there to do the drawing. And here, too, the reason is that the recipient was not there to go through the process of acquiring the title as specified.*

K.   *Well, then, why not transfer title to him through a third party?*

L.   *He didn't want to rely on a third party, fearing that he would take off and eat up the gift!*

M.   *So what's the sense of the language, he had no remedy...?*

N.   *This is the sense of the matter: Because he had no confidence in a third party,* under those circumstances he had no remedy except to transfer the goods along with a piece of real estate.

O.   *Come and take note:* **There was the case involving   Rabban**

Gamaliel and the elders, traveling on a ship when the time for removal of the agricultural gifts had come, requiring their transfer to their proper recipients. Said Rabban Gamaliel, "The tenth I intend to measure out and designate as first tithe is given [27A] t o Joshua [who is a Levite], and the place in which it is located is rented to him. The other tenth which I intend to remove and designate as poor man's tithe is given to Aqiba ben Joseph, who will make it available to the poor, and the place in which it is located is rented to him" [M. M.S. 5:9C]. *Now this surely proves that the goods must be heaped up on the real estate.*

P. *No, this case is exceptional, for he didn't want to put them to any trouble.*

Q. *Come and take note of what* Rabbah bar Isaac said Rab said, "There are two classifications of deeds. If someone says, 'Take possession of the field in behalf of Mr. So-and-so [as my gift to him], and also write a deed for him,' he may retract on the deed [Slotki: if the donor, having given instructions to the witnesses, desires to have no written con-

firmation of the gift,
he may recall the deed
at any time before it
reaches the donee],
but he may not retract
on the gift of the land.
If he says, 'Take
possession of the field
on condition that you
write a deed for him,'
he may retract both
the deed and the
field." And R. Hiyya
bar Abin said R. Huna
said, "There are three
classifications of
deeds, *the two that we
have said just now, and
the following:* If the
seller prior to the sale
went ahead and wrote
a deed, [Slotki: being
anxious to sell, and in
order to expedite the
transaction on ob-
taining the consent of
the buyer, he requests
a scribe to prepare the
deed before he knows
whether the person to
whom he wishes to
sell would consent to
buy], in line with that
which we have
learned in the Mish-
nah: **They write a writ
of sale to the seller,
even though the
buyer is not with
him. But they do not
write a writ of sale for
the purchaser, unless
the seller is with him
[M. B.B. 10:3H-I].**
Then, once the buyer
has taken possession
of the land, he
acquires the deed as
well, without regard
to the location of the
deed." *That proves that*

> we do not require that
> the goods be piled up on
> the land.
>
> R. *The case of a deed is
> exceptional, since it has
> a bearing on the land
> itself.*
>
> S. *But lo, in that regard
> there is a Tannaite
> statement:* And that is
> in line with what we
> have learned:
> "Movable property
> may be acquired
> along with landed
> property through
> transfer of money,
> deed, and exercising a
> right of possession."
>
> T. *That is decisive proof.*

The issue is whether movables are acquired along with real estate, and how we know that fact. Y.'s inquiry finds a prooftext to prove that when the movables and real estate are together, the transfer of the former takes place along with the latter. If they were in different places, we have to prof the same point. This is shown by appeal to Eliezer's precedent. That is further examined. Then our second proof, and a better one, is supplied by Aqiba's ruling. The Bavli's framers utilized the same Tannaite stories concerning Eliezer and Aqiba. But the use of the stories in the Yerushalmi in no way prepares us for the way they serve in the Bavli's composition. To the contrary, the entire argument follows its own lines. First we frame our question, now not in the framework of the Mishnah rule at all. Then we find Aqiba's ruling, but instead of treating that as the conclusive demonstration, we conduct an argument about the pertinence of the reasoning that has led us to appeal to Aqiba to begin with, C, D. Then, E, we accept the challenge and proceed to Eliezer's proof (the variation from Eliezer to Eleazar need not detain us). This evidence is also subjected to searching analysis and criticism. So a third governing precedent is supplied, and that, too, is overturned. At Q we have yet another formulated authoritative rule, and that one stands.

Any claim that, even where the two Talmuds ask the same question and invoke the same precedents, the documents intersect, has now to be abandoned. The Yerushalmi finds its precedent and settles its question. The Bavli settles the question, too – but it does so only after a searching, corrosive examination of the precedents that are adduced in evidence. The two Talmuds do not differ on the sources upon which they draw –

the Mishnah, the Tosefta, Scripture, some episodic sayings – but they differ profoundly in the morphology and structure of analysis and argument.

6

Mishnah-Tractate Qiddushin 1:6
in the Yerushalmi and the Bavli

1:6

A. Whatever is used as payment for something else –

B. once this one has effected acquisition [thereof]

C. the other has become liable for what is given in exchange.

D. How so?

E. [If] one exchanged an ox for a cow, or an ass for an ox,

F. once this one has effected acquisition, the other has become liable for what is given in exchange.

G. The right of the Most High is effected through money, and the right of ordinary folk through usucaption.

H. One's word of mouth [dedication of an object] to the Most High is equivalent to one's act of delivery to an ordinary person.

I. M. Qiddushin 1:6 in the Talmud of the Land of Israel

[I.A] There we have learned: This is the general rule: All movable property effects acquisition of all other movable property [M. B.M. 4:1].

[B] R. Ba, R. Huna in the name of Rab: "Even a whole pile of merchandise [that has not been evaluated item by item serves in exchange for some other pile of merchandise]."

[C] "Said to him R. Eleazar, 'We have learned only: Whatever is used as payment for something else, and this implies something that is subject to assessment.'"

[D] The opinion of R. Huna accords with that of R. Yohanan, and R. Eleazar is consistent with views held by him elsewhere.

[E] [To understand what follows, we must begin with a passage quoted only later in the unfolding of the argument, M. Bekh. 9:3: What is purchased or what is given to someone as a gift is exempt from the law to tithe cattle. Brothers in partnership who are liable to a surcharge [in paying the sheqel (explained below)] are exempt from tithe of cattle. And those who are liable to tithe of cattle are exempt from the surcharge. If they acquired cattle from the property of the

245

estate of their father, they are liable, and if not, they are exempt. If they divided the estate and then went and formed a partnership, they are liable to surcharge and exempt from tithe of cattle. Now when someone pays a half-sheqel to the Temple, he is liable to a surcharge, to cover the cost of changing the money for the Temple's purposes. Individuals are liable to a half-sheqel plus the surcharge. The issue is whether the brothers, like other partners, together give the Temple tax of a half-sheqel, paying a whole sheqel to the Temple. If so, they pay the surcharge over and above the sheqel; they are deemed two strangers, not joint owners of the estate. Now if they are regarded as strangers, then they are exempt from tithing herds they jointly own. Why? Because of the opening statement: What is purchased – for example, in the formation of a partnership – is exempt. At issue therefore is the point at which they form their partnership. If they form the partnership before the division of the estate, they are liable to tithe the cattle. Hence they are exempt from the surcharge, since they are deemed one entity (joint heirs). If they form the partnership after the division of the estate, when all the cattle have entered their respective domains, they are exempt from tithing offspring born to their partnership, and, as is obvious, they are also liable to pay the surcharge as individuals in a re-formed partnership. So the critical point will be when the partnership is formed and whether, in its formation, the contribution of each party is assessed for purposes of forming the partnership. The discussion commences with the citation of M. Sheq. 1:7's statement on this same matter:] For we have learned there: Brothers who are partners who are liable to the surcharge are exempt from tithe of cattle. But when they are liable to tithe of cattle, they are exempt from the surcharge [M. Sheq. 1:7]. [What has happened, as is clear, is that the brothers take their share in the estate, then go and form a partnership to tend their cattle together. Then they are true partners, so they are liable to pay the surcharge, but, as we know, they are not liable to tithe the shared herd. If, by contrast, they have not yet divided the estate, they are not partners but are deemed one corporate body. The herd, undivided, is liable to the tithe as it was when the father owned it. But they also do not pay the surcharge. Now Eleazar will gloss this statement in such wise as to restate his established principle, that any sort of valid commercial exchange requires an assessment of the goods introduced into the exchange.]

[F] Said R. Eleazar, "[The rule that, once they have divided the estate and formed a partnership, they are liable to the surcharge but exempt from the tithing of their herd] applies when they divide up and contribute to the partnership lambs for rams and rams for lambs. [Why? Because in this case there has been a proper appraisal of the value of the contribution of each to the partnership. In that case we do not allege that this party has contributed what was already his. That is, when the father died each brother acquired ownership of half of all the lambs and half of all the rams. If there is a division of diverse types of animals, there must be an appraisal, since it cannot be done on a one-for-one basis. Then we have a true partnership, and the offspring of the herd belong to partners and are not subject to tithe. The herd itself is exempt, since it is deemed to have been purchased (appraised, exchanged), in line with M. Bekh. 9:1A. So the need to appraise the division to each brother sets the herd into the status of something that has been purchased.]

[G] "But [Eleazar continues] if they split up lambs for lambs and rams for rams, it is as if the herd in common were contributed from the very outset. That is, all we have is the inheritance of each brother, joined together as it always was in their father's domain. When they formed their partnership, they did not establish a new entity but re-formed the existing one. There is no need to appraise the whole, so the status of a purchase and trade has not been established. When the herd comes to the tithing season, the beasts are not in the status of something that has been purchased. Accordingly, we have no true partnership here. Tithing is required. Then, as we know, the surcharge on the sheqel paid to the Temple will not apply.]"

[H] Said R. Yohanan, "But even if one party contributed lambs against another party's lambs, or rams against rams, they remain in the status of purchasers, [and the beasts, purchased beasts, so, as we know, the conception of F is not invoked. It follows that, from Yohanan's viewpoint, an appraisal of the value of the division to each is not required. Mere exchange suffices to establish that we have a new entity, created by the exchange of each party for a share in the whole herd]."

[I] For we have learned there: What is purchased or what is given to one as a gift is exempt from the law to tithe cattle. Brothers in partnership who are liable to a surcharge are exempt from tithe of cattle. And those who are liable to tithe of cattle are exempt from the surcharge. If they acquired cattle from the property of the estate of their father, they are liable. And if not, they are exempt. If they divided the estate and then went and formed a partnership, they are liable to surcharge and exempt from tithe of cattle [M. Bekh. 9:3].

[II.A] R. Ba in the name of R. Judah in the name of Samuel: "If this party has a cow and that party has an ass, and they exchanged what belongs to this party for what belongs to that party, and what belongs to that party for what belongs to this party,

[B] "if the owner of the ass drew [and so acquired] the cow, and the owner of the cow came to draw the ass and it turned out that the ass had died,

[C] "the owner of the ass has to bring proof that his ass was alive at the time that the owner of the ass had drawn the cow.

[D] "For whoever wishes to extract property from his fellow bears the burden of proof, except in a case of an exchange. [That is, here the owner of the ass wishes to keep the cow and must bring proof.]

[E] "And whoever does not grasp this matter knows nothing at all in the laws of torts."

[F] Said R. Zeira, "But I don't grasp this at all!"

[G] Said R. Ba to R. Zeira, "The following Mishnah pericope differs from the rule of Samuel:

[H] "If there were blemishes while she was yet in her father's house, the father [who holds a lien for the marriage settlement] must bring proof that after she was betrothed, these blemishes made their appearance on her [M. Qid. 7:8A-B].

[I] "But does not the husband also have to bring proof to extract the money he paid for betrothal festivities from the domain of the father?"

[J] The disciples of R. Jonah said, "Interpret the law to speak of a case where the festivity funds are a small sum [not equivalent to the marriage settlement, so the husband is not the principal plaintiff]. [The father wants to collect the marriage settlement, so he must bring proof. This contradicts Samuel's position.]"

[K] Now when R. Huna, R. Phineas, and R. Hezekiah went up to inquire after the welfare of R. Joseph, to study with him, they said to him, "The following Mishnah pericope supports the position of Samuel:

[L] "If she had entered the domain of the husband, then the husband has to bring proof that, before she was betrothed, these blemishes were on her body [M. Ket. 7:8C].

[M] "And it is not the father who has to bring proof to extract the money owing on the marriage settlement [owed by the husband] from the domain of the husband."

[N] He said to them, "Does Samuel not agree that, if the owner of the cow had drawn the ass, he has to bring proof? And this one, since he has married the girl, it is as if he has drawn the beast and acquired ownership of it, [so there is no support for Samuel's view at all].

[O] "So he has to bring proof that these blemishes were on her before she entered his domain."

[III.A] R. Ada bar Ahva in the name of Rab: "If he had sold him the cow for money [and the debt is not yet paid] –

[B] "[the debtor] avoided payment [DHQ] –

[C] "He said to him, 'Give me the money' –

[D] [61a] "He said to him, 'What do you want to do with it?' –

[E] "He said to him, 'To buy an ass' –

[F] "If the owner of the cow drew an ass [from the debtor], the cow would not now be acquired [for it had been acquired at the earlier transaction, and the debtor merely owes the creditor money]?

[G] "What is the law as to the ass's being acquired [without its being drawn that is, do we now view the ass as an exchange for the cow]?"

[H] R. Ba said, "It has been acquired."

[I] R. Yosé says, "It has not been acquired."

[J] R. Ba assumed that it was a case of an exchange, but it was not a case of an exchange.

[IV.A] R. Mana in the name of R. Yosé, "There are times that the beginning of the purchase is assigned to this party, and the beginning of the purchase is assigned to that party [and no acquisition is effected, as will be explained].

[B] "What would be a concrete case?

[C] "If one sold him a cow for money, and he left [the money] with a money-changer.

[D] "On the next day he found him standing [to collect the money]. [Translation follows Leiden MS and Epstein 6:1, p. 3].

[E] "He said to him, 'What are you doing, standing here?'

[F] "He said to him, 'I want my money.'

[G] "He said to him, 'What do you want to do with it?'

[H] "He said to him, 'Buy an ass.'

[I] "He said to him, 'Here is an ass before you.'

[J] "If this one drew it, that party has not made acquisition. If that party drew it, this party has not made acquisition.

[K] "But this party effects acquisition for himself, and that party effects acquisition for himself. [The debt did not cover the entire cost of the purchase of the ass. It is not a debt by reason of the prior sale. So acquisition in no way falls under the law of exchange [M. 1:6E-F].]"

[V.A] The right of the Most High is effected through money [M. Qid. 1:6G] – how so?

[B] **The Temple treasurer who paid over coins of the Sanctuary for movables – the Sanctuary has made acquisition wherever [the movables] may be.**

[C] **But in the case of an ordinary person, he has not made acquisition until he will have drawn [the object] [T. Qid. 1:9C-E],**

[D] as it is said, "The earth is the Lord's and the fullness thereof, the world and those that dwell therein" (Ps. 24:1).

[E] **One's word of mouth [dedication of an object] to the Most High is equivalent to one's act of delivery to an ordinary person [M. 1:6H].**

[F] How so?

[G] If one has purchased a cow from the sanctuary for two hundred zuz and did not suffice to bring the two hundred zuz before the price of the cow fell to a maneh [a hundred], he pays two hundred.

[H] That illustrates the statement, one's word of mouth to the Most High is equivalent to an act of delivery to an ordinary person.

[I] [If he purchased] a cow from the sanctuary for a maneh, and did not suffice to bring the maneh before the price went up to two hundred, he brings the two hundred.

[J] This is in line with what is written, "And he shall add a fifth of the valuation in money to it, and it shall be his" (Lev. 27:15).

[K] If he has added, lo, it is his, and if not, it is not his.

[L] **One's word of mouth [dedication of an object] to the Most High is equivalent to one's act of delivery to an ordinary person [M. Qid. 1:6H] – how so?**

[M] **[If one said,] "This ox is sanctified ['WLH]," "This house is sanctified [QRBN]" – even if it is at the end of the world, the Sanctuary has made acquisition wherever it is situated, as it is written, "The earth is the Lord's and the fullness thereof."**

[N] **But in the case of an ordinary person, he makes acquisition only when he effects ownership through usucaption [T. Qid. 1:9F-H].**

The facts of unit I require somewhat extended explanation, but the issue is clear – whether an (independent) appraisal is required in a swap. Eleazar maintains that to give a trade the status of a purchase and sale, a price must be established for the goods that are exchanged from one party to the other. Unit II moves on to an independent but relevant issue, clarifying the point in a trade at which ownership shifts from one party to the other, in line with M. 1:6E-F. Unit III gives us a middle case, between an exchange and a sale. Since there is to be an exchange of a cow and an ass, the sale is deemed by one authority to fall under the law of exchange. Consequently, as soon as the second party has carried out his obligation by laying hands on the beast he must forthwith deliver, the beast he has taken over immediately belongs to the person awaiting payment. But, as III.J observes, this really is not an exchange at all, so the stated rule does not apply. Unit IV gives yet another instance in which we do not invoke the rule of acquisition through exchange of M. 1:6E-F. Unit V, finally, turns to M. 1:6G-H, the way the Temple effects acquisition.

II. Mishnah Qiddushin 1:6A-F, G-H in the Talmud of Babylonia

1:6A-F

A.   Whatever is used as payment for something else –
B.   once this one has effected acquisition [thereof]
C.   the other has become liable for what is given in exchange.
D.   How so?
E.   [If] one exchanged an ox for a cow, or an ass for an ox,
F.   once this one has effected acquisition, the other has become liable for what is given in exchange.

I.1   A.   [**Whatever is used as payment for something else:**] *What is subject to barter? Money.* [Freedman: It is assumed that the language, **Whatever is used as payment for something else** includes money. Hence the point is: If A exchanges a cow for B's money, the money not being given as payment but as barter, just as an ox might be given, then as soon as A gets the money, B accepts liability for whatever happens to the cow, which is now subject to his title; that is the case even though if the money had been given as payment, the receipt of the money by A would not have transferred title of the cow to B.] *That then proves* money may be treated as an object of barter.

   B.   *Said R. Judah, "This is the sense of the passage:* Whatever may be assessed as the value of another object, [excluding money, which, by definition, requires no assessment, since its value is explicit], [28B] once one party has taken possession of that object, the other becomes liable for what is given in exchange. *And that reading is reasonable, for lo, the passage proceeds as follows:* **How so? If one has exchanged an ox for a cow or an ass for an ox** [once one party has taken possession of that object, the other becomes liable for what is given in exchange]."

   C.   *That's decisive proof.*

D. *And with respect to what we originally imagined, which is that* money may serve as an object of barter, *what is the meaning of the language,* How so?

E. *This is the sense of the matter:* Produce, too, can serve to effect a barter. How so? If one has exchanged an ox for a cow or an ass for an ox [once one party has taken possession of that object, the other becomes liable for what is given in exchange].

F. *Well, that reading poses no problem to R. Sheshet, who does indeed maintain that produce may serve for the purposes of barter. But from the viewpoint of R. Nahman, who has maintained that produce cannot effect a barter, what is the sense of the matter?*

G. *This is the sense of the matter:* Money may sometimes serve as a medium of barter. How so? If one has exchanged an ox for a cow or an ass for an ox [once one party has taken possession of that object, the other becomes liable for what is given in exchange].

H. *And what's the operative consideration in his mind?*

I. *He shares the viewpoint of R. Yohanan, who has said, "By the law of the Torah, the transfer of cash serves to transfer title."*

J. Then how come they have said that only drawing a beast transfers title?

K. It is a precautionary decree, lest the other say to him, "Your grain has burned up in the silo."

L. *Rabbis made a precautionary decree only to cover what is commonplace, but not for what is uncommon* [and therefore biblical law pertains (Freedman)].

M. *And from the perspective of R. Simeon b. Laqish, who* has said, "The medium of acquiring title through drawing a beast is explicitly required by the Torah," *then there is no problem if he concurs with R. Sheshet's view that produce can effect a barter, for the matter can be explained as does R. Sheshet. But if he concurs with R. Nahman, that produce cannot effect a barter, while money does not transfer title at all, then how is the matter to be worked out?*

N. *You really have to say that he concurs with R. Sheshet.*

I.1 investigates the relationship between our case and a general rule, finding in our case proof of the prevailing principle.

1:6G-H

G. The right of the Most High is effected through money, and the right of ordinary folk through usucaption.

H. One's word of mouth [dedication of an object] to the Most High is equivalent to one's act of delivery to an ordinary person.

I.1 A. *Our rabbis have taught on Tannaite authority:*

B. How is the right of the Most High effected through money? If the Temple treasurer handed over money for a beast, even if the animal is located on the other side of the world, he acquires title to it, but an ordinary person acquires title only by performing the act of drawing the beast.

C. How is it so that one's word of mouth [dedication of an object] to the Most High is equivalent to one's act of delivery to an ordinary person? He who says, "This ox is a burnt-offering," "This house is sanctified," even if they are at the other side of the world, the sanctuary acquires title. In the case of an ordinary person, he acquires title only [29A] by performing an act of drawing or usucaption.

D. If a common person performed the act of drawing when the beast was worth a maneh but did not suffice to redeem the beast, paying the money, until the price rose to two hundred zuz, he must pay the two hundred. How come? Scripture says, "And he will pay the money and depart," meaning, if he has given the money, lo, these belong to him, but if not, they do not belong to him. If he performed the act of drawing when it was worth two hundred zuz but did not suffice to redeem it before the price fell to a maneh, he still has to pay two hundred zuz. How come? So that the rights of a common person should not be stronger than those of the sanctuary. If he redeemed it when it was worth two hundred but did not suffice to draw the beast before the price went down to a maneh, he has to pay the two hundred zuz. How come? Scripture says, "And he will pay the money and depart." If he redeems it at a maneh and did not suffice to perform the act of drawing before it went up to two hundred zuz, what he has redeemed is redeemed, and he pays only a maneh [T. Ar. 4:4A-G].

E. *Why? Here, too, should we not just say, So that the rights of a common person should not be stronger than those of the sanctuary?*

F. *But doesn't an ordinary person have to submit to the curse, "He who punished the generation of the blood will punish him who does not stand by his word"?*

I.1 provides a Tannaite complement, spelling out the rule of the Mishnah paragraph.

III. The Exegetical Programs of Yerushalmi and of the Babli Compared

Let us now outline the two Talmud's presentations of M. Qiddushin 1:6.

1:6 I This composition is included because it draws upon our Mishnah rule for evidence for an argument focused on a distinct proposition.

1:6 I This composition is included because it draws upon our Mishnah rule for evidence for an argument focused on a distinct proposition.

1:6 II Clarification and refinement of the Mishnah rule that once one has effected acquisition, the other becomes liable for what is given in exchange. Case of unclarity resolved by maintaining, whoever wishes to

1:6A-F I.1 Gloss of the Mishnah rule, in assuming that the Mishnah refers to money. This yields the question of how our rule intersects with a prevailing principle.

1:6G-H I.1 Tannaite complement.

extract property from the other
bears the burden of proof.

1:6 III If money is promised
and not paid....

1:6 I IV Further problem on
exchange of money for a cow.

1:6 V Toseftan complement
to the Mishnah rule.

Now we have a chance to see how the two Talmuds address the
same Tannaite materials:

[V.A] The right of the Most High is effected through money [M. Qid. 1: 6G] – how so?

[B] The Temple treasurer who paid over coins of the Sanctuary for movables – the Sanctuary has made acquisition wherever [the movables] may be.

[C] But in the case of an ordinary person, he has not made acquisition until he will have drawn [the object] [T. Qid. 1:9C-E],

[D] as it is said, "The earth is the Lord's and the fullness thereof, the world and those that dwell therein" (Ps. 24:1).

[E] One's word of mouth [dedication of an object] to the Most High is equivalent to one's act of delivery to an ordinary person [M. 1:6H].

[F] How so?

[G] If one has purchased a cow from the sanctuary for two hundred zuz and did not suffice to bring the

I.1 A. *Our rabbis have taught on Tannaite authority:*

B. How is the right of the Most High effected through money? If the Temple treasurer handed over money for a beast, even if the animal is located on the other side of the world, he acquires title to it, but an ordinary person acquires title only by performing the act of drawing the beast.

C. How is it so that one's word of mouth [dedication of an object] to the Most High is equivalent to one's act of delivery to an ordinary person? He who says, "This ox is a burnt-offering," "This house is sanctified," even if they are at the other side of the world, the sanctuary acquires title. In the case of an ordinary person, he acquires title only [29A] by performing an act of drawing or usucaption.

D. If a common person

two hundred zuz before the price of the cow fell to a maneh [a hundred], he pays two hundred.

[H] That illustrates the statement, One's word of mouth to the Most High is equivalent to an act of delivery to an ordinary person.

[I] [If he purchased] a cow from the sanctuary for a maneh, and did not suffice to bring the maneh before the price went up to two hundred, he brings the two hundred.

[J] This is in line with what is written, "And he shall add a fifth of the valuation in money to it, and it shall be his" (Lev. 27:15).

[K] If he has added, lo, it is his, and if not, it is not his.

[L] One's word of mouth [dedication of an object] to the Most High is equivalent to one's act of delivery to an ordinary person [M. Qid. 1:6H] – how so?

[M] [If one said,] "This ox is sanctified ['WLH]," "This house is sanctified [QRBN]" – even if it is at the end of the world, the Sanctuary has made acquisition wherever it is situated, as it is written, "The earth is the Lord's and the fullness thereof."

[N] But in the case of an

performed the act of drawing when the beast was worth a maneh but did not suffice to redeem the beast, paying the money, until the price rose to two hundred zuz, he must pay the two hundred. How come? Scripture says, "And he will pay the money and depart," meaning, if he has given the money, lo, these belong to him, but if not, they do not belong to him. If he performed the act of drawing when it was worth two hundred zuz but did not suffice to redeem it before the price fell to a maneh, he still has to pay two hundred zuz. How come? So that the rights of a common person should not be stronger than those of the sanctuary. If he redeemed it when it was worth two hundred but did not suffice to draw the beast before the price went down to a maneh, he has to pay the two hundred zuz. How come? Scripture says, "And he will pay the money and depart." If he redeems it at a maneh and did not suffice to perform the act of drawing before it went up to two hundred zuz, what he has redeemed is ordinary person, he makes acquisition only when he effects ownership through usucaption [T. Qid. 1:9F-H].

E. *Why? Here, too, should we not just say, So that the rights of a common person should not be stronger than those of the sanctuary?*

F. *But doesn't an ordinary person have to submit to the curse, "He who punished the generation of the blood will punish him who does not stand by his word"?*

redeemed, and he pays only a maneh [T. Ar. 4:4A-G].

The difference is small but important, and it is at B. 1:6G-H I.E-F: a secondary challenge and response, that is to say the second Talmud takes as its task a process of dialectical inquiry, treating a Tannaite statement not as a point at which an argument closes, but as the occasion at which an analysis – challenge, response – commences.

7

Mishnah-Tractate Qiddushin 1:7 in the Yerushalmi and the Bavli

1:7

A. For every commandment concerning the son to which the father is subject – men are liable, and women are exempt.

B. And for every commandment concerning the father to which the son is subject, men and women are equally liable.

C. For every positive commandment dependent upon the time [of year], men are liable, and women are exempt.

D. And for every positive commandment not dependent upon the time, men and women are equally liable.

E. For every negative commandment, whether dependent upon the time or not dependent upon the time, men and women are equally liable,

F. except for not marring the corners of the beard, not rounding the corners of the head (Lev. 19:27), and not becoming unclean because of the dead (Lev. 21:1).

G. [The cultic rites of] laying on of hands, waving, drawing near, taking the handful, burning the fat, breaking the neck of a bird, sprinkling, and receiving [the blood] apply to men and not to women,

H. except in the case of a meal-offering of an accused wife and of a Nazirite girl, which they wave.

I. Mishnah Qiddushin 1:7 in the Talmud of the Land of Israel

[I.A] What is a commandment pertaining to the father concerning the son [M. 1:7A]?

[B] To circumcise him, to redeem him, and to teach him Torah, and to teach him a trade, and to marry him off to a girl.

[C] And R. Aqiba says, "Also to teach him how to swim" [T. Qid. 1:1 1E-G].

[D] To circumcise him, in line with the following verse of Scripture: "And on the eighth day the flesh of his foreskin shall be circumcised" (Lev. 12:3).

257

[E]   To redeem him, in line with the following verse of Scripture: "Every firstborn of man among your sons you shall redeem" (Ex. 13:13).

[F]   To teach him Torah, in line with the following verse of Scripture: "And you shall teach them to your children [talking of them when you are sitting in your house, and when you are walking by the way, and when you lie down, and when you rise]" (Deut. 11:19).

[G]   To teach him a trade: R. Ishmael taught, "[I call Heaven and earth to witness against you this day, that I have set before you life and death, blessing and curse;] therefore choose life, [that you and your descendants may live]" (Deut. 30:19).

[H]   "This [refers to] learning a trade."

[I]   To marry him off to a girl, in line with the following verse of Scripture: "[Only take heed, and keep your soul diligently, lest you forget the things which your eyes have seen, and lest they depart from your heart all the days of your life;] make them known to your children and your children's children" (Deut. 4:9).

[J]   In what circumstances do you have the merit [of seeing] children and grandchildren? When you marry your children off when they are young.

[K]   R. Aqiba says, "Also to teach him how to swim," in line with the following verse of Scripture: "[I call Heaven and earth to witness against you this day, that I have set before you life and death, blessing and curse; therefore choose life,] that you and your descendants may live" (Deut. 30:19).

[L]   What [is the status of the statement about the father's obligations]? Is it a religious duty, or are these absolute requirements, [which a person is compelled to carry out, with special reference to marrying off the son]?

[M]   Let us derive the answer from the following case:

[N]   Bar Tarimah came to R. Immi. He said to him, "Persuade father to get me a wife."

[O]   He went and tried to persuade him, but the father was not agreeable [to the project].

[P]   That is to say that it is a mere religious duty, for if you say that it was an absolute requirement, he should have forced him to comply.

[Q]   How do we know that, if his father did not do his duty, the son is liable to do it for himself?

[R]   Scripture states, "Every firstborn of man among your sons you shall redeem."

[S]   "You shall be circumcised [in the flesh of your foreskin, and it shall be a sign of the covenant between me and you]" (Gen. 17:11).

[T]   "And you shall teach them to your children."

[U]   "And make them known to your children."

[V]   "That you and your descendants may live."

[II.A]   There we have learned: **The father endows his child with beauty, strength, riches, wisdom, and length of years [M. Ed. 2:9].**

[B]   How do we know beauty?

[C]   "Let thy work be manifest to thy servants, [and thy glorious power to their children]" (Ps. 90:17).

[D]   Strength: "His descendants will be mighty in the land; [the generation of the upright will be blessed]" (Ps. 112:2).

[E] Riches: "I have been young and now I am old; yet I have not seen the righteous forsaken or his children begging bread" (Ps. 37:25).

[F] Wisdom: "And you shall teach them to your children, speaking of them..." (Deut. 11:19).

[G] Years: "That your days and the days of your children may be multiplied in the land which the Lord swore to your fathers to give them" (Deut. 11:20).

[H] And just as the father endows his children with five traits, so the children are liable to him in five regards, and these are they: Food, drink, clothing, shoes, and guidance.

[I] This is in line with what is written, "May it fall upon the head of Joab, [and upon all his father's house; and may the house of Joab never be without] one who has a discharge, or who is leprous, or who holds a spindle, or who is slain by the sword, or who lacks bread" (2 Sam. 3:29).

[J] "One who has a discharge" is weak.

[K] "One who is leprous" is abandoned [on account of ugliness].

[L] "One who holds a spindle" is feebleminded.

[M] "Who is slain by the sword" is short-lived.

[N] "Who lacks bread" is poor.

[O] When Solomon came to kill Joab, [Joab] said to him, "Your father made five evil decrees against me [those at 2 Sam. 3:29]. You accept them, and I shall accept the death penalty from you. Solomon accepted them, and all of them were fulfilled in the house of David."

[P] "One who has a discharge" applies to Rehoboam: "And King Rehoboam made haste to mount his chariot, to flee to Jerusalem" (1 Kgs. 12:18).

[Q] There is he who says he had a discharge, and there is he who says he was spoiled.

[R] As to "a leper," this is Uzziah: "And King Uzziah was a leper to the day of his death, [and being a leper dwelt in a separate house, for he was excluded from the house of the Lord]" (2 Chr. 26:21).

[S] "One who holds a spindle" applies to Joash: "[Though the army of the Syrians had come with few men, the Lord delivered into their hand a very great army, because they had forsaken the Lord, the God of their fathers.] Thus they executed judgment on Joash" (2 Chr. 24:24).

[T] R. Ishmael taught, "This teaches that they set up against him sadists, who had never known a woman in their lives, and they inflicted suffering on him as they inflict suffering on a woman."

[U] This is in line with what is written, "The pride of Israel testifies to his face; [Israel and Ephraim shall stumble in his guilt; Judah also shall stumble with them]" (Hos. 5:5). [The meaning is,] they tormented the pride of Israel in his face.

[V] "One who is slain by the sword" refers to Josiah, in line with the following verse of Scripture: "And the archers shot King Josiah; [and the king said to his servants, 'Take me away, for I am badly wounded']" (2 Chr. 35:23).

[W] R. Yohanan says, "This teaches that they made his body into a sieve."

[X]   R. Ishmael taught, "Three hundred arrows did they shoot into the anointed of the Lord."

[Y]   "Who lacks bread" refers to Jehoiachin, as it is written, "[And every day of his life he dined regularly at the king's table;] and for his allowance, a regular allowance was given him [by the king, every day a portion, as long as he lived]" (2 Kgs. 25:30).

[III.A] There we have learned: If [before the start of the Sabbath] they began, they do not interrupt the process] [M. Shab. 1:5].

[B]   What is the point at which the bath begins?

[C]   R. Zeriqan in the name of R. Haninah: "Once he has removed his belt."

[D]   Rab said, "Once he has removed his sandal."

[E]   R. Joshua b. Levi would hear the lesson of his grandson every Friday afternoon. One time he forgot and went into the bath of Tiberias. Now he was leaning on the shoulder of R. Hiyya b. Ba. He remembered while he was in the bath [that he had not heard the child's lesson] and he went out of the bath. What happened?

[F]   R. Daromi said, "It was this way. R. Eleazar b. Yosé said, 'He had already removed his garments.'"

[G]   Said to him R. Hiyya bar Ba, "Did not Rabbi teach us, 'If before the start of the Sabbath they began, they do not interrupt?'"

[H]   He said to him, "Hiyya, my son, is it a small thing in your eyes that whoever hears a passage of Torah from his grandson is as if he hears it from Mount Sinai?

[I]   "What is the scriptural basis for this statement? 'Make them known to your children and your children's children – how on the day that you stood before the Lord your God at Horeb' (Deut. 4:9-10).

[J]   "That is to say, 'It is like the day on which you stood before the Lord your God at Horeb.'"

[IV.A] R. Hezekiah b. R. Jeremiah, R. Hiyya in the name of R. Yohanan: "If you can trace the authority behind a tradition to Moses, do so, and if not, put the first [name you hear] first, and the last, last."

[B]   Giddul said, "Whoever says a tradition in the name of the one who said it should see himself as if the one who is the authority for the tradition is standing before him."

[C]   What is the scriptural basis for that statement?

[D]   "Surely a man goes about as a shadow! [Surely for nought are they in turmoil] man heaps up, and knows not who will gather."

[E]   "Many a man proclaims his own loyalty, but a faithful man who can find?" (Prov. 20:6).

[F]   This refers to R. Zeira, for R. Zeira said, "We pay no attention to the traditions of R. Sheshet, [which he says in the names of those who originally said them,] because he is blind [and may err in identifying the voices]."

[G]   And R. Zeira said to R. Yosa. "Do you know Bar Pedaiah, that you cite traditions in his name?"

[H]   He said to him, "R. Yohanan said them in his name."

[I]   Said R. Zeira to R. Ba, bar Zabeda, "Does my lord know Rab, that you cite traditions in his name?"

[J]   He said to him, "R. Ada bar Ahva said them in his name."

[V.A] Every commandment concerning the father to which the son is liable [M. 1:7B]:

[B] What is the way one expresses reverence for the father?

[C] He does not sit in his place or speak in his place, he does not contradict him.

[D] And what is the form of honor owing to the father?

[E] Giving him food to eat and something to drink and clothing him and covering him and taking him out and bringing him in and washing his face, his hands, and his feet [T. Qid. 1:1 IB].

[F] Whose [food and the like must be given to the father]? [Does the son have to provide it?]

[G] Hunah bar Hiyya said, "It is the old man's."

[H] And there are those who wish to say, "It is his [the son's]."

[I] Did not R. Abbahu say in the name of R. Yosé b. R. Haninah, "How do we know that even if the father said to him, 'Throw this purse into the sea,' the son must listen to him?" [So the son bears unlimited obligations.]

[J] That applies to a case in which the father has another such purse, and in which the son gives pleasure to the father by doing what he wants.

[K] All the same are husband [61b] and wife, but the husband has sufficient means to do these things [for the aged parent], and the wife does not have sufficient means to do them,

[L] for others have power over her [T. Qid. 1:1].

[M] If the daughter was widowed or divorced, she enters the status of one who has sufficient means to carry out what is required.

[VI.A] To what extent does the requirement of honoring the father and mother extend?

[B] He [Eleazar, Y. Pe. 1:1] said to them, "Are you asking me? Go and ask Damah b. Netinah. He was the chief of the patroboule of his town. One time his mother was slapping him before the entire council, and the slipper she was beating him with fell from her hand, and he got down and gave it back to her, so that she would not be upset."

[C] Said R. Hezekiah, "He was a gentile from Ashkelon, and head of the patroboule of his town. Now if there was a stone on which his father had sat, he would never sit on it. When [his father] died, he made the stone into his god."

[D] One time the Benjamin's jewel in the high priest's breastplate was lost [cf. Jastrow, p. 601]. They said, "Who has one as fine as that one? They said that Damah b. Netinah had one. They went to him and made a deal with him to buy it for a hundred denars. He went to get it for them, and he found that his father was sleeping [on the box containing the jewel].

[E] And some say that the key to the box was on the finger of his father, and some say that his foot was stretched out over the jewel cask.

[F] He went down to them and said, "I can't bring it to you." They said, "Perhaps it is because he wants more money." They raised the price to two hundred, then to a thousand. Once his father woke up from his sleep, he went up and got the jewel for them.

[G]   They wanted to pay him what they had offered at the end, but he would not accept the money from them. He said, "Shall I sell you [at a price] the honor I pay to my father? I shall not derive benefit by reason of the honor I pay to my father."

[H]   How did the Holy One, blessed be He, reward him?

[I]   Said R. Yosé b. R. Bun, "That very night his cow produced a red cow, and the Israelites paid him its weight in gold and weighed it [for use for producing purification water]."

[J]   Said R. Shabbetai, "It is written, '[The Almighty – we cannot find him; he is great in power and justice,] and abundant righteousness he will not violate' (Job 37:23).

[K]   "The Holy One, blessed be He, will not long delay the reward that is coming to gentiles for the good they do."

[L]   The mother of R. Tarfon went down to take a walk in her courtyard on the Sabbath, and her slipper fell off, and R. Tarfon went and placed his two hands under the soles of her feet, so that she could walk on them until she got to her couch.

[M]   One time sages went to call on him. She said to them, "Pray for Tarfon, my son, who pays me altogether too much honor."

[N]   They said to her, "What does he do for you?" She repeated the story to them.

[O]   They said to her, "Even if he did a thousand times more than this, he still would not have paid even half of the honor of which the Torah has spoken."

[P]   The mother of R. Ishmael went and complained to the rabbis about him. She said, "Rebuke Ishmael, my son, because he does not pay respect to me."

[Q]   At that moment the faces of our rabbis grew dark. They said, "Is it at all possible that R. Ishmael does not pay honor to his parents?"

[R]   They said to her, "What did he do to you?"

[S]   She said, "When he comes home from the council house, I want to wash his feet in water and drink the water, and he does not let me do it."

[T]   They said, "Since that is what she deems to be the honor she wants for herself, that indeed is just the kind of honor he must pay to her."

[U]   Said R. Mana, "Well do the millers say, 'Everyone's merit is in his own basket.' [That is, there is a different way of doing good for every man (following Pené Moshe and Jastrow).]"

[V]   "The mother of R. Tarfon said one thing to them, and they responded thus, and the mother of R. Ishmael said something else to them, and they responded so."

[W]   R. Zeira was distressed, saying, "Would that I had a father and a mother, whom I might honor, and so inherit the Garden of Eden." When he heard these two teachings [about Tarfon and Ishmael], he said, "Blessed be the All-Merciful, that I have no father and mother. I could not behave either like R. Tarfon or like R. Ishmael."

[X]   Said R. Abin, "I am exempt from the requirement of honoring father and mother."

[Y]   They say that when his mother became pregnant, his father died, and when his mother gave birth, she died.

[Z] There is he who feeds his father fattened [birds] and inherits Gehenna, and there is he who ties his father to the millstones [to pull them] and inherits the Garden of Eden.

[AA] How does one feed his father fattened [birds] and inherit Gehenna?

[BB] There was a man who gave his father fattened chickens to eat. One time the father said to him, "My son, how do you come by these things?"

[CC] He said to him, "Old man, eat and shut up, just like dogs that eat and shut up."

[DD] So he turns out to feed his father fattened [birds] and to inherit Gehenna.

[EE] How does he tie his father to the millstones and inherit the Garden of Eden?

[FF] There was a man who was a miller, pulling the stones. The government orders came to the millers [for the corvée]. He said to him, "Father, go and pull the wheel in my place. If the [labor for the government] should be dishonorable, it is better that I do it and not you, and if there should be floggings, it is better that I get them and not you."

[GG] So he turns out to tie his father to the millstones and inherits the Garden of Eden.

[VII.A] "Every one of you shall revere his mother and his father, [and you shall keep my Sabbaths]" (Lev. 19:3).

[B] And it is said, "You shall fear the Lord your God; [you shall serve him and swear by his name]" (Deut. 6:13).

[C] Scripture so compares the reverence owing to father and mother to the reverence owing to the Omnipresent.

[D] It is said, "Whoever curses his father or his mother shall be put to death" (Ex. 21:17).

[E] And it is said, "[And say to the people of Israel,] 'Whoever curses his God shall bear his sin'" (Lev. 24:15).

[F] Scripture so compares the penalty for cursing the father and mother to the penalty for cursing the Omnipresent.

[G] But it is not possible to introduce the matter of smiting Heaven.

[H] But these [C, F] are reasonable, for the three of them are partners.

[VIII.A] What is the way one expresses reverence for the father? He does not sit in his place or speak in his place, he does not contradict him.

[B] **And what is the form of honor owing to the father?**

[C] **Giving him food to eat, something to drink, clothing him, and covering him and taking him out and bringing him in and washing his face, his hands, and his feet [T. Qid. 1:1 lB].**

[D] Whose [food and the like must be given to the father]? [Does the son have to provide it?]

[E] Huna bar Hiyya said [that the father must supply what is needed for himself].

[F] The following saying of R. Hiyya bar Ba differs, for R. Hiyya bar Ba [said], "R. Judah, son of the daughter of R. Simeon b. Yohai taught that R. Simeon b. Yohai taught: 'Great is the honor owing to father and mother, for the Holy One, blessed be He, gave preference to it, even over the honor owing to God.'

[G] "Here is stated, 'Honor your father and mother, [that your days may be long in the land which the Lord your God gives you]' (Ex. 20:12).

[H] "And elsewhere it is stated, 'Honor the Lord with your substance [and with the firstfruits of all your produce]' (Prov. 3:9).

[I] "How then do you honor God? It is with your substance. You set aside gleanings, the forgotten sheaf, and the corner of the field. You set aside heave-offering and first tithe, second tithe and poor man's tithe, dough-offering, you make a tabernacle [for the festival of Sukkot], and take a lulab, a shofar, phylacteries and show fringes, feed the hungry and give drink to the thirsty. Now if you have enough, you are liable for all these things, and if you do not have, you are not liable for any one of them.

[J] "But when it comes to the matter of honoring father, and mother, whether you have sufficient or whether you do not have, you must honor your father and mother,

[K] "even if you have to go begging at doorways."

[IX.A] R. Aha in the name of R. Abba bar Kahana, "It is written, 'She does not take heed to the path of life, her ways wander and she does not know it' (Prov. 5:6).

[B] "The Holy One, blessed be He, took [and kept to himself] the reward that is coming to those who carry out their religious duties, so that they should do them in true faith [and without expecting a reward]."

[C] R. Aha in the name of R. Isaac, "'Keep your heart with all vigilance; for from it flows the springs of life' (Prov. 4:23).

[D] "[The meaning is this:] 'As to all the things about which I spoke to you in the Torah, keep [and do them all], for you do not know from which of them the springs of life will flow to you.'"

[E] Said R. Abba bar Kahana, "The Scripture has compared the easiest of all the religious duties to the most difficult of them all.

[F] "The easiest of them all is sending forth the dam from the fledglings.

[G] "The most difficult of them all is honoring father and mother.

[H] "Yet in regard to both of them, the same reward is specified: 'That your days may be long.'"

[I] Said R. Abun, "Now if in respect to a matter that is tantamount to paying back a debt [that is, the debt one owes one's father and mother], it is written, '[You shall walk in all the way which the Lord your God has commanded you, that you may live,] and that it may go well with you, and that you may live long in the land which you shall possess' (Deut. 5:33),

[J] "as to a matter that involves a loss of money and endangerment to life [as some religious duties may require], how much the more so [will there be the reward of long life]."

[K] Said R. Levi and an [unnamed] rabbi. "A matter that is tantamount to paying back a debt is still greater than a matter that is not tantamount to paying back a debt."

[L] It was taught: R. Simeon b. Yohai says. "Just as the reward that is coming for doing the two of them is equivalent, so the punishment applying to not doing the two of them is the same: 'The eye that mocks a father and scorns to obey a mother will be picked out by the ravens of the valley and eaten by the vultures' (Prov. 30:17).

[M] "The eye that has ridiculed the notion of honoring the father and mother and that scorns [61c] the duty of not taking the dam with the fledglings.

[N] "'Will be picked out by the ravens of the valley': Let the raven come, which is cruel, come and pluck it, but not derive benefit from it.

[O] "'And eaten by the vultures': Let the vulture come, which is merciful, and eat it and derive benefit from it."

[P] R. Yannai and R. Jonathan were in session. Someone came and kissed the feet of R. Jonathan. R. Yannai said to him, "What is the meaning of this [honor that] he pays you today?"

[Q] [Jonathan] said to him, "One time he came to complain to me about his son, so that the son would support him. I said to him to go to the synagogue and get some people to rebuke him [and tell him to support his father]."

[R] [Yannai] said to him, "And why did you not force [the son to do so, by court order]?"

[S] He said to him, "And do they force [children to do so]?"

[T] [Yannai] said to him, "And are you still [in doubt about] that?"

[U] They say that R. Jonathan reverted and established the tradition on the matter in his [Yannai's] name.

[V] [So, too, did] R. Jacob bar Aha come [and give evidence].

[W] R. Samuel b. Nahman said in the name of R. Jonathan that they force the son to support the father.

[X] Said R. Yosé, "Would that all the traditions I know were so clear and self-evident to me as this one, that they do force the son to support the father."

[X.A] **What is a positive commandment dependent upon the time [of year, for which men are liable and women are exempt] [M. Qid. 1:7C]?**

[B] **For example, building the sukkah, taking the lulab, putting on tefillin.**

[C] **What is a positive commandment not dependent upon the time [of year] [M. Qid. 1:7D]?**

[D] **For example, restoring lost property to its rightful owner, sending forth the bird, building a parapet, and putting on sisit.**

[E] **R. Simeon declares women exempt from the requirement of wearing sisit [show fringes], because it is a positive commandment dependent upon time [T. Qid. 1:10].**

[F] Said to them R. Simeon, "Do you not concur with me that it is a positive commandment dependent upon time? For lo, one's nightgown is exempt from the requirement of having sisit."

[G] Said R. Hila, "The reasoning behind the position of the rabbis is that if [the garment] was designated by him for use by day and by night, it would be liable for sisit."

[XI.A] Said R. Eleazar, "The Passover-offering to be prepared for women is a matter of optional performance, [and even so] if they set aside the restrictions of the Sabbath."

[B]   R. Jacob bar Aha in the name of R. Eleazar, "The Passover-offerings to be prepared for women and slaves are a matter of optional performance."

[C]   Then [shall we say] all the more so do they override the restrictions of the Sabbath on their account? [Obviously not.]

[D]   What is the status of unleavened bread prepared for them?

[E]   He said to him, "It is an obligation."

[F]   R. Zeira said, "That is subject to dispute."

[G]   R. Hila said, "That is a matter of unanimous opinion."

[H]   There is a Tannaite teaching that supports the position of this party, and there is a Tannaite teaching that supports the position of that party.

[I]   There is a Tannaite teaching that supports the position of R. Zeira.

[J]   **Lettuce, unleavened bread, and the Passover lamb –**

[K]   **on the first night, [eating them] is an obligation.**

[L]   **And on the other days, it is optional matter.**

[M]   R. Simeon says, **"For men it is an obligation, and for women it is an optional matter"** [T. Pisha 2:22].

[N]   The following Tannaite teaching supports the position of R. Hila:

[O]   It is said, "You shall eat no leavened bread with it; seven days you shall eat it with unleavened bread, the bread of affliction – [for you came out of the land of Egypt in hurried flight – that all the days of your life you may remember the day when you came out of the land of Egypt]" (Deut. 16:3).

[P]   One who is subject to the requirement not to eat leaven, lo, he is subject to the positive requirement of eating unleavened bread.

[Q]   Now lo, since women are subject to the negative commandment of not eating leaven, lo, they are subject to the positive commandment of eating unleavened bread.

[R]   Now we have learned: **For every positive commandment dependent upon the time, men are liable, and women are exempt** [M. 1:7C]. [That would seem to contradict the conclusion just now reached, since the positive commandment of eating unleavened bread depends upon the time of year.]

[S]   Said R. Mana, "A more strict rule applies to a positive commandment that comes in the wake of a negative commandment."

[XII.A] [What follows relates to M. Hal. 4:11, which states, Joseph the Priest also brought his sons and household to keep the Lesser Passover (Num. 9:10ff.) in Jerusalem, and they turned him back, lest it should be established as an obligation.]

[B]   Now this accords with the view of him who says, "The Passover-offering of women ['his household'] is an optional matter." [Offering the Passover-offering on the first Passover is an optional matter. On the second Passover they turned him back. Why? For on the second Passover women do not make the offering at all (E). That is, to do it at its normal time is optional, and to do it at the later time is not permitted at all.]

[C]   It was taught: "[The woman's obligation on the first Passover is firm, and therefore] a woman prepares the Passover-offering on the first Passover for herself, and on the second, she is ancillary to others [but shares their Passover-offering]. [But it is optional for her to observe the second Passover, if she has missed the first one,]" the words of R. Meir.

[D] R. Yosé says, "A woman prepares the Passover-offering on the second Passover for herself [as a matter of obligation]. It is hardly necessary to specify that she does the same on the first."

[E] R. Eleazar b. Simeon says, "A woman prepares the Passover-offering on the first Passover as an ancillary matter [joining in the Passover-offering done for males], and she does not prepare a Passover-offering on the second Passover, [should she miss the first one,] at all."

[F] What is the scriptural basis for the position of R. Meir [C]?

[G] "Tell all the congregation of Israel that on the tenth day of this month they shall take every man a lamb according to their fathers' houses, [a lamb for a household]" (Ex. 12:2). [House is understood to mean wife.] Then, if they wished, [they do it] for the wife, [who has the right to do it for herself].

[H] What is the scriptural basis for the position of R. Yosé?

[I] "A lamb according to their fathers' houses"– all the more so for his house [his wife].

[J] What is the scriptural basis for the position of R. Eleazar b. R. Simeon?

[K] "Man" – not a woman.

[L] How do the other rabbis interpret the language "man"?

[M] "Man" – not a minor.

[N] Said R. Jonah, "Even in accord with the one who said that it is an obligation [for a woman to keep the Passover the first time around, B], the present case is different.

[O] "For the matter was based on a limited consideration: So that the matter [as done by Joseph the Priest] should not be established as an obligation. "

[XIII.A] **Except for not marring the corners of the beard. not rounding the corners of the head (Lev. 19:27), and not becoming unclean because of the dead (Lev. 21:1).**

[B] Issi says, "[Women are also not liable for transgressing the prohibition of] 'They shall not make bald spots upon their heads.'"

[C] What is the scriptural basis for this? 'They shall not make bald spots upon their heads nor shave off the edges of their beards" (Lev. 21:5).

[D] One who is subject to the negative commandment against marring the corners of the beard is subject to the prohibition of a bald spot.

[E] Women, who have no beards, are exempt from the negative commandment regarding a bald spot.

[F] And there is yet a further matter: "Sons," not daughters.

[G] Said R. Eleazar, "Women are liable not to make a bald spot."

[H] What is the scriptural basis for this position?

[I] "For you are a holy people to the Lord your God, [and the Lord has chosen you to be a people for his own possession, out of all the peoples that are on the face of the earth]" (Deut. 14:2).

[J] All the same are men and women.

[K] How does R. Eleazar interpret the reference to "sons"?

[L]   When Israel does the will of the Holy One, blessed be He, they are called his children, and when Israel does not do the will of the Holy One, blessed be He, they are not called his children.

[M]   Rab instructed the members of the household of R. Ahi, R. Hamnuna gave instructions to the associates: "Tell your wives that when they are standing before the deceased, they should not tear out their hair, so that they should not produce a bald spot, [which they are forbidden to do, just like men]."

[N]   How large is a bald spot?

[O]   There is a Tannaite authority who teaches, "Any size at all."

[P]   And there is a Tannaite authority who teaches, "The size of a bean."

[Q]   One who says it is of any size at all derives that from the language "bald spot," which indicates any size at all.

[R]   One who says it is the size of a bean proves it as follows: "Bald spot" is mentioned in two different contexts, both in regard to the present prohibition and in respect to the appearance of leprosy (Lev. 13:42).

[S]   Just as "bald spot" stated later is one the size of a bean, so the one here is the size of a bean.

[T]   R. Yosé bar Mamel: "A priest girl is permitted to go abroad."

[U]   What is the scriptural basis for that position?

[V]   [Lev. 21:1 says,] "Say to the priests," and not to the priest girls.

[W]   [That must be the case,] for if you do not say so, shall we conclude that, since she is subject to the general decree, she should not go abroad? If you say so, you turn out to set aside the entire chapter dealing with the matter of uncleanness. [Women in general are not subject to the prohibitions of uncleanness in the Temple cult, for they do not participate in the cult. So the proposed conclusion is the only possible one.]

[XIV.A]   [With reference to M. 1:7I: Except in the case of a meal-offering of an accused wife and of a Nazirite girl, which they wave:] The priest puts his hand under hers and she waves [the offering].

[B]   Is that not a disgrace [that the priest should touch the woman]?

[C]   He brings a cloth.

[D]   But it will not sufficiently interpose.

[E]   They bring an old priest.

[F]   And even if you say it is a young priest [that poses no problem], for concupiscence will not be troublesome for that brief moment.

[G]   R. Hiyya taught, "If the accused wife has no arms, two priests come and wave the offering in her behalf."

Once more the Talmud presents a protracted essay on the themes of the Mishnah, sometimes also touching on the specific allegations of the Mishnah as well. But what is before us has the character of a thematic anthology, not an exegetical essay. Unit I, for its part, introduces the Tosefta's elucidation of the Mishnah and then undertakes to clarify the Tosefta. Unit II turns to another passage of the Mishnah entirely, relevant to the present one in a general way. Why units III and IV are inserted I do not know. Unit V brings us back to the Mishnah, which is cited and then glossed, and, as usual, the Tosefta's amplification of the Mishnah is the focus of interest. Because the matter of honoring father and mother is introduced in clarifying the Mishnah, the Talmud at units VI-IX gives us an extensive repertoire of materials on that theme. Unit X returns to the Mishnah, once more citing the Tosefta for that purpose. Unit XI presents a secondary development of the Mishnah theme, the obligation of women. Unit XII is attached because it is part and parcel of unit XI. Units XIII and XIV, finally, conclude the elucidation of the Mishnah.

II. Mishnah Qiddushin 1:7 in the Talmud of Babylonia

1:7A-F [For Bavli M. 1:8A = Yerushalmi's M. 1:7G-H, covered below]

A. For every commandment concerning the son to which the father is subject – men are liable, and women are exempt.

B. And for every commandment concerning the father to which the son is subject, men and women are equally liable.

C. For every positive commandment dependent upon the time [of year], men are liable, and women are exempt.

D. And for every positive commandment not dependent upon the time, men and women are equally liable.

E. For every negative commandment, whether dependent upon the time or not dependent upon the time, men and women are equally liable,

F. except for not marring the corners of the beard, not rounding the corners of the head (Lev. 19:27), and not becoming unclean because of the dead (Lev. 21:1).

I.1 A. *What is the meaning of* For every commandment concerning the son to which the father is subject...? *Should we say, from every religious duty that the son is required to do for the father, women are exempt? But hasn't it been taught on Tannaite authority:* "Every man his mother and his father you shall fear" (Lev. 19:27) – I know only that that applies to the man. How do I know that it applies to the woman? When Scripture says, "His mother and his father you shall fear," lo, both of them are included?

B. *Said R. Judah, "This is the sense of the statement:* For every commandment concerning the son to which the father is subject to do for his son – men are liable, and women are exempt."

I.2 A. *Thus we learn as a Tannaite statement here that which our rabbis have taught on Tannaite authority:*

B. The father is responsible with respect to his son to circumcise him, to redeem him, to teach him Torah, to marry him off to a woman, and to teach him a trade.

C. And there are those who say, also to teach him to swim.

D. R. Judah says, "Anyone who does not teach his son a trade is as though he trains him to be a gangster" [T. Qid. 1:11F-H].

I.3 A. ...To circumcise him: *How on the basis of Scripture do we know that he must do so?*

B. *As it is written,* "And Abraham circumcised Isaac, his son" (Gen. 21:4).

C. *And how do we know that if his father did not circumcise him, the court is liable to circumcise him?*

D. *As it is written,* "Every male among you shall be circumcised" (Gen. 17:10).

E. *And how do we know that if the court did not circumcise him, he is liable to circumcise himself?*

F. *As it is written,* "And the uncircumcised male who will not circumcise the flesh of his foreskin, that soul shall be cut off" (Gen. 17:14).

G. *And how do we know that his mother is not liable to do so?*

H. *As it is written,* "And Abraham circumcised his son...as God had commanded him" (Gen. 21:4) – him, not her.

I. *So we have shown on the basis of Scripture that that was the rule governing that time, but how do we know that it is the rule for all time?*

J. *A Tannaite authority of the household of R. Ishmael:* "Wherever the language, 'command,' is used, the sole purpose is to encourage obedience both at that time and for all generations: As for encouragement, 'But charge Joshua and encourage him and strengthen him' (Deut. 3:28); both at that time and for all generations: 'From the day that the Lord gave commandment and onward throughout your generations' (Num. 15:23)."

I.4 A. **To redeem him:** *How on the basis of Scripture do we know that he must do so?*

B. *As it is written,* "And all the firstborn of man among your sons you shall redeem" (Ex. 13:13).

C. *And whence do we know that if the father did not redeem him, he is liable to redeem himself?*

D. *As it is written,* "Nevertheless the firstborn of man you shall surely redeem" (Num. 18:15).

E. *And how do we know that his mother is not liable to do so?*

F. *As it is written,* "you shall redeem" which through a shift in vowels may be read, "you shall redeem yourself," so, one who is charged with redeeming himself is liable to redeem others, while one who is not obligated to redeem herself is not obligated to redeem others.

G. *So how do we know that she is not required to redeem herself?*

H. *As it is written,* "you shall redeem" which through a shift in vowels may be read, "you shall redeem yourself," thus: One whom others are commanded to redeem is commanded to redeem himself, one whom others are not commanded to redeem is not commanded to redeem herself.

I. *So how do we know that others are not commanded to redeem her?*

J. *As it is written,* "And all the firstborn of man among your sons shall you redeem" (Ex. 13:13) – your sons, not your daughters.

I.5 A. *Our rabbis have taught on Tannaite authority:*

B. [M. Bekh. 8:6M-P: **If a man who was firstborn son had a firstborn son and was told that he had not been redeemed so that [he is] to redeem himself and [he is] to redeem his son, he comes before his son. R. Judah says, "His son comes before him. For the requirement of redeeming him [the father] falls upon *his* father, while the requirement of redeeming his son falls on him."**] If he was to be redeemed and his son was to be redeemed, he takes precedence over his son.

C. R. Judah says, "His son takes precedence over him, for the religious duty pertains to his father, and the religious duty involving the son pertains to the father."

D. *Said R. Jeremiah, "All parties concur* [29B] *that in a case in which there are only five selas in hand, he takes precedence over his son. What is the reason? The religious duty involving himself is of greater importance. Where there is a disagreement, it concerns a case in which there are five selas worth of encumbered property, and five selas worth of unencumbered property. R. Judah takes the view that* a debt that derives from what is written in the Torah is classified within the same category as one that is obligated in a note, and therefore the five selas due for himself does the priest go and seize from encumbered property, and with the five selas of unencumbered property he redeems his son. Rabbis take the position that a debt that derives from what is written in the Torah is not classified within the same category as one that is obligated in a note [but is treated only as a verbal loan], and therefore the religious duty of redemption pertaining to the father takes precedence."

I.6 A. *Our rabbis have taught on Tannaite authority:*

B. **If a man was obligated to redeem his son and to make a pilgrimage for the festival, he first redeems his son and then makes the pilgrimage for the festival.**

C. **R. Judah says, "He makes the pilgrimage for the festival and then he redeems his son, for the former is a religious duty that will pass with the passage of time, but the other is a religious duty that will not pass with the passage of time" [T. Bekh. 6:10A-C].**

D. *Now there is no problem understanding the position of R. Judah, for he has stated the operative consideration in so many words, but what is the source in Scripture for the view of rabbis?*

E. Scripture said, "All the firstborn of your sons shall you redeem" (Ex. 34:20), and only then it is stated, "And none shall appear before me empty handed" (Ex. 34:20).

I.7 A. *Our rabbis have taught on Tannaite authority:*

B. How do we know that of a man had five firstborn sons by five wives, he is required to redeem all of them?

C. Scripture states, "All the firstborn of your sons shall you redeem" (Ex. 34:20).

D. *Well, what else is knew? Obviously, Scripture has invoked as the criterion, the one that opens the womb first!*

E. *What might you otherwise have supposed? We should establish a verbal analogy between the meaning of firstborn here and that in the matter of inheritance, so that, just as in that case, the sense is, "the beginning of his strength" (Deut. 21:17), the same meaning applies here too. So we are informed that that is not the case.*

I.8 A. **To teach him Torah:** *How on the basis of Scripture do we know that fact?*

B. "And you shall teach them to your sons" (Deut. 11:19).

C. *And that in a case in which his father did not teach him, he is liable to teach himself?*

D.   "And you shall study" (Deut. 5:1).

E.   *And that she is not liable to do so?*

F.   "You shall teach" can be read "and you shall study," with the consequence: Whoever is commanded to study is commanded to teach, and whoever is not commanded to study is also not commanded to teach.

G.   *And how do we know that she herself is not obligated to teach herself?*

H.   "And you shall teach" can be read, "And you shall learn": One whom others are commanded to teach is commanded to teach himself, and one whom others are not commanded to teach is not commanded to teach herself.

I.   So how do we know that others are not commanded to teach her?

J.   Because it is written, "And you shall teach them to your sons" – not your daughters.

I.9   A.   *Our rabbis have taught on Tannaite authority:*

B.   If he had to study Torah and his son likewise, he takes precedence over his son.

C.   R. Judah says, "If his son was an eager student, gifted and retentive, his son takes precedence over him" [T. Bekh. 6:10F-H].

I.10 A.   *That is in line with the case of R. Jacob b. R. Aha bar Jacob, whose father sent him to Abbayye. When he came home, his father observed that his traditions were not very sharp. He said to him, "I'm better than you are. So you stay here, and I'll go."*

B.   *Abbayye heard that he was coming. Now there was a certain demon in the household of rabbis that Abbayye consulted, so when only two disciples came in to study, even in daylight, they were harmed. Abbayye ordered, "Nobody rent him a room [so he'll have to sleep in the schoolhouse], maybe there'll be a miracle."*

C.   *So he came and spent the night in the schoolhouse. The demon appeared to him like a seven-headed dragon. Every time he fell on his knees, one head fell off. But the next day he rebuked them: "So if there weren't a miracle, you would have endangered my life."*

I.11 A.   *Our rabbis have taught on Tannaite authority:*

B.   If someone had to study the Torah and get married, let him study the Torah and then get married. But if he can't live without a wife, let him get married and then study the Torah. [T. Bekh. 6:10D-E].

I.12 A.   Said R. Judah said Samuel, "The law is: One marries a wife and then studies Torah."

B.   R. Yohanan said, "With a millstone around his neck, is he going to study much Torah?"

C.   *But there is really no disagreement. The one refers to us, the other to them [in the Land of Israel].*

I.13 A.   *R. Hisda praised R. Hamnuna before R. Huna as a major authority. He said to him, "When he comes to hand, bring him to me."*

B.   *When he came, he saw that he wasn't wearing a head covering. "Why don't you have a head covering?" he asked.*

C.   *He said to him, "Because I'm not married."*

D.   *He turned his face away: "See that you don't come before me until you are married."*

E. *R. Huna was consistent with views expressed elsewhere, for he said,* "Someone twenty years old and not married spends his whole day in sin."

F. *Do you really think, in sin?! Rather:* Spends his whole day thinking about sin.

I.14 A. Said Raba, *and so did a Tannaite authority of the household of R. Ishmael:* "Until someone is twenty years old, the Holy One blessed be He sits and looks forward to when a man will marry a wife. But once he reaches the age of twenty and has not married, he says, 'Blast be his bones.'"

I.15 A. *Said R. Hisda, "The fact that I am better than my fellows is because I got married at sixteen, and if I'd married at fourteen, [30A] I'd be able to say to Satan, 'An arrow in your eye.'"*

I.16 A. *Said Raba to R. Nathan bar Ammi, "While your hand is still on your son's neck, marry him off, that is, between sixteen and twenty-two." Others say, "Eighteen and twenty-four."*

I.17 A. *There is a conflict of Tannaite statements on the same matter:*

B. "Raise up a youth in the way he should go" (Prov. 22:6):

C. *R. Judah and R. Nehemiah –*

D. *One said, "[Youth means] from sixteen to twenty-two."*

E. *The other: "From eighteen to twenty-four."*

I.18 A. To what extent is a man obligated to teach his son Torah?

B. Said R. Judah said Samuel, "The exemplary case is Zebulun b. Dan, whose grandfather taught him Scripture, Mishnah, talmud analysis, law and lore."

C. *An objection was raised:* If he taught him Scripture, he need not teach him Mishnah, and said Raba, "Scripture refers to Torah, as in the case of Zebulun b. Dan, but also not as in the case of Zebulun b. Dan: As in the case of Zebulun b. Dan, whose grandfather taught him, but not as in the case of Zebulun b. Dan, *for in that case involved were lessons in Scripture, Mishnah, talmud analysis, laws and lore, but here involved is only Scripture alone."*

D. *And is the grandfather so obligated? And hasn't it been taught on Tannaite authority:* "And you shall teach them to your sons" (Deut. 11:19) – and not to your grandsons. And how am I to interpret, "And you shall make them known to your sons and your sons' sons" (Deut. 4:9)? This lets you know that whoever teaches his son Torah is regarded by Scripture as though he had taught not only him but also his son and his son's son to the end of all generations.

E. *He made his statement in line with the position of the following Tannaite authority, as has been taught on Tannaite authority:* "And you shall teach them to your sons": I know only that this applies to your sons. How do I know that it applies to your sons' sons? It is said, "And you shall make them known to your sons and your sons' sons." Then why say, "And you shall teach them to your sons"? To teach: Your sons but not your daughters.

I.19 A. Said R. Joshua b. Levi, "He who teaches his grandson Torah is credited by Scripture as though he had received [Torah] from Mount Horeb. For it is said, 'And you shall make them known to your children and your children's children' (Deut. 4:9), and, juxtaposed next, it is written, 'The day that you stood before the Lord your God in Horeb' (Deut. 4:10)."

B.   *R. Hiyya bar Abba came across R. Joshua b. Levi, wearing a plain cloth on his head [not a kerchief indicative of his status as a major authority] and bringing a child to the house of assembly. He said to him, "So what's going on?"*

C.   *He said to him, "So is it such a small thing that is written in Scripture,* 'And you shall make them known to your children and your children's children' (Deut. 4:9), and, juxtaposed next, it is written, 'The day that you stood before the Lord your God in Horeb' (Deut. 4:10)?"

D.   *From that time onward R. Hiyya bar Abba didn't taste breakfast sausage before hearing a child review his lesson and adding a verse to it.*

E.   *Rabbah bar R. Huna didn't taste breakfast sausage before he brought a child to the schoolhouse.*

I.20   A.   *Said R. Safra said R. Joshua b. Hananiah, "What is the meaning of the verse,* 'and you shall teach them diligently to your children' (Deut. 6:7)? Read the letters to yield not 'repeat' but rather 'divide into three,' so that a person should always divide years into three parts: a third for Scripture, a third for Mishnah, a third for talmud."

B.   *So does someone know how many years he will live?*

C.   *The teaching is required for days [not years].*

I.21   A.   Therefore the early masters were called scribes [those who numbered], because they would count up all the letters in the Torah. For they would say, "The W in the word belly (gahon) [Lev. 11:42: 'Whatever goes on the belly'] is the midpoint among all of the letters of a scroll of the Torah. The words 'diligently enquire' [at Lev. 10:16] mark the midpoint among the words; the word 'he shall be shaven' (Lev. 13:33) marks half the verses; in the verse, 'the boar out of the wood does ravage it' (Ps. 80:14), the ayin of the word for forest marks the midpoint of the Psalms; 'but he, being full of compassion, forgives their iniquity' (Ps. 78:38) marks the midpoint of all of the verses [of Psalms]."

I.22   A.   *R. Joseph raised this question: "Is the W in the word belly assigned to the first half or the second half?"*

B.   *They said to him, "Let's get a scroll of the Torah and count them up. Didn't Rabbah bar R. Hannah state, 'They didn't move from the spot until they brought a scroll of the Torah and counted them up?'"*

C.   *He said to them, "Well, they were experts in the matter of the defective and full spellings of words, but we're not [so even if we counted, we wouldn't know]."*

I.23   A.   *R. Joseph raised this question: "Is the word 'he shall be shaven' (Lev. 13:33) assigned to the former half or the latter half?"*

B.   *Said to him Abbayye, "As to the count of the verses, in any event, we certainly can bring a scroll and count them up."*

C.   *As to counting up the verses, we're no experts, for when R. Aha bar Ada came, he said, "In the West the following verse is divided into three parts, each counted on its own:* 'And the Lord said to Moses, Lo, I come to you in a thick cloud' (Ex. 19:9)."

I.24　A.　*Our rabbis have taught on Tannaite authority:* There are 5,888 verses in the Torah; the Psalms are longer by eight, Chronicles are less by eight.

I.25　A.　*Our rabbis have taught on Tannaite authority:*

　　　B.　["And you shall teach them diligently to your children" (Deut. 6:7)]: "[That is to say, 'Impress them upon your children':]

　　　C.　[The meaning of "impressing," or "repeating," is that] the teachings of the Torah should be so sharp in your mouth that when someone asks you something, you should not stammer.

　　　D.　But you should give a reply forthwith.

　　　E.　So Scripture says, [30B] "Say to wisdom, 'You are my sister,' and call understanding your kinswoman" (Prov. 7:4).

　　　F.　"Bind them on your fingers, write them on the table of your heart" (Prov. 7:3).

　　　G.　"You arrows are sharp" (Ps. 45:6).

　　　H.　"The peoples fall under you, they sink into the heart of the king's enemies" (Ps. 45:6).

　　　I.　"As arrows in the hand of a mighty man, so are the children of one's youth" (Ps. 127:4).

　　　J.　And concerning these children: "Happy is the man who has his quiver full of them, they shall not be put to shame when they speak with their enemies in the gate" (Ps. 127:5) [Sifré Deut. XXXIV:I.1-2].

　　　K.　*What is the meaning of* their enemies in the gate?

　　　L.　Said R. Hiyya bar Abba, "Even father and his son, master and his disciple: When they are engaged in Torah study in the same topic, they turn into mutual enemies, but they don't leave the spot until they come to love one another, as it is said, 'Wherefore it is said in the book of the wars of the Lord, love is at the end' (Num. 21:14)."

I.26　A.　*Our rabbis have taught on Tannaite authority:*

　　　B.　"Therefore impress these my words upon your very heart; [bind them as a sign on your hand and let them serve as a symbol on your forehead; and teach them to your children, reciting them when you stay at home and when you are away, when you lie down and when you get up, and inscribe them on the doorposts of your house and on your gates, to the end that you and your children may endure in the land that the Lord swore to your fathers to assign to them, as long as there is a heaven over the earth]" (Deut. 11:18-21):

　　　C.　This use of the word [impress, which can be read to sound like "medicine, ointment"] indicates that words of Torah are compared to a life-giving medicine.

　　　D.　The matter may be compared to the case of a man [Sif. Deut.: king] who grew angry with his son and gave him a severe blow, but then put a salve on the wound and said to him, "My son, so long as this bandage is on the wound, eat whatever you like, drink whatever you like, and wash in either warm or old water, and nothing will do you injury. But if you remove the bandage, the sore will immediately begin to produce ulcers."

E. So the Holy One, blessed be He, said to Israel, "My children, I have created in you an impulse to do evil, than which nothing is more evil.

F. "'Sin crouches at the door and to you is its desire' (Gen. 4:7).

G. "Keep yourselves occupied with teachings of the Torah, and [sin] will not control you.

H. "But if you leave off studying words of the Torah, lo, it will control you, as it is said, 'And to you is its desire' (Gen. 4:7).

I. "And not only so, but all of its undertakings concern you. But if you want, you will control it, as it is said, 'But you may rule over it' (Gen. 4:7)."

J. And Scripture says, "And if your enemy is hungry, give him bread to eat, and if he is thirsty, give him water to drink, for you will heap coals of fire upon his head" (Prov. 25:21-22) [Sifré Deut. XLVI.I.2].

I.27   A.   *Our rabbis have taught on Tannaite authority:*

B. So formidable is the lust to do evil that even its creator has called it evil, as it is written, "For that the desire of man's heart is evil from his youth" (Gen. 8:21).

C. Said R. Isaac, "The desire to do evil renews itself daily against a person: 'Every imagination of the thoughts of his heart was only evil every day' (Gen. 6:5)."

D. And said R. Simeon b. Levi, "A man's inclination [to do evil] prevails over him every day and seeks to kill him. For it is said, 'The wicked watches the righteous and seeks to slay him' (Ps. 37:32). And if the Holy One, blessed be He, were not there to help him, he could not withstand it. For it is said, 'The Lord will not leave him in his hand nor suffer him to be condemned when he is judged' (Ps. 37:32)."

I.28   A.   *A Tannaite of the household of R. Ishmael:* "If that vile one meets you, drag it to the house of study. If it is a stone, it will dissolve. If it is iron, it will be pulverized. If it is a stone, it will dissolve," as it is written, "Ho, everyone who is thirsty, come to water" (Isa. 55:1). And it is written, "The water wears down stones" (Job 14:19). "If it is iron, it will be pulverized," as it is written, "Is not my word like fire, says the Lord, and like a hammer that breaks the rock into pieces" (Jer. 23:29).

I.29   A.   **To marry him off to a woman:**

B. *What is the source in Scripture?*

C. Because it is said in Scripture, "Take wives for yourselves and produce sons and daughters, and take wives for your sons and give your daughters to husbands" (Jer. 29:6).

D. *Well, there's no problem about marrying off a son, the decision is his. But as regards the daughter, does the matter depend on him? [You have to find the husband, too.]*

E. *This is the sense of Jeremiah's statement: "Give her a dowry, clothes, ornaments, so men will come looking for her."*

I.30   A.   **And to teach him a trade:**

B. *What is the source in Scripture?*

C. Said Hezekiah, "Said Scripture, 'See to a livelihood with the wife whom you love' (Qoh. 9:9)."

| | D. | If this refers literally to a wife, then, just as the father is obligated to find a wife for him, so he is obligated to teach him a trade. If the meaning of "wife" is as a metaphor for Torah, then just as he is obligated to teach him Torah, so he is obligated to teach him a trade. |

I.31 A. And there are those who say, also to teach him to swim:
      B. *How come?*
      C. *Because it can save his life.*

I.32 A. R. Judah says, "Anyone who does not teach his son a trade trains him to be a gangster":
      B. *Can you imagine, to be a gangster?! Rather, is as though he trains him to be a gangster.*
      C. And what's at issue here?
      D. *At issue here is training him in commerce [Judah rejecting commerce].*

II.1 A. And for every commandment concerning the father to which the son is subject, men and women are equally liable:
      B. *What is the definition of for every commandment concerning the father to which the son is subject? Should we say, for all of the religious duties that a father is obligated to do for his son, women are obligated as well? But hasn't it been taught on Tannaite authority:* The father is responsible with respect to his son to circumcise him, to redeem him – the father, not the mother.
      C. *Said R. Judah, "This is the sense of the statement:* For every commandment concerning the father to which the son is subject, men and women are equally liable. *Thus we learn the Tannaite statement in line with that which our rabbis have taught on Tannaite authority:* '"You shall fear every man his father and his mother" (Lev. 19:3) – I know that that is so only for a man. How do I know it applies to a woman? Scripture states, 'you shall fear,' covering both. Then why state 'man'? A man has the possibility of carrying this out, but a woman doesn't, since she is subject to the authority of a third party."
      D. Said R. Idi bar Abin said Rab, "If she was divorced, however, both of them are equally obligated."

II.2 A. *Our rabbis have taught on Tannaite authority:*
      B. It is said, "Honor your father and your mother" (Ex. 20:12), and it is further said, "Honor the Lord with your wealth" (Prov. 3:9).
      C. Scripture thereby establishes an analogy between the honor of father and mother and the honor of the Omnipresent.
      D. It is said, "He who curses his father or his mother will certainly die" (Prov. 20:20), and it is said, "Any person who curses his God will bear his sin" (Lev. 24:15).
      E. Scripture thereby establishes an analogy between cursing father and mother and cursing the Omnipresent.
      F. But it is not possible to refer to smiting Heaven [in the way in which one is warned not to hit one's parents].
      G. And that is entirely reasonable, for all three of them are partners [in a human being] [Sifra Qedoshim CXCV:II.3].

II.3 A. *Our rabbis have taught on Tannaite authority:*
      B. Three form a partnership in the creation of a human being, the Holy One, blessed be He, one's father and one's mother. When someone honors father and mother, said the Holy One, blessed be He, "I

credit it to them as though I had lived among them and they honored me."

II.4   A.   *It has been taught on Tannaite authority:*

    B.   Rabbi says, "It is perfectly self-evident to the One who spoke and brought the world into being that the son honors his mother more than his father, because [31A] she influences him with kind words. Therefore the Holy One blessed be He gave precedence to honoring the father over honoring the mother. But it also is perfectly self-evident before the One who spoke and brought the world into being that the son fears the father more than the mother, because he teaches him Torah. Therefore the Holy One, blessed be He, gave priority to fear of the mother over fear of the father."

II.5   A.   *A Tannaite authority repeated before R. Nahman:* "When someone gives anguish to his father or his mother, said the Holy One, blessed be He, 'I did well in not living among them, for if I lived among them, they would have given me anguish too.'"

II.6   A.   Said R. Isaac, "Whoever secretly carries out a transgression is as though he stepped on the feet of the Presence of God: 'Thus said the Lord, the Heaven is my throne, and the earth is my footstool' (Isa. 66:1)."

II.7   A.   Said R. Joshua b. Levi, "It is forbidden to walk about stiffly erect, even for four cubits, for it is written, 'The whole earth is full of his glory' (Isa. 6:3)."

    B.   R. Huna b. R. Joshua wouldn't walk four cubits bareheaded. He said, "The Presence of God is above my head."

II.8   A.   A widow's son asked R. Eliezer, "If father says, 'Give me a glass of water,' and mother says, 'Give me a glass of water,' to which of them do I give precedence?"

    B.   He said to him, "Ignore the honor owing to your mother and carry out the act of respect owing to your father, for you and your mother are equally obligated to pay respect to your father."

    C.   He came before R. Joshua, who said the same to him.

    D.   "My lord, if she is divorced, what is the law?"

    E.   He said to him, "From the character of your eyelids, it's obvious that you're a widow's son. Pour out some water for them in a basin and cackle for them like chickens."

II.9   A.   *Ulla the elder gave this exposition at the gate of the patriarch:* "What is the meaning of Scripture, 'All the kings of the earth shall praise you, Lord, for they have heard the words of your mouth' (Ps. 138:4)? What is stated is not, 'the word of your mouth,' but 'the words of your mouth.' So when the Holy One, blessed be He, said, 'I am the Lord your God' 'you shall have no other Gods before me,' (Ex. 20:2-3), said the nations of the world, 'All he wants is his own self-aggrandizement.' When he said,' Honor your father and your mother' (Ex. 20:12), they retracted and confessed to the validity of the first statements as well."

    B.   *Raba said, "From the following verse [the same point can be drawn, namely:]* 'The beginning of your word is true' (Ps. 119:160) – the beginning but not the end? But what comes at the end of your word – the truth of the beginning of your word is understood."

II.10   A.   *They asked R. Ulla, "To what extent is one obligated to honor father and mother?"*

          B.   He said to them, "Go and observe how a certain gentile has treated his father in Ashkelon, and Dama b. Netinah is his name. On one occasion sages wanted to do business with him in the amount of six hundred thousand but the keys were lying under his father's pillow, and he would not disturb him."

          C.   Said R. Judah said Samuel, "They asked R. Eliezer, to what extent is one obligated to honor one's father and one's mother? He said to them, 'Go and observe how a certain gentile has treated his father in Ashkelon, and Dama b. Netinah is his name. On one occasion they wanted to buy from him precious stones for the ephod, in the amount of six hundred thousand (R. *Kahana repeated as the Tannaite version,* eight hundred thousand) but the keys were lying under his father's pillow, and he would not disturb him. Another year the Holy One, blessed be He, gave him his reward, for a red cow was born to him in his corral, and sages of Israel came to him. He said to them, "I know full well of you that if I should demand of you all the money in the world, you will give it to me. But now I ask of you only that sum of money that I lost in honor of my father."'"

          D.   And said R. Hanina, "Now if someone who is not subject to commandments acts in such a way, then if someone who is subject to the commandment acts in such a way, all the more so! For said R. Hanina, 'Greater is he who is commanded and acts on that account than he who is not commanded and acts on that account.'"

II.11   A.   *Said R. Joseph, "To begin with, I thought that if someone said to me, the decided law accords with R. Judah, that a blind person is exempt from the obligation of the commandments, I should have made a big party for all the rabbis, since I'm not obligated to do them but I do them anyhow. But now that I've heard the statement of R. Hanina, 'Greater is he who is commanded and acts on that account than he who is not commanded and acts on that account,' to the contrary, if someone will tell me that the decided law is not in accord with R. Judah, I'll make a big party for all the rabbis."*

II.12   A.   *When R. Dimi came,* he said, "Once [Dama] was dressed in a gold embroidered silk coat, sitting among the Roman nobles, and his mother came along and tore it from him and hit him on the head and spat in his face, but he did not in any way answer back to her."

II.13   A.   *A Tannaite statement of Abimi b. R. Abbahu:* There is he who feeds his father pheasant to eat but this drives the son from the world, and there is he who binds his father up to the grinding wheel, [31B] and this brings the son into the world to come. [Someone fed the father pheasants but when the father asked how he could afford them, said, "It's none of your business, chew and eat." By contrast, someone was grinding on a mill and the father was summoned for the corvée, so the son said to the father, "You grind for me and I'll go in your place."]

II.14   A.   Said R. Abbahu, "For instance, my son Abimi carried out in an exemplary manner the religious duty of honor of parents."

B. *Abimi had five ordained sons when his father was yet alive, but when R. Abbahu came and called at the gate, he ran and opened for him, saying, "Coming, coming," until he got there.*

C. *Once he said to him, "Bring me a glass of water." Before he got there, the father dozed off. So he bent over him until he woke up. This brought it about that Abimi succeeded in explaining* "a song of Asaph" (Ps. 79:1).

II.15 A. *Said R. Jacob bar Abbuha to Abbayye, "How about someone like me? For when I come home from the household of the master, father pours a cup for me, and mother mixes – what am I supposed to do?"*

B. He said to him, "Well, take it from your mother but not from your father, *since he, too, is obligated to study the Torah, it may be an insult to him.*"

II.16 A. *R. Tarfon's mother – whenever she wanted to get into bed, he would bend down and let her climb up on his back, and when she wanted to get out, she would step down on him. He went and praised himself in the schoolhouse.* They said to him, "So you still haven't got to half the honor that is owing: Has she thrown down a money bag in your presence into the sea, without your answering back to her?"

II.17 A. *R. Joseph – when he heard the sound of his mother's steps, he said, "Let me arise before the Presence of God, who approaches."*

II.18 A. Said R. Yohanan, "Happy is he who never knew his parents [since it is so hard properly to honor them]."

II.19 A. R. Yohanan – when his mother was carrying him, his father died, and she his mother bore him, she died.

B. The same is so of Abbayye.

C. *But how can that be so,* when he was always saying, "Mother told me"?

D. *That was his stepmother.*

II.20 A. *R. Assi had an aged mother. She said to him, "I want some jewelry."* So he made it for her.

B. *"I want a man."*

C. *"I'll go looking for someone for you."*

D. *"I want a man as handsome as you."*

E. *At that he left her and went to the Land of Israel. He heard that she was coming after him. He came to R. Yohanan and asked him,* "What is the law on my leaving the Land and going abroad?"

F. He said to him, "It is forbidden."

G. "What is the law as to going to greet my mother?"

H. He said to him, "I don't know."

I. *He waited a bit and then went and came back.* He said to him, "Assi, you obviously want to go. May the Omnipresent bring you back here in peace."

J. *Assi came before R. Eleazar. He said to him,* "God forbid! Maybe he was mad?"

K. "What did he say to you?"

L. "May the Omnipresent bring you back here in peace."

M. He said to him, "Well, if he had been angry, he wouldn't have given you a blessing."

N. *In the meanwhile he heard that it was her coffin that was coming. He said,* "If I had known that, I wouldn't have gone out."

II.21 A. *Our rabbis have taught on Tannaite authority:*

B.   The child must honor the parent in life and after death.

C.   In life: How so? If one is obeyed somewhere because of his father, he shouldn't say, "Let me go for my own sake," "Wish me Godspeed for my own sake," "Free me for my own sake," but only, "For my father's sake."

D.   And after death: How so? If one was saying something he had heard from his father's own mouth, he should not say, "This is what my father said," but rather, "This is what my father, my teacher, for whose resting place may I be an atonement, said."

E.   *But that is the rule* only during the first twelve months after his death. From that point onward, he says only, "Of blessed memory, for the life of the world to come."

II.22 A.   *Our rabbis have taught on Tannaite authority:*

B.   A sage changes the name of his father and the name of his teacher, but the interpreter doesn't change the name of his father or the name of his teacher. [The sage when using an interpreter to give a teaching he heard from his father does not refer to his father by name but by the formula, "my father and my teacher," but the interpreter doesn't do that (Freedman).]

C.   *Whose father? Should I say, the father of the interpreter? Isn't the interpreter obligated to honor his parents?*

D.   Rather, said Raba, "The name of the sage's father or the name of the sage's teacher."

E.   *That would be like the case of Mar b. R. Ashi, when he would gave an exposition in the assembly, he would say to the interpreter, "This is what my father, my teacher said," and the interpreter would say, "This is what R. Ashi said."*

II.23 A.   *Our rabbis have taught on Tannaite authority:*

B.   What is the form of reverence that is owing?

C.   The son should not sit in his place, speak in his place, contradict him.

D.   What is the form of honor that is owing?

E.   The son should feed him, give him drink, dress him, cover him, bring him in and take him out [Sifra CXCIX.I.5].

II.24 A.   *The question was raised:* [32A] "At whose expense [must he feed him and so on]?"

B.   R. Judah said Samuel said, "The son's."

C.   R. Nathan bar Oshayya said, "The father's."

D.   *Rabbis gave a ruling to R. Jeremiah, some say, to the son of R. Jeremiah, in accord with him who said, "The father's."*

E.   *An objection was raised:* "Honor your father and your mother" (Ex. 20:12), and further, "Honor the Lord with your property" (Prov. 3:9) – just as the latter means, at one's own expense, so the former has the same meaning. But if you say that it is at the father's expense, *then what does it cost the son?*

F.   It costs him time off from his own work.

G.   *Come and take note:* Two brothers, two partners, a father and a son, a master and his disciple redeem one another's second tithe; and feed one another with the tithe set aside for the poor [T. M.S. 4:7A]. But if you say that it is at the son's expense, then it will turn out that this fellow is paying off his debt out of what belongs to the poor.

H. *This speaks only of what is excess [over and above the father's needs, over and above what is ordinarily expected].*

I. *If so, then what's the point of the continuation of the Tannaite formulation:* Said R. Judah, "May a curse come upon someone who feeds his father tithe set aside for the poor?" *Now if it speaks only of what is excess [over and above the father's needs, over and above what is ordinarily expected], then what difference does it make?*

J. *It's a disgrace for the father.*

K. *Come and take note:* They asked R. Eliezer, "To what extent does the obligation of honoring father and mother extend?" He said to them, "To the extent that he might take a money bag and toss it into the sea in his presence, and the child will not yell at him." *Now if you maintain that the money belongs to the father, what difference does it make to the son?*

L. It is a case in which the son is supposed to inherit the father's estate.

M. *That would be like the case of Rabbah b. R. Huna. For R. Huna tore up silk in the presence of Rabbah his son. He said, "I will go and see whether he gets mad or not."*

N. *But if he got mad, then wouldn't he violate the commandment, "You shall not put a stumbling block before the blind" (Lev. 19:14) [by baiting the son to treat him disrespectfully]?*

O. *He renounced the honor owing to him.*

P. *But didn't [Huna] violate the commandment, "You shall not destroy the trees thereof" (Deut. 20:19) [wasting property]?*

Q. *He did it in the seam.*

R. *So maybe that's why he didn't lose his temper.*

S. *He did it when he was already upset about something [and yet he didn't insult the father].*

II.25 A. **If those to be stoned were confused with those to be burned [M. San. 9:3D]:** *R. Ezekiel repeated the passage at hand for Rami, his son, as follows:* "'If those to be burned were confused with those to be stoned, **R. Simeon says, "They are judged to be executed by stoning, for burning is the more severe of the two modes of execution" [M. 9:3E].'"**

B. *Said R. Judah to him, "Father, do not repeat it in this way. Why give as the reason, 'Because burning is more stringent'? Rather, derive the fact that the larger number of those who are put to death are put to death through stoning.* [Freedman, p. 536, n. 3: For 'if criminals condemned to burning became mixed up with others condemned to stoning' implies that the latter were in the majority, as the smaller number is lost in the larger.] *Instead, this is how it should be repeated:* **If those to be stoned were confused with those to be burned, R. Simeon says, 'They are judged to be executed by stoning, for burning is the more severe of the two modes of execution' [M. 9:3D-E]."**

C. *He said to him, "Then take up the concluding clause:* **But sages say, 'They are adjudged to be executed by burning, for stoning is the more severe mode of execution of the two' [M. 9:3F].** *Why invoke the criterion that stoning is the more severe penalty? But derive that point*

from the simple fact that the greater number of those who are put to death
are put to death through burning?"

D. He said to him, "In that case, it is rabbis who frame matters so as to state
to R. Simeon, "In accord with your view, for you maintain that burning is
more severe, but to the contrary, **stoning is the more severe**
[Freedman, p. 536, n. 4: But their ruling could be deduced from the
fact that the majority are to be executed through burning]."

E. *Said Samuel to R. Judah, "Sharp one! Do not say things in this way to
your father! This is what has been taught on Tannaite authority:* Lo, if
one's father was violating the teachings of the Torah, he should not
say to him, 'Father, you have violated the teachings of the Torah.'
Rather, one should say to him, 'Father, this is what is written in the
Torah.'"

F. *Still, he's giving him grief!*

G. Rather, he says to him, "Father, there is a verse of Scripture that is
written in the Torah, and this is what it says. [He does not state the
law directly but lets the father draw his own inference (Freedman,
p. 536, n. 8)]."

II.26 A. Eleazar b. Matthias says, "If father says, 'Give me a drink of water,'
and I have a religious duty to carry out, I ignore the honor owing to
father and I carry out the religious duty, for both father and I are
obligated to carry out religious duties."

B. Issi b. Judah says, "If it is possible for the religious duty to be done
by someone else, then let it be done by someone else, and he should
go and carry out the honor owing to his father."

C. Said R. Mattenah, "The decided law is in accord with Issi b. Judah."

II.27 A. Said R. Isaac b. Shila said R. Mattenah said R. Hisda, "If a father
renounced the honor that is coming to him, the honor that is coming
to him is validly renounced. If the master renounced the honor that
is coming to him, the honor that is coming to him is not
renounced."

B. And R. Joseph said, "Even if a master renounced the honor that is
owing to him, the honor that is owing to him is renounced: 'And
the Lord went before them by day' (Ex. 13:21)."

C. *Said Raba, "But how are the cases comparable? In that case, the Holy
One, blessed be He – the world is his, and the Torah is his, so he can well
renounced the honor that is owing to him. [32B] But in this case, does the
Torah belong to the master [that he can renounce the honor owing to it]?"*

D. *Said Raba, "Yessiree, the Torah belongs to him, for it is written, 'And in
his Torah he meditates day and night' (Ps. 1:2)."*

E. *Well, is that so! For Raba was serving drinks at the celebration of his son's
wedding, and when he offered a cup to R. Pappa and R. Huna b. R. Joshua,
they arose in his honor; when he offered it to R. Mari and R. Phineas b. R.
Hisda, they didn't get up in his honor, so he got mad and said, "Are these
rabbis rabbis, but those rabbis not rabbis?"*

F. *Furthermore, R. Pappa was serving drinks at the wedding celebration of
Abba Mar his son, and he offered a cup to R. Isaac b. R. Judah and he
didn't arise in his honor, and he got mad.*

G. *Nonetheless, they ought to have paid him respect.*

II.28 A. *Said R. Ashi, "Even from the perspective of him who has said, 'The
master who has renounced the honor coming to him – the honor*

coming to him is renounced,' nonetheless, the patriarch who has renounced the honor coming to him – the honor coming to him is not renounced."

B.   *An objection was raised:* There was the case concerning R. Eliezer, R. Joshua, and R. Sadoq, who were reclining at the banquet of the son of Rabban Gamaliel, and Rabban Gamaliel was standing and pouring drinks for them. He gave the cup to R. Eliezer, and he did not take it. He gave it to R. Joshua and he accepted it. Said to him R. Eliezer, "What's going on, Joshua! Should we recline while Rabban Gamaliel is standing and serving drinks to us?"

C.   He said to him, "We find that a greater one than he served as a waiter, namely, Abraham, the greatest one of his generation, did so, and concerning him it is written, 'And he stood over them' (Gen. 18:8). And should you say, they appeared to him as ministering angels [on which account he acted as he did], they appeared to him only in the guise of Arabs. So in our case, shouldn't the majestic Rabban Gamaliel stand and pour drinks for us?"

D.   Said to them R. Sadoq, "How long are you going to ignore the honor owing to the Omnipresent and concentrated only on the honor owing to mortals? The Holy One, blessed be He, brings back the winds and causes the mists to ascend, rain to fall, earth to yield, so setting a table before every single person, and, as to us, shouldn't the majestic Rabban Gamaliel stand over us and pour?"

E.   *Rather, if there was such a statement, this is what the statement actually said:*

F.   *Said R. Ashi, "Even from the perspective of him who has said, 'The patriarch who has renounced the honor coming to him – the honor coming to him is renounced,' the king who has renounced the honor coming to him – the honor coming to him is not renounced, for it is said, 'You shall surely set a king over you' – his authority shall be over you."*

II.29 A.   *Our rabbis have taught on Tannaite authority:*

B.   **"You shall rise up before the hoary head" (Lev. 19:32):**

C.   **Might one suppose that one is obligated to rise up even before a malefactor?**

D.   **Scripture says, "elder."**

E.   **An "elder" is only a sage,**

F.   **as it is said, "Collect for me seventy men of the elders of Israel" (Num. 11:16).**

G.   **R. Yosé the Galilean says, "An 'elder' is only one who has acquired wisdom, as it is said, 'The Lord created me at the beginning of his way' (Prov. 8:22)."**

H.   **Might one suppose that one should rise up before him only from a distance?**

I.   **Scripture says, "And honor the face of an elder."**

J.   **If then it is to "Honor the face of an elder," might one suppose that one should honor him with money?**

K.   **Scripture says, "Rise up... and honor...."**

L.   **Just as "rising up" does not involve an expenditure of money, so "honoring" does not involve an expenditure of money.**

M. Might one suppose that he has to rise up before him in the toilet or bathhouse?

N. Scripture says, "You shall rise up and you shall honor": I have commanded you to rise up only in a place in which that confers honor.

O. Might one suppose that if one saw him, one may close his eyes as though he had not seen him?

P. Lo, the matter is handed over to the heart, for it is said, "You shall fear your God, I am the Lord" –

Q. in connection with anything that is handed over to the heart, the fear of God is invoked.

R. R. Simeon b. Eleazar says, "How do we know that an elder should not make trouble for others?

S. "Scripture says, 'An elder and you shall fear your God'" [Sifra CCIV:III.1].

T. Issi b. Judah said, "You shall rise up before the hoary heard' means, any hoary head [not only a master]."

II.30 A. *What R. Yosé the Galilean says is the same as what the first Tannaite authority says!*

B. *At issue between them is a youngster who is a sage. The first Tannaite authority maintains that a youngster who is a sage is not included, while R. Yosé the Galilean maintains that he is.*

C. *What's the operative reading of Scripture behind the position of R. Yosé the Galilean?*

D. *If matters were otherwise, Scripture should have written, "Before the hoary head of an old man you should rise up and pay respect." How come the All-Merciful treated these categories separately? To teach that one hoary head is not the same as the other, and vice versa. This proves that even a sage who is a younger is included.*

E. *And the first Tannaite authority?*

F. *The reason that matters are formulated as they are is that Scripture wanted to keep "old man" together with "and you shall fear."*

G. *And the first Tannaite authority – what is the scriptural basis for his position?*

H. *If it should enter your mind that matters are as R. Yosé the Galilean claims, then the All-Merciful should have written,* [33A] *"You shall rise up before and honor the hoary head, you shall rise up before and honor the old man." But since that is not how matters are written out, it proves that the two categories are one and the same.*

II.31 A. The master has said: "Might one suppose that one should honor him with money? Scripture says, "Rise up... and honor...." Just as "rising up" does not involve an expenditure of money, so "honoring" does not involve an expenditure of money":

B. *But as to rising, is there never monetary consideration? Wouldn't it even speak of one who is involved in piercing pearls, and, if he rises up before him, he will be disturbed in his work?*

C. Rather, Scripture compares rising to honoring: Just as honoring involves an interruption in one's work, so rising, too, would involve no interruption in one's work.

D. Why not compare honoring to rising in this way: Just as rising involves no monetary costs, so honoring should involve no monetary cost? So on that basis sages have said, Craftsman are not permitted to rise before disciples of sages when the craftsman are engaged in doing their work.

E. *Well aren't they now? And haven't we learned in the Mishnah:* **And all the craftsmen of Jerusalem stand before them and greet them, [saying], "Brothers, men of such and such a place, you have come in peace" [M. Bik. 3:3]]?**

F. Said R. Yohanan, "Before such as those mentioned here they arise, but before disciples of sages they don't arise."

G. Said R. Yosé bar Abin, "Come and see how valued is a religious duty done at the proper time. For lo, 'Before such as those mentioned here they arise, but before disciples of sages they don't arise.'"

H. *But maybe the case there is exceptional, since you may otherwise make them stumble in the future [deciding not to come to Jerusalem with the first fruits].*

II.32   A. Said the master, "Might one suppose that he has to rise up before him in the toilet or bathhouse? Scripture says, 'You shall rise up and you shall honor': I have commanded you to rise up only in a place in which that confers honor":

B. *But don't we rise up under those circumstances? And lo, R. Hiyya was seated in a bathhouse, when R. Simeon b. Rabbi went by and he did not rise before him. The other was angered and came and told his father, "I taught him two of the Five Parts of the Book of Psalms, and he doesn't stand before me!"*

C. *And furthermore, Bar Qappara, and some say, R. Samuel bar R. Yosé, was sitting in a bathhouse. R. Simeon b. Rabbi came in and went by, and the other did not rise before him. The other was angered and came and told his father, "Two-thirds of a third of the Torah of the Priests [Leviticus] I taught him, and he didn't rise before me!"*

D. He said to him, "But maybe he was sitting and reflecting on them."

E. *So the operative consideration is that he was sitting and reflecting on them, lo, otherwise, it would not be proper?*

F. *No problem, the one speaks of inner rooms, the other, outer rooms [in the inner rooms people have no clothes on so they don't rise, in the outer rooms they are clothed and show respect].*

G. *That moreover stands to reason, for* said Rabbah bar bar Hannah said R. Yohanan, "In every place it is permitted to reflect on Torah teachings except for the bathhouse and the toilet."

H. *But it may be exceptional if [reflecting on one's Torah study under such circumstances] is involuntary.*

II.33   A. Might one suppose that if one saw him, one may close his eyes as though he had not seen him? Lo, the matter is handed over to the heart, for it is said, "you shall fear your God, I am the Lord" – in connection with anything that is handed over to the heart, the fear of God is invoked:

B. *So are we dealing with genuinely wicked people?*

C. Rather: Might one suppose that he may shut his eyes *before the time at which the obligatory greeting comes about, so that, when the obligation takes effect, he will not see him to stand up before him?*

D. Scripture said, "You shall rise up and you shall fear."

II.34 A. *A Tannaite statement:* What is the rising up that expresses honor? One must say, it is in the space of four cubits [when the sage comes that close, in which case it is only in the sage's honor that one has arisen].

B. Said Abbayye, "We have made that rule only in the case of his master who was not his principal teacher, but in the case of his master who was his principal teacher, it should be from as far a distance as he can see."

C. *As to Abbayye, when he saw the ear of the ass of R. Joseph, he would get up.*

D. *Abbayye was riding on an ass and going along the bank at the Sagya Canal. R. Mesharshayya and other sitting on the other side and didn't arise in his presence. He said to them, "Am I not your principal master?"*

E. *They said to him, "We weren't thinking about it."*

II.35 A. R. Simeon b. Eleazar says, "How do we know that an elder should not make trouble for others? Scripture says, 'An elder and you shall fear your God'":

B. *Said Abbayye, "We hold in hand the tradition that if the sage took a circuitous route, he will have a long life."*

C. *Abbayye took a circuitous route. R. Zira took a circuitous route. Rabina took a circuitous route. Rabina was sitting before R. Jeremiah of Difti; a certain man went by and didn't cover his head. He said, "What gall that man has!"*

D. *He said to him, "Well, maybe he's from Mata Mehassaya, where people treat rabbis arrogantly."*

II.36 A. Issi b. Judah said, "'You shall rise up before the hoary heard' means, any hoary head [not only a master]":

B. Said R. Yohanan, "The decided law accords with Issi b. Judah."

C. *R. Yohanan would rise before gentile sages, saying, "How many troubles have washed over these."*

D. *Raba, while he would not get up, he did pay them respect.*

E. *Abbayye would give his hand to the aged.*

F. *Raba would send his messengers.*

G. *R. Nahman would send his bodyguards, saying, "But for the Torah that I know, how many Nahman bar Abbas are there in the market."*

II.37 A. Said R. Aibu said R. Yannai, [33B] "A disciple of a sage is allowed to stand up before his master only morning and night, so that the honor accruing to the master is no more than the honor owing to heaven."

B. *An objection was raised:* R. Simeon b. Eleazar says, "How do we know that an elder should not make trouble for others? Scripture says, 'An elder and you shall fear your God'"! *Now if you say that it is only morning and night, why should he not trouble people? It would be an obligation. So it would follow that one would have to rise any time during the day.*

C. *No, it is morning and evening only, yet even so, so far as people, one should not impose on people.*

II.38 A. Said R. Eleazar, "Any disciple who does not arise before his master is called wicked and will not live a long time, and his learning will be forbidden: 'But it shall not be well with the wicked, neither shall he prolong his days which are as a shadow, because he doesn't fear

God' (Qoh. 8:13). Now I don't know the meaning of this 'fear,' but when Scripture says, 'You shall rise up before the hoary head... and fear your God' (Lev. 19:32), then 'fear' means 'rising.'"

B. *But why not say:* Fear of usury or dishonest weights?

C. *R. Eleazar forms a verbal analogy between the two matters since the word "before" occurs in both instances.*

II.39 A. *The question was raised:* If his son was also his master, what is the law about his standing before his father?

B. *Come and take note of what Samuel said to R. Judah,* "Smartass, get up before your father."

C. *R. Ezekiel was exceptional, since he also had good deeds to his credit, for even Mar Samuel would arise before him.*

D. *Then what is the sense of the statement that he made to him?*

E. *This is the sense of the statement that he made to him:* Sometimes he may come up behind me. Then you rise before him, and don't worry about the honor owing to me.

II.40 A. *The question was raised:* What if his son was his master, should his father stand before him?

B. *Come and take note that* said R. Joshua b. Levi, "As for me, it is not appropriate for me to stand up before my son, but it is because of the honor that is owing to the household of the patriarch." *So the operative consideration is that I am his teacher, but if he were my teacher, I would rise before him.*

C. *This is the sense of his statement:* "As for me, it is not appropriate for me to stand up before my son, *even if he were my master, since I am his father,* but it is because of the honor that is owing to the household of the patriarch."

II.41 A. *The question was raised:* Is riding equivalent to walking [so the disciples stand when the master rides by], or is that not the case?

B. *Said Abbayye,* "Come and take note: **The unclean [person] stands under the tree, and the clean person passes – he is unclean. The clean person stands under the tree, and the unclean passes – he is clean. And if the unclean person sat down, the clean person is unclean. And so with the stone which is afflicted with plague – he is clean. And if he put it down, lo, this one is unclean [M. Neg. 13:7]. And said R. Nahman bar Kohen, "That is to say, 'Riding equivalent to walking.'"**

C. *That settles the question.*

II.42 A. *The question was raised:* What is the law about rising before a scroll of the Torah?

B. R. Hilqiah, R. Simon, and R. Eleazar say, "It is an argument a fortiori: If people stand up before those who study the Torah, shouldn't they stand up before the Torah itself?!"

C. *R. Ilai and R. Jacob bar Zabedi were sitting when R. Simeon b. Abba passed by. He said to them,* "First of all, you are sages and I am merely an associate; second, should the Torah rise before its students? [So you shouldn't have paid me that respect.]"

D. *He concurs with R. Eleazar, who said,* "A disciple of a sage is not permitted to rise before his master when he is engaged in study of the Torah."

E. *Abbayye cursed that teaching.*

II.43 A. "And when Moses went into the tent, all the people rose up and stood and looked after Moses until he was gone into the tent" (Ex. 33:8):

B. R. Ammi and R. Isaac Nappaha –

C. One said, "It was derogatory."

D. The other said, "It was a compliment."

E. *As to the one who said it was derogatory, that is as is [Moses was disparaged, but we're not going to say so].*

F. *As to the view of the one who said it was to pay a compliment,* said Hezekiah, "Said to me R. Hanina b. R. Abbahu said R. Abbahu said R. Abdimi of Haifa, 'When a sage passes, one has to rise before him at a distance of four cubits, and when he has passed by for a distance of four cubits, he sits down; when a principal of a court passes, one stands up before him when he comes in sight and as soon as he has gone on four cubits, he may sit down; when the patriarch passes, one rises when he comes into sight and sits down only after he has taken his seat: "And when Moses went into the tent, all the people rose up and stood and looked after Moses until he was gone into the tent."'"

III.1 A. **For every positive commandment dependent upon the time [of year], men are liable, and women are exempt:**

B. *Our rabbis have taught on Tannaite authority:*

C. **What is the definition of a positive commandment dependent upon the time [of day or year]? Building a tabernacle at the festival of Tabernacles, carrying the palm branch on that festival, sounding the ram's horn, wearing show fringes, [34A] putting on phylacteries. And what is the definition of a positive commandment not dependent upon time? The fixing of an amulet to the doorpost, the erection of a parapet (Deut. 22:8), returning lost property, sending forth the dam from the nest [T. Qid. 1:10A-C].**

III.2 A. *Is this an encompassing generalization here?* But what about unleavened bread, rejoicing on the festivals, and assembly on the Festival of Sukkot in the Seventh Year (Deut. 31:12) [which include women, but which] depend on a particular time, and for which women are obligated! *And furthermore:* What about study of the Torah, procreation, and the redemption of the firstborn, which are not religious duties that depend on a particular time, and yet women are exempt from these?

B. Said R. Yohanan, "We may not establish analogies resting on encompassing principles, and that is so even though exceptions are explicitly stated, *for we have learned in the Mishnah:* **With any [food] do they prepare an erub and a shittuf [partnership meal], except for water and salt [M. Er. 3:1A].** *Now aren't there any other exceptions? Lo, there is the matter of mushrooms and truffles. So it must follow,* We may not establish analogies resting on encompassing principles, and that is so even though exceptions are explicitly stated."

IV.1 A. **For every positive commandment dependent upon the time [of year], men are liable, and women are exempt:**

B. *How do we know this rule?*

    C.   We derive an analogy from the matter of phylacteries: Just as women are exempt from the requirement to put on phylacteries, so they are exempt from every positive commandment dependent upon the time of day or year.

    D.   And the rule in respect to phylacteries itself derives from the matter of study of the Torah: Just as in the case of study of the Torah, women are exempt, so in the case of phylacteries, women are exempt.

    E.   *But why not draw an analogy to the mezuzah from phylacteries [exempting a woman there as well]?*

    F.   Phylacteries are treated as comparable to study of the Torah in both the first and the second sections (Deut. 6:4-9, Deut. 11:13-21), but they are not comparable to the mezuzah in the second section.

    G.   *But why not draw an analogy to the mezuzah from study of the Torah [exempting a woman there as well]?*

    H.   *Don't let it enter your mind, for it is written,* "That your days may be long" (Deut.11:21) – *so do men need a long life but not women?*

IV.2   A.   What about the building of the tabernacle, which is a positive commandment dependent upon the time of year?

    B.   Scripture says, "You shall dwell in booths for seven days" (Lev. 23:42). *Now the reason for women's being exempt from this obligation is that Scripture referred to* "the homeborn" [males, not females], *but otherwise, women would be liable!*

    C.   *Said Abbayye, "It is necessary to make that exclusion explicit. I might have thought, since it is written,* 'You shall dwell in booths for seven days,' 'you should dwell' *is comparable to* 'you should live in a house,' *and just as normal living in a house involves a husband and wife together, so the sukkah must be inhabited by husband and wife together."*

    D.   *And Raba said,* [34B] *"It is necessary to make that exclusion explicit. I might have thought,* we should establish a verbal analogy involving the fifteenth of the month from another holiday in which there is the requirement that it be on the fifteenth of the month. Just as in that other holiday, that is, Passover, women are subject to the obligation, so here, too, women are subject to the obligation. *So it was necessary."*

IV.3   A.   But what about the pilgrimage, which is a positive commandment dependent upon the time of year?

    B.   *Now the reason that a woman is exempt is that Scripture said,* "Three times in the year all your males shall appear" (Ex. 23:17) – excluding women. *But if it were not for that fact, women would be liable!*

    C.   *It is necessary to make that exclusion explicit, for otherwise I would have thought that we derive the rule governing the appearance on the festival from the rule governing assembling once in seven years, which a woman is obligated to do.*

    D.   *Well, then, instead of deriving an exemption from phylacteries, why not deduce that she is obligated based on the requirement of participation in the rejoicing of a festival [which a woman is obligated to do by Deut. 16:14]?*

E. Said Abbayye, "As to a woman, the obligation is on her husband to provide for her rejoicing."

F. *So what are you going to say of a widow?*

G. It would speak of the one with whom she is living.

H. *Why not derive the obligation of a woman from the religious duty of assembling every seven years on Tabernacles?*

I. The reason is that the obligation to eat unleavened bread on Passover and the obligation of assembling are two verses of Scripture that go over the same matter, and where you have a case in which two verses of Scripture go over the same matter, they do not establish an analogy for other cases [but the rule is limited to those explicit cases].

J. *If that's so, then phylacteries and the pilgrimage also are two verses that go over the same matter and these two cannot serve to establish an analogy governing other matters!*

K. *Both matters are required. For if the All-Merciful had made reference to phylacteries but not made reference to the pilgrimage, I might have thought we should establish an analogy between the meaning of the pilgrimage and the requirement of assembling every seven years. If the All-Merciful had made reference to pilgrimage but not phylacteries, I might have supposed: Let the matter of phylacteries be treated as comparable to the mezuzah. So both are required.*

L. *If so, then why shouldn't we say that it was necessary for Scripture to make reference to both the requirement of eating unleavened bread and also to gathering once in seven years. [Then these two are not items that go over the same matter, as we originally alleged.]*

M. *Well, then, what are they required to show us? For if the All-Merciful had made reference to assembling every seven years, but not to the requirement of eating unleavened bread on Passover, it would make the latter unnecessary, for I would maintain, deduce the rule governing a holiday on the fifteenth from the feast of Tabernacles on the fifteenth. But if the All-Merciful had written unleavened bread, with the reference to assembling needless, I would have reasoned: If it is required for children, all the more so, women. So it really is a case of two verses that go over the same matter, and they cannot serve to establish a generative analogy.*

N. *Well, now, that poses no problems from the perspective of him who maintains that they cannot serve to establish a generative analogy. But from the perspective of him who has said they can serve to establish a generative analogy, what is to be said? And furthermore, as to the fact that* for every positive commandment not dependent upon the time, women are liable – *how do we know that fact?*

O. *We derive that fact from the matter of fear of parents:* Because women as much as men are required to fear their parents (Lev. 19:3): Just as fearing parents is required for women, so for every positive commandment not dependent upon time women are liable.

P. *But why not draw your generative analogy from the matter of study of Torah?*

Q. Because the study of Torah and the requirement of procreation are two verses of Scripture that go over the same matter, and wherever there are two verses of Scripture that cover the same matter, they cannot serve to establish a generative analogy.

R.   **[35A]** *Well, from the perspective of* R. Yohanan b. Beroqa, who has said, "The religious duty applies to them both: 'And God blessed them...be fruitful and multiply,' (Gen. 1:28)" *what is to be said?*

S.   *Well, the reason is that* study of the Torah and redeeming the first both are two verses of Scripture that go over the same matter, and wherever there are two verses of Scripture that cover the same matter, they cannot serve to establish a generative analogy.

T.   *And then, also, from the perspective also of R. Yohanan b. Beroqa,* the commandment concerning procreation and the commandment concerning fear of parents are two verses of Scripture that go over the same matter, and wherever there are two verses of Scripture that cover the same matter, they cannot serve to establish a generative analogy.

U.   *In point of fact, those two matters both had to be spelled out [and do not therefore fall into the classification of two verses of Scripture that go over the same matter]. For if the All-Merciful had made reference to fear of parents but not to procreation, I might have supposed that when Scripture referred to* "and conquer it" (Gen. 1:28), Scripture spoke of man, whose nature it is to conquer, and not to woman, whose nature it is not to conquer, *so she would be omitted. And if Scripture had spoken of procreation but not of fear of parents, I might have thought that a man, who has the capacity to carry it such a requirement, would be covered by that requirement, but a woman, who has not got the means to carry out that commandment, since she has not got the means to do it, would be exempt from that requirement in any way at all. So it was necessary.*

V.   *Well, now, that poses no problems from the perspective of him who maintains that* two verses of Scripture that go over the same matter cannot serve to establish a generative analogy. *But from the perspective of him who has said,* they can serve to establish a generative analogy, *what is to be said?*

W.   *Said Raba, "The Papunian knows the reason for this item, and who might that be? It is R. Aha bar Jacob:* 'Said Scripture, "And it shall be a sign for you upon your hand and for a memorial between your eyes, that the Torah of the Lord may be in your mouth" (Ex. 13:9) – Thus the whole of the Torah is treated as analogous to phylacteries. Just as the rules governing phylacteries are an affirmative action dependent on a particular time, from which women are exempt, so are women exempt from all affirmative actions dependent upon a particular time. And, since women are exempt from all affirmative actions dependent on a particular time, it must follow that they also are subject to all of those affirmative actions that are not limited to a particular time.'"

X.   *Well, now that poses no problem to those who maintain that* phylacteries are an affirmative action that depends on a particular time, *but from the perspective of him who maintains that* wearing phylacteries is an affirmative action that does not depend upon a particular time, *what is to be said?*

Y.   *Whom have you heard who takes the view that* wearing phylacteries is an affirmative action that does not depend upon a particular time?

Z.	*It is R. Meir, and R. Meir takes the position that* there are two verses that go over the same matter and these do not generate an analogy serving other cases.
AA.	And from the perspective of R. Judah, who has said, "Two verses that go over the same matter do establish a generative analogy for other cases, and, further, that wearing phylacteries is an affirmative action that does not depend upon a particular time," *what is to be said?*
BB.	Since eating unleavened bread, rejoicing on the festivals, and assembling every seven years on Tabernacles represent three verses that go over the same matter [namely, positive duties, dependent on a particular time, but binding on women (Freedman)], as such, they do not generate an analogy governing any other case.

V.1	A.	**And for every positive commandment not dependent upon the time, men and women are equally liable. For every negative commandment, whether dependent upon the time or not dependent upon the time, men and women are equally liable:**
	B.	*What is the scriptural basis for this rule?*
	C.	R. Judah said Rab said, *and so, too, did the Tannaite authority of the household of R. Ishmael state:* "'When a man or a woman shall commit any sin that men commit' (Num. 5:6) – in this way Scripture has treated women as equal to men in regard to all penalties that are in the Torah."
	D.	*The household of R. Eleazar repeated as its Tannaite formulation:* "'Now these are the ordinances that you shall set before them' (Ex. 21:1) – in this language, Scripture has treated the woman as comparable to the man for the purpose of all the laws that are imposed by the Torah."
	E.	*The household of Hezekiah and R. Yosé the Galilean presented as a Tannaite formulation,* "Said Scripture, 'It has killed a man or a woman' (Ex. 21:1) – in this language, Scripture has treated the woman as comparable to the man for the purpose of all the forms of the death penalty that are specified in the Torah."
	F.	*And all three proofs are required to make the point. For had we heard only the initial one, we might have thought that it is in that area in particular that the All-Merciful has taken pity on a woman, so that she will have a means of atonement, but so far as civil laws in general, a man, who is engaged in business transactions, would be subject to the law, but I might have thought that a woman is not.*
	G.	*And had we been given the rule concerning the civil law, I might have thought that that is so that a woman should have a way of making a living, but as to atonement, since a man is responsible to carry out the religious duties, he would be given the means of making atonement for sin, but a woman, who is not responsible for keeping [all] religious duties, is not under the law.*
	H.	*And had we been given these two, the one because of making atonement, the other because of making a living, but as to the matter of manslaughter, a man, who is subject to the religious duty of paying a ransom in the case of manslaughter,* [35B] *would be subject to the law, but a woman would not.*

I.   *And had we been given the matter of ransom, it might have been thought because in that matter, it is because a soul has perished, but as to these other matters, in which there is no issue of a soul's having perished, I might have thought that that was not the case. So all of them are required.*

VI.1   A.   ...Except for not marring the corners of the beard, not rounding the corners of the head (Lev. 19:27), and not becoming unclean because of the dead (Lev. 21:1):

B.   *There is no problem understanding the exception of defiling oneself to bury a corpse, since it is explicitly written that this applies only to males:* "Speak to the priests, the sons of Aaron: No one shall defile himself for the dead among his people" (Lev. 21:1) – the sons of Aaron, not the daughters of Aaron. *But how on the basis of Scripture do we know that the same pertains to not marring the corners of the beard, not rounding the corners of the head?*

C.   "You shall not round the corner of your heads nor mar the corners of your beard" (Lev. 19:27) – anyone who is subject to the prohibition of marring the corners of the beard is covered by the prohibition of rounding, *but women, who obviously are not subject to the prohibition of marring the corners of the beard, also are not subject to the prohibition of rounding.*

D.   *So how do we know that women are not subject to the prohibition against marring the beard?*

E.   *Well, friend, if you want, I'll just say it's a matter of common sense, since they don't have beards. Or, if you need it, I'll cite a verse of Scripture:* "You shall not rend the corner of your heads, nor shall you mar the corner of your beard" (Lev. 19:27) – since Scripture has varied its usage, moving from the you plural to the you singular, [clearly the latter does not apply to both genders]. *Otherwise, the All-Merciful should speak of* "the corner of your beards." *Why* "your beard"? *It means,* "your beard, but not your wife's beard."

F.   *So is the woman's beard not covered? But hasn't it been taught on Tannaite authority:* A woman or a eunuch's beard that produced hair – lo, they are classified as an ordinary beard for all purposes affecting them? *Doesn't this mean, in respect to marring the beard?*

G.   Said Abbayye, *"Well, now, you can't say that it is in regard to marring, for we derive the verbal analogy out of the rule governing the 'corner' of that of the sons of Aaron:* Just as there women are exempt from the commandment, so here, too."

H.   *Yes, but if we take for granted that the language,* "sons of Aaron," *is stated with regard to everything covered in this section* [Israelites in general: "Nor shall you mar the corner of your beard," priests in particular: "Neither shall they shave off the corner of their beard," with "sons of Aaron" governing the whole section], *then let Scripture fall silent, and we should produce the same result by an argument a fortiori. For this is what I might propose:* If in the case of priests, for whom Scripture has provided an abundance of religious duty, yield the argument, "sons of Aaron" and not daughters of Aaron, then a fortiori the same rule should apply to ordinary Israelites!

I.   *But if it were not for the verbal analogy, I might have said that the matter is interrupted* [so that "sons of Aaron" does not refer to "they shall not shave"]. *So here, too, why not say that the matter is interrupted, and, so far as the argument resting on the verbal analogy, it is required for another purpose altogether, namely, for that which has been taught on Tannaite authority:*

J.   "Neither shall the priests shave off the corner of their beard" (Lev. 21:5):

K.   Might one suppose that he is liable even if he shaved it off with scissors?

L.   Scripture says, "Neither shall you mar..." (Lev. 19:27).

M.   Might one suppose if one removed it with tweezers or pincers he is liable?

N.   Scripture says, "Neither shall you mar" – which involves destruction.

O.   How so? It must be a kind of shaving that involves destruction, and that is with a razor.

P.   *If it were the case that the verbal analogy covers only shaving and marring but not those to whom these acts apply, Scripture should have said, "You shall not round the corner of your heads nor should you mar that of your beard." Why say, "the corner of your beard"? It is to yield both points.*

Q.   *Well, then, what about that which has been taught on Tannaite authority:* A woman or a eunuch's beard that produced hair – lo, they are classified as an ordinary beard for all purposes affecting them? *What purpose does this law serve?*

R.   Said Mar Zutra, "It pertains to the uncleanness brought on by the skin ailment" (Lev. 13:1-17, 29-37.) [Freedman: If a woman or eunuch grows a beard, though normally their chins are free of hair, the test of the skin ailment are the symptoms of hair, not those of skin.]

S.   *But the symptoms of uncleanness brought on by the skin ailment so far as these affect skin or hair are explicitly stated by Scripture:* "If a man or a woman have a mark of the skin ailment on head or beard (Lev. 13:29)."

T.   Rather, said Mar Zutra, "These serve to indicate the marks of purification from the skin ailment" [Freedman: when a woman becomes clean from the marks of skin ailment of the beard, she must undergo the same ritual as a man].

U.   *Well, that, too, is a pretty obvious point since she can become unclean, she obviously can be made clean!*

V.   *It was necessary to make the point nonetheless, for without this statement, I might have assumed that it covers distinct subjects, that is,* "If a man or a woman has a mark of the skin ailment on the head," *while when reference is made to* "or the beard," *it would revert to the man alone; so we are informed to the contrary.*

VI.2 A.   *Isi taught as a Tannaite statement:* "So, too, are women excempt from the prohibition of baldness" (Lev. 21:5).

B.   *What is the scriptural basis for Isi's view?*

C.   *This is how he expounds the matter:* "'You are sons of the Lord your God, you shall not cut yourselves nor make any baldness between your eyes for the dead, for you are a holy people to the Lord your God' (Deut. 14:1) – sons, but not daughters, in the matter of baldness.

D.   "You maintain that it is in respect to baldness. But maybe it is in respect to cutting yourselves?

E.   "When Scripture says, 'For you are a holy people to the Lord your God,' cutting is covered. So how do I interpret the sense of 'sons,' but not daughters? It is in respect to baldness.

F.   "Well, why do you prefer to extend the law to cutting and to exclude from the law the matter of baldness?

G.   "I extend the law to cutting, which is possible both where there is hair and where there is none, but I exclude the matter of baldness, which pertains only instead of hair."

H.   *But why not say:* "Sons and not daughters" in regard to both baldness and cutting, and the phrase, "for you are a holy people to the Lord your God," *pertains to an incision* [Lev. 21:5: Priests are not to make any incision]?

I.   *Isi takes the view that* incisions and cuttings **[36A]** are the same thing.

J.   *Said Abbayye, "This is the scriptural basis for the position of Isi: He derives a verbal analogy from the appearance in both contexts of the phrase, 'sons of Aaron,' in regard to baldness* [both at Deut. 14:1-2, for Israelites, and Lev. 21:5, for priests]. *Just as in the one case, women are exempt, so in the other, women are exempt."*

K.   *But if we assume that Scripture refers to the entire matter in making reference to* "the sons of Aaron," *then let Scripture just fall silent, and the exemption of women I would derive from an argument a fortiori, as follows:* If in the case of priests, for whom Scripture has provided an abundance of religious duty, yield the argument, "sons of Aaron" and not daughters of Aaron, then a fortiori the same rule should apply to ordinary Israelites!

L.   *But if it were not for the verbal analogy, I might have said that* the matter is interrupted [so that "sons of Aaron" does not refer to "they shall not shave"]. *So here, too, why not say that the matter is interrupted, and, so far as the argument resting on the verbal analogy, it is required for another purpose altogether, namely, for that which has been taught on Tannaite authority:*

M.   "They shall not make tonsures [upon their heads, nor shave off the edges of their beards, nor make any cuttings in their flesh]":

N.   Might one suppose that for making four or five tonsures, one should be liable only on one count?

O.   Scripture refers to "tonsure" in the singular, so imposing liability for each cut.

P.   "Upon their heads":

Q.   What is the point of Scripture here?

R.   Since it is said, "[You are the sons of the Lord your God: You shall not cut yourselves nor make any baldness on your foreheads for the dead" (Deut. 14:1),

S.   one might have thought that liability is incurred only for a cut on the forehead.

T.   How do we know that the prohibition extends to the entire head?

U.   Scripture says, "upon their heads,"

V.   to encompass the entire head.

W.   Might one suppose that in the case of priests, for whom Scripture has specified numerous supererogatory commandments, liability extends to each cut and also to the entire head,

X.   while for ordinary Israelites, for whom Scripture has not specified supererogatory commandments, liability should be incurred only on one count for however many cuts and only for a cut on the forehead?

Y.   Scripture refers to "tonsure" in several passages [here and at Deut. 14:1, here speaking of the priests, there speaking of Israelites as well], so establishing grounds for the following analogy:

Z.   Just as in the case of "cutting" stated with reference to priests, liability is incurred for each cut and is incurred for a cut on any part of the head as much as on the forehead, so for "cut" spoken of in connection with an Israelite, liability is incurred for each cut and is incurred for a cut on any part of the head as much as on the forehead.

AA.   And just as "cutting" stated with reference to an Israelite imposes liability only if it is made for a deceased, so "cutting" stated with reference to priests imposes liability only if it is made for a deceased [Sifra CCXII:I.1-3].

BB.   [Abbayye responds:] *"If so, Scripture should write 'baldness' [in abbreviated form. Why say 'baldness' in a fully spelled out form]? It is to yield both points."*

CC.   *Said Raba, "This is the scriptural basis for the position of Isi: He derives how the consideration of the phrase* 'between your eyes' *applies from the case of phylacteries. Just as in the latter case, women are exempt, so here, too, they are exempt."*

DD.   *And how come Raba doesn't state matters as does Abbayye?*

EE.   *Because he doesn't see any point in the variation of spellings of the word for baldness.*

FF.   *And how come Abbayye doesn't state matters as does Raba?*

GG.   *He will say to you, "The matter of phylacteries themselves derives from this very passage, namely:* Just as in that context 'between the eyes' means, a place where a bald spot can be made, which is the upper part of the head, so here, too, the place at which phylacteries are locates is the upper part of the head."

HH.   *Now in regard to both Abbayye and Raba, how do they deal with the phrase,* "you are sons" *[since they make the same point on the basis of other language altogether]?*

II.   *They require it in line with that which has been taught on Tannaite authority:*

JJ.   "You are children of the Lord your God. You shall not gash yourselves or shave the front of your heads because of the dead. For you are a people consecrated to the Lord your God: The Lord your God chose you from among all other peoples on earth to be his treasured people" (Deut. 14:1-2):

KK.   R. Judah says, "If you conduct yourselves in the way good children do, then you are children, and if not, you are not children [of the Lord your God]."

LL. R. Meir says, "One way or another, 'You are children of the Lord your God.'"

MM. And so Scripture says, "Yet the number of the children of Israel shall be as the sand of the sea... it shall be said to them, 'You are the children of the living God' (Hos. 2:1)" [B.'s version: "They are sottish children" (Jer. 4:22); "They are children in whom is no faith" (Deut. 32:20), "A seed of evil doers, sons that deal corruptly" (Isa. 1:4), then Hos. 2:1] [Sifré Deut. XCVI:IV.1].

NN. *Why all these further verses?*

OO. *If you should reply, then only when they are foolish are they classified as sons, but not when they lack faith, come and note:* "They are children in whom is no faith" (Deut. 32:20).

PP. *If you should reply, then only when they have no faith they are classified as sons, but when they serve idols they are not classified as sons, then come and hear:* "A seed of evil doers, sons that deal corruptly" (Isa. 1:4).

QQ. *And should you say, well, they're called sons that act corruptly, but not good sons, then come and hear:* "Yet the number of the children of Israel shall be as the sand of the sea... it shall be said to them, 'You are the children of the living God' (Hos. 2:1)."

I.1+2, supplied with its talmud and appendix on the theme of the talmud, at Nos. 3-32, begin with the required exegesis of the Mishnah's reference. II.1+2-43 then go through the same inquiry as I.1, with the usual anthology of thematically pertinent compositions, formed into an enormous composite. III.1-2 explain the rule of the Mishnah by appeal to a Tannaite complement. IV.1-2+3 go over the same sentence, now providing a scriptural basis for the rule. V.1, VI.1 ask for the scriptural basis for the rule of the Mishnah. No. 2 continues the exposition of the law of the Mishnah, now extending its coverage.

1:8

A. [The cultic rites of] laying on of hands, waving, drawing near, taking the handful, burning the fat, breaking the neck of a bird, sprinkling, and receiving [the blood] apply to men and not to women,

B. except in the case of a meal-offering of an accused wife and of a Nazirite girl, which they wave.

I.1 A. Laying on of hands:

B. *For it is written,* "Speak to the sons of Israel...and he shall lay his hand upon the head of the burnt-offering" (Lev. 7:29-30) –

C. The sons of Israel, not the daughters of Israel do it.

II.1 A. Waving:

B. *For it is written,* "Speak to the sons of Israel...the fat...may be waved" (Lev. 6:7).

C. The sons of Israel, not the daughters of Israel do it.

III.1 A. Drawing near:

B. *For it is written,* "And this is the law of the meal-offering: The sons of Aaron shall offer it –

C. The sons of Aaron, not the daughters of Aaron do it.

IV.1 A. **Taking the handful:**

B. *For it is written,* "And he shall bring it to Aaron's sons, the priests, and he shall take out of it his handful of the fine flour" (Lev. 2:2) –

C. The sons of Aaron, not the daughters of Aaron do it.

V.1 A. **Burning the fat:**

B. *For it is written,* "And Aaron's sons shall burn it" (Lev. 2:2)

C. The sons of Aaron, not the daughters of Aaron do it.

VI.1 A. **Breaking the neck of a bird, sprinkling:**

B. *For it is written,* "And he shall wring off his head and burn it on the altar" –

C. *Treating as comparable wringing the neck and burning the fat.*

VII.1 A. **And receiving [the blood]:**

B. *For it is written,* "And the priests, the sons of Aaron," *and a master has said,* [36B] "'And they shall bring' refers to receiving the blood."

VIII.1 A. **Sprinkling:**

B. *Sprinkling what? If it is the blood of the red cow, "Eleazar" [the priest] is written in that connection. And if it is the blood that is sprinkled in the inner sanctum of the Temple [for example, on the veil and golden altar], then* the anointed priest *is required for that [for example, Lev. 4:5].*

C. *It is the sprinkling of the blood of fowl, deriving a fortiori from the case of the beast:* If an animal, for slaughter of which a priest is not specified, has to have a priest for sprinkling its blood, then fowl, for the wringing of the neck of which a priest is required, surely should have to have a priest for sprinkling the blood.

IX.1 A. **Except in the case of a meal-offering of an accused wife and of a Nazirite girl, which they wave:**

B. *Said R. Eleazar to R. Josiah, his contemporary, "You may not take your seat until you explain the following matter:* How do we know that the meal-offering of the accused wife had to be waved?"

C. [He replied,] "How do we know indeed! It is written, 'And he shall wave' (Num. 5:25)!"

D. [No, the question is,] "How do we know that it must be done by the owner [explaining why the priest puts the woman's hand on the utensil of service, along with his own, so that she may wave the offering as he does]?"

E. "The proof derives from the appearance of the word 'hand' both in the present context and in the setting of the peace-offerings. *Here it is written,* 'And the priest will take from the hand of the woman' (Num. 5:25) *and in that other connection it is written,* 'His own hands shall bring...' (Lev. 7:30). Just as, in the present instance, it is the priest who does the waving, so, in that other instance, it is the priest who does the waving. Just as, in that other context, the owner joins in, so here, too, the owner joins in. How so? **The priest puts his hand under the hand of the owner and waves [the meal-offering] [M. Sot. 3:1B]."**

F. *So we have found the case of the accused wife. How about the Nazirite woman?*

G. We derive the sense of "palm" from the meaning in connection with the accused wife.

I.1-VII provide scriptural foundations for the Mishnah's details. VIII.1 clarifies the rule of the Mishnah. IX.1 reverts to the established inquiry.

III. The Exegetical Programs of Yerushalmi and of the Babli Compared

The enormous size of the Bavli's treatment of M. 1:7 is not the only difference between the two Talmuds; the more profound difference is that even though answering the same questions, the framers of the Talmuds' compositions and (in the case of the Bavli) composites simply go their own way, each group of writers using its own language to make its own points in response to the logical necessities that motivate its work. The Bavli is different in form; different in program; different in interpretation of the literary task; different in modes of exposition and different in manner of argument. The Yerushalmi tends to cite; the Bavli, to argue; the Yerushalmi is happy to lay out possibilities; the Bavli insists on settling questions. All the two Talmuds have in common is that both are talmuds.

1:7 I A Tannaite complement to the Mishnah is systematically glossed, with its talmud.

1:7 II Citation of M. Ed. 2:9, which deals with the allegation of our Mishnah rule; talmud to that Mishnah sentence.

1:7 III Citation of M. Shab. 1:5 and secondary amplification.

1:7 IV Continuation of foregoing.

1:7 V M. 1:7B clarified: how does one show reverence for the father; with Tannaite complement.

1:7 VI To what extent does the requirement of honoring father and mother extend? Sequence of stories.

1:7 VII Lev. 19:3 and other relevant verses.

1:7 VIII What is the way one expresses reverence for the father?

1:7A-F I.1 What is the meaning of **for every commandment concerning the son to which the father is subject...?**

1:7A-F I.2 Tannaite complement to the foregoing.

1:7A-F I.3-5 Talmud to the cited Tannaite complement.

1:7A-F I.6-7 Topical appendix to foregoing complement.

1:7A-F I.8 Continuation of talmud to the cited Tannaite complement.

1:7A-F I.9+10-20 Free-standing Tannaite statement relevant to foregoing, with its talmud and topical appendix at the following numbers.

1:7A-F I.21+22-24: Contrast of teaching between early masters and later masters; fully exposed in terms of a topical appendix.

1:7 IX Prov. 5:6, 4:23.

1:7 X Gloss of M. 1:7C, cit. of Tosefta: religious duties that depend on a particular time.

1:7 XI Passover-offering prepared for women is optional.

1:7 XII Continuation of foregoing issue.

1:7 XIII M. 1:7F: Except for not marring + Women also are not liable for parallel rules.

1:7 XIV Gloss of M. 1:7 I: how the waving of the rite is gone.

1:7 XV Same as foregoing: how can the priest touch the woman.

1:7A-F I.25 Tannaite statement on teaching children.

1:7A-F I.26 Same as above.

1:7A-F I.27 Tannaite statement inserted as complement to the foregoing.

1:7A-F I.28 Same as above.

1:7A-F I.29-32: Completion of sustained gloss of No. 2.

1:7A-F II.1 What is the definition of..., as at I.1.

1:7A-F II.2 Tannaite complement to the foregoing: honoring father and mother.

1:7A-F II. 3, 4, 5 Tannaite complements.

1:7A-F II.6 As best as I can tell, this is a footnote to the foregoing, so, too, Nos. 7-9.

1:7A-F II.10 To what extent is one obligated to honor father & mother + exemplary story.

1:7A-F II.11-12 Footnotes to foregoing.

1:7A-F II.13 Tannaite statement on same issue as No. 10.

1:7A-F II.14-20 Footnotes, stories, and other supplements to the foregoing.

1:7A-F II.21 Tannaite statement: Child must honor parent in life and after death.

1:7A-F II.22 Tannaite statement on priority of father's honor.

1:7A-F II.23, 24 Tannaite statement and talmud, intersects with Yerushalmi: What is the form of reverence that is owing? Not sit in father's place, etc.

1:7A-F II.25, 26 Cases illustrative of honor owing to father.

1:7A-F II.27 Said X, if father renounced honor....

1:7A-F II.28 Talmud to the foregoing.

1:7A-F II.29 Tannaite statement amplifying Lev. 19:32.

1:7A-F II.30 Talmud to the foregoing.

1:7A-F II.31-35, 36 As above.

1:7A-F II.37 Said X, a disciple is allowed to stand up only..., so that the honor owing to the master is no more than that owing to Heaven.

1:7A-F II.38 Said X, any disciple who does not rise before the master....

1:7A-F II.39 Theoretical question: If son was also the master, what is the law?

1:7A-F II.40 Theoretical question: if son was father's master.

1:7A-F II.41 Theoretical question: is riding equivalent to walking.

1:7A-F II.42 Theoretical question: on rising before scroll of the Torah.

1:7A-F II.43 People arose before Moses (Ex. 33:8).

1:7A-F III.1 Tannaite complement to the Mishnah rule.

1:7A-F III.2 Talmud to the foregoing.

1:7A-F IV.1 How do we know the Mishnah's rule? An argu-ment by analogy.

1:7A-F IV.2-3 Amplification of the Mishnah rule: What about an interstitial case?

1:7A-F V.1 Scriptural source

of the Mishnah's rule.

1:7 A-F VI.1 How on the basis of Scripture do we know an issue precipitated by the Mishnah's rule.

1:7A-F VI.2 Tannaite complement; Scriptural basis therefor.

1:7G-H [=B. M. 1:8] I.1 Scriptural basis for the Mishnah's detail.

1:7G-H [=B. M. 1:8] II.1 Scriptural basis for the Mishnah's detail.

1:7G-H [=B. M. 1:8] III.1 Scriptural basis for the Mishnah's detail.

1:7G-H [=B. M. 1:8] IV.1 Scriptural basis for the Mishnah's detail.

1:7G-H [=B. M. 1:8] V.1 Scriptural basis for the Mishnah's detail.

1:7G-H [=B. M. 1:8] VI.1 Scriptural basis for the Mishnah's detail.

1:7G-H [=B. M. 1:8] VII.1 Scriptural basis for the Mishnah's detail.

1:7G-H [=B. M. 1:8] VIII.1 Clarification of the sense of the Mishnah's rule.

1:7G-H [=B. M. 1:8] IX.1 Scriptural basis for the Mishnah's rule.

We note that the Bavli's enormous composition on the obligations of the father, 1:7A-F I.2-32, has no counterpart in the other Talmud. This is a massive talmud to a Tannaite complement to the Mishnah statement, complete with secondary expansions and accretions, little footnotes and sizable appendices; the entire composite fully pertinent, for obvious reasons, to the Mishnah's main point – and utterly unknown to the Yerushalmi. Where there is an intersection, as indicated on the chart, it is in the setting of a received writing; but then, as we note, Bavli's secondary talmud goes its own way, addressing a question interesting to the Yerushalmi but answering it entirely in the Bavli's own way.

[V.A] Every commandment concerning the father to which the son is liable [M. 1:7B]:

[B] What is the way one expresses reverence for the father?

[C] He does not sit in his place or speak in his place, he does not contradict him.

[D] And what is the form of honor owing to the father?

[E] Giving him food to eat and something to drink and clothing him and covering him and taking him out and bringing him in and washing his face, his hands, and his feet [T. Qid. 1:1 IB].

[F] Whose [food and the like must be given to the father]? [Does the son have to provide it?]

[G] Hunah bar Hiyya said, "It is the old man's."

[H] And there are those who wish to say, "It is his [the son's]."

[I] Did not R. Abbahu say in the name of R. Yosé b. R. Haninah, "How do we know that even if the father said to him, 'Throw this purse into the sea,' the son must listen to him?" [So the son bears unlimited obligations.]

[J] That applies to a case in which the father has another such purse,

II.23 A. *Our rabbis have taught on Tannaite authority:*

B. **What is the form of reverence that is owing?**

C. **The son should not sit in his place, speak in his place, contradict him.**

D. **What is the form of honor that is owing?**

E. **The son should feed him, give him drink, dress him, cover him, bring him in and take him out [Sifra CXCIX.I.5].**

II.24 A. *The question was raised:* [32A] "At whose expense [must he feed him and so on]?"

B. R. Judah said Samuel said, "The son's."

C. R. Nathan bar Oshayya said, "The father's."

D. *Rabbis gave a ruling to R. Jeremiah, some say, to the son of R. Jeremiah, in accord with him who said, "The father's."*

E. *An objection was raised:* "Honor your father and your mother" (Ex. 20:12), and further, "Honor the Lord with your property" (Prov. 3:9) – just as the latter means, at one's own expense, so the former has the same meaning. But if you say that it is at the father's expense, *then what does it cost the son?*

F. It costs him time off

and in which the son gives pleasure to the father by doing what he wants.

[K] **All the same are husband [61b] and wife, but the husband has sufficient means to do these things [for the aged parent], and the wife does not have sufficient means to do them,**

[L] for others have power over her [T. Qid. 1:1].

[M] If the daughter was widowed or divorced, she enters the status of one who has sufficient means to carry out what is required.

from his own work.

G. *Come and take note:* **Two brothers, two partners, a father and a son, a master and his disciple redeem one another's second tithe; and feed one another with the tithe set aside for the poor [T. M.S. 4:7A]. But if you say that it is at the son's expense, then it will turn out that this fellow is paying off his debt out of what belongs to the poor.**

H. *This speaks only of what is excess [over and above the father's needs, over and above what is ordinarily expected].*

I. *If so, then what's the point of the continuation of the Tannaite formulation:* Said R. Judah, "May a curse come upon someone who feeds his father tithe set aside for the poor?" *Now if it speaks only of what is excess [over and above the father's needs, over and above what is ordinarily expected], then what difference does it make?*

J. *It's a disgrace for the father.*

K. *Come and take note:* They asked R. Eliezer, "To what extent does the obligation of honoring father and mother extend?" He said to them, "To the extent that he might take a money bag and toss it into the sea in his presence, and the child will not yell at

him." Now if you
maintain that the money
belongs to the father,
what difference does it
make to the son?

L. It is a case in which
the son is supposed to
inherit the father's es-
tate.

M. *That would be like the
case of Rabbah b. R.
Huna. For R. Huna tore
up silk in the presence of
Rabbah his son. He said,
"I will go and see
whether he gets mad or
not."*

N. *But if he got mad, then
wouldn't he violate the
commandment, "You
shall not put a stum-
bling block before the
blind" (Lev. 19:14) [by
baiting the son to treat
him disrespectfully]?*

O. *He renounced the honor
owing to him.*

P. *But didn't [Huna] violate the commandment,
"You shall not destroy
the trees thereof"
(Deut. 20:19) [wasting
property]?*

Q. *He did it in the seam.*

R. *So maybe that's why he
didn't lose his temper.*

S. *He did it when he was
already upset about
something [and yet he
didn't insult the father].*

The Yerushalmi at IV.F asks exactly the same question as the Bavli at
II.24. But the compositions have nothing in common. The Yerushalmi
cites two conflicting opinions, F-H. Then, I, we have an indication that
the son's obligation is unlimited. J qualifies the foregoing. K-L then
continue the citation of the Tannaite formulation, and M glosses. So
much for the Yerushalmi – show-and-tell of Tannaite rules in response to
a logically important question. The Bavli presents the same conflicting
positions, II.24A-C, D. Then we present an objection to one of these
positions, and a counter to the objection. Another piece of evidence is

introduced, G, and that, too, is countered. K goes through the same process. This runs parallel to Y.'s case, but is explained away, with an illustrative case, M, bearing in its wake yet another dialectical argument, in which each position is met with a counterposition, each argument with a contrary argument. The upshot of our little exercise in futility is the familiar one: there is nothing to compare; the second Talmud is made up of materials that scarcely intersect with those of the first Talmud. And when the second Talmud uses materials that occur, also, in the prior one, it uses them for its own purposes, in a pattern of thought, argument, and expression with no counterpart in the earlier Talmud. It suffices to repeat, in the context of an enormous comparison, the simple conclusions I stated up front: the Talmuds differ because they differ.

8

Mishnah-Tractate Qiddushin 1:8 in the Yerushalmi and the Bavli

Y. 1:8=B. 1:9

A. Every commandment which is dependent upon the Land applies only in the Land,

B. and which does not depend upon the Land applies both in the Land and outside the Land,

C. [37A] except for orlah [produce of a fruit tree in the first three years of its growth] and mixed seeds (Lev. 19:23, 19:19).

D. R. Eliezer says, "Also: Except for [the prohibition against eating] new [produce before the omer is waved on the sixteenth of Nisan] (Lev. 23:14)."

I. Mishnah Qiddushin 1:8 in the Talmud of the Land of Israel

[I.A] It is written, "These are the statutes and ordinances that you shall be careful to do in the land that the Lord, the God of your fathers, has given you to possess, all the days that you live upon the earth]" (Deut. 12:1).

[B] In the Land you are obligated to do them, but you are not obligated abroad.

[C] To this point we rule that commandments that depend upon the Land apply only in the Land. Is it possible to maintain that even commandments that do not depend upon the Land should apply also only in the Land?

[D] Scripture states, "Take heed lest your heart be deceived, [and you turn aside and serve other gods and worship them,] and the anger of the Lord be kindled against you" (Deut. 11:16).

[E] "You shall therefore lay up these words of mine in your heart and in your soul" (Deut. 11:18).

[F] Even when you are exiles, "You shall therefore bind up these words of mine upon your heart and in your soul. "

[G] [Since the cited verse reads, "And you shall bind them as a sign upon your hands and they shall be as frontlets between your eyes, and you shall teach them to your children" (Deut. 11:18),] what do

309

you derive from the verse? It is, for example, putting on phylacteries and studying Torah.

[H] Accordingly, just as putting on phylacteries and studying Torah, which do not depend upon being in the Land, apply both in the Land and abroad, so also every matter that does not depend upon being in the Land should apply both in the Land and abroad.

[I] If that is so, then when they are redeemed they should be exempt [from doing them].

[J] It is written, "And all the assembly of those who had returned from the captivity made booths and dwelt in the booths, for from the days of Jeshua the son of Nun to that day the people of Israel had not done so. And there was very great rejoicing" (Neh. 8:17).

[K] Why Jeshua [lacking the expected H]? [Not YHWS' but YS'.]

[L] It was Scripture's way of impairing the honor owing to one righteous man who was in his grave on account of the honor owing to another righteous man in his day.

[M] [It is on account of the honor owing to a righteous man in his time, namely:] The Scripture has compared the coming of the Israelites to the Land in the time of Ezra to the coming of the Israelites to the Land in the time of Joshua.

[N] Just as when they came in the time of Joshua, they had been exempt from the religious requirement [of obligations tied to the land of Israel], but they became liable to do so, so when they came in the time of Ezra they had been exempt from the religious requirement [of obligations tied to the land of Israel] His tabernacle, and they now became liable to do so. [Now since the verse observes that they did not do so in Ezra's time but did do so in Nehemiah's, it follows that, to avoid dishonoring Ezra, they impaired the honor owing to Joshua and so dropped a letter from his name.]

[O] On what grounds did they become liable?

[P] R. Yosé b. R. Haninah said, "It was on the strength of the teaching of the Torah that they became liable."

[Q] This is in line with what is written, "And the Lord your God will bring you into the land which your fathers possessed, that you may possess it; [and he will make you more prosperous and numerous than your fathers]" (Deut. 30:5).

[R] The Scripture thereby has compared your inheriting the Land to the inheriting of the Land by your fathers.

[S] Just as inheriting the Land on the part of the fathers was on the basis of the Torah's teaching, so your inheriting the Land likewise is on the basis of the Torah's teaching.

[T] "He will make you more prosperous and numerous than your fathers" (Deut. 30:5). They had been exempt, and they became liable, so, too, you had been exempt, and now you have become liable.

[U] As to your fathers, they had not been subject to the yoke of the kingdom, but you, even though you are subject to the yoke of the kingdom [are in a different situation, for] your fathers became liable only after fourteen years, seven while they conquered the Land and seven while they divided it, but you are liable as soon as you buy a piece of Land.

[V] Said R. Eleazar, "They accepted the requirement to separate tithes on their own initiative."

[W] What is the scriptural basis for this position?

[X] "Because of all this we make a firm covenant and write it, [and our princes, our Levites, and our priests set their seal to it]" (Neh. 10:1).

[Y] And how does R. Eleazar interpret the following verse: "[We obligate ourselves to bring the first fruits of our ground and the first fruits of all fruit of every tree, year by year, to the house of the Lord; also to bring to the house of our God, the firstborn of our sons and of our cattle, as it is written in the law,] and the firstlings of our herds and of our flocks" (Neh. 10:36-37).

[Z] [61d] Since they accepted responsibility for matters for which they were not liable, even as to matters for which they were liable, the Omnipresent credited it to them as if they had accepted the obligation on their own initiative.

[AA] How does R. Yosé b. R. Haninah interpret the verse, "Because of all this we make a firm covenant and write it" (Neh. 10:1)?

[BB] Since they accepted their responsibilities in a willing spirit, the Omnipresent credited it to them as if they had accepted the obligation to separate tithes on their own initiative.

[CC] How does R. Eleazar interpret the verse, "More than your fathers"?

[DD] He interprets it to speak of the world to come.

[EE] For R. Helbo, Simeon bar Ba in the name of R. Yohanan: "Your fathers inherited the Land from seven peoples, but you are destined to inherit the Land from ten peoples."

[FF] Who are the other three?

[GG] "[To your descendants I give this land, from the river of Egypt to the great river, the river Euphrates,] the land of the Kenites, the Kenizzites, the Kadmonites, [the Hittites, the Perizzites, the Rephaim, the Amorites, the Canaanites, the Girgashites, and the Jebusites]" (Gen. 15:18-21).

[HH] R. Judah said, "The Shalmaites, the Arabs, and the Nabateans."

[II] R. Simeon said, "Asia, Aspamaea, and Damascus."

[JJ] R. Eliezer b. Jacob says, "Asia, Carthage, and Thrace [following Jastrow]."

[KK] Rabbi says, "Edom, Moab, and the beginning of the area of the Ammonites."

[LL] "More than your fathers." As to your fathers, even though they were redeemed, they once more went and were subjected, but as to you, once you have been redeemed, you will never again be subjugated.

[MM] What is the scriptural proof for that statement?

[NN] "Ask now and see, can a man bear a child?" (Jer. 30:6).

[OO] Just as a male cannot give birth, so you, once you have been redeemed you will never again be subjugated.

[II.A] **Except for orlah and mixed seeds. R. Eliezer says, "Also: Except for the prohibition against eating new produce before the omer is waved on the sixteenth of Nisan " (Lev. 23:14) [M. 1:8C-D].**

[B] What is the scriptural basis for the position of R. Eliezer?

[C] "[And you shall eat neither bread nor grain parched or fresh until this same day, until you have brought the offering of your God: It is a statute forever throughout your generations] in all your dwellings" (Lev. 23:14) – whether in the land or abroad.

[D] How do rabbis interpret "in all your dwellings"?

[E] They apply it to the rule governing new produce deriving from the land of Israel that is taken outside the boundaries of the land. [Such produce may not be eaten before the omer.]

[F] R. Yonah raised the question, "And why do we not learn, 'Also dough-offering'?"

[G] Said to him R. Yosé, "We have learned the rule governing only matters that apply to Israelites' crops and also to gentiles' [crops]. But separating dough-offering applies to Israelites' [food] and not to gentiles'."

[H] What is the scriptural basis for that statement?

[I] "Of the first of your coarse meal you shall present a cake as an offering; [as an offering from the threshing floor, so shall you present it]" (Num. 15:20) – and not the first of gentiles' coarse meal.

The Talmud's principal interest is in discovering and interpreting the scriptural foundations for the Mishnah's statements. Unit I is a rather long account, but its starting point is clear. Unit II deals with some minor details of the Mishnah.

II. Mishnah-Qiddushin 1:8 in the Talmud of Babylonia

I.1 A. *What is the meaning of,* which is dependent upon, *and what is the meaning of,* which does not depend upon? *If I say that the sense of* which is dependent upon *pertains where the language,* "entering the land" *is used, and the sense of* which does not depend upon *pertains where the language,* "entering the land" *is not used, then what about the matters of phylacteries and the disposition of the firstling of an ass, which pertain both in the Land of Israel and abroad, even though the language* "entering the land" *is used in their connection?*

     B. *Said R. Judah, "This is the sense of the statement:*Every religious duty that is an obligation of the person applies whether in the Land or abroad, but if it is an obligation that is incumbent upon the soil, it applies only in the Land."

I.2 A. *What is the scriptural basis for that rule?*

     B. *It is in line with what our rabbis have taught on Tannaite authority:*

     C. ["These are the laws and rules that you must carefully observe to do in the land that the Lord, God of your fathers, is giving you to possess, as long as you live on earth. You must destroy all the sites at which the nations you are to dispossess worshiped their gods, whether on lofty mountains and on hills or under any luxuriant tree. Tear down their altars, smash their pillars, put their sacred posts to the fire, and cut down the images of their gods, obliterating their name from that site" (Deut. 12:1-3)]:

     D. "These are the laws":

     E. This refers to the midrash exegeses.

     F. "And rules":

     G. These are the laws.

H. "...That you must carefully observe":

I. This refers to studying.

J. "...To do":

K. This refers to doing the deeds.

L. "...In the land [that the Lord, God of your fathers, is giving you to possess, as long as you live on earth]":

M. Might one suppose that all of the religious duties without exception pertain abroad?

N. Scripture says, "To do in the land."

O. Might one suppose that all of the religious duties without exception pertain solely in the land [and not abroad]?

P. Scripture says, "...As long as you live on earth."

Q. After Scripture has stated matters in encompassing language, Scripture has further stated matters in limiting language, on which account we learn from the stated context.

R. In context, it is stated, "You must destroy all the sites at which the nations you are to dispossess worshiped their gods."

S. Just as the matter of idolatry is singular in that it is a religious duty pertaining to one's person and not dependent upon one's being situated in the Land, thus pertaining both in the Land and also abroad, so all religious duties that are incumbent upon the person and do not depend upon one's being located in the Land apply both in the Land and abroad [Sifré Deut. LIX:I.1-2].

II.1 A. Except for orlah [produce of a fruit tree in the first three years of its growth] and mixed seeds (Lev. 19:23, 19:19). R. Eliezer says, "Also: Except for [the prohibition against eating] new [produce before the omer is waved on the sixteenth of Nisan] (Lev. 23:14)":

B. *The question was raised: Is the dissenting opinion of R. Eliezer meant to yield a lenient ruling or a strict ruling?*

C. *It is meant to yield a strict ruling, and this is the sense of the passage: The initial authority says,* except for orlah and mixed seeds, *these deriving from a traditional law; that is so, even though one might argue, to the contrary, these represent an obligation that is connected with the soil, but the consideration of the use of new produce only after the waving of the barley sheaf is practiced only in the Land but not overseas. How come? "Dwelling" means, after taking possession and settling down [Lev. 23:14: "It shall be a statute throughout your generations in all your dwellings," and that might mean, even outside of the Land; but even in the Land this rule came into force only after the Israelites had settled down, not while they were fighting for and dividing up the country (Freedman)]. And then R. Eliezer comes along to say: Also the consideration of the use of new produce only after the waving of the barley sheaf is practiced both in the Land but not overseas. How come? "Dwelling" means, anywhere where you dwell.*

D. *Well, maybe his ruling is meant to yield a lenient ruling, and this is the sense of the passage: The initial authority says,* except for orlah and mixed seeds, *these deriving from a traditional law – and all the more so does the rule governing not eating new produce prior to the waving of the barley sheaf of new grain, for the sense of the word "dwelling" is, anywhere where you dwell. And then R. Eliezer comes along to say: Also the consideration of the use of new produce only after the waving of* the barley sheaf is practiced only in the Land but not overseas. How come? "Dwelling" refers to the situation that prevailed only after the Israelites had settled down, not while they were fighting for and dividing up the country.

E. *And what is the reference point of also here [in this theory of matters]?*

F. *It refers to the first clause only* [the consideration of not eating new grain before the waving of the sheaf of barley is included in the general principle that all precepts and so on (Freedman)].

G. *Come and take note, for said Abbayye, "Who is the Tannaite authority who differs from R. Eliezer? It is R. Ishmael, for it has been taught on Tannaite authority:*

H. ["When you come into the land of your dwellings, which I give to you, and will make an offering burnt by fire to the Lord, then shall he who offers offer a meal-offering and libations" (Num. 15:2ff.):] "This serves to teach you that wherever the word 'dwelling' appears, it refers only to the period after taking possession and settling down in the Land," the words of R. Ishmael.

I. Said to him R. Aqiba, "Lo, there is the matter of the Sabbath, concerning which 'dwellings' occurs, and that applies both in the Land and abroad."

J. He said to him, "The matter of the Sabbath derives from an argument a fortiori: If there are less important religious duties that apply both in the Land and abroad, the Sabbath, which is a weighty commandment, all the more so."

K. *Well, now, since said Abbayye, "Who is the Tannaite authority who differs from R. Eliezer? It is R. Ishmael," it must follow that R. Eliezer's dissenting opinion is meant to yield a strict ruling.*

L. *It certainly does prove the point.*

M. *Well, to what does R. Ishmael make reference? It is to libations. But in connection with libations,* [37B] *the language* "coming into the land" *and also* "dwelling" *are used.* [Freedman: Maybe only "dwelling" extends the law to all places only when it stands alone, but here, used along with "coming," it limits the applicability of the law to the Land of Israel.]

N. *This is the sense of the statement:* "This serves to teach you that wherever the words 'coming' and 'dwelling' appear, Scripture refers only to the period after the inheritance and settlement of the Land," the words of R. Ishmael.

O. *If so, then the language we have is inappropriate, namely:* Said to him R. Aqiba, "Lo, there is the matter of the Sabbath, concerning which 'dwellings' occurs, and that applies both in the Land and abroad." He said to him, "The matter of the Sabbath derives from an argument a fortiori: If there are less important religious duties that apply both in the Land and abroad, the Sabbath, which is a weighty commandment, all the more so." *Rather, what should be said is this:* "I was referring to 'coming' and 'dwelling'"!

P. *The force of his statement was, first – and furthermore, namely:* "I was referring to 'coming' and 'dwelling,'" *and, furthermore, as to your statement,* "Lo, there is the matter of the Sabbath, concerning which 'dwellings' occurs" *– The matter of the Sabbath derives from an argument a fortiori.*

II.2   A.   *What is at issue between them?*

       B.   *Whether or not they offered libations in the wilderness. R. Ishmael takes the view that* they didn't offer libations in the wilderness, *and R. Aqiba maintains that* they did offer libations in the wilderness.

       C.   *Said Abbayye, "This Tannaite authority of the household of R. Ishmael differs from another Tannaite authority of the household of R. Ishmael, for a Tannaite authority of the household of R. Ishmael [stated],* 'Since there are unspecified "comings" stated in the Torah, but Scripture also has qualified the meaning of one of them, indicating that it refers to the time after the Land was inherited and the people settled down, so all other references are to the period after inheriting and settling down in the Land.'"

       D.   *And as to the other Tannaite authority?*

       E.   *It is because* the rules governing the king and the presentation of first fruits represent two verses of Scripture that go over the same matter, and wherever there are two verses of Scripture that go over the same matter, they do not generate an analogy governing other matters [but the rule is limited to the case].

       F.   *And as to the other Tannaite authority?*

       G.   *Both verses are required to make the same point. For if the All-Merciful had made reference only to the king but not to first fruits, I would have supposed, since in the case of first fruits, the obligation is immediate [upon entry into the Land, prior to settling down], for there is immediate enjoyment of the crop. [So the rule is special to the case.] But if the case of the first fruits were stated and not that of the king, I might have supposed, since the king's nature is to go out and conquer, he has to be appointed immediately on entering the Land, but the obligation to present first fruits comes only when the people will have settled down.*

       H.   *And as to the other Tannaite authority?*

       I.   *Let Scripture specify the case of the king and it would be needless to give the rule for first fruits, for I would have reasoned as follows: If a king, who by nature goes out and conquered, is appointed only after inheriting and settling down in the Land, then how much are first fruits obligatory only when people have inherited and settled down in the land.*

       J.   *And as to the other Tannaite authority?*

       K.   *Had Scripture laid that matter out in such a way, I would have thought that first fruits are governed by the analogy supplied by the dough-offering [which was obligatory as soon as they had entered the Land]. So we are told that that is not the case.*

II.3   A.   *Now that you have taken the position, Every religious duty that is an obligation of the person applies whether in the Land or abroad, [but if it is an obligation that is incumbent upon the soil, it applies only in the land,] then what is the point of "dwelling" that the All-Merciful spelled out in connection with the Sabbath?*

       B.   *It was indeed required. For it might have entered your mind to maintain, since it is written in connection with the passage on festivals, therefore it requires an act of sanctification as do the festivals [which require an act of sanctification of the new month of the month in which they occur, and that is done by a sanhedrin]. So we are informed to the contrary.*

II.4   A.   *And what is the point of "dwelling" that the All-Merciful spelled out in connection with the forbidden fat and blood [at Lev. 3:17]?*

B.   *It was indeed required. For it might have entered your mind to maintain,
      since it is written in connection with the passage on sacrifices, then, so
      long as sacrifices are carried out, the forbidden fat and blood are not to be
      used, but since the sacrifices are not carried out, there is no further
      prohibition. So we are informed to the contrary.*

II.5   A.   *And what is the point of "dwelling" that the All-Merciful spelled out in
            connection with unleavened bread and bitter herbs for Passover [at Ex.
            12:20]?*

       B.   *It was indeed required. For it might have entered your mind to maintain,
            since it is written, "They shall eat the Paschal Lamb with unleavened
            bread and bitter herbs" (Num. 9:11), that pertains only where the
            Passover sacrifice is offered, not otherwise. So we are informed to the
            contrary.*

II.6   A.   *And what is the point of "dwelling" that the All-Merciful spelled out in
            connection with the phylacteries and the firstling of an ass [which are not
            limited to the Land of Israel]?*

       B.   *That is required in connection with that which a Tannaite authority of the
            household of R. Ishmael [stated]:* "Carry out this religious duty, on
            account of which you will enter the Land."

II.7   A.   *Now from the viewpoint that "dwelling" means, wherever you live,
            there are no problems; that is in line with the statement, "And they ate of
            the new produce of the land on the day after the Passover" (Josh.
            5:11). They ate on the day after Passover, but not before, and that proves
            [38A] that the sheaf of first barley was offered and then they ate. But from
            the perspective of him who maintains that "dwelling" means, after the
            inheritance and settling down on the Land, why did they not eat the
            new produce forthwith?*

       B.   *Well, as a matter of fact, they didn't need to, for it is written,* "And the
            children of Israel ate the manna forty years, until they came to a
            land inhabited; they ate the manna until they came to the borders of
            the land of Canaan" (Ex. 16:35). It is not possible to take literally the
            statement, "until they came into the land inhabited," since it is said,
            "until they came to the borders of the land of Canaan." And it is
            not possible to take literally the language, "unto the borders of the
            land of Canaan," since it is said, "until they came to a land
            inhabited." So how hold the two together? Moses died on the
            seventh of Adar, the manna stopped coming down, but they used
            what they had in hand until the sixteenth of Nisan [Freedman: so
            "until they came to a land inhabited" refers to the actual period of
            eating it, but it descended only "until they came to the border,"
            where Moses died].

II.8   A.   *It has further been taught on Tannaite authority:*

       B.   "And the children of Israel ate the manna forty years, until they
            came to a land inhabited; they ate the manna until they came to the
            borders of the land of Canaan" (Ex. 16:35):

       C.   Well, did they really eat it for forty years? Didn't they eat it for
            forty years less thirty days?

       D.   But this is to teach you that they could taste the taste of manna even
            in the cakes that they had brought with them from the land of
            Egypt.

II.9   A.   *It has further been taught on Tannaite authority:*

B.   "On the seventh of Adar, Moses died, and on the seventh of Adar, he was born.

C.   How do we know that on the seventh of Adar, Moses died? "So Moses the servant of the Lord died there" (Deut. 34:5); "And the children of Israel wept for Moses in the plains of Moab thirty days" (Deut. 34:8); "Moses my servant is dead, now therefore arise, go over this Jordan" (Josh. 1:2); "Pass through the midst of the camp and command the people saying, Prepare you food for within three days you are to pass over this Jordan" (Josh. 1:11); "And the people came up out of the Jordan on the tenth day of the first months [Nisan]." Deduct from the tenth of Nisan the prior thirty-three days, and you learn that on the seventh of Adar, Moses died.

D.   How do we know that on the seventh of Adar, he was born?

E.   "And he said to them, I am a hundred and twenty years old this day, I can't go out and come in" (Deut. 31:2) – "this day" is hardly required, so why does Scripture say it? It is to teach you that the Holy One, blessed be He, goes into session and fills out the years of the righteous from day to day and month to month: "The number of your days I will fulfil" (Ex. 23:26) [so he was exactly a hundred and twenty years old when he died, so he was born on that day, too, (Freedman)].

II.10   A.   *It has been taught on Tannaite authority:*

B.   R. Simeon b. Yohai says, "Three religious duties were assigned to Israel when they entered the Land, and they apply both to the Land and abroad:

C.   "And it is logical that they should apply:

D.   "If the consideration of new grain [to be eaten only after the waving of the sheaf of barley on the fifteenth of Nisan], which is not forbidden forever [but only until that rite], and from which it is not forbidden to derive any kind of benefit whatsoever, and from which the prohibition can be raised [through the rite], applies both in the Land of Israel and abroad, then the prohibition of mixed seeds, the prohibition of which is permanent, and the prohibition of which extends to deriving any sort of benefit from the crop, and from which it is not possible to raise the prohibition, surely should apply both in the Land and abroad; and the same logic on two grounds applies also to orlah fruit."

II.11   A.   R. Eleazar b. R. Simeon says, [38B] "Every commandment for which the Israelites became liable before they entered the Land applies in the Land and abroad, and every commandment for which the Israelites became liable only after they came into the Land applies only in the Land, except for the forgiveness of debts, the redemption of fields that have been sold, and the sending forth free of the Hebrew slave in the Seventh Year. For even though they became liable to them only after they had come into the Land, they do apply in the Land and abroad" [T. Qid. 1:12A-C].

II.12   A.   Except for the forgiveness of debts: But that's a personal duty [and applies even before entry into the Land]!

B.   *It had nonetheless to be made articulate because of that which has been taught on Tannaite authority, for it has been taught on Tannaite authority:* Rabbi says, "This is the manner of release: Release [by every creditor of that which he has lent his neighbor' (Deut. 15:2) – it is of two different acts of release that Scripture speaks, one, the release of lands, the other, the release of debts. When you release lands you release debts, and when you do not release lands, you do not release debts."

C.   *But why not say:* In a place in which you have to remit ownership of the land, you release debts, but in a place in which you do not remit ownership of the land, which is to say, abroad, you also do not release debts?

D.   Scripture says, "Because the Lord's release has been proclaimed" (Lev. 25:10) – under all circumstances.

II.13   A.   **The sending forth free of the Hebrew slave in the Seventh Year:** But that's a personal duty [and applies even before entry into the land]!

B.   *It might have entered your mind to think,* since Scripture states, "and you shall proclaim liberty throughout the Land," that requirement applies only in the Land but not abroad; therefore Scripture says, "It is a jubilee" – under all circumstances.

C.   Then why does Scripture make reference to "the Land"?

D.   When the emancipation of slaves applies in the Land, it applies abroad; when it does not apply in the Land, it does not apply abroad.

II.14   A.   *We have learned in the Mishnah:* [Consumption] in any locale [of] new produce, that is, that on behalf of which the omer has not yet been offered, is forbidden by Scripture. And the [prohibition against eating produce which is] orlah [that is, deriving from fruit trees in the first three years of their growth] applies outside of the Land of Israel] by law. And [the prohibition against planting together] diverse kinds [in a vineyard applies outside of the Land of Israel] by authority of the scribes [M. Orl. 3:9Kff.].

B.   [With reference to the clause, **and the [prohibition against eating produce which is] orlah [applies outside of the Land of Israel] by law],** *what is the meaning of* by law?

C.   Said R. Judah said Samuel, "It means, a law practiced in the province [as matter of local custom]."

D.   Ulla said R. Yohanan [said], "It is a law given to Moses at Sinai."

E.   *Said Ulla to R. Judah, "From my perspective, in maintaining that* it is a law given to Moses at Sinai, *there is no problem in distinguishing between orlah that is subject to doubt and mixed seeds' produce that is subject to doubt, in line with what we have learned in the Mishnah:* [Fruit about which there is] a doubt [whether or not it is in the status] of orlah – [if it is] in the Land of Israel [the fruit in question] is forbidden [deemed to have the status of orlah]. But in Syria [the fruit] is permitted [not in the status of orlah]. And outside of the Land [of Israel], one may go down [to the orchard] and purchase [such fruit], provided that he does not see him [the seller] pick [the fruit] [M. Orl. 3:9A-D], *while with respect to mixed seeds, we have learned in the Mishnah:* [As to] a vineyard which was planted with vegetables [which are of diverse kinds], and outside of [this vineyard] vegetables [of like kinds] are sold – [if it is] in the Land

of Israel [the produce] is forbidden [under the law of diverse
kinds]. But in Syria, it is permitted. And outside of the Land [of
Israel], one may go down and buy [this produce], provided that he
[the Israelite] does not pick [it] with his hand [M. Orl. 3:9F-J]. *But,
by contrast, from your perspective,* [39A] *the Tannaite formulation should
present in both cases:* Either this party [the Israelite] may enter the
field and make a purchase, or that party [the gentile] may enter the
field and gather the produce [since produce in both classifications
falls into the same classification, neither one resting on the law of
the Torah]."

F. *Well, didn't Samuel say to R. Anan, "Repeat as the Tannaite formulation:
'Either this party* [the Israelite] *may enter the field and make a
purchase, or that party* [the gentile] *may enter the field and gather
the produce'?"*

G. *Mar b. Rabana repeated this rule to yield a lenient result:* "Either this
party [the Israelite] may enter the field and make a purchase, or that
party [the gentile] may enter the field and gather the produce,
provided that he [the Israelite] does not pick [it] with his hand."

II.15 A. *Said Levi to Samuel, "Your eminence, provide me with produce that may
or may not be orlah fruit and I'll eat it."*

B. *R. Avayya and Rabbah bar R. Hanan supplied one another with produce
that may or may not be orlah fruit.*

C. *Say the sharpest wits in Pumbedita,* "The prohibition of orlah produce
does not apply outside of the Land of Israel."

D. *R. Judah sent word to R. Yohanan reporting this ruling, to which he sent
word in reply,* "Shut away the rule governing produce that may or may
not be orlah fruit, suppress the rule as it concerns produce that certainly
are orlah fruit, and announce that produce in this classification must be
stored away and not eaten. And whoever takes the view, the prohibition
of orlah produce does not apply outside of the Land of Israel – may
he have no children or grandchildren 'that shall cast the line by lot
in the congregation of the Lord' (Mic. 2:5)."

E. *Well, then, in accord with which authority do the sharpest wits in
Pumbedita make their decision?*

F. *They make their ruling in accord with the following, which has been
taught on Tannaite authority:* R. Eleazar b. R. Yosé says in the name
of R. Yosé b. Durmasqah, who made the statement in the name of
R. Yosé the Galilean, who made the statement in the name of R.
Yohanan b. Nuri, who made the statement in the name of R.
Eliezer the Elder: "The prohibition of orlah produce does not
apply outside of the Land of Israel [T. Orl. 1:8P]."

G. *Isn't there now! And haven't we learned in the Mishnah:* R. Eliezer
says, "Also: Except for [the prohibition against eating] new
[produce before the omer is waved on the sixteenth of Nisan]
(Lev. 23:14)"?

H. *Repeat the Tannaite formulation as:* Except for the prohibition against
eating new produce.

II.16 A. Said R. Assi said R. Yohanan, "The prohibition of orlah produce
abroad derives from a law revealed to Moses at Sinai."

B. *Said R. Zira to R. Assi, "But haven't we learned in the Mishnah:* [Fruit
about which there is] a doubt [whether or not it is in the status] of

orlah – [if it is] in the Land of Israel [the fruit in question] is forbidden [deemed to have the status of orlah]. But in Syria [the fruit] is permitted [not in the status of orlah]. And outside of the Land [of Israel], one may go down [to the orchard] and purchase [such fruit], provided that he does not see him [the seller] pick [the fruit] [M. Orl. 3:9A-D]?"

C. *He was struck dumb for the moment, but then he said to him,* "Maybe this is how the law was formulated: Produce that may or may not be subject to the prohibition of orlah is permitted in the diaspora; produce that certainly is orlah fruit is forbidden."

II.17 A. Said R. Assi said R. Yohanan, "By the ruling of the Torah, violators of the prohibition of mixed seeds [in the exile] are flogged."

B. *Said to him R. Eleazar b. R. Yosé,* "But lo, we have learned in the Mishnah: And [the prohibition against planting together] diverse kinds [in a vineyard applies outside of the Land of Israel] by authority of the scribes [M. Orl. 3:9M]?"

C. *No problem, the one speaks of mixed seeds in a vineyard, the other speaks of grafting heterogeneous trees.*

D. *That accords with Samuel, for* said Samuel, "Scripture states, 'You shall keep my statutes...' (Lev. 19:19), meaning 'the statutes that I have already ordained for you,' hence: 'You shall not let your cattle breed with a diverse kind; you shall not sow your field with mixed seed' (Lev. 19:19). Just as for your beast, the prohibition is against hybridization, so in respect to your field, the prohibition is against hybridization. Just as the prohibition applies to your beast whether in the Land or outside of the Land, so with respect to your field, the prohibition applies whether it is in the Land or outside of the Land."

E. *But isn't the word "your field" written [meaning, what belongs to you alone, hence in the Land of Israel]?*

F. *That serves to exclude from the prohibition the planting of mixed seeds outside of the Land of Israel.*

II.18 A. *R. Hanan and R. Anan were engaged in discussion and walking along the way. They saw someone sowing mixed seeds together. He said to him,* "Well, will the master join me in excommunicating him?"

B. *He said to him,* "You don't see this matter clearly."

C. *Then again they saw someone who was sowing wheat and barley among vines. He said to him,* "Well, the master join me in excommunicating him?"

D. *He said to him,* "Don't we accept as established what R. Josiah said, for he said, 'The law of diverse kinds is not violated unless one has sowed a wheat seed, barley seed, and grape kernel, with one and the same throw'?"

II.19 A. *R. Joseph would mix seeds and sow them. Said to him Abbayye,* "But haven't we learned in the Mishnah, And [the prohibition against planting together] diverse kinds [in a vineyard applies outside of the Land of Israel] by authority of the scribes [M. Orl. 3:9M]?"

B. *He said to him,* "No problem, the rule just cited speaks of mixed seeds in the vineyard, but what I'm doing is mixing seeds. Mixed seeds in the vineyard, of which all benefit, are forbidden by the authority of rabbis

outside of the Land; mixing other seeds, of which in the Land benefit is not
forbidden, is not forbidden by the rule of rabbis outside of the Land."

C. *But then R. Joseph retracted, saying, "What I said is nonsense. For Rab*
sowed the garden patches for the household of Rab in separate beds. How
come? Obviously, to avoid mixing seeds."

D. *Said to him Abbayye, "Well, there is no problem if we had in hand the*
tradition that [39B], he sowed four distinct species on four sides of
the bed and one in the middle [thus keeping the species distinct].
But here, he did so only because it would look pretty or to save work for the
worker."

I.1-2 explain the meaning of the Mishnah sentence's language, and
No. 2 moves on to discover the scriptural foundations for the stated rule.
II.1-2 clarify the intent of the dispute in the Mishnah. In the context of
the discussion of No. 2, Nos. 3-7, with an appendix at Nos. 8-9 then take
up the conclusion concerning the sense of the Mishnah language that I.1
established, which certainly proves that the entire, huge composite is in
fact a composition worked out under uniform auspices and for a single
purpose. Nos. 10-11, with its talmud at Nos. 13, 14 then proceed to
Tannaite complements. Following the familiar logic of the document,
Nos. 15-17, ending up with concrete cases at Nos. 18-19, move on to the
intersecting rules pertinent to our Mishnah problem.

III. The Exegetical Programs of Yerushalmi and of the Babli Compared

1:8 I Scriptural basis for the rule of the Mishnah.	1:9 I.1 Clarification of the meaning of the Mishnah's word choices.
1:8 II As above.	1:9 I.2 Scriptural basis for the rule of the Mishnah.
	1:9 II.1 Speculative question on the intent of a statement in the Mishnah: Is it for a strict or a lenient ruling?
	1:9 II.2-7 Continuation of foregoing.
	1:9 II.8-10 Topical appendix tacted on to the foregoing.
	1:9 II.11 Tannaite complement to the Mishnah rule.
	1:9 I.II.12-13 Talmud to the foregoing.
	1:9 I.II.14 Intersecting Mishnah rule analyzed in its own terms.

1:9 II.15 Story relevant to foregoing.

1:9 II 16 Continuation of the problem of II.14.

1:9 II.17 Secondary problem attached to foregoing.

1:9 II.18 Case illustrative of foregoing.

1:9 II.19 As above.

The one possible point of comparison is at the scriptural proof, to which we turn forthwith:

[I.A] It is written, "These are the statutes and ordinances that you shall be careful to do in the land that the Lord, the God of your fathers, has given you to possess, all the days that you live upon the earth]" (Deut. 12:1).

[B] In the Land you are obligated to do them, but you are not obligated abroad.

[C] To this point we rule that commandments that depend upon the Land apply only in the Land. Is it possible to maintain that even commandments that do not depend upon the Land should apply also only in the Land?

[D] Scripture states, "Take heed lest your heart be deceived, [and you turn aside and serve other gods and worship them,] and the anger of the Lord be kindled against you" (Deut. 11:16).

[E] "You shall therefore lay up these words of mine in your heart and in your soul"

I.2 A. *What is the scriptural basis for that rule?*

B. *It is in line with what our rabbis have taught on Tannaite authority:*

C. ["These are the laws and rules that you must carefully observe to do in the land that the Lord, God of your fathers, is giving you to possess, as long as you live on earth. You must destroy all the sites at which the nations you are to dispossess worshiped their gods, whether on lofty mountains and on hills or under any luxuriant tree. Tear down their altars, smash their pillars, put their sacred posts to the fire, and cut down the images of their gods, obliterating their name from that site" (Deut. 12:1-3)]:

D. "These are the laws":

E. This refers to the midrash exegeses.

F. "And rules":

G. These are the laws.

H. "...That you must

(Deut. 11:18).

[F] Even when you are exiles, "You shall therefore bind up these words of mine upon your heart and in your soul. "

[G] [Since the cited verse reads, "And you shall bind them as a sign upon your hands and they shall be as frontlets between your eyes, and you shall teach them to your children" (Deut. 11:18),] what do you derive from the verse? It is, for example, putting on phylacteries and studying Torah.

[H] Accordingly, just as putting on phylacteries and studying Torah, which do not depend upon being in the Land, apply both in the Land and abroad, so also every matter that does not depend upon being in the Land should apply both in the Land and abroad.

[I] If that is so, then when they are redeemed they should be exempt [from doing them].

[J] It is written, "And all the assembly of those who had returned from the captivity made booths and dwelt in the booths, for from the days of Jeshua the son of Nun to that day the people of Israel had not done so. And there was very great rejoicing" (Neh. 8:17).

carefully observe":

I. This refers to studying.

J. "...To do":

K. This refers to doing the deeds.

L. "...In the land [that the Lord, God of your fathers, is giving you to possess, as long as you live on earth]":

M. Might one suppose that all of the religious duties without exception pertain abroad?

N. Scripture says, "To do in the land."

O. Might one suppose that all of the religious duties without exception pertain solely in the land [and not abroad]?

P. Scripture says, "...As long as you live on earth."

Q. After Scripture has stated matters in encompassing language, Scripture has further stated matters in limiting language, on which account we learn from the stated context.

R. In context, it is stated, "You must destroy all the sites at which the nations you are to dispossess worshiped their gods."

S. Just as the matter of idolatry is singular in that it is a religious duty pertaining to one's person and not dependent upon one's being situated in the Land, thus pertaining both in the

> Land and also abroad,
> so all religious duties
> that are incumbent
> upon the person and
> do not depend upon
> one's being located in
> the Land apply both
> in the Land and
> abroad [Sifré Deut.
> LIX:I.1-2].

Even where the two Talmuds appeal to the same prooftexts for the same purpose, they still pursue distinct paths; the Bavli's materials, deriving from Sifré to Deuteronomy, take their own direction, incidentally making the point that is besought. So here the two Talmuds say pretty much the same thing, appeal to the same prooftext, and yet manage not to intersect in any substantive way.

For our purpose, it is the simple fact that the Bavli is not second to the Yerushalmi and does not depend upon the prior Talmud; it makes its own statement in its own way, here choosing what its framers preferred to make the point they wished to make – in preference to the Yerushalmi's manner of making the same point with the same materials (if the Bavli's framers knew the Yerushalmi's proof at all). Once more, the Talmuds differ because they're different. And the difference is, the Bavli's sages in no way considered themselves bound by the Yerushalmi's program, sources, or initiatives (if they knew them to begin with).

9

Mishnah-Tractate Qiddushin 1:9 in the Yerushalmi and the Bavli

Y. 1:9 = B. 1:10A-D

A. Whoever does a single commandment – they do well for him and lengthen his days.

B. And he inherits the Land.

C. And whoever does not do a single commandment – they do not do well for him and do not lengthen his days.

D. And he does not inherit the Land.

E. Whoever has learning in Scripture, Mishnah, and right conduct will not quickly sin,

F. since it is said, "And a threefold cord is not quickly broken" (Qoh. 4:12).

G. And whoever does not have learning in Scripture, Mishnah, and right conduct has no share in society.

I. Mishnah Qiddushin 1:9 in the Talmud of the Land of Israel

[I.A] Lo, whoever sits and does not commit a transgression – they pay him a reward like that of him who does a commandment [M. Mak. 3:15].

[B] And you say this [that one must do it]?

[C] But thus do we interpret the matter: [It speaks of a case in which one has] an even number [of credits and debits, in which case, by doing a single commandment, he is given the additional credit he needs to incline the balance in his favor].

[D] Whoever does a single commandment – they do well for him and lengthen his days and his years, and he inherits the Land [M. Qid. 1:10A-B].

[E] And whoever commits a single transgression – they do ill to him and cut off his days, and he does not inherit the Land [T. Qid. 1:13].

[II.A] There we have learned, Lo, whoever sits and does not commit a transgression – they pay him a reward like that of him who does a commandment.

[B] Said R. Zeira, "This speaks of someone who had the opportunity to do something that may or may not be a transgression, and who did not do it."

[C] Said R. Yosé b. R. Bun, "This speaks of someone who designated for himself a given religious duty and never in his life transgressed it."

[D] What would be examples of such a thing?

[E] Said R. Mar Uqban, "For example, honoring father and mother."

[F] Said R. Mana, "'Blessed are those whose way is blameless, who walk in the law of the Lord' (Ps. 119:1). [They are] like those who walk in the law of the Lord."

[G] Said R. Abun, "'Who also do no wrong, but walk in his ways.' It is as if they walk in his ways."

[H] R. Yosé b. R. Bun, "What is the meaning of the following verse of Scripture: 'Blessed is the man who walks not in the counsel of the wicked' (Ps. 1:1)? Since he did not walk in the counsel of the wicked, it is as if he walked in the council of the righteous."

[I] Ben Azzai interpreted the following verse: "'Dead flies make the perfumer's ointment give off an evil odor' (Qoh. 10:1).

[J] "Now will a single dead fly not make the perfumer's ointment give off an evil odor? [Of course it will.] Now this one, because he did a single sin, he has lost all the merit that was in his possession."

[K] So did R. Aqiba interpret the following verse: " 'Therefore Sheol has enlarged its appetite and opened its mouth beyond measure' (Isa. 5:14).

[L] "'Beyond measures' is not written here, but rather, 'beyond measure.' This may be compared to a person who did not have in his hand a single religious duty to incline the balance in his favor."

[M] What you say applies to the world to come. But as to this world, even if 999 angels argue against him and a single angel argues for him, the Holy One, blessed be He, inclines the balance in his favor.

[N] And what is the scriptural basis for that statement?

[O] "If there be for him an angel, a mediator, one of the thousand, to declare to man what is right for him; and he is gracious to him, and says, 'Deliver him from going down into the pit, I have found a ransom' (Job 33:23-24)."

[P] Said R. Yohanan, "If you hear a teaching of R. Eliezer, son of R. Yosé the Galilean, incline your ear like a water clock and listen carefully."

[Q] For R. Yohanan said, "R. Eliezer, son of R. Yosé the Galilean, says, 'Even if 999 angels argue against a person, and a single angel argues in his favor, the Holy One, blessed be He, inclines the scales in his favor.'

[R] "And that is not the end of the matter as to that angel. But even if 999 aspects of the argument of that single angel argue against a man, but a single aspect of his case of that single angel argues in favor, the Holy One, blessed be He, still inclines the scales in favor of the accused."

[S] What is the scriptural basis for that statement? "'If there be for him an angel.' One of the thousand" is not written, but rather "one part of the thousand," meaning one-thousandth of the aspects of the arguments of that single angel.

[T] What is written immediately following? "And he is gracious to him and says. 'Deliver him from going down into the pit, I have found a ransom.'"

[U] "Deliver him" through the atonement of suffering.

[V] "I have found a ransom"– he has found a ransom for himself.

[W] What you have said applies in this world, but as to the world to come, if the man has a larger measure of merits, he inherits the Garden of Eden, and if he has a larger measure of transgressions, he inherits Gehenna.

[X] If they were equally balanced?

[Y] R. Yosé b. Haninah said, "forgiving sin" (Mic. 7:18).

[Z] R. Abbahu said, "It is written, 'forgiving' (Mic. 7:18)."

[AA] What does the Holy One, blessed be He, do?

[BB] He snatches one of his bad deeds, so that his good deeds outweigh the balance.

[CC] Said R. Eleazar, "'To thee, O Lord, belongs steadfast love, for thou dost requite a man according to his work' (Ps. 62:12).

[DD] "And if he has no works you give them to him out of your own store."

[EE] That is the opinion of R. Eleazar, for R. Eleazar said "'Abundant in mercy' (Ex. 34:6) teaches that he inclines the scale in favor of mercy."

[III.A] R. Jeremiah said R. Samuel b. Isaac raised the question, "'Righteousness guards him whose way is upright, but sin overthrows the wicked' (Prov. 13:6).

[B] "'Misfortune pursues sinners, but prosperity rewards the righteous' (Prov. 13:21).

[C] "'He will guard the feet of his faithful ones, but the wicked shall be cut off in darkness' (1 Sam. 2:9).

[D] "'Toward the scorners he is scornful, but to the humble he shows favor. The wise will inherit honor, but fools exalt disgrace' (Prov. 3:34-35).

[E] "Now is it possible that they build up the fence and lock the gates [so that the Holy One helps the sinner to sin]?

[F] "It is thus, that they build up the fence and lock the gate."

[G] But thus did R. Jeremiah say in the name of R. Samuel bar R. Isaac, "[If] a man keeps himself from transgression one time, then a second and a third time, the Holy One, blessed be He, keeps him from transgressing further; as it is said, 'Behold, God does all these things twice, three times, with a man, to bring his soul from the pit, that he may see the light of life' (Job 33:29)."

[H] Said R. Zeira, "And that is on condition that the man not go back upon himself and repeat what he has done: 'A threefold cord is not broken forever' (Qoh. 4:12) is not written, but rather 'A threefold cord is not quickly broken.' But if you apply pressure to it, it will snap."

[I] R. Huna in the name of R. Abbahu: "The Holy One, blessed be He – before him there [truly] is no such thing as forgetting. But it is as if, on account of Israel, he becomes forgetful, for it is said, 'Who is a God like thee, forgiving sin, and passing over transgression, for the remnant of his inheritance?' (Mic. 7:18). "

[J]   It is written Ns' [i.e., forgetting sin].

[K]   And so David said, "You did forgive the iniquity of your people; you did pardon all their sin. Selah" (Ps. 85:2).

The Talmud compares the Mishnah's view with that elsewhere, unit I, then richly glosses the cited passage, unit II. I assume that unit III is inserted because III.H refers to a verse also cited in the Mishnah.

II. Mishnah Qiddushin 1:9 in the Talmud of Babylonia

1:10A-D

A.   Whoever does a single commandment – they do well for him and lengthen his days.

B.   And he inherits the Land.

C.   And whoever does not do a single commandment – they do not do well for him and do not lengthen his days.

D.   And he does not inherit the Land.

I.1   A.   *By way of contradiction:* These are things the benefit of which a person enjoys in this world, while the principal remains for him in the world to come: [Deeds in] honor of father and mother, [performance of] righteous deeds, and [acts which] bring peace between a man and his fellow. But the study of Torah is as important as all of them together [M. Pe. 1:1C-E]. [Freedman: Thus only for these is one reward in this world, while the Mishnah says that that is so of any precept.]

      B.   *Said R. Judah, "This is the sense of the matter:* Whoever does a single commandment – over and above the advantaged deriving from his inherited merits – they do well for him, and he is as though he had carried out the entire Torah."

      C.   *Then does it follow that for these other deeds, one is rewarded even for a single one [with no other deeds to one's credit]?*

      D.   Said R. Shemaiah, "It is to say that if there is an equal balance, then that one deed tips the scale in his favor."

I.2   A.   *But is it really true that* if there is an equal balance, then that one deed tips the scale in his favor? *And by way of contradiction:* In the case of anyone whose merits are more than his sins, they punish him, and it is as though he had burned the entire Torah, leaving of it not even a single letter, and whoever's sins outnumber his merits – they do good for him, and it is as though he observed the entire Torah, and did not leave out a single letter of it [so he gets his reward in this world and suffers in the world to come]?

      B.   *Said Abbayye, "The Mishnah paragraph before us means, they make for him a happy day and a miserable day"* [Freedman: the Mishnah means he is punished in this world, the punishment being a happy day for him, since he thereby wholly enjoys the next].

      C.   *Raba said, "Lo, who is the authority behind this ruling? It is R. Jacob, who has said, 'There is no reward in this world for carrying out the religious duties. For it has been taught on Tannaite authority:* R. Jacob says, "You have not got a single religious duty that is written in the

Torah, the reward of which is not specified alongside, that does not depend for its fulfillment on the resurrection of the dead. For example, with reference to honor of father and mother, it is written, 'That your days may be prolonged and that it may go well with you' (Deut. 5:16); with regard to sending forth the dam out of the nest: 'That it may be well with you and that you may prolong your days' (Deut. 22:6). Now, if someone's father said to him, 'Climb up into the loft and bring me the pigeons,' and he went up to the loft, sent away the dam and took the young, and climbing down, fell and was killed – what are we to make of this one's 'happiness' and 'length of days'"? But the language, "in order that it may be well with you" refers to a day that is wholly good; and "in order that your days may be long" means, on the day that is entirely long.'"

D.   *But maybe such a thing never really happened?*

E.   *R. Jacob saw such an incident.*

F.   *Well, maybe the victim was thinking about doing a sin [at the time of the accident].*

G.   A wicked thought the Holy One blessed be He does not join with a virtuous deed.

H.   *Well, maybe the victim was thinking about idolatry [at the time of the accident,] and it is written, "That I may take the house of Israel in their own heart" (Ezek. 14:5)?*

I.   *That is precisely what he meant to say: "If you ever imagine that the reward of a religious duty comes in this world, then how come keeping the religious duties didn't protect him from being led to such wicked meditations?"*

J.   But lo, said R. Eleazar, "Those who are engaged in carrying out a religious duty are not harmed."

K.   *There, while they are en route to carry out the religious duty, it is different [but here, he was climbing back down, having done the duty].*

L.   But lo, said R. Eleazar, "Those who are engaged in carrying out a religious duty are not harmed – coming or going."

M.   *It was a rickety ladder, so the possibility of an accident was ready at hand, and wherever the possibility of accident is ready at hand, there is no relying on miracles, for it is written, "And Samuel said, how can I go? if Saul hears it, he'll kill me" (1 Sam. 16:2).*

I.3   A.   *Said R. Joseph, "If the Apostate [Elisha b. Abbuya] had interpreted this verse of Scripture in the way that R. Jacob, the son of his daughter, did, he would never have fallen into sin."*

B.   *So what's the story with the Apostate?*

C.   *There are those who say that he saw an incident like this one, and there are those who say, he saw the tongue of Huspit the Interpreter being dragged by a pig. He said, "Should the tongue that brought forth pearls lick the dust?" He apostatized and so sinned.*

I.4   A.   *R. Tobi bar R. Qisna contrasted for Raba the following rules: "We have learned in the Mishnah,* **whoever does a single commandment – they do well for him.** *So if he does it, that is so, but if not, not, and by contrast: If one sits and does not transgress, they give him a reward like that going to one who does a religious duty!"*

B.   *He said to him, "The latter speaks of a case in which* an opportunity to sin comes to hand and he is saved from it."

C.   *It is like the case of R. Hanina bar Pappi, whom a certain Roman lady propositioned. He said something that brought up boils and scabs over his whole body. She did something that healed him. He ran away and hid in a bathhouse where, even if two people came in together, even by day, they would suffer harm [from the local demon, but he wasn't injured]. The next day, the rabbis said to him, "So who protected you?"*

D.   He said to them, "Two [40A] of Caesar's armor bearers guarded me all night long."

E.   They said to him, "Maybe you had a chance to score and you were saved from it? *For we have learned as a Tannaite statement:* Whoever has a chance to score and is saved from it – they do a miracle for him."

I.5 A.   "Bless you the Lord, you messengers of his, you mighty in strength, who fulfil his word, obeying the voice of his word" (Ps. 103:20): For example, R. Sadoq and his companions.

B.   *A Roman lady propositioned R. Sadoq. He said to her, "I feel faint and I can't do it, maybe you've got something to eat?"*

C.   *She said to him, "Well, there's something unclean."*

D.   *He said to her, "So what conclusion am I supposed to draw, that someone who does this sin can eat that?"*

E.   *She was lighting the oven to put the meat in it, but he went and sat in the oven. She said to him, "So what's going on?"*

F.   *He said to her, "Someone who does this [act you want of me is so punished that he] falls into that [oven]."*

G.   *She said to him, "If I'd known it was such a big deal for you guys, I wouldn't have bothered you."*

I.6 A.   *R. Kahana was selling baskets. A certain Roman lady propositioned him. He said to her, "I'll go and get ready." He went up to the roof and threw himself down, but Elijah came along and caught him.*

B.   *He said to him, "You made me rush four hundred parasangs to do this!"*

C.   *He said to him, "So what made it happen? Isn't it poverty [that makes me go sell baskets to women]?"*

D.   *He gave him a basketful of denars.*

I.7 A.   *Raba pointed out to R. Nahman the following contrast: "We have learned in the Mishnah:* **These are things the benefit of which a person enjoys in this world, while the principal remains for him in the world to come: [Deeds in] honor of father and mother, [performance of] righteous deeds, and [acts which] bring peace between a man and his fellow. But the study of Torah is as important as all of them together [M. Pe. 1:1C-E].** And with respect to honor of parents, it is written, 'That your days may be long and that it may go well with you' (Deut. 5:16); of performance of righteous deeds: 'He who pursues righteousness and loving kindness finds life, righteousness, and honor' (Prov. 21:21). As to bringing peace, it is said, 'Seek peace and pursue it' (Ps. 34:15), and said R. Abbahu, 'We learn by verbal analogy the meaning of pursuing in two distinct passage; here, 'Seek peace and pursue it,' and elsewhere, 'He who pursues after righteousness and loving kindness' (Prov. 21:21). As to study of the Torah: 'For that is your life and the length of your days' (Deut. 30:20). But as to sending forth the dam from the nest it is written, 'That it may be well with you and that you may prolong your days' (Deut. 22:7). *So why not add this item to the list?"*

B.   *"The Tannaite authority has left out some appropriate items."*

C.   *"Yes, but he's used the language,* **These** [in particular] **are things,** *and you maintain,* **The** *Tannaite authority has left out some appropriate items!?"*

D.   *Said Raba, "R. Idi explained it to me in these terms:* "'Say you of the righteous when he is good that they shall eat the fruit of their doings" (Isa. 3:10) – so is there a righteous man who is good and a righteous man who isn't? But he who is good to Heaven and good to people is a righteous man who is good, but good to Heaven and not good to human beings – that's a righteous person who's not good. So too: "Woe to the wicked man who is evil, for the reward of his hands shall be given to him" (Isa. 3:11) – so is there a wicked person who is wicked and a wicked person who isn't? But one who is wicked to Heaven and wicked to people is a wicked person who is wicked; and one who is wicked to Heaven but not wicked to people is a wicked person who is not wicked.'"

I.8   A.   Merit has both principal and interest: "Say you of the righteous when he is good that they shall eat the fruit of their doings" (Isa. 3:10).

B.   Wickedness has principal but no interest: "Woe to the wicked man who is evil, for the reward of his hands shall be given to him" (Isa. 3:11).

C.   So how do I interpret the language, "Therefore shall the wicked eat of the fruit of their own way and be filled with their own devices" (Prov. 1:31)?

D.   A transgression that produces results has results, but one that does not produce results has no results.

I.9   A.   Good intention joins with deeds: "Then they that feared the Lord spoke with one another, and the Lord listened and heard and a book of remembrance was written before him for those who feared the Lord and who thought about his name" (Mal. 3:16).

B.   *What is the meaning of* and who thought about his name?

C.   Said R. Assi, "Even if a person has given thought to doing a religious duty but was prevented from doing it, Scripture credits him as though he had done it."

D.   As to bad intention, the Holy One does not join it together with a deed, as it is said, "If I regarded iniquity in my heart, the Lord would not hear" (Ps. 66:18).

E.   Then how do I interpret the verse, "Lo, I bring evil upon this people, even the fruit of their intentions" (Jer. 6:19)?

F.   In the case of intention that bears fruit the Holy One, blessed be He, combines the intention with action; in the case of intention that does not bear fruit, the Holy One, blessed be He, does not join intention with action.

G.   Then how do I interpret the verse, "That I may take the house of Israel in their own heart" (Ezek. 14:5)?

H.   *Said R. Aha bar Jacob, "That is written with reference to idolatry. For* a master has said, 'The sin of idolatry is so weighty that one who denies idolatry is as though he had confessed to the entirety of the whole Torah.'"

I.   *Ulla said, "It is in line with what R. Huna said, for* said R. Huna, 'Once a man has committed a transgression and gone and repeated it, it is permitted to him.'"

J.   "It is permitted to him" – *can you possibly imagine it?*

K.   Rather: "It is treated as though it were permitted."

I.10   A.   Said R. Abbahu in the name of R. Hanina, "It is better for someone to transgress in private but not profane the Name of Heaven in public: 'As for you, house of Israel, thus says the Lord God: Go, serve every one his idols, and hereafter also, if you will not obey me; but my holy name you shall not profane' (Ezek. 20:39)."

       B.   Said R. Ilai the Elder, "If someone sees that his impulse to sin is overpowering him, he should go somewhere where nobody knows him and put on ordinary clothing and cloak himself in ordinary clothing and do what he wants, but let him not profane the Name of Heaven by a public scandal."

       C.   *Is that so now! And hasn't it been taught on Tannaite authority: Whoever has no concern for the honor owing to his Creator is worthy of not having come into the world. And what would be such a case?* Rabbah says, "This refers to someone who stares at a rainbow." R. Joseph says, "This refers to someone who commits a transgression in secret."

       D.   *There is no contradiction, the one speaks of a case in which he can control his urge, the other, a case in which he cannot control his urge.*

I.11   A.   *We have learned in the Mishnah there:* They do not allow credit in connection with profaning the name of God, whether it was done unwittingly or intentionally. *What is the meaning of* they do not allow credit?

       B.   Said Mar Zutra, "They don't keep books like a shopkeeper [and give credit; they exact the penalty immediately]."

       C.   Mar b. Rabana said, "It is to say that if one's account of sin and merit is in balance, then profaning God's name tips the scale."

I.12   A.   *Our rabbis have taught on Tannaite authority:*

       B.   **One should always [40B] see himself as if he is half meritorious and half guilty. If he did a single commandment, happy is he, for he has inclined the balance for himself to the side of merit. If he committed a single transgression, woe is he, for he has inclined the balance to the side of guilt. Concerning this one it is said, "One sinner destroys much good" (Qoh. 9:18), for on account of a single sin that he commits, much good is lost to him.**

       C.   R. Eleazar b. R. Simeon says, "For the world is judged by the conduct of the majority in it, and an individual is judged by the majority of the deeds that he has done; if he did a single commandment, happy is he, for he has inclined the balance for himself and for the world as well to the side of merit. If he committed a single transgression, woe is he, for he has inclined the balance to the side of guilt for himself and for the world, for it is said, 'One sinner destroys much good' (Qoh. 9:18) – for on account of a single sin that he commits, much good is lost to him and to the whole world."

D. R. Simeon b. Yohai says, "If a man was righteous his entire life but at the end he rebelled, he loses the whole, for it is said, 'The righteousness of the righteous shall not deliver him in the day of his transgression' (Ezek. 33:12). And even if one is completely wicked all his life but repents at the end, he is not reproached with his wickedness, for it is said, 'And as for the wickedness of the wicked, he shall not fall thereby in the day that he turns from his wickedness' (Ezek. 33:12)" [T. Qid. 1:13-15].

E. Well, why not regard the case of the righteous one who rebels at the end as one that is half transgression and half merit?

F. *Said R. Simeon b. Laqish, "It is a case of his regretting his former, good deeds."*

I.1+2-3, 4 work out the expected interest in intersecting Mishnah rulings. A sequence of thematically pertinent compositions form a large composite as an appendix, Nos. 5-6. Once the secondary materials are added, Nos. 7+8-12 then bring us to a secondary expansion on the intersecting Mishnah passage cited at the outset, another example of the closely woven character of the composite.

1:10E-G

E. Whoever has learning in Scripture, Mishnah, and right conduct will not quickly sin,

F. since it is said, "And a threefold cord is not quickly broken" (Qoh. 4:12).

G. And whoever does not have learning in Scripture, Mishnah, and right conduct has no share in society.

I.1 A. Said R. Eliezer bar Sadoq, "To what are the righteous compared in this world? To a tree that is standing in a clean place, with its foliage extending from it to an unclean place. What do people say? 'Cut off the foliage from the tree so that the whole of it may be clean, as is its character.'

B. "Thus the Holy One, blessed be He, brings suffering upon the righteous in this world so that they will inherit the world to come: 'And though your beginning is small, yet the latter end shall greatly increase' (Job 8:7).

C. "To what are the wicked compared in this world? To a tree that is standing in an unclean place, with its foliage extending from it to a clean place. What do people say? 'Cut off the foliage from the tree, so that the whole of it may be unclean, as is its character' [Abot deR. Nathan XXXIX.X.1].

D. "Thus the Holy One, blessed be He, brings prosperity on the wicked in this world, so as to destroy them and throw them out to the nethermost rung: 'There is a way that seems right to man, but at the end of it are the ways of death' (Prov. 14:12)."

I.2 A. Once R. Tarfon and the elders were reclining at a banquet in the upper room of the house of Nitezeh in Lud. This question was raised for them: "Is study greater or is action greater?"

B. T. Tarfon responded: "Action is greater."

C.   R. Aqiba responded: "Study is greater."

D.   All responded, saying, "Study is greater, for study brings about action."

I.3   A.   *It has been taught on Tannaite authority:*

B.   R. Yosé says, "Great is study, for it preceded the commandment to separate dough-offering by forty years, the commandments governing priestly rations and tithes by fifty-four years, the commandments covering remission of debts by sixty-one years, the commandment concerning the Jubilee year by one hundred and three years." [Freedman: The Torah was given to Israel two months after the Exodus from Egypt, but liability to dough-offering came into force forty years later, and so throughout.]

C.   ...One hundred and three years? *But it was a hundred and four.*

D.   *He takes the view that* the Jubilee effects the release of slaves and land at the outset.

E.   And just as study of the Torah came prior to the actual practice of it, so judgment on that account takes precedence over judgment concerning practice of the Torah.

F.   *That accords with R. Hamnuna, for* said R. Hamnuna, "The beginning of a person's judgment comes with the issue of study of Torah, for it is said, 'The beginning of judgment concerns the letting out of water' (Prov. 17:14) [and water stands for Torah]."

G.   And just as judgment concerning study takes priority over judgment concerning practice, so, too, the reward for studying the Torah takes priority over the reward for practice: "And he gave them the lands and nations, and they took the labor of the people in possession, that they might keep his statutes and observe his laws" (Ps. 105:44-45).

II.1   A.   **And whoever does not have learning in Scripture, Mishnah, and right conduct has no share in society:**

B.   Said R. Yohanan, "And he is invalid to give testimony."

II.2   A.   *Our rabbis have taught on Tannaite authority:*

B.   He who eats out in the marketplace – lo, he is like a dog.

C.   And there are those who say, "He is invalid to give testimony."

D.   Said R. Idi bar Abin, "The decided law is in accord with the view of those who say."

II.3   A.   Expounded Bar Qappara, "A temperamental person [41A] gets nothing but his anger. To a good man they feed the good taste of the fruit of his deeds.

B.   "And whoever does not have learning in Scripture, Mishnah, and right conduct – forbid yourself by a vow from having any good from him: 'Nor sits in the seat of the scorners' (Prov. 1:1) – such a person is the very seat of the scorners."

I.1 adds a Tannaite complement. Nos. 2-3 pursue the theme invited by the statement of the Mishnah. II.1 provides a minor gloss for the Mishnah's rule, and No. 2, a Tannaite complement to No. 1. No. 3 provides a secondary expansion on the Mishnah sentence's language.

III. The Exegetical Programs of Yerushalmi and of the Babli Compared

We compose the usual side-by-side précis, looking for an appropriate point of contact, even a tangential one.

1:9 I Contrast of M. 1:9A-D and M. Mak. 3:15 and harmonization of the two statements.

1:9 II Further clarification of M. Mak. 3:15 speaks of someone who had a chance to do something that may or may not be a transgression and who refrained from doing the deed; or someone who designated for himself a given religious duty and never once violated it + examples, verses.

1:9 III Clarification of Prov. 3:6, 13:21, 1 Sam. 2:9, Prov. 3:34-35, inserted because the composition refers to a verse cited in the Mishnah paragraph.

1:10A-D I.1 Contrast of M. 1:10A-D & M. Pe. 1:1C-E.

1:10A-D I.2 Continuation of foregoing.

1:10A-D I.3 Story of the apostate, joined to foregoing through shared verse of Scripture.

1:10A-D I.4 Clarification of M. 10A.

1:10A-D I.5 Ps. 103:20 illustrated by reference to Sadoq.

1:10A-D I.6 Comparable story.

1:10A-D I.7 Intersection of M. Pe. 1:1C-E, Deut. 5:16, Prov. 21:21, Ps. 34:15, Deut. 30:20, Deut. 22:7.

1:10A-D I.8 Merit has both principal and interest.

1:10A-D I.9 Good intention joins with deeds.

1:10A-D I.10 Said X, it is better to transgress in private but not profane the name of Heaven in public.

1:10A-D I.11 They don't keep in abeyance punishment for profaning name of God but exact the penalty immediately.

1:10A-D I.12 Tannaite complement to the Mishnah rule: one should always see himself as if half-meritorious and half-guilty.

1:10E-G I.1 Said X, to what are righteous compared in this world/to what are wicked compared in this world; Tannaite complement to the Mishnah's theme.

1:10E-G I.2 Which matters more, study or deed of Torah.

1:10E-G I.3 Same issue.

1:10E-G II.1 Gloss of Mishnah rule.

1:10E-G II.2 Tannaite supplement: he who eats out in the marketplace.

1:10E-G II.3 Expounded..., a temperamental person gets nothing but his anger, to a good man they feed the good taste of the fruit of his deeds. Secondary expansion of the statement of the Mishnah sentence.

There is no reason to compose parallel columns for this Mishnah pericope, since, so far as I can see, there is nothing to compare. The two Talmuds intersect at the Mishnah.

10

The Bavli's Unique Voice

I. The Talmuds Differ Because They're Different

The Bavli's voice is unique because, at its foundations, the Bavli is different from the Yerushalmi. The two Talmuds differ not in detail, but in origin: the Bavli's statement belongs to its compositions' authors and to its composites' compilers and to its penultimate and ultimate authorship – to them, to them alone, to them uniquely.

What makes the Bavli unique, therefore, is that it forms a statement distinctive and particular to those who framed the whole, and, also, in very great measure, to those who wrote up the principal parts of the document: nearly all of the composites, and the vast majority of the compositions. It stands for different people, talking to different people about different things, from the Yerushalmi's authors, their address, their audience, their intent.

The simple fact is that the Bavli is made up of cogent compositions and large-scale composites, as well as massive miscellanies of compositions, brought together for other than analytical purposes, mainly as agglutinations. In the samples of which this monograph is comprised, not a single massive miscellany of the Bavli occurs also in the Yerushalmi, and, furthermore, I cannot identify a single composite in the Talmud of Babylonia that finds a place also in the Talmud of the Land of Israel. As to compositions, it is rare for the same composition to occur in the earlier and then in the later document. But, when that is the case, it is difficult to show, for more than a saying or a brief story, that the earlier document's version of the composition has been taken over and revised line by line in the later document's version of the same matter. Where the Talmuds share materials other than passages of Scripture, the Mishnah, the Tosefta, or compilations of formulations of rules accorded Tannaite status, the points of intersection are few and far between.

That means that the second Talmud stands autonomous and free of the first. Both appeal to some sources in common, Scripture, Mishnah, episodic passages that we now find, also, in the Tosefta, and a few sayings; the framers of the compositions, all the more so, of the composites, of the second Talmud do precisely what they wish with such shared sayings or stories, and so far as I can discern in the sample examined in these five volumes, they rarely, if ever, respond to, carry forward, or build on, a composition, all the more so, a composite, shared with the earlier Talmud. They do precisely what they like, they make their own statement, and in all, the Talmud of Babylonia speaks with a single voice to deliver a message unique to itself, by which I mean, to the authors of its compositions and the compilers of its composites and the authorships of its massive and whole statements: chapters, tractates – the lot.

II. The Talmuds' Localized Sources:
Composites and Compositions that Do Not Intersect

We may state as the operative hypothesis of this work that the Bavli speaks about its region's reading of the Mishnah; its particularity is the localization of the Torah to its place. The compositions and composites that comprise the Babylonia occasionally use imported sayings but are manufactured at home – and the document all the more so. The one whole Torah of Moses, our rabbi – written, in Scripture, oral, in the Mishnah and related sayings classified as Tannaite – divides by place, and traditions are bound by place, and the Torah governs here in particular, if everywhere else, also and equally in all due particularity.

To spell out the first results of this five-volume monograph, we begin with the recognition that both Talmuds are made up of materials – compositions and also composites[1] – composed before the final forming of the talmudic composites: the documents as we know them. Each draws upon an indeterminate volume of compositions, made up of completed units of thought, whether free-standing sayings or disputes or little stories or extensive and sustained analyses.[2] So the comparison of

---

[1]This distinction is critical to all analysis of all rabbinic writings of late antiquity; it is set forth in *The Rules of Composition of the Talmud of Babylonia. The Cogency of the Bavli's Composite* (Atlanta, 1991: Scholars Press for South Florida Studies in the History of Judaism).

[2]My reference system for the Bavli serves very well to identify these various types of formations; the one for the Yerushalmi did not, and that accounts for the less clear marking of completed units of thought in the Yerushalmi. For the present work, however, I determined not to provide the Yerushalmi with a more adequate reference system than the one I originally invented for it. But any further translation is going to have to do just that. Not one review of the

the two Talmuds really requires the contrast of the character of the available compositions and even composites. And that is precisely where, entireliy and consistently and nearly ubiquitously, the Bavli differs from the Yerushalmi. The results of our analysis of Mishnah tractate Qiddushin in the two Talmuds – forty folios of the Bavli! – yield a simple but now ineluctable hypothesis: the framers of the Bavli drew upon their distinctive, local sources for compositions and composites, and the framers of the Yerushalmi drew upon their equivalently distinctive, local sources for compositions and composites. The two Talmuds treat the same Mishnah but only very rarely intersect other than at a given Mishnah paragraph.

The reason is that the penultimate and ultimate framers of the two Talmuds utilized what they had in hand, and each document's framers drew upon a corpus of materials utterly different from thaused by (therefore also: available to) the other. Whether or not the framers of the Bavli "knew" the Yerushalmi is not at issue here. I cannot understand why they should not have known the document as a whole, since, we all assume, it was composed and completed two centuries before the closure of the Yerushalmi. What matters is, what difference did the document make to them? And they answer is, no difference at all. If they knew the document, they certainly were not so impressed by it as to turn themselves into its continuators and commentators; theirs is no commentary to the Yerushalmi. I do think that the work of Mishnah commentary is common to the sages of both countries, and it is clear that that work involved an interest, among the authors of compositions and even framers of composites, in details of Mishnah rules, and other Tannaite rules, as these were read in the other country: the Babylonian writers very frequently address opinion formulated in the Land of Israel on this, that, and the other thing.

That makes all the more stunning the fact that, for the bulk of their thirty-seven tractates, they simply go their own way, utilizing what they received from the Land of Israel for their own purposes, in their own idiom, and on their own terms. That fact begins with the Babylonian sages' choice of tractates and divisions, since they ignore an entire

---

Yerushalmi translation noted the inadequacy of the reference system, probably because it was such a remarkable advance over the blundering "system" that preceded: 59C, at the top; or Y. 1:1, meaning, reference to the printed page, on the one side, or the Mishnah paragraph served by an indeterminate amount of material, on the other. But then, what did the Bavli have before my system, other than B. 59B, at the top [!]. What is even more interesting is that some of the reviews of my Bavli and Midrash translations objected to the reference systems I provided, not because they were inadequate (and I think they serve fairly well), but because they were unneeded.

division covered in the other Talmud, the first, and they treat an entire division ignored in the other Talmud, the fifth. And we shall take account in a later volume of the Babylonian masters' systematic reading of an entire tractate treated only briefly (if extant evidence is to be believed) and perfunctorily by the other Talmud, tractate Niddah. Nor can we ignore the extraordinary difference in the character of the Bavli's treatment of the Babas and the Yerushalmi's simply routine and third-rate reading of the same tractates. So it is really not an interesting question to find out whether the later Talmud's framers knew the earlier document – the answer being slightly embarrassing, if they did: they knew it and thought it third rate. I prefer to think they had ample access to episodic sayings and even brief compositions, but went their own way, using the sayings and revising the compositions as they liked.[3]

Since the Bavli's framers produced their document, it is generally agreed, hundreds of years after the Yerushalmi's finished their work, we may conclude that, if they had access to the Yerushalmi's compositions and composites, they chose not to use them but preferred to make their own statement in their own way and for their own purpose. Where sayings are shared by the two Talmuds, they are episodic, ad hoc, singular; rarely do entire compositions make their way from the former to the latter document, and whole composites, never. Referring in common with the authors of the Yerushalmi's composites and even compositions to the same Scripture, Mishnah, Tosefta, Sifra, and the two Sifrés, the Bavli's authorship drew upon composites and compositions that differed, beginning to end and top to bottom, from the Yerushalmi's counterparts. The materials shared in common are episodic and seldom. The sustained comparisons undertaken in these five volumes leaves no doubt of that fact. Short of a complete comparison of the two dozen tractates or so shared by both Talmuds, the probe undertaken here provides sufficient evidence to sustain that claim; any counter-reading of matters will have to give us not two or three examples of something or other, but an equally sustained and massive probe. But I have no doubt

---

[3]How they made such revisions of compositions is spelled out in rich detail in my comparative studies of versions of the same saying or story in these works:

Development of a Legend. Studies on the Traditions Concerning Yohanan ben Zakkai. Leiden, 1970: Brill.

The Rabbinic Traditions about the Pharisees before 70. Leiden, 1971: Brill. I-III.

   I.   *The Rabbinic Traditions about the Pharisees before 70. The Masters.*

   II.   *The Rabbinic Traditions about the Pharisees before 70. The Houses.*

   III. *The Rabbinic Traditions about the Pharisees before 70. Conclusions.*

Eliezer ben Hyrcanus. The Tradition and the Man. Leiden, 1973: Brill.

   I.   *Eliezer ben Hyrcanus. The Tradition and the Man. The Tradition.*

   II.   *Eliezer ben Hyrcanus. The Tradition and the Man. The Man.*

that such a probe will replicate my results. This work demonstrates the simple propositions stated just now: a sustained, elaborate, and massive demonstration that the Talmuds differ because they differ, thus, the Bavli's unique voice.

III. Differentiating the Bavli from the Yerushalmi: The Results to Date

Let me now place this work into the context of completed research: in four prior works I have compared and contrasted the two Talmuds, the two Talmuds, the Talmud of the Land of Israel, a.k.a. the Yerushalmi, and the Talmud of Babylonia, a.k.a. the Bavli, and so begun to address the problem of their relationship of These were, *Judaism: The Classical Statement. The Evidence of the Bavli* (Chicago, 1986: University of Chicago Press), a phenomenological approach of a fairly elementary order, and, second, *The Bavli and Its Sources: The Question of Tradition in the Case of Tractate Sukkah* (Atlanta, 1987: Scholars Press for Brown Judaic Studies). This second item is reproduced as Volume Two of this monograph, because of its critical place in the unfolding of my present argument and analysis. In it I show that while both Talmuds refer back to a common document, the Mishnah, the second of the two in no way responds to the issues important to the first or identifies the first Talmud as a guide and model. Not only so, but, faced with a topic treated in Midrash compilations produced long before its own day, the Bavli's authorship treated that topic in a completely independent way, in no way raising the questions earlier deamed important or guided by lines of thought (let alone results) that dominated in treating that topic in prior writings. The result of *the Bavli and Its Sources* is so important to me that, in the present monograph, I go over the work I produced there.

Third and fourth, in the monographs just prior to this set, which are *The Torah in the Talmud. A Taxonomy of the Uses of Scripture in the Talmuds. Tractate Qiddushin in the Talmud of Babylonia and the Talmud of the Land of Israel. I. Bavli Qiddushin Chapter One* (Atlanta, 1992: Scholars Press for South Florida Studies in the History of Judaism) and *The Torah in the Talmud. A Taxonomy of the Uses of Scripture in the Talmuds. Tractate Qiddushin in the Talmud of Babylonia and the Talmud of the Land of Israel. II. Yerushalmi Qiddushin Chapter One. And a Comparison of the Uses of Scripture by the Two Talmuds* (Atlanta, 1992: Scholars Press for South Florida Studies in the History of Judaism), I pursued the problem of the comparison of the two documents. This I do by choosing as a fixed reference point the utilization of Scripture in each. What I found was that, in general, the two documents make use of the same forms to accomplish the same goals. But, it turned out, in detail, the documents scarcely intersect; they do the same things, but they produce results that do not bear comparison at all.

My attention was drawn, at the same time as *The Bavli and Its Sources*, to the matter of Scripture. A systematic comparison from a phenomenological perspective between the two Talmuds yielded *Judaism: The Classical Statement. The Evidence of the Bavli* (Chicago, 1986: University of Chicago Press). There I concluded that there are significant structure differences between the two Talmuds, in that the later one built large-scale composites around verses of Scripture (ordinarily, in sequence, that is, as a commentary), and the earlier one tended not to do that. I drew from that fact a number of conclusions, but the results remained sketchy and tentative; I determined that, at a later time, I would return to that matter, and I did so in *The Torah in the Talmud*.

What emerged in my comparison of the two Talmuds' uses of Scripture in *The Torah in the Talmud* was the simple fact that, when it comes to the Torah in the Talmud or utilizing Scripture, the two Talmuds intersect only at a few points. Most of the Scripture compositions and composites of the Talmuds stand by themselves and do not intersect with, or even address the same verses of Scripture as, most of the compositions and composites of the Talmud of Babylonia. As I looked for passages that may plausibly be set side by side and stand comparison, I realized that most of the items on the one list bore so little in common with those on the counterpart list that side by side comparison would prove absurd. When it comes to Scripture, we find ourselves in mostly separate worlds, worlds that do not collide but float, each in its own orbit around the same sun: distant planets, reflecting the same light through such different atmospheres that the light of each, seen from afar, appears to form its own spectrum, and, seen from close up, dazzles eyes accustomed to the glow of the other.

That fact is surprising indeed when we realize that both documents are organized, and fully intend to serve, as commentaries to the Mishnah. But even when they do just that, the result is negligible: they intersect at only a few points, and then along lines that, so far as I can see, begin within the program of Mishnah exegesis and are governed by the dictates of the substrate of that program (whether logical, whether topical). The two Talmuds use Scripture in the same way, but each for its own purpose. First, the uses of Scripture form no point of differentiation between the two Talmuds. Framers of compositions and composites used in the one document take for granted the same premises and propositions a those of the other. If we wish to compare the two writings, the present point of differentiation will not serve. The reason, as I have argued in Volume One of this study, is that to begin with we have asked a question in categories not native to this writing: the Torah in the Talmud being incomprehensible.

If, therefore, we wish to compare the two Talmuds and to find out how the second differs from the first, we shall find our answers not in Scripture exegesis but Mishnah exegesis. And that is hardly surprising, since, after all, both documents represents themselves as commentaries to the Mishnah, and, further, the Talmud of Babylonia also presents itself as an autonomous commentary to that same writing. The upshot is that when we wish to explain how the one Talmud differs from the other, we have to turn to issues of Mishnah exegesis, and when these issues have come to resolution, we shall also find it possible to explain the differences in Scripture exegesis such as impressed us so forcefully in the brief comparisons given just now. That is why the necessary next step – taken in this volume and its companion – is yet another comparison of the treatment of Mishnah-tractate Qiddushin in the two Talmuds, now from the perspective of Mishnah exegesis. But what, precisely, is at issue?

IV. The Problem of Differentiation

Now to the problem of differentiation – and that means, the differentiation of the Bavli from the Yerushalmi – in the end for solid, historical purposes, not merely the froth of literary analysis. In the second part of this monograph, recapitulating *The Bavli and Its Sources*, we ask whether the Bavli tractate under discussion emerged from a continuous process of tradition, that is, an incremental and linear process that step by step transmitted out of the past statements and wordings that bear authority and are subject to study, refinement, preservation and transmission. In Chapter Two of that work we see the opposite, namely, the framers of the Bavli tractate on Sukkah addressed the same Mishnah tractate as had been dealt with two centuries earlier by the authors of the Yerushalmi tractate, and also drew episodically and infrequently on a common corpus of sayings, most of them identified as originating from a Tannaite memorizer, but the second of the two Talmuds simply went its own way, in no aspect continuing the program of the first of the two or even acknowledging any prior address to the Mishnah tractate under discussion.

For the case at hand, while the Bavli is connected with earlier documents – not the Yerushalmi alone, but also the Tosefta and some sort of set of circulating corpus of Tannaite sayings, and also with some received sayings not written down in a systematic way in prior compilations – whatever is shared with prior writings, the connections appear episodic and haphazard, not systematic, except in respect to the

Mishnah, The Bavli cannot be shown systematically and generally to continue the program and inquiry of predecessors. In few ways does the Bavli give evidence of taking its place within a process of tradition. To the contrary, the appeal of the authorship of the Bavli is to the ineluctable verity of well-applied logic, practical reason tested and retested against the facts, whether deriving from prior authorities, or emerging from examples and decisions of leading contemporary authorities.

True enough, the Bavli contains ample selections from available writings. The authorship of the Bavli leaves no doubt that it makes extensive use of extant materials, sayings and stories. Readers who review the sizable sample before us will see numerous indications – much like footnotes and references – of that fact. For example, the authorship of the Bavli invokes verses of Scripture. It further takes as its task the elucidation of the received code, the Mishnah. More to the point, frequent citations of materials now found in the Tosefta as well as allusions to sayings framed in Tannaite Hebrew and attributed to Tannaite authority – marked, for instance, by TN' – time and again alert us to extensive reference, by our authorship, to a prior corpus of materials. The authorship of the Bavli would be hard put to demonstrate in detail that its fundamental work of literary selection and ordering, its basic choices on sustained and logical discourse, its essential statement upon the topics it has selected – that anything important in their document derives from long generations past. For instance, we should open the Tosefta's treatment of, or counterpart to, a given chapter of the Mishnah and look in vain for a systematic, orderly, and encompassing discourse, dictated by the order and plan of the Tosefta, out of which our authorship has composed a sizable and sustained statement.

The Bavli in relationship to its sources is simply not a traditional document, in the plain sense that most of what it says in a cogent and coherent way expresses the well-crafted statement and viewpoint of its authorship. Excluding, of course, the Mishnah, to which the Bavli devotes its sustained and systematic attention, little of what our authorship says derives cogency and force from a received statement, and most does not. The Bavli's authorship's cogent, rigorously rational reading of the received heritage has demonstrably emerged *not* from a long process of formulation and transmission of received traditions, in each generation lovingly tended, refined and polished, and handed on essentially as received. The system comes first. In the present context, that means that the logic and principle of orderly inquiry take precedence over the preservation and repetition of received materials, however holy. The mode of thought defined, the work of applied reason and practical rationality may get under way. Nothing out of the past can be shown to have dictated the Bavli's program, which is essentially the work of its authorship.

That is to say, what, exactly, do we compare when we compare the two Talmuds? We have to identify how they are like, before we may explain where they differ. As writings, they are alike in a variety of ways, in appealing to a common corpus of prior writings (Scripture, the Mishnah and other sayings bearing the status of Tannaite formulation). All this is spelled out in the introduction, and the case for comparison is formidable and beyond refutation. But as I have explained, the prior studies of consequence told me only that the Talmuds look alike but are different from one another. And, we now realize, the point of difference emerges not in formal traits, which, being superficial, are easy to identify. It is at the intellectual foundations of the second of the two Talmuds, which so profoundly differs from the first as to establish itself as a wholly autonomous statement. Both Talmuds comment on the Mishnah, organizing nearly all of the materials they comprise in the form of a commentary to the Mishnah. Then what is it that the first Talmud failed to do, but that the framers of the second undertook?

Questions of comparison and contrast may be addressed only through systematic and orderly classification of data. The alternative is ad hoc and episodic guesswork.[4] It follows that the answer to that question requires us to compose a classification of types of Mishnah commentary characteristic of each writing. To classify, we must describe each specimen in terms sufficiently general so that other specimens may be shown to fall into the same class of things or to differ in some way, either fundamental, hence forming a distinct genus, or superficial, so constituting a species or subspecies. The movement from the specific case to an account of sufficient generality to warrant comparison and contrast with other data requires a measure of caution. For if we generalize into utter abstraction, we shall emerge with platitudes; everything will be like everything else, being insufficiently differentiated. On the other side, if we generalize too timidly, mutatis mutandis, nothing will be like anything else, in the end not having been classified at all – but only paraphrased.

These results establish the negative fact that the two Talmuds are not like one another. But I do not know the answer to the positive question, in what ways is the second Talmud different from the first? It is only through finding the answer to that question that I can hope accurately to

---

[4]A review of prior research will be found in Baruch M. Bokser, "The Palestinian Talmud," in J. Neusner, ed., *The Study of Ancient Judaism* (New York 1981: Ktav. Second printing: Atlanta, 1992: Scholars Press for South Florida Studies in the History of Judaism). II. *The Palestinian and Babylonian Talmuds.*

describe the second Talmud, a project that has, to date, defied the intellectual powers of all those who have tried. For up to now we have mere impressions, on the one side, or episodic aperçus, on the other, and what we require is a systematic, orderly, and well-grounded account. The planned parts in continuation of this first part of the monograph are in the following six more parts:

The Bavli's Unique Voice. A Systematic Comparison of the Talmud of Babylonia and the Talmud of the Land of Israel. Volume Two. *Yerushalmi's, Bavli's, and Other Canonical Documents' Treatment of the Program of Mishnah-Tractate Sukkah Chapters One, Two, and Four Compared and Contrasted. A Reprise and Revision of* The Bavli and its Sources (Atlanta, 1993: Scholars Press for South Florida Studies in the History of Judaism).

The Bavli's Unique Voice. A Systematic Comparison of the Talmud of Babylonia and the Talmud of the Land of Israel. Volume Three. *Bavli and Yerushalmi to Selected Mishnah Chapters in the Division of Moed. Erubin and Hagigah* (Atlanta, 1993: Scholars Press for South Florida Studies in the History of Judaism).

The Bavli's Unique Voice. A Systematic Comparison of the Talmud of Babylonia and the Talmud of the Land of Israel. Volume Four. *Bavli and Yerushalmi to Selected Mishnah Chapters in the Division of Nashim. Gittin and Nedarim. And Niddah* (Atlanta, 1993: Scholars Press for South Florida Studies in the History of Judaism).

The Bavli's Unique Voice. A Systematic Comparison of the Talmud of Babylonia and the Talmud of the Land of Israel. Volume Five. *Bavli and Yerushalmi to Selected Mishnah Chapters in the Division of Neziqin. Baba Mesia and Makkot* (Atlanta, 1993: Scholars Press for South Florida Studies in the History of Judaism).

The Bavli's Unique Voice. A Systematic Comparison of the Talmud of Babylonia and the Talmud of the Land of Israel. Volume Six. *Bavli and Yerushalmi to a Miscellany of Mishnah Chapters. Gittin Chapter One, Hagigah Chapter Three, and Qiddushin Chapter Two* (Atlanta, 1993: Scholars Press for South Florida Studies in the History of Judaism).

The Bavli's Unique Voice. A Systematic Comparison of the Talmud of Babylonia and the Talmud of the Land of Israel. Volume Seven. *The Uniqueness of the Bavli in the Context of the Canon of Judaism* (Atlanta, 1993: Scholars Press for South Florida Studies in the History of Judaism).

V. Circumstance ("History") Intervenes: Different People Talking to Different People in Different Ways about Different Things

When we compare the Mishnah to the Talmud we find two intertwined documents, quite different from one another both in style and in values. Yet they are so tightly joined that the Talmud appears in the main to provide mere commentary and amplification for the Mishnah. So the two Talmuds are indistinguishable. In fact, on the strength of the comparisons of Bavli and Yerushalmi to Mishnah-tractate Qiddushin Chapter One, they have nothing in common except for form. But writings that exhibit formal congruence await differentiation as to substantive, and with the two Talmuds, that work is exceptionally simple, since, in fact, they intersect at only a few points, each set of writers doing pretty much whatever it likes with sayings, stories, and even compositions that it shares with the other. The Talmuds differ because they are different from one another. Is that result limited to their treatment of one topic, or one Mishnah tractate, and is it limited to a single division? A probe of other tractates in the division of Women and other divisions altogether will provide definitive answers to that question.

Still, the reader will forgive my projecting the answer even now: no, the result is not limited to a topic or a tractate. Yes, the Talmuds differ everywhere for only one reason: they are different. That is to say, they draw on distinct bodies of compositions and composites, localized and particular to their regions – the Land of Israel, Babylonia, respectively. They are called by the name of their regions because they are regional. They scarcely intersect, except at the Torah they have in common, that is to say, the Written Torah, which we know as the Hebrew Scriptures or Tanakh, and the Oral Torah, which we know as the Mishnah (together with other sayings bearing the mark of Tannaite authority). That is where they intersect – there alone. They form two species of a single genus, to be sure; but the species common form belies their utterly different character. Species ordinarily are alike except where they differ. The Talmuds differ except where they are alike. And why should that not be the fact, since they were written, each by different people talking about different things and in different ways to different people? Is that true everywhere? In Volume Two we proceed to another comparison of the Bavli with the Yerushalmi and also of the Bavli with other prior documents.

Index

South Florida Studies in the History of Judaism